Agrarian Reforms, Land Markets and Rural Poor

About the Editor

D. Narasimha Reddy recently retired as Professor in Economics and Dean, School of Social Sciences, University of Hyderabad. Labour Economics and Political Economy of Development have been his areas of research interest. Besides a number of publications, he supervised a large number of M.Phil. and Ph.D. dissertations in these areas. During the last decade he has done extensive work on globalization, WTO and Agrarian Crisis. His latest publication includes *Agrarian Crisis in India* (OUP), a jointly edited volume. Presently, he is Visiting Professor, Institute for Human Development, New Delhi.

About the Centre

The Centre for Rural Studies (formerly Land Reforms Unit) of the Lal Bahadur Shastri National Academy of Administration was set up in the year 1989 by the Ministry of Rural Development, Government of India, with a multifaceted agenda that included among others, the concurrent evaluation of the ever-unfolding ground realities pertaining to the implementation of the Land Reforms and Poverty Alleviation Programmes in India. Sensitizing the officer trainees of the Indian Administrative Service in the process of evaluating of land reforms and poverty alleviation programmes by exposing them to the ground realities; setting up a forum for regular exchange of views on land reforms and poverty alleviation between academicians, administrators, activists and concerned citizens and creating awareness amongst the public about the various programmes initiated by the Government of India through non-governmental organizations are also important objectives of the Centre for Rural Studies. A large number of books, reports related to land reforms, poverty alleviation programmes, rural socio-economic problems etc. published both externally and internally bear testimony to the excellent research quality of the Centre.

Agrarian Reforms, Land Markets and Rural Poor

Edited by

D. Narasimha Reddy

Published for

Centre for Rural Studies
Lal Bahadur Shastri National Academy of Administration, Mussoorie

by

CONCEPT PUBLISHING COMPANY, NEW DELHI-110059

ISBN 13-978-81-8069-604-6 **ISBN 10-81-8069-604-9**

First Published 2009

Published and Printed by

Concept Publishing Company

Regd. Office:

A/15-16, Commercial Block, Mohan Garden

New Delhi-110059 (India)

Phones : 25351460, 25351794, *Fax* : 091-11-25357109

Email : publishing@conceptpub.com,
website: www.conceptpub.com

Editorial Office:

H-13, Bali Nagar, New Delhi-110 015, India.

Cataloging in Publication Data--*Courtesy:* D.K. Agencies (P) Ltd. <docinfo@dkagencies.com>

National Workshop on Land Markets and Rural Poverty (2004 :Mussoorie, India)
Agrarian reforms, land markets and rural poor / edited by D. Narasimha Reddy.
p. cm.
Revised version of papers presented at the National Workshop on Land Markets and Rural Poverty, held at Mussoorie during 10-11 August 2004.
Includes bibliographical references and index.
ISBN 13: 9788180696046 ISBN 10: 8180696049

1. Land reform--India--Congresses. 2. Land tenure--India--Congresses. 3. Farm tenancy--India--Congresses. 4. Land use, Rural--Government policy--India--Congresses. 5. Rural development--India--Congresses I.Narasimha Reddy D. II. Lal Bahadur Shastri National Academy of Administration. Centre for Rural Studies. III. Title.

DDC 333.30954 22

Preface

This book is largely an outcome of the papers presented at the National Workshop on "Land Markets and Rural Poverty" organised during 10-11 August 2004 at Mussoorie by the Centre for Rural Studies (CRS) of the Lal Bahadur Shastri National Academy of Administration. The book in taking the present shape is made possible by the help, encouragement and cooperation of a large number of persons. Manoj Ahuja, the then Coordinator-cum-Vice-Chairman of the CRS is instrumental in initiating the Workshop, in evincing keen interest that the papers would take publishable form and facilitating the editorial process and publication. I am also grateful to S.R. Sankaran and B.N. Yugandhar for their valuable comments. I thank Binod Kumar, the then Chairman of CRS, who took keen interest not only in the Workshop but also in the publication of the papers. I also owe my debt to B.K. Sinha, former Coordinator and Vice-Chairman of the CRS, for permission to incorporate a few papers in the book, including one of his own, from the National Workshop he conducted on "Whither Tenancy?" (24-25 September 1999). I am grateful to all the participants in the Workshop who cooperated in not only by revising their papers but also patiently bearing with the unforeseen delay in the publication. Now, it is my pleasant duty to thank Dr. D. Narasimha Reddy, editor of the book and the staff of the CRS, particularly Dr.Varunendra Vikram Singh who bore the burden of coordination between the editor, authors and the administration.

Yatendra Kumar, IAS
Deputy Director &
Coordinator-cum-Vice Chairman
Centre for Rural Studies
Lal Bahadur Shastri National Academy of Administration
Mussoorie

Contents

Preface v

List of Contributors ix

Introduction xi

1. Land Reforms: The Next Phase 1
   V. S. Vyas
2. The Land Question and Globalization: Some Reflections on the Relevance of Redistributive Land Reforms 13
   V. B. Athreya
3. The Problem of Tenancy Reforms and Land Reforms in Relation to Productivity and Rural Poverty 31
   Utsa Patnaik
4. Some Aspects of Tenancy Debate: Implications for Policy Reforms 47
   Pushpendra and *B. K. Sinha*
5. Volatility in Land Markets and Rural Poverty 70
   C. S. Murty
6. Changing Tenancy Relations in Rural India 88
   H. R. Sharma
7. Tenancy and Rural Poor: Some Important Issues 123
   R. P. Singh
8. Operation Barga and Rural Poverty: West Bengal Experience 138
   Sankar Kumar Bhaumik
9. Emerging Land Lease Market in Haryana 152
   P. C. Bansil
10. Changes in Land Holding Structure, Farm Size, Productivity and Tenancy in Punjab 163
    Ramesh Chand

11. Sharecropping Tenancy and Terms of Access to Land to the Poor: A Comparative Study 175
A. P. Singh

12. Poverty Alleviation: Relative Roles of Land Lease and Sales Markets in a Prosperous Part of UP 190
Gyanendra Mani and *V. K. Pandey*

13. Access to Land, Land Markets and Poverty: The Orissa Experience 204
Basanta K. Sahu

14. Land Markets, Agrarian Structure and Poverty in Andhra Pradesh 240
R. Vijay

15. Changing Land-Caste-Class Relations and Rural Poverty in Bihar 271
Anup K. Karan

16. Land Reforms and Land Policy Issues in the Context of Karnataka 299
R. S. Deshpande

17. Conceptualizing Land and Rural Poverty Linkages with Some Reflections on Madhya Pradesh and Chhattisgarh 318
Praveen Jha

18. Land Distribution and Tenancy in Orissa 332
R. K. Panda and *S. Tripathy*

19. Land Relations and Conflicts in North Eastern India: A Look at Modernisation, Immigration and Livelihood Loss 350
Walter Fernandes

20. Land Holdings and Tenancy in North-Eastern States 364
S. Tripathy

21. State and NGO Interventions in the Distribution of Land to the Poor: A Study of Tamil Nadu 383
M. Thangaraj

22. Globalization and Contract Farming: The Experience of Some States 399
K. Gopal Iyer

Index 409

List of Contributors

V. S. Vyas, Professor Emeritus, Institute of Development Studies, Jaipur.

V. B. Athreya, Professor of Economics, Bharatidesan University, Tiruchirapalli.

Utsa Patnik, Centre for Economic Studies and Planning, Jawaharlal Nehru University, New Delhi.

Pushpendra, Currently Fellow, Institute of Human Development, New Delhi and formerly Consultant, Centre for Rural Studies, LBSNAA, Mussoorie.

B. K. Sinha, Earlier Coordinator-cum-Vice Chairperson, Centre for Rural Studies, LBSNAA, Mussoorie and presently Director General, National Institute of Rural Development, Ministry of Rural Development, Hyderabad.

C. S. Murty, Fellow (Professor), Centre for Economic and Social Studies, Hyderabad.

H. R. Sharma, Professor, Department of Agricultural Economics, Himachal Pradesh Agricultural University, Palampur, Kangra-176 062.

R. P. Singh, Former Director, Centre for Sustainable Economic Development, National Institute of Rural Development, Rajendranagar, Hyderabad-500 030 and presently Senior Faculty, Indian Institute of Management, Lucknow.

Sankar Kumar Bhaumik, Professor, Department of Economics, Calcutta University, Kolkata.

P. C. Bansil, Ex-Senior Staff Member of the Indian Economic Service and of the Food and Agricultural Organization (FAO, Rome) and is Founder Member and Head of the Techno-Economic Research Institute (TERI, New Delhi).

Ramesh Chand, Currently ICAR National Professor and Theme Area Leader for Market and Trade at NCAP, India and formerly Principal Scientist, National Centre for Agricultural Economics and Policy Research, New Delhi.

A. P. Singh, Former Assistant Professor, Centre for Rural Studies, Lal Bahadur Shastri National Academy of Administration, Mussoorie and presently Associate Professor, NIAR, LBSNAA, Mussoorie.

Gyanendra Mani and V. K. Pandey, Agricultural Economists, National Bank for Agriculture & Rural Development (NABARD), UP RO, Lucknow and Professor (Retd.), Department of Agriculture and Technology, Pantnagar, respectively.

Basanta K. Sahu, Formerly Assistant Professor, CFDA, Ahmedabd-380054,

India and currently Assistant Professor of Economics at Indian Institute of Foreign Trade, New Delhi.

R. Vijay, Reader in Economics, University of Hyderabad, Hyderabad, Andhra Pradesh.

Anup K. Karan, Fellow, Institute for Human Development, New Delhi.

R. S. Deshpande, Professor and Head, ADRT Unit, Institute for Social and Economic Change, Nagarbhavi, Bangalore.

Praveen Jha is at the Centre for Economic Studies and Planning, Jawaharlal Nehru University, New Delhi. This paper draws substantially on an earlier work, i.e. Jha (ed.), 2002.

Prof. R. K. Panda, Professor of Economics, Utkal University, Orissa.

Walter Fernandes, Director, North Eastern Social Research Centre, Guwahati.

S. Tripathy, Former Assistant Professor, Centre for Rural Studies, Lal Bahadur Shastri National Academy of Administration, Mussoorie and presently Associate Faculty, Entrepreneurship Development Institute of India, Gandhinagar, Gujarat.

M. Thangaraj, is Professor, Dr. Ambedkar Centre for Economics, University of Madras, Chennai.

K. Gopal Iyer, Retired Professor, Department of Sociology, Punjab University, Chandigarh.

Introduction

D. NARASIMHA REDDY

LAND REFORMS AND RURAL POVERTY

Most of the overpopulated underdeveloped countries like India, which became independent after the Second World War, recognized the need for reforming the agrarian structure as a precondition for agricultural growth and rural development. Beginning with the 1950s, thus, land reforms became an important agenda of development, and a number of measures were inititated in India. By late 1960s, it was clear that but for abolition of intermediaries, much of the other reforms like tenancy and ceilings were only perfunctory in implementation and deliberately defective in legislation. The early 1970s saw some corrective legislative measures. However, by late 1970s, much before an assessment of the extent of completion of the agenda and its impact on rural poverty, land reforms, as if these were obsolete, had gradually vanished from the policy priorities. But, what is of more interest is that during the last few years as if to make amendments for the premature pass over of land reforms policy, 'land' is reappearing as an important ingredient of the strategies for rural development and poverty alleviation. The objective of the present proposal for a workshop is not only to explore the reasons and significance of this revival of interest in land, but also to re-examine the potential of the 'land' question in alleviating rural poverty.

The theoretical foundations for redistributive land reforms, both on the grounds of equity and efficiency, were never under severe dispute. Much of the criticism of land reforms is directed towards implementational failures. It is argued that a precondition for land reforms to be feasible and effective in improving beneficiaries' livelihoods is that such programmes should fit into a broader policy aimed at reducing poverty and establishing favourable environment for the development of productive small holder agriculture by the beneficiaries. A recent World Bank Report (2003), which tries to rediscover the importance of 'land' in improving the living conditions of rural poor through the role of 'land policies' identifies a number of characteristics as essential for effective redistributive land reforms which include land reform programmes need to be integrated into a broader strategy for rural development and cannot be limited to providing land, but should put households on a viable trajectory of development; incentives to maximize productivity gains including labour intensive modes of land use should become part of the strategy; there is need for multiplicity of paths, including land markets, towards the objective of equitable operational holdings; state should provide secure and unconditional rights; there should be a level playing field by extending complementary services, access to markets and technology supportive of small holder agriculture; extension of complementary grants for enabling investment, including working capital, and rule of law with clearly defined property rights.

Ironically, the implicit conclusion is that land reforms as implemented in countries like India suffered a setback because of lack of these characteristics. It is in this context that "land market" route is brought-in as a part of "land policy".

LAND MARKETS AND RURAL POVERTY

The development of markets for land takes two forms, *viz*. the 'land sales markets' and the 'land lease/rental markets'. The Marxist analysis is focused on the '*land sales markets*' as a part of the process of capitalist development in agriculture. Land sales facilitate transfer of land from the peasantry to capitalists through dispossession, pauperization and proletarianization. There will thus emerge concentration of land and polarization of classes. Small and middle peasantry may still persist by enduring self-deprivation. In India there had been a history of dispossession of direct producers through forced commercialisation, and because of generation and accumulation of debt through consumption loans bearing usurious interest rates under conditions of informal credit markets. In the post-independence period, though there are wide regional variations, in general there has not been much of a tendency towards emergence of concentration in land. On the contrary, there is persistence, and even growth, of small holder agriculture along with the phenomenon of increase in the proportion of agricultural labour in rural population. Whether it is dry land regions or the relatively better-endowed irrigated regions, there appears to be a tendency towards decrease in the land inequality. In West Bengal, since late 1970s for instace, the effective implementation of ceilings and the registration of sharecroppers and the enforcement of minimum wages along with the improved functioning of the local self-government created conditions in which land sales markets facilitated redistribution of land by enabling the poor and the landless to purchase land, though in small fragments. In some regions, peasantry appear to be in debt, not for consumption, but for acquiring assets including land. In tribal areas, dispossession or alienation of land appear to be in favour of moneylenders and traders without much hint of development of capitalist agriculture. The place of land sales markets in the face of persistence of small and medium peasantry in spite of distressing agrarian conditions needs to be analysed in relation to the nature of other markets including credit, labour and other inputs. The role of State intervention through land reforms, and through input and output markets, in determining the emerging tenurial structure and relations needs assessment. Yet another important aspect to be examined is whether public intervention by way of purchase of land for distribution to the poor could still be an option.

Though it has very little to offer in analysing 'land sales markets', the neoclassical economic analysis suggests that land rental markets would increase productivity and equity because of low cost land-transfers to more productive producers, by enabling some to lease land, some others to move on to non-farm economic activities and also by improving the ability of the poor to face consumption shocks through employment and income from the leased-in land. However, fixed rent contracts are seen as not feasible for the poor because of the wealth constraints. Thus, the emphasis is laid on share-tenancy based rental markets as an option that brings operational distribution of land closer to optimum. Land rental markets are seen as a means of reaching optimal size of operational holdings, where family labour could be fully employed. Rental markets are expected to equalize returns to non-tradable factors of production, such as family labour and bullocks in the traditional farms of India. Further, land rental markets are seen as more advantageous than sales markets since rental markets are flexible and involve low transaction costs, rental markets demand only limited capital outlay, therefore poor can participate by using a part of capital for productive working capital than being locked in land, rental markets facilitate easy reallocation of land towards more efficient users than current users, and rental markets provide a stepping-stone for the poor towards land ownership.

The argument in favour of land rental markets emphasizes, that under conditions of clearly defined property rights, free operation of rental markets will bring about optimal allocation of land across households with differential endowments or abilities and result in significant gains in efficiency and equity. The protagonists also argue that state should ensure tenure security, and explore options for eliminating unjustified restrictions on the operation of land rental markets. The intellectual itinerary of the neoclassical journey into land rental markets extends to contract farming or even corporate farming. The neoclassical theory, however, is blind to institutional dimensions and market distortions that arise out of caste-class discrimination and the interlocking of lease-market with other markets.

In the context of renewed debate on the ability of land reforms, the doubts about the land sales markets, and the claims of efficacy of rental markets in alleviating rural poverty and achieving rural development, the present book discusses wide ranging issues which include the performance of the State and other institutions in providing access to credit, technology and other critical inputs to land reform beneficiaries; the role of grassroots movements and decentralised democratic institutions in effective implementation of equitable land reforms, role of NGOs in enabling the land reform beneficiaries to access credit, inputs and product markets; the impact of ceilings legislation on land sales markets; the tenancy legislation *vis-à-vis* the operation of land rental markets; land policy and the ability of small-marginal farmers to adopt modern farming practices and to diversify their farming to a higher level of productivity; land reforms *versus* rural development and anti-poverty programmes—alternatives or integral parts?, persistence of semi-feudal and other forms of agrarian relations; nature of interaction between land markets and other markets—especially credit, other inputs, product and labour markets, and their impact on the poor peasants; the place of contract farming or corporate farming in rural poverty alleviation; implications of extending land markets to Tribal/Agency areas; and place of land policy in Agricultural and Rural Development—Past and Present experiences.

Chapter 1

Land Reforms: The Next Phase

V. S. VYAS

In current discussion on agricultural and rural development hardly any mention is made of the structural features of our agriculture and how they impinge on income and welfare of the rural people. It is rather surprising. In a predominantly rural society like ours questions pertaining to agrarian structure, particularly those centring on land should have attracted much more attention. One can have different views on the nature and content of land reforms or the process of implementing changes in agrarian structure, but to deny that the relationship between tiller of soil and the land s/he tills is of no consequence is to adopt an ostrich-like attitude. The prevailing indifference to these questions is in sharp contrast to the stance taken by the intellectuals and policy makers concerned with the growth of Indian economy in previous decades. A time has come to bring back the issues of ownership and access to land on the centre stage in our discussion of rural economy.

LAND REFORMS: THE FIRST PHASE

In the years preceding and following Independence significant measures of land reforms were undertaken. This was mainly because a large part of land was controlled by the functionless intermediaries; skewness in land holding pattern was worsening. Even in *ryotwari* areas layers of intermediaries enjoying various rights but hardly any obligation were rampant. Because of the plethora of tenures and several rungs of the intermediaries, relationship in land had become very complex and litigation was thriving. First set of land reform legislations were aimed at correcting this situation. Because there was a national consensus on the direction of land reforms, actual legislation followed more or less same content and sequence through out the country. Practically in all states of the country, the reforms proceeded in following stages:

- Abolition of functionless intermediaries (such as *zamindars* and *jagirdars*);
- Protection of tenants' rights, and regulation of rent;
- Ceiling on land holdings and distribution of surplus land among small farmers and landless labourers;
- Legislation aimed at "land to the tiller"; and
- Further lowering of the ceiling on land.

Some states, such as Haryana, Punjab, Maharashtra and Uttar Pradesh took the programme of consolidation of fragmented holdings quite serious. A few states, with the blessing of the Central government, also encouraged experiments in cooperative farming. The guiding force in all land related legislation during this period was equity and social justice.

Of these various reforms, measures to remove functionless intermediaries were quite successful. Results of tenancy reforms present a mixed picture. A large number of small tenants were ejected by the landowners taking advantage of the provisions for 'self cultivation'.

At the same time a sizeable group of tenants, particularly the medium and large tenants tilling the land of absentee landowners, could secure tenancy rights and avail of lower rents. The same group could acquire the land they were cultivating once the legislation on 'land to the tiller' came into force. The worst sufferers were share croppers and tenants-at-will. In most parts of the country open tenancy was replaced by concealed tenancy; long term lease contract to short term leases; annual to seasonal lease; written to oral arrangements, and formal to informal contracts. Ceiling legislation was effective in hardly one or two states. Cooperative farming was largely a failure (Vyas, 1993).

There were two basic reasons for this less than expected success. With few exceptions, there was no mobilisation of beneficiaries to enable them to claim the rights provided in the legislation. In a system which was dominated by the vested interests this was a major failing.

Second, with the pre-occupation with equity the aspect of productivity was not addressed in any meaningful way. Even the sections who benefited from the reforms in terms of better access to land and more secure rights in land did not have wherewithal to make productive use of land.

Processes described above were not without some favourable outcome. For example, we now have in the country a more or less uniform land tenure system approximating to *rayotwari* system. The reforms have, at least indirectly, contributed to the reduction in inequality in land holdings, as some evidence of the lower value of gini coefficient imply; Land reforms might have also helped in the emergence of a medium size holding group at the expense of the large land holders. With all these favourable features, reforms have not helped in removing poverty and destitution among the small and marginal farmers. Nor they seem to have contributed to the growth of non-farm employment. To address these questions we have to look into the present agrarian structure and the forces which have contributed to its evolution.

EMERGING AGRARIAN STRUCTURE

Agrarian structure in India has undergone significant changes during last few decades. The major changes in the pattern of land ownership as revealed in the latest Agricultural Census (1995-96) and NSS rounds can be summarised as follows:

- Proportion of landless agricultural households in the rural area has stabilised around 11 to 12 per cent. Trend towards prolitarianisation has halted.
- Nearly 80 per cent of the cultivators own marginal (less than 1 ha.) and small (between I and 2 ha.) holdings. Their number as well as area has increased. They accounted for 36 per cent of the total cultivated area in 1995-96. The cultivated area in these holding groups might have reached 40 per cent by now. A large majority among these are the marginal farmers, with average holding size of .4 ha.
- Nearly 18 per cent of cultivating households own semi-medium (between 2 to 4 ha.) and medium (between 4 to 10 ha.) holdings, and accounted for 49 per cent of the

cultivated area in 1995-96. There is no perceptible decline in their number or in the area owned by them in recent years.

- Number and area under large holdings (10 ha. and above) has continuously declined.

Information on operational holdings, as revealed by the NSS rounds, suggest the similar pattern in operational holdings. Additionally, it has been revealed that tenancy is a widespread phenomenon, and most of it is 'concealed'. All groups of farmers operate in the lease market; marginal and small farmers are more active as lessor as well as lessee (Chadha *et al.,* 2004).

Thus, significant changes are taking place in access to land by different groups in the rural area. For a large and diverse country like India, it is natural that certain trends will be specific to individual regions. However, the over all developments are easily recognisable. A large proportion of holdings are marginal and small holdings; progressively more and more area is being cultivated in these holding groups. Agriculture in India is a small farm dominated activity, and this characteristic is not likely to change in near future.

These observations are based on periodic censuses and surveys. At best they give comparative picture at different points of time. They do not reveal the processes which account for such changes, nor do they indicate inter-group or intra-group dynamics which results in the observed changes. Only panel data over large parts of the country could have yielded such information. In the absence of regularly monitored intra-group data we have to make qualitative assessment of the structural changes in land holdings and access to land by different groups by analysing the likely impact of some of the determining factors. These factors can be broadly categorised as: (i) market transactions, (ii) legislative measures, and (iii) demographic factors.

Land Market

In traditional societies transactions in land are not very common because until a dire need arises a peasant will not like to sell his land. Provisions of various legislations have further contributed to restricting land market. For example, a scheduled tribe land owner cannot sell his land to non scheduled tribe person. In spite of these restrictions and inhibitions large chunks of land had passed over to the money lenders and bigger land owners in the pre-Independence years. During the post-Independence period this process seems to have been slow down. The threat of ceiling legislation acted as a deterrent to further purchase of land by large farmers. Opportunities for intensification of farming, especially in the irrigated areas, lured cultivators with cash surpluses to invest in existing holdings rather than expand their holdings. On the other hand tenancy legislation made it possible for the landless or marginal tenants to purchase land which they were cultivating on lease. Admittedly this was not a universal phenomenon, but in the areas where absentee landlords were lessors it was not an uncommon feature. This tendency was more prominent when the credit institutions, i.e. Land Development Banks, advanced credit to tenants for purchase of land, e.g. in parts of former Bombay and Saurashtra states. Available evidence suggests that after land reforms the land market has tended to work in favour of the small and marginal land owners rather than against them.

Land Reforms

Land reforms legislation played a much more important role in influencing the ownership pattern. Market related factors at best supplemented the impact of the land legislation. The direct implication of the ceiling legislation in sequestering land of the large owners and its distribution to the small and marginal farmers, as is well known, was not significant except in Jammu and Kashmir and West Bengal. But the indirect pressure exercised by the legislation was very significant. In spite of fictitious transfers and other subterfuges devised by the large land owners, enactment of land ceiling legislation led to disposal of land by those owning large holdings, particularly the absentee landlords. As the tenancy legislation gave right of purchase of land to the tenants the process of breaking up of the above-ceiling holdings was further accentuated. In any event, the ceiling legislation made it more risky to enlarge holdings beyond the stipulated area and to that extent curbed the tendency to further enlarge the holdings by dispossessing the small owners and acquiring their land. It is reasonable to infer that the small farmers could retain their holdings against the machination of the large farmers, and they as well as the landless labourers were the main beneficiaries once the larger land owners decided to dispose of part of their land to be on the right side of law. Again, the process did not unfold in a neat fashion. There were large numbers of cases of ejection of small tenants as there were numerous cases of acquisition of land by small farmers. However, in large parts of the country small land owners and landless tenants were the gainers due to land reform legislation.

Demographic Pressure

While the increase in the area under marginal and small holding group could be largely explained by legislative measures supplemented by market processes, increase in their number is basically due to population increase in these households and lack of alternative employment opportunity in the country side. An expansion of the household or, more commonly, death of the head of the household leads to division of holdings among the legal heirs. Unfortunately, there are no systematic studies of household dynamics in the rural areas to arrive at a precise measure of subdivision of holdings over a period of time due to demographic factors. However, it is reasonable to assume that the combined effect of the two factors, population growth and lack of non-farm employment opportunity, largely explain the increase in the number of small and marginal holdings. There could also be a possibility of a 'ladder'; i.e. landless labourers, or more likely landless tenants acquiring small plots of land. In the circumstances discussed above this possibility cannot be ruled out. Similarly, decline in the number of and area under large and big holding groups could be due to division of the households leading to subdivisions of the holdings and their sliding to the lower holding group. At the same time, reduction of the number of the households in these holding groups due to their opting for non-farm activities could also be one of the reasons for the diminishing numbers in the large holding group (Vyas, 1979).

Complex of factors described above have resulted in small farm dominated agriculture in our country. This tendency is likely to continue. Given the present social and political milieu, it may be possible to stop the erosion of holdings of the small farmers, but it will not be possible to stop the division of large holdings, and their further expansion to any meaningful extent is out of question—the noise about the corporatisation of agriculture or removal of ceiling notwithstanding. Small farm dominate agriculture will be a reality in India for quite some time to come.

The moot question therefore is that how do we improve the dismal living conditions of vast section of rural population subsisting on the small and marginal holdings.

Experience in India in this regard is opposite to that in China, where the break up of the Communes in small peasant holdings (the average size of these holdings was less than one-third of the average size of holdings in India), lead to a spurt in the non-farm activities. The main reason for the growth of the non-farm activities in China was that along with the introduction of the household responsibility system severe price distortions in agricultural produce were also removed to a considerable extent. Both these developments provided the needed incentive to boost agricultural productivity which was already very high, especially in comparison to India. With increase in production and better prices the cash income of the farmers increased significantly leading to an upsurge in their demand for non-farm goods and services. There were other factors responsible for the phenomenal growth of the non-farm sector in China, the most important among these being a much higher investment in human resources, in education and health, which preceded the institution of 'household responsibility system'. Also, a much more effective technological support was available to the small peasant holdings. However, the main reason was the strong demand-induced linkages forged between agricultural and non-agricultural sectors (Vyas, 2003).

In India nothing of that sort happened. Income, particularly the cash income, of the majority of the cultivators remained abysmally low. Naturally, they could not provide markets for non-agricultural goods and services. Only the rural rich could provide markets for non-farm sectors, and their consumption pattern, as that of the richer sections of urban population, is dominated by goods with high capital and high import components. It is not surprising that such goods find an expanding market in the rural areas, while the rural arts and crafts languish. For the survival of the latter several other preconditions have to be fulfilled, e.g. better quality, reduced cost, institutional support, infrastructure development etc., but the most important component in reviving rural non-farm activities would be an increase in the income of the large mass of the small and marginal farmers. Growth of other major non-farm activity, i.e. agro-processing, is conditioned, among other factors, by the availability of sizable surpluses of uniform quality and standard together with the infra-structural and technical support. According to 1992 Agricultural

Census, 68 per cent of the total cultivated area of marginal farmers and 64 per cent of the cultivated area of the small farmers was devoted to cereals, presumably for self-consumption. With large majority of producers having self-provisioning as the major objective, there was little chance of emergence of large surpluses for processing and catering to external demand. Any reform of the agrarian structure has to keep these conditions in the forefront.

Improving productivity on these farm holdings is an obvious component of strategy to improve income of the small cultivators. At the same time, it should be recognised that for minuscule holdings included in the marginal holding group even a sizable increase in productivity, i.e. in yield per hectare, will not be able to lift them above the poverty line. As it is, a large part of income for this group comes from wage labour and livestock rearing rather than from cultivation. The solution for this group is the expansion of farm and non-farm employment opportunities. The small farm groups are potentially viable in most of the ecological regions in our country provided institutional support is provided to them in terms of extension, credit and marketing. The task of providing viable income from farming is easier still on the semi-medium and medium holdings. On the other hand the cultivators in the large holding groups take recourse to non-farm activities, e.g. trade, money lending, dealings in real estate, provision of services etc. (though for tax purposes they may declare all their income as the agricultural income!) to a large extent. Thus, non-farm activities are important at the two ends of the spectrum, i.e. for very small farmers and for very large farmers. The nature of non-farm activities which these groups opt for, naturally, differs. For the semi-medium and medium holdings agriculture is the main source of their income.

SUGGESTED DIRECTIONS IN LAND REFORMS

If above description of the rural scene is correct a three pronged strategy for improving the lot of small farmers and strengthening farm non-farm linkages is indicated:

- Marginal farmers should be encouraged to sale or lease out their lands and should be provided with gainful employment.
- Small farmers should be encouraged to expand their holdings by purchase or by leasing in land.

- The large farmers should be encouraged to sell or lease out land and facilitated to start non-farm rural enterprises.

The agrarian structure in our country is dominated by the marginal holdings (i.e. holdings with less than 1 ha of cultivated land). Although with declining importance of land in agriculture the size of holding is not the decisive criterion for remunerative farming, but it can be safely assumed that baring some exceptional circumstances the 'handkerchief holdings', say of less than a hectare, will not be viable. Our objective should be to create as many viable holdings as possible. It should not lead to a conclusion that estate farming is the better alternative. There is enough evidence to suggest that large holdings do not have any intrinsic advantage in crop production (Sen, 2004). We should aim at an agrarian structure characterised by small and medium size holdings and enable them to go for high value remunerative agriculture.

A major step forward in that direction will be if the marginal farmers are permitted to lease out their land to the small and medium size holdings on a long term basis, without losing their ownership right. The marginal holdings account around three million ha. of land, a large part of it can be leased to small and medium farmers. This will not be workable unless the marginal farmers are given right to lease out their land without losing ownership right, and enough opportunities for non-farm employment is available to them. For latter to happen large farmers should be encouraged to vacate (lease out) the land in favour of small and medium farmers and specialise in post-harvest operations, in trade, agro-processing and other rural industries. This group has resources, access to institutional support and capacity to bear risk, all of which are important to start an enterprise.

The suggested changes will be in accordance with what is actually happening at the ground level. At the two ends of the spectrum, i.e. among the marginal farmers and the large farmers, agriculture is not the main source of income. Of course, the sources of non-agricultural income differ in the two cases. The present arrangements of leasing out of land by the marginal as well as the large farmers are, in most of the circumstances, illegal and lead to sub-optimal results as the premium for the risk entailed in such arrangements has to be added on. In the past, i.e. in the initial phase of land reforms in our country, rural cooperative credit societies, especially the Land Development

Banks, assisted small farmers and tenants to buy land or to secure proprietorship rights. Such schemes exist even to day but they hardly figure in the portfolio of the rural financial institutions.

In order to make this a viable strategy, the State will have to take following action.

UNFREEZING THE LEASE MARKET

Objective is to enable small farms to increase their operational area. In order to ensure that it is not used to defeat the purpose of ceiling on agricultural holdings, it may be stipulated that the operational holdings with leased-in land should be within the ceiling limits. Further, three preconditions are necessary to reach the objective of the 'free lease markets': (a) proper record of rights; (b) clear annunciation of rights and obligations of the land owner and tenant; and (c) an effective machinery for monitoring and adjudication, at the ground level.

A Programme for Ensuring Employment for the Landless and Marginal Farmers

There is enough scope to use labour intensive methods for strengthening land and water resources. Ingenuity lies is designing ways to make people who benefit from these improvements to pay for the benefits. Experience of the current employment programme should be utilised to develop a viable employment programme. The proposed Employment Guarantee Bill provides excellent opportunity to offer gainful employment to marginal farmers along with landless workers while strengthening the land and water resources in the rural areas.

An Active Land Market to Enable Small Farmers to Enlarge their Holdings

Small farmers on their own will find it difficult to negotiate land purchase deals. Some agency of the state may purchase land at market price from large farmers and sale it to small farmers.

Financial Support to Small Farmers to Expand their Holdings

Credit agencies should be encouraged to advance credit for purchase of land by the small farmers. This was done in the past, and is being done even today in some selected regions. Provisions for financing land purchases by the Land Development Banks and refinancing of these advances by NABARD already exist. These have to be made more effective.

Improvements in Delivery Systems

The objective in this phase of land reforms is not simply to perpetuate a small holding's agrarian structure; the aim is to make the small farms economically viable. Small farm agriculture will depend more on the institutional support. Thus, reforming the institutions of credit, marketing and extension to make them congruent to a small farm agriculture is as important as reforms in the land and lease markets. State policies in this as in other respects should be consciously designed to support the small farm system.

Encouragement to Contract Farming

Contract farming is not a new innovation in Indian agriculture, it was introduced decades back by cooperative sugar factories and milk unions. Recent interest in contract farming by private sector should be encouraged. However, fair terms for contracting parties have to be ensured and an effective adjudication mechanism has to be established.

Risk Mitigation

Without proper and effective instruments of risk mitigation to ask the bulk of the farmers to go for high input intensive high risk prone high value crops is to compound their difficulties. In such circumstances the better alternative will be to propagate mixed farming with emphasis on self-provisioning, and 'commercial crops' or commercial enterprises playing only a supplementary role. This is the model which bulk of the farmers in risk prone areas are adopting on their own. Propagation of high value agriculture in Indian agricultural setting is predicated on the access to reliable instruments of crop and income insurance.

A Massive Programme of Rural Industrialisation

With the participation of large farmers and technical and institutional support by relevant agencies at the *taluk* and district level a demand driven programme of rural industrialisation should be mounted. We can learn valuable lessons in this regard from the Chinese experience.

Time is ripe for instituting the next phase of land reforms on the lines suggested above. With several favourable factors such as adequate food and non-food resources with the government, a vast institutional network for providing credit, marketing and extension, large number of trained people, improved infrastructure of roads and communication, and relevant experience in implementing various programmes we can launch bold actions in favour of those who have been left out of the mainstream of development, to theirs as well as country's disadvantage.

REFERENCES

Chadha G. K., Suchitra Sen & H. R. Sharma, (2004). *Land Resources. State of the Indian Farmers—A Millennium Study*. Volume 2. Academic Foundation, New Delhi.

Sen Abhijit & M. S. Bhatia, (2004). *Cost of Cultivation and Farm Income. State of the Indian Farmers—A Millennium Study*. Volume 14. Academic Foundation, New Delhi. 2004.

Vyas V. S. (1979). "Some Aspects of Structural Changes in Indian Agriculture". Presidential Address delivered at 38th Annual Conference of the Indian Society of Agricultural Economists held under the auspices of the Assam Agricultural University, Jorhat (Assam), on January 18, 1979.

Vyas V. S, (1993). "Agricultural Policies for the Nineties: Issues and Approaches". A paper prepared for the Ministry of Finance, Government of India. Institute of Development Studies.

Vyas V. S. (2003). *India's Agrarian Structure: Economic Policies and Sustainable Development*. Academic Foundation, New Delhi.

Chapter 2

The Land Question and Globalization: Some Reflections on the Relevance of Redistributive Land Reforms

V. B. ATHREYA

I
RENEWED INTEREST IN LAND REFORMS

Land reforms were on the political agenda of the country through much of the period of the freedom struggle and the decades after independence till about the late 1970s. Since then, however, despite the fact that the remarkable achievements of Operation Barga received widespread recognition nationally and internationally, land reforms have not figured prominently on the political agenda of the country for over two decades now. Of late, however, there has been a flurry of moves in the area of land legislation by several state governments and discussions at various levels on the questions of land ceilings and tenurial reform (Ramachandran and Ramakumar, 2000; D. N., 2002; Brian Lobo, 2002; Government of Tamil Nadu, 2002). The new measures, both those legislated and those proposed, are altogether different in character from land reforms as generally understood in both academic and political discussions in the country. While the issue of land reforms as posed during the freedom movement and afterwards, both by bourgeois and by left political forces (though from their respective, distinct viewpoints), stressed redistribution of land from landlords to the actual tillers, and provision of security of tenure, fixation of fair rent and conferment of ownership to the cultivating tenantry, the current proposals for "land reform" are primarily concerned with liberalizing land markets and raising ceilings to enable corporate agri-business, both domestic and foreign, to enter agriculture in a big way.

Elsewhere in the developing world also, there has been a revival of the land reforms agenda, although in this case, for the most part, land reforms of a redistributive kind are being proposed, but within a neoliberal perspective. The World Bank has declared itself to be in favour of greater equity in land ownership, and has rediscovered a new compatibility between equity and "efficiency" (K. Deininger and G. Feder, 2002; Monica Das Gupta *et al.*, 2002; K. Deininger *et al.*, 2002). A great deal of laboured research has been sponsored by the Bank to demonstrate something that should be self-evident, namely that access to land can reduce the incidence of poverty and strengthen the poor (Mearns, 2002). But there is, of course, a catch. Measures to bring about greater access to land for the poor, in the view of the Bank, must not be state-driven, but market-driven. The State should not be involved, or involved at best as a facilitator, and as a provider of the necessary legal framework. Land must get distributed from "willing sellers" to "willing buyers" through a market transaction. The State may facilitate some land transfer to the poor by providing them loan finance on concessional terms to purchase land. It is not difficult to see how this would work out in a situation where the large landowners have considerable political and economic clout, which is of course almost always the case. Except for revolutionary land reforms of the kind that occurred during the socialist transformations of former USSR, China, Vietnam, DPRK and Cuba, and the land reforms carried out in Japan, South Korea and Taiwan under very special political conditions, landlords have largely been able to sabotage (at least partially) reforms even when the State has been the agency bringing about the reforms. In a market setting, the landlords/ capitalist farmers will be able to strengthen themselves in a "land reform" process of the kind being pushed by the Bank, and the result may well be a redistribution of wealth, and over time, the lands as well as the new landed poor sell out under the pressure of market forces, from the poor to the rich.

Available evidence from Central and South America, as well as South Africa and countries like Egypt demonstrate that the Bank's much touted market assisted land reforms neither benefit the poor nor are they fiscally sustainable (V. K. Ramachandran and

M. Swaminathan, 2002). But the real agenda of the Bank model is not redistribution anyway. It is much more concerned with creating a land market, or more broadly, a "free" market in land rights. What this means is that sale, lease and mortgage of land must not be restricted in any way by the legal system/the State. Such a neoliberal regime will facilitate the purchase/lease of land by corporates, both MNC and domestic, from the weaker landholders, and enable them to engage in "captive farming". Where political conditions are not conducive to direct ownership or leasing in by MNCs, they may settle for contract farming to ensure supplies of crops necessary for their export operations.

In this paper, we proceed as follows. In the next section, we shall provide a brief review of India's record in implementation of land reforms since independence upto the period of commencement of vigorous pursuit of neoliberal policies in 1991, focusing primarily on redistributive reform. We then examine the implications of the changed global context since the late 1980s, marked by the rise to dominance of finance capital and the collapse of East European and Soviet Socialist regimes for the issue of redistributive land reforms, and locate the current moves towards land market liberalization in that context. In the final section, we seek to reflect on the issue of land reforms in India in the current context.

II
LAND REFORMS IN INDIA

The case for redistributive land reform can be made on many grounds. In the course of discussions at an international conference on 'Agrarian Relations and Rural Development in Less-Developed Countries' held at Kolkata in January 2002, Professor Prabhat Patnaik referred to three types of argument for land reforms: the populist, which argues the case on the grounds of the alleged superior efficiency of small farms over the large; the redistributive, which sees land reform as an anti-poverty measure; and the viewpoint of the political Left, which sees land reform as part of the democratic revolution that seeks to eliminate all forms of economic exploitation and social oppression in the countryside, and unleash the productive energies of the primary producers. One may also add that the argument for land reforms can never be a purely productionist one, but one that places human development at the centre, as Professor Bagchi has noted

(Ramachandran and Swaminathan, 2002). Interestingly, referring to possible objections to redistribution of lands expropriated from large estates to small peasants in the course of a social revolution on the ground that large scale farming is technically superior, Lenin says, in the 'Preliminary Draft Theses on the Agrarian Question',

> 'To achieve this revolution, the proletariat should not shrink from a temporary decline in production', and further that, 'What is most important to the bourgeois is production for the sake of production; what is most important to the working and exploited population is the overthrow of the exploiters and the creation of conditions that will permit the working people to work for themselves, and not for the capitalists'(Lenin, 1975).

The Indian bourgeoisie was of course not looking at land reforms in this perspective. It had to deal with pressure for land reform from below at the dawn of independence, in the context of the Tebaga, Telengana and Warli struggles of the peasantry as well as other peasant struggles. Further, the growth of Indian capitalism needed a reformation of the agrarian structure to promote capitalist farming, with a view to ensuring adequate marketed supplies of wage goods as well as agricultural raw materials needed for industrialisation. In the political context of the early independence years, the *zamindars* who were basically huge absentee landlords with a record of being greatly reviled oppressors of the peasantry, and who had moreover collaborated with the hated colonial regime, could be targeted, using the slogan of 'land to the tiller'. Not surprisingly, the thrust of the early land reform legislation was on the abolition of intermediaries, meaning essentially the abolition of various forms of *zamindari*, known by different names in different parts of the country. While this particular aspect of land reforms was relatively successful in the sense that a large number of ex-tenants on the *zamindari* estates were able to acquire ownership of the land they had possession of under the *zamindars*, it must also be noted that, given the considerable extent of sub-infeudation, it was mostly the tenants with superior rights who benefited, and not necessarily the actual cultivators. In fact, the considerable time over which the desirability of various alternative land reform measures were debated before the actual passing of legislation gave the *zamindars* time enough to organize a certain degree of evasion. Besides, they were able, in the first instance, to retain a large amount of lands in their possession in the name of so-called sir or *khud-kasht* ('home farm') cultivation. In this process, a large number of tenants-at-will, who had been cultivating these lands were thrown into the ranks of the landless. Further, the *zamindars* managed to extract a large amount of compensation from the State, reported as around rupees 670 crores by official sources—no mean amount in the 1950s! Nevertheless, the old feudal estates, by and large, were abolished over a period of time in most parts of the country, and the superior tenants—many of whom were from the cultivating peasantry—gained a firm access to land. The official claim is that 20 million cultivators were benefited in the process (Ministry of Rural Development, 1992). A large amount of land under the *zamindari* estates also reverted to the State.

The second important component of land reforms was concerned with tenancy, which was widespread in the so-called ryotwari areas as well. There were three declared objectives of tenancy reform, namely provision of security of tenure, fixation of fair rent and conferment of ownership to the tenant. However, the tenancy legislation also provided for the right of resumption of cultivation by the owner on several grounds, which were systematically misused, where the tenants' movements were weak, to evict tenants on a large scale. The scandalously liberal definition of 'personal cultivation' facilitated this process greatly, while enabling tenancy on onerous terms for the tenant to continue in a concealed manner. Poor land records and the notorious method of extracting so-called "voluntary surrenders" from the weak tenants also contributed to minimizing the progressive impact of tenancy legislation. Many of the failures of tenancy legislation in terms of declared intent have been admitted in several official documents, most notably successive plan documents of the 1960s to the 1980s which never failed to pay ritual homage to the objectives of land reform. The official assessment on tenancy reforms is that an estimated 77.21 lakh cultivators had been conferred ownership rights on 138 lakh acres of land by 1991. Besides, in what remains a unique achievement, 14 lakh *bargadars* had been brought on record in West Bengal by then.

The third and most widely discussed component of land reforms has been the ceiling on landholdings. There was a great deal of vacillation on the part of the government in the early years following independence on this question (P. S. Appu,1996). The First Plan showed considerable ambivalence on this issue. In the end, the principle of imposing a limit on the size of landholding was ultimately accepted. However, it was only in the late 1950s/early 1960s that land ceiling legislations came to be passed. By this time, the wave of peasant militancy, so evident from the mid-1940s to the mid-1950s, had subsided. The Communist movement was heading for a split. The legislation and implementation of land ceilings became a largely administrative affair, with the honourable exception of Kerala where the undivided communist party initiated serious land reforms. With the undemocratic dismissal of the Kerala Government in 1960, another nine years had to pass before the second EMS ministry could carry out a thorough reform (which was mainly concerned with the abolition of tenancy, and did not lead to any significant extent of ceiling-surplus land for distribution to the landless and the land-poor; the provision of house-sites and a minimum of five cents of land to the landless labourers was, however, an extremely important measure). As already noted, the long period over which the land ceilings legislations were debated and passed, with various pro-landlord provisions, by the various state legislatures, gave landlords plenty of time to conceal large amounts of land, with the connivance of the local revenue administration and the collusion of the party in power.

For a while, it seemed as if the land ceilings issue was over and done with, even though hardly any ceiling surplus land had been unearthed. While the first three plan documents had copious references to land reform policies and their implementation, the fourth plan was practically silent on the issue, and was instead almost wholly devoted to discussions of the "new agricultural strategy" and the technocratic route to increasing productivity in agriculture. However, with the implementation of the new agricultural strategy in the mid-1960s in the context of a serious foodgrains crisis, there was a fresh round of evictions of peasants on a large scale by landlords who had discovered that cultivation could be quite profitable with the new technology and the new policies. This naturally led to renewed mass struggles by the peasantry. The sharpening of rural class struggles which was evident in the late 1960s and the early 1970s, as well as the compulsions of bourgeois inner party conflicts, led to the reemergence of land reforms on the political agenda as part of the *garibi hatao* rhetoric (F. T. Januzzi, 1994). The significant political advance of the Left in West Bengal, Tripura and Kerala, and the emergence of Left-led peasant and agricultural labour struggles in different parts of the country were important among the factors which led to the convening of the conference of chief ministers in 1972 by the then prime minister to discuss land reforms implementation. The conference agreed upon a new set of national guidelines for land ceilings, which sought to lower the ceiling limits, remove some of the more patently unjustifiable exemptions, and invest the whole process with a certain degree of political seriousness. (P. S. Appu, 1996). Unlike the Fourth Plan document where the emphasis was almost entirely on growth, the Fifth and Sixth Plan documents spoke at length of land reforms. Estimates of of ceiling-surplus were once again made. It may be recalled that, based on a 20 acre uniform ceiling, it had been suggested in the late 1960s that as much as one-sixth of India's 400 million acres of cultivable land—63 million acres—could be made available for distribution (AIKS, 1979). By the early seventies, this figure was not making the rounds any more, but the estimates in circulation (*all figures in acres*) varied from 12 million (26th Round, NSS, 1971-72) to 30 million (Agricultural Census 1970-71).

What actually happened is another, unsurprising story. By end-September 1991, 72.49 lakh acres had been declared surplus, 62.53 lakh acres had been taken possession of, and 48.12 lakh acres had been actually distributed to 45.98 lakh persons (Ministry of Rural Development, 1992). Has the picture changed much since then? It has not, except for what has been done in West Bengal. As of March 31, 2002, 73.73 lakh acres had been declared surplus, 65 lakh acres had been taken over, and 53.94 lakh acres had been distributed to a total of 56.47 lakh persons (Ministry of Rural Development, 2002). West Bengal accounted for 10.64 lakh acres in terms of land distributed and 26.52 lakh persons had received ceiling surplus land in the State.

The achievement in respect of distribution of government wastelands was considerably higher in absolute terms. As of September 30, 1991, 124.61 lakh acres of such lands had been distributed, the bulk of it from Andhra Pradesh (30.4 lakh acres), Uttar Pradesh (22.28), Gujarat (13.73), Karnataka (13.22) and Maharashtra (10.23) (Ministry of Rural Development, 1992). By March 31, 2002, the total amount of government wastelands distributed had risen to 147.47 lakh acres, with Andhra Pradesh contributing the largest chunk of 42.02 lakh acres (Ministry of Rural Development, 2002).

The implication of the fact that relatively little land has been distributed as ceiling surplus, together with the distribution of wastelands and the conferment of ownership on over 8 million erstwhile tenants, is that while landlessness would have decreased to some extent on this account, land concentration would have not declined significantly.[1] When we take into account the processes of peasant differentiation under way for over five decades, and the negative impact of overall macroeconomic policies over this period, one would not even be surprised if the land concentration ratio had marginally increased. In fact, between 1970-71 and 1990-91, the Gini-concentration ratio for operational holdings rose from 0.586 to 0.641 while that for ownership holdings increased marginally from 0.709 to 0.710 (V. K. Ramachandran and R. Ramakumar, 2000). The picture for 1995-96 is not very different. A comparison of the distribution of operational holdings in 1985-86, 1990-91 and 1995-96 is provided below:

Size	Class of Holdings	Year		
		1985-86	1990-91	1995-96
Marginal	Share of Holdings (%)	57.8	59.4	61.6
(< 1 Hectare)	Share of Area Operated (%)	13.4	15.0	17.2
Small	Share of Holdings (%)	18.4	18.8	18.7
(1-2 Hectares)	Share of Area Operated (%)	15.6	17.4	18.8
Semi-medium	Share of Holdings (%)	13.6	13.1	12.3
(2-4 Hectares)	Share of Area Operated (%)	22.3	23.2	23.8
Medium	Share of Holdings (%)	8.2	7.1	6.1
(4-10 Hectares)	Share of Area Operated (%)	28.6	27.1	25.3
Large	Share of Holdings (%)	2.0	1.6	1.2
(> 10 Hectares)	Share of Area Operated (%)	20.1	17.3	14.8

It can be seen that there is no radical change in the concentration of operational holdings, although there is some subdivision of holdings leading to a slightly greater bulge in the proportion of holdings in the smaller size categories and some corresponding thinning in the highest brackets. In 1995-96, the bottom 61.6 per cent of operational holdings accounted for only 17.2 per cent of the total operated area as against 40.1 per cent accounted for by the top 7.3 per cent. The picture in respect of ownership holdings is unlikely to show any dramatic change. In fact, taking into account the relatively greater concentration of non-land assets, especially pumpsets, tractors and other agricultural machinery, the concentration of productive assets in agriculture would most certainly have risen.

This is not to say that there have been no significant changes in agrarian structure even in terms of landholding. In fact, it is well known that there has been a real process of social churning in land ownership, with intermediate peasant castes replacing the upper castes in states like Tamil Nadu, and even dalits getting some access to land (K. Nagaraj, 2000). However, taking an overall view, land concentration and land monopoly remain substantially intact. The degree of land monopoly does of course vary considerably across the regions, as does the implication of such monopoly for agricultural growth.

Summing up the record of land reforms, and without going into such important issues as distribution of homestead land, the state of land records and land consolidation, we can remind ourselves that, as of 1992:

- Less than 2 per cent of total area operated has been redistributed.
- Other than in three states, the area redistributed is less than 1 per cent of the area operated in the state.
- Ownership rights over only 3.8 per cent of total area operated were conferred on the tenants.

(V. K. Ramachandran and R. Ramakumar, 2002)

III
LAND REFORMS AND THE AGRARIAN QUESTION

In 1991, the country's rulers embarked on an accelerated programme of liberalization, privatization and globalization. The basic philosophy behind this programme was clearly inimical to any serious redistributive land reform, but since ideas usually lag behind objective circumstances, there was a brief flurry of conferencing activity around the issue of land reforms in the early 1990s. In 1992, a national workshop was convened jointly by the National Institute of Rural Development and the Indian Association of Social Science Institutions to discuss land reforms (IASSI, n.d.). The overwhelming majority of participants at the workshop including those who generally supported the neoliberal policies of the regime in power reiterated the need for serious implementation of land reforms, and opposed the entry of large Indian and multinational companies into agriculture. But the late Professor Dandekar, in his inimitable style, fired the first salvo on behalf of the liberalizers. He stated, in the course of his remarks, that, 'An essential condition for an industry to grow is that a firm engaged in it must have the capacity to grow; in agriculture, a farm or a farmer must have the capacity to create a surplus and plough it back in agriculture and thus grow as a farmer. This he cannot do if there is a ceiling on his landholding. Hence, the first thing to do is to remove the ceiling.' More over, in his view, '...like the country, agriculture needs outside capital in the form of investment...This can be done only by private capital. This needs to be permitted.' (IASSI, n.d, p.182).

Although Dandekar was in a minority at the conference, and although the officials of the Ministry of Rural Development made an elaborate presentation to the Prime Minister and State Revenue Ministers in 1992 arguing the case for serious steps to unearth benami ceiling surplus land and ensure security for tenants and sharecroppers across the land, the tide had definitely changed (Ministry of Rural Development, 1992). By the mid-1990s, the academics were not the only ones calling for reversal of some aspects of earlier land reforms in order to promote agricultural growth through corporate investments. As already noted, several state governments had gone further and changed the land laws accordingly. Karnataka, Maharashtra and Gujarat were among the first ones to legislate such changes. A more recent case is Tamil Nadu. In a series of government orders issued between October 2001 and July 2002, the government announced its policy of leasing out waste lands to the tune of 20 lakh hectares to private companies in blocks of upto 1000 hectares for a period of 30 years, on very nominal lease rates.[2] To deflect opposition to the move, the government has also offered to provide blocks of upto 20 hectares for co-operatives, self-help groups and so on. There is an emerging consensus in ruling circles and among academics supporting neoliberal policies that all restrictions on land leasing should be removed (A. Virmani, 2002). As for redistributive land reforms, that is simply not on the agenda. Even writers generally sympathetic to the idea take the view that there is simply not enough land to go around (F. T. Januzzi, 1996). On the other hand, in a recent review of India's land reforms, Sukumar Das (B. K. Sinha and Pushpendra, 2000) argues that there is indeed enough land for distribution even if we want to provide every agricultural household with 3 hectares of land. This is of course based on the arithmetic of available wastelands, *bhoodan* lands and taking away all lands in excess of 3 hectares from the 9.3 million holdings in the top bracket operating 73.9 million hectares of land in 1991! Such arithmetic of course does not clinch the issue, given the lopsided distribution of such lands across the different regions of the country. In any event, land reform is not an issue of arithmetic, but the exercise is an interesting counter to the opposite refrain of "There is simply just not enough land"!

At an altogether different, theoretical level, Henry Bernstein has recently argued that the last great wave of redistributive land reforms under the aegis of the developmentalist state probably came to an end with the decade of the 1970s, with the possible exception of the South African case (H. Bernstein, 2002). With the collapse of the developmentalist state consequent to the rise to dominance of finance capital and its processes of centralization and globalization, Bernstein argues, the question of agrarian transition has to be seen in an altogether new perspective. Posing the question of "...why and how changes in capitalism since the end of developmentalism...may have transcended the conditions of the 'classic' agrarian question that had persisted until then, at least in certain zones of the South". Bernstein argues that '...the classic agrarian question is no longer a concern of capital on a global scale.' Bernstein argues that overproduction is a key problem of contemporary capitalist agriculture, and that "...the circuits of domestic/'national' economies intersect with, and are increasingly shaped by those of global patterns of production, divisions of labour, markets for finance and commodities, and forms of regulation by transnational capital." Bernstein argues that the new-found enthusiasm of some international agencies for land reforms based on a populist understanding ('the small peasant is more efficient' etc.,) is misplaced in terms of practical effectiveness, given the dominance of globalized agriculture under the aegis of metropolitan capital. Arguing implicitly that one must explore forms of class and popular struggle that relate, no longer to an agrarian question of the peasantry, but to the role of various classes of labour—with even rural labour no longer being entirely or even predominantly peasant in character—in issues of land redistribution, Bernstein suggests that the Latin American experience—of the MST in Brazil or the Zapatistas of Chiapas in Mexico, with their mobilization of landless labourers and poor peasants, may be relevant in this context. He contrasts this type of movement—which, in his view, addresses agrarian questions of labour—to the 'new' farmers' movements of India whose programmatic centre strongly on prices and subsidies rather than on land. His broad conclusion is that regardless of what happens to the current dominance of neoliberal ideology and the political forces underlying it, the old, classic agrarian question is no longer relevant. By implication, the agrarian question is no longer of the peasantry, but of labour.

While the argument is provocative and merits serious engagement, it will not be possible to go into it here, except to say that at one level it may be too sweeping an assertion, and at another level, not all that different from the classical Marxist position of relying on the poor peasants and agricultural labourers as the axis of the agrarian movement. Bernstein may also be writing off the third world state in such large countries as India prematurely. There is a strong dose of what Byres has called 'the determinism of global industrial capital' in Bernstein's argument (Byres in V. K. Ramachandran and M. Swaminathan, 2002). Against Bernsten's view, it can well be argued that the classic agrarian question—which, in the contemporary epoch, cannot be a question of the transition to capitalism in the third world, given the impossibility of the bourgeoisie completing the democratic revolution, and can, therefore, be only a question of the agrarian revolution under the leadership of the working class—has been made very complex by the present phase of imperialist globalization, but not rendered irrelevant.

In any event, it is certainly true that the new global situation and its political economy have to be taken into account while reflecting on the question of land reforms. It is to this aspect that we now turn.

IV
LAND REFORMS AND THE NEOIMPERIALIST CONTEXT

Professor Prabhat Patnaik has pointed out that with the rise to dominance of finance capital in the global economy, we have entered a new phase of imperialism in which the liberalization process serves as '...a mechanism for centralization of capital on a world scale: metropolitan capital-in-production ousts third world producers, while metropolitan capital-as-finance (which is the dominant component of globalized finance) gets control over third world resources and enterprises (built up earlier at public cost) at throwaway prices.' (P. Patnaik, 1999, p. 65). The implication of the new phase of imperialism is that '...the opportunity for a Third World bourgeoisie to pursue a relatively autonomous trajectory of development no longer exists.'(*Ibid*, p.76) Further, 'Stagnation punctuated by acute crises ...is the fate of the periphery in the era of globalized finance.'(*Ibid.*, p. 70).

Professor Utsa Patnaik has brought out the disastrous consequences of these contemporary globalization processes, both with respect to the dominance of finance capital and the deflationary macroeconomic policies that integration with such a system entails, and with respect to the specific features of globalization of agriculture and its implications for such issues as food security and famine (U. Patnaik, 2003a, 2003b, and references cited therein). We shall therefore not dwell on these aspects, except to note the consensus among progressive forces that over the last decade, strongly deflationary and unashamedly pro-global capital and pro-corporate policies have destroyed Indian agriculture to a considerable degree, and its victims include especially the rural poor, but also practically all sections of the peasantry. Both theoretical arguments and empirical validation to these propositions have been provided by a number of scholars.[3] In such a context, what should be our assessment of the question of redistributive land reforms?

Given the enormous heterogeneity and uneven development of capitalist agrarian relations across the different regions of the country, redistributive land reform cannot have a uniform significance across the country. However, with the continued existence of land and asset monopoly in large parts of the country, redistributive land reform is an issue that remains relevant, if mass deprivation in the country is to be eliminated and the productive energies of the primary producers are to be unleashed to achieve humane development. In a situation where an emerging economic regime in India, tied to the apron strings of global capital, and pursuing massive deflationary policies, is never going to ensure rapid absorption of the rural labour force, and with such a high degree of landlessness, redistributive land reform can never be off the agenda in a basic and long-term sense.[4] The route to it will involve a number of different kinds of struggles, including especially struggle against the neoliberal regime and its policies, and imperialism. In several of these struggles, sections of rural exploiters may be allied with progressive forces against imperialism. After all, the rich peasantry is not assumed to be an enemy of the people's democratic front at the present stage of struggle. But surely, the line of peasant unity against imperialism cannot be interpreted to mean abandonment of the struggle 'for abolition of landlordism and distribution of land gratis to the poor peasantry and agricultural labourers'. One could go further, and argue that where the agricultural labourers and poor peasants are willing to enter the struggle for land, a la MST, for instance (though it must be recognized that conditions in India are very different), it is incumbent on progressive forces to bring redistributive land reforms on the agenda. It is of course not being argued that such reform, by itself, will solve the agrarian question. But when it occurs as part of a rapidly advancing struggle of the agrarian proletariat and semi-proletariat, and is meant to be carried out quickly, and by a mass mobilizational process, it is a key component.

In short, in agrarian societies characterized by considerable land monopoly, regardless of the global conjuncture, redistributive land reform has to be part of the agrarian revolution. The global conjuncture may have implications for agency. If Bernstein is right about the nature of the agrarian question as being one destined for resolution by labour, it still cannot be a vision of waiting for the world proletariat to carry it out. Given the unequal relationship of the Third World to the metropolitan powers in the imperialist system, the poor peasantry and the agricultural proletariat will be the key agencies to resolve the agrarian question, together with the working class.

A few qualifying remarks are in order while concluding this *Note*. We have exclusively focused on the need for redistributive reforms as an integral part of the resolution of the agrarian question in a democratic way. However, this is not to argue that such a redistributive reform can be the immediate agenda nor that redistributive land reform by itself will resolve the land question. Given the current crisis of the rural economy—rising input prices, falling output prices, decline in institutional credit and collapse of public investment for agriculture, and more generally, macro deflationary policies, decline in rural employment and development expenditure and collapse of the public distribution system for the rural economy, there are other urgent problems at hand. Rather than the 'land question', in at least parts of the country (such as Kerala, for example), the 'price question' and the 'wage question' may in fact be more urgent. In the context of a concerted attempt by the large Indian corporations and international capital to grab or otherwise access land, to bring Indian agriculture under their hegemony, fighting back "redistributive reform" of a different kind—from the poor to the rich—may well be a more urgent task. Similarly, fighting for policy changes to reverse the decline in public investment in agriculture and rural infrastructure may be a more immediate need. But all of these things do not obviate the need for a massive redistribution of land to break land monopoly and strengthen democracy in the countryside as part of the agrarian revolution. Experience has shown that for genuine democracy and human development, and for elimination of deprivation, redistributive land reform is absolutely necessary. To put an end to caste and gender oppression and a whole host of precapitalist constraints to development, such land reform is clearly a must. It is of course not a stand-alone measure. It has to be viewed as part of a larger process, and moreover, as being brought about by powerful mass movements of the poor peasantry and agricultural labour and not as an administrative measure. Its positive role will be enhanced by decentralized democracy and by investments in human development as experience has shown. The route to developing the subjective consciousness for such a reform may well lie through a number of other struggles on wage, price, social oppression, public investment and so on. But at the end of the day, there can be no agrarian revolution without massive land redistribution, no matter what the global conjuncture may be.

END NOTES

1. It is of course also true that the process of capitalist development over the several decades since independence and the large scale eviction of tenants in the wake of tenurial reform processes referred to earlier would have led, overall, to a larger degree of rural landlessness now than was the case at independence, which is indeed the case (V. K. Ramachandran and M. Swaminathan, 2002).
2. See G. O. (Ms) No. 189 dated July 2, 2002 of the Department of Agriculture, Government of Tamil Nadu.
3. See the contributions by U. Patnaik and A. Sen in V. K. Ramachandran and M. Swaminathan, 2002.
4. If land monopoly was a constraint to capitalist development in the predominantly rural periphery even earlier, it clearly cannot cease to be a fetter on development in the current conjuncture. (Cf. U. Patnaik, in T. J. Byres, 1998).

REFERENCES

All India Kisan Sabha, (1979). *General Secretary's Report to the 23rd Conference*, A. K. Gopalan Nagar, Varanasi.

Appu, P. S. (1996). *Land Reforms in India*, Vikas Publishing House.

Aziz, Abdul and Sudhir Krishna (1997). *Land Reform in India, Volume 4—Karnataka—Promises Kept and Missed*, Sage Publications.

Barraclough, Solon L. (1999). *Land Reform in Developing Countries: The Role of the State and Other Actors* UNIRSD Discussion Paper No. 101.

Bernstein, H. (2002). "Land Reform: Taking a Long (er) View", *Journal of Agrarian Change*, Volume 2, No. 4, October.

Besley, T. and R. Burgess (1998). "Land Reforms, Poverty Reduction and Growth: The Evidence from India, Development Economics", Discussion Paper 13, London School of Economics.

Bhalla, G. S. and Gurmail Singh (2001). *Indian Agriculture: Four Decades of Development,* Sage.

Chakravarty, Sukhamoy (1997). *Writings on Development*, Oxford University Press.

Chen, Fu and John Davis (1998). "Land Reform in Rural China Since the Mid-1980s", *Land Reform,* Volume 2.

D. N. (2002). "Breaking the Deadlock: Land Reform Revisited", *Economic and Political Weekly,* Volume XXXVII, No.26, June 29-July 5, pp. 2545-2549.

Das Gupta, Monica, Heleno Grandvoinnet and Mattia Romani (2001). *State-Community Synergies in Development: laying the basis for collective action*, World Bank.

Deininger, K. (1999). "Making Negotiated Land Reform Work: Initial Experience from Colombia, Brazil, and South America", *World Development*, Volume 27, No. 2.

Deininger, K. and Gershon Feder (2002). *Land Institutions and Policy: Key Messages of the Policy Research Report*, World Bank.

Deininger, K., Pedro Olinto and Miet Maertens (2002). *Redistribution, Investment and Human Capital Accumulation: The Case of Agrarian Reform in the Philippines,* World Bank.

Dogra, Bharat (2002). "Land Reforms, Productivity and Farm Size", *Economic and Political Weekly*, Volume XXXVII, No. 6, February 9-15, pp. 532-533.

Dorner, Peter and Don Kanel (1971). "The Economic Case for Land Reform: Employment, Land Distribution and Productivity", Report No. 74, Land Tenure Center, University of Wisconsin, Madison, USA.

Ghose, A. K. (1984). *Agrarian Reform in Contemporary Developing Countries*, Select Book Service Syndicate.

Gill, Sucha Singh (2001). *Land Reforms in India, Volume 6—Intervention for Agrarian Capitalist Transformation in Punjab, Haryana*, Sage Publications.

Gill, Sucha Singh and Ranjit Singh Ghuman (2001). "Hanging Agrarian Relations in India: Some Reflections from Recent Data", *Indian Journal of Labour Economics*, Volume 44, No. 4, October-December, pp. 809-826.

Government of India (No date). *Report of the 9th Plan Sub-Group on Land Reforms, Land Use and Land Management.*

Government of India (Planning Commission). *Five Year Plan Documents* (First to Tenth).

Government of Tamil Nadu (2002). *G. O. (Ms) No. 189*, July 2.

Harashima, S. (2000). "Issues in Agricultural Reform: Public Investment and Land Market Development", *Economic and Political Weekly*, October 28.

Herring, R. J. (1983). *Land to the Tiller*, Oxford University Press.

Indian Association of Social Science Institutions (no date). *Land Reform and Rural Change.*

Jannuzi, F. T. (1994). *India's Persistent Dilemma: The Political Economy of Agrarian Reform.* West View Press.

K., Nagaraj (2000). "Tamil Nadu Economy", Mimeo.

Lehmann, D. (1974). *Agrarian Reform and Agrarian Reformism*, Faber & Faber, London.

Lenin, V. I. (1975). *On the Alliance of the Working Class and the Peasantry*, Novosti Press Agency Publishing House, Moscow.

Lobo, Brian (2002). "Maharashtra: Land Reforms—Turning the Clock Back", *Economic and Political Weekly*, Volume XXXVII, No. 4, February 9-15, pp. 529-532.

Mearns, R. (1998). *Access to Land in India*, World Bank.

Ministry of Rural Development, (1992). *Conference of Revenue Ministers, March 14, 1992, Agenda Notes*, Government of India.

Ministry of Rural Development (2002). *Annual Report.*

N. Rajasekaran (1998). "Land Reforms in Maharashtra: A Regional Analysis", *Review of Development and Change*, Volume III, No.2, July-December.

National Book Agency, Kolkata (1969). *A Collection on the Agrarian Question.*

Patnaik, P. (1998). "Critical Reflections on Some Aspect of Structural Change in the India Economy" in T. J. Byres (ed.), *The State, Development Planning and Liberalisation in India*, Oxford University Press.

Patnaik, Prabhat (1999). "Capitalism in Asia at the end of the Millennium", *Monthly Review*, Volume 51, No.3, July-August, pp. 59-78.

Patnaik, Utsa (1998). "India's Agricultural Development in the Light of Historical Experience" in T. J. Byres (ed.), *The State, Development Planning and Liberalisation in India*, Oxford University Press.

Patnaik, Utsa (2003a). *Global Capitalism, Deflation and Agrarian Crisis in Developing Countries*, Social Policy and Development Paper No.15, UNRISD.

Patnaik, Utsa (2003b). "Food Stocks and Hunger", *Social Scientist*, 362-363, Volume 31, No. 7-8, July-August.

Ramachandran, V. K. and Madhura Swaminathan (2002). *Agrarian Studies*, Tulika, 2002.

Ramachandran, V. K. and R. Ramakumar (2000). "Agrarian reforms and Rural Development Policies in India: A Note", Mimeo.

Sen, Bhowani (1962). *Evolution of Agrarian Relations in India*, People's Publishing House.

Sen, Nirupam (2002). "Agricultural Reforms in West Bengal—Some Issues", Paper presented at the International Conference on Agrarian Studies, Kolkata, January.

Sinha, B. K. and Pushpendra (2000). *Land Reforms in India. Volume 5—An Unfinished Agenda*, Sage Publications.

Thorner, Daniel (1976). *The Agrarian Prospect in India*, Allied Publishers.

Virmani, A. (1999). *Reform of Agriculture and Agricultural Processing Policy*, Chintan Policy Paper no. 11, available at <www.chintan.india.org>.

World Bank (1974). *Land Reform*, World Bank.

Xing, Li (1999). "Socialist Foundations of Market Reforms: Assessing Chinese Past", *Economic and Political Weekly*, Volume XXIV, No.49, December 4-10.

Chapter 3

The Problem of Tenancy Reforms and Land Reforms in Relation to Productivity and Rural Poverty

UTSA PATNAIK

I
TENANCY : THE REFORM PATHS

In the post-World War II era, all third world developing countries have faced a common *general* problem of abolishing feudal and semi-feudal relations of production and of securing a more democratic, egalitarian distribution of land and water resources. Feudal relations involving land monopoly by landowners who extract rent from small tenants, act as a fetter in productivity and the removal of this fetter is a basic task both on the grounds of equity and of development. The question is, how do landlord-tenant relations act as a fetter? They do so because the landowners with substantial rent incomes have no economic incentive to invest and to improve productivity; and the tenant paying high tent is left with too little income to invest, while the incentive to do so even when it is feasible, is lost because the fruits of any improvements by the tenant embodied in the soil are taken by the landowner. In addition to the common general problem of semi-feudal relations, Orissa has faced certain specific problems arising from its large tribal population and the existence of the second highest level of poverty in India.

The general of archaic semi-feudal relation and tenures have been tackled historically in different countries through two main alternative paths or strategies: landlord-dominated redistribution and peasant—dominated redistribution respectively. In the first, there is no radical take-over of landlord land by peasants; the landlords continue to monopolise land and may give up only a part of it against compensation; but they begin themselves to turn into capitalist producers, evicting their former tenants the employing them as hired workers. In the second, more democratic path the land is seized without compensation from the landlords and distributed to the landless and land-poor peasants, while the rural capitalists are thrown up in large numbers from the ranks of the well-to-do sections of the peasants themselves. In the western context the two paths are known as the Prussian Junker path and the American path, respectively. In the Asian context we may characterise the conservative path as the Meiji Japan path, and that followed in the same country itself after World War II and also in China, as the second, democratic path.

Thus in Japan after the 1868 Meiji restoration even though the feudal high nobility known as *daimyo* lost their rights, they were compensated heavily with cash and bonds and very little land went to the actual tillers, for mainly the village-level non-cultivating bigger landowners were given the *chiken*, certificates of modern ownership. Under this conservative landlord-dominated reforms, small tenancy grew rapidly to cover over a third of the rice area and high rents along with tenurial insecurity became such a fetter on productivity that rice output started stagnating. Japan turned to colonised Korea which by 1937 was made to supply 65 per cent of the increasing rice imports on which the urban areas depended heavily. By contrast, the post-World War II land reform in Japan itself was a peasant-dominated radical redistribution in which the ceiling for the landlord's personal ownership was placed at 1 *cho* or 2.45 acres, and the remainder amounting to one-third of total cultivated area was given to the tenants. The data show that as tenant area fell to below 5 per cent of total cultivated area, rice yields spurted upwards. In China an even more comprehensive peasant-dominated redistribution took place in which an estimated 45 per cent of total cultivated area passed from the landowners to the landless and land-poor, creating a highly egalitarian distribution. Cooperatives permitted investment to be stepped up especually in water management; much of China's good growth and reduction in rural poverty can be traced to the initial land reform and its consolidation through the cooperative system up to 1978.[1]

II
TENANCY REFORMS IN SELECTED STATES IN INDIA

In India we can usefully analyse our own land reforms in terms of the two-paths conceptualisation sketched above. Without doubt in most states it is the path of landlord-dominated redistribution that has taken place. When intermediary tenures were abolished, it was the former intermediaries who got automatic ownership rights over their *khud-kasht* land and were well compensated with cash and bonds for the small part of the land they gave up to the state. An estimated maximum of one-eighth or about 12 per cent of total cultivated area has been redistributed at the all-India level in the four decades of reforms to 1990, through the market mechanism, viz. after vesting in the government land has been sold to the better-off tenants who already had some owned land and who could afford to pay the purchase price. The ex-intermediaries continued to monopolise land ownership and extract rent from both recorded and unrecorded tenants in many states while going in for hired-labour cultivation in other states.

In Orissa too, as elsewhere, the problem of land monopoly continues and redistribution has been much less than the all-India average. Looking at the NSS data on land operated we find that in 1970-71 the top 20 per cent of holdings operating above 2 ha. controlled 54 per cent of total area and at the bottom 54.5 per cent of holdings operating below 1 ha. held only 18.6 per cent of the total area. Twenty years later in 1991-2 the holdings above 2 ha. comprised 16 per cent of the total number and had 48 per cent of the total area while holdings below 1 ha. were 60 per cent of the total number and held 22 per cent of the area (see Table 3.1). For a more exact comparison of the position at the two dates we have constructed the Lorenz curves of concentration for 1970-71 and 1991-92 from the data of Table 3.1. We find that in the lower range the two curves are identical but they cross at the upper end owing to some redistribution amounting to about one-twentieth of total area, from the top to the medium group of farmers. Thus the top decile of all holdings had 38 per cent of total area operated in 1970-71 while the top decile in 1991-92 had 33 per cent, a decline of 5 per cent. Correspondingly the share of the next 25 per cent of all holdings had gone up 5 per cent points from 37 per cent to 42 per cent over the period. It is noteworthy that the poorer mass of the cultivators, the bottom 65 per cent had gained nothing at all and continued to account for

25 per cent of the total area at both dates (Table 3.2). A redistribution of 5 per cent of area, that too not to the really poor, is far too small to make an impact on productivity.

Table 3.1: Percentage distribution of operational holdings and area operated by size level of operational holdings in Orissa

Size of Farm (Hec.)	*Per cent of Holdings*		*Per cent of Area*	
	1970-71	*1991-92*	*1970-71*	*1991-92*
< 1.01	54.5	60.0	18.6	22.1
1.01—2.00	25.8	24.3	27.3	30.1
2.01—4.00	13.9	12.0	27.1	27.9
4.01—10.00	5.2	3.4	21.5	16.2
> 10.00	0.6	0.3	5.5	3.7
All	100	100	100	100

Source: NSS Reports on Landholding, 26th Round and 48th Round.

Table 3.2: Per cent distribution of holdings ranked by area and area operated, from lorenz curves for specified fractile groups in Orissa

Household Type	*Per cent of Holdings*		*Per cent of Area*	
	1970-71	*1991-92*	*1970-71*	*1991-92*
Well-to-do (top)	10	10	38	33
Middling	25	25	37	42
Poor (bottom)	65	65	25	25
All	100	100	100	100

Source: Lorenz curves of concentration were constructed by taking the cumulative percentages of holdings and area from Table 3.1 data.

It is sometimes argued that tenancy is not longer important in Orissa because according to the 1991-92 NSS data it has dropped to some 10-11 per cent of total area operated and this leased land is with about 18-19 per cent of total holdings. This argument of the non-importance of tenancy is fallacious on two counts. First, it is fallacious because widespread unrecorded tenancy exists with, it is thought, a higher incidence in the coastal districts in particular. The system of collection of agricultural statistics and the NSS survey data are no worse in West Bengal than it is in Orissa and W. Bengal too had shown falling recorded tenancy. Yet it was found necessary to carry out Operation Barga in Bengal in 1978 because the actual, *de facto* extent of tenancy was far higher than the recorded extent. Since in Orissa the 1965 Act made tenancy, illegal there is every reason to think that there is concealed tenancy. Enough micro-studies also exist showing a very high extent of *de facto* leasing-in villages where the records show much lower figures.

The second reason that the fall in recorded area under tenancy cannot be used to infer that the tenancy problem is minor, has to do with the *reason* for the fall in recorded tenancy. This fall reflects the fact that a handful of well-to-do farmers who leased-in land in addition to operating substantial owned land, could afford to purchase ownership rights to their formerly leased lands after these vested with the government. Since the quantum of land every such farmer leased-in was higher than the average, the acquisition of ownership by them showed up in a substantial fall in area leased. But such better off farmers were in any case not the people who were over-exploited and grounds down to below poverty level. It is the lakhs of poor and marginal farmers who could not afford tenants (most of the 18 per cent of holdings recorded as leasing-in land); but many after suffering eviction when landowners resumed land under the 'personal cultivation' clause, were re-engaged on oral informal leases to prevent their acquiring any legal rights. It is precisely these poorer farmers, who are either pure tenants or with little owned land of their own, for whom rent payment becomes a sufficiently heavy burden to prevent any improvement on their land, and for whom insecurity of tenure inhibits any dynamism even if they somehow scrape together some funds.

The fact that it is landlord-dominated redistribution which has taken pace and *de facto* leasing is much higher than recorded leasing, means that the barrier of rent to growth of productivity remains, output growth rates are low and poverty levels are high while social indicators remain poor. Further, the parts of the agricultural economy are articulated together through the lease and labour markets into an organic whole and it is incorrect to think mechanically about it and say that if tenancy covers say 20 per cent of the area, the remaining 80 per cent of area is unaffected. The existence of a mass of small farmers paying high rents will affect the decision regarding investment even of those bigger owners who do not themselves lease-out. To say that tenanted area is minor part of the total and therefore, it is unimportant is somewhat like that one's right hand is a small part of the body and if it is infected with gangrene the rest of the body can function normally.

What is the theoretical analysis of *ground rent as a barrier to investment*? Ever since the times of Adam Smith and Ricardo, continuing through to Alfred Marshall, the economists have stressed that land monopoly and rent extraction is *barrier* to investment and raising of productivity. A capitalist needs only to make profit to cultivate, but if he needs to lease land to cultivate he must also make a surplus profit over and above average profit to be able to pay the rent on leased land. Price-cost conditions, which permit a piece of land to be cultivated under ownership, will not permit the same land to be cultivated when rent has to be paid.

The security or insecurity of lease, which is related to the period of the lease contract, is as important as the fact of lease. Even when price-cost conditions are such that a tenant has something left over to invest after paying rent to the owner, he will not have the incentive to invest in anything apart from very short-term improvements which give their full return within the period of lease (season or year), for with any other type of improvement which permanently raises productivity (e.g. irrigation investment, contour-bunding, fruit trees), the landowner can evict him and use his improvement to charge a higher rent from the next tenant; or he may capitalise the higher income from the land by selling it at a higher price.

The barrier of rent operates even more strongly in a developing economy like ours with a mass of poor people who are forced to pay very high rent amounting to half or more of the gross output to those who monopolise land. The tenants themselves are left with a bare subsistence and have no funds to put even into inputs like more HYV and fertilisers to improve the yields; longer term improvements are out of the questions. If the tenant was to put in his sweat and money in digging, say a shallow tubewell, or in planting trees for firewood and fruit, he faces the risk of being evicted and the landowner benefiting from his outlays by charging a higher rent from the next tenant. Such investment in raising productivity or diversifying output is, therefore, never undertaken by the tenant as long as there is uncertainty regarding tenure.

As regards the landowner himself, supposing him to be a substantial owner, his incentive to cultivate directly is low. The owner is already getting Rs. R say of rent from an acre of land leased-out, without making any outlays in production at all. He also has his money capital say Rs. M, free to invest in any income-yielding way, such as moneylending, trade, shares term deposit etc.; let us suppose the average return or profit obtainable on this sum of Rs. M to be Rs. P. For him to think in terms of direct cultivation with hired labour, putting his Rs. M into the working capital requirements, the return of Rs. P alone will not be enough; the return has to be at lease Rs. P + R, that is, it has to give not only average profit but also that rent foregone by going in for direct cultivation. The fact that direct capitalist cultivation has to give a surplus profit equal to rent in addition to average profit, is what constitutes the barrier of rent. From empirical studies carried out as part of our doctoral research in the late sixties we had found that a profit rate as high as 49 per cent on capital outlays was required (where land value was not included in capital). [2]

The small owner cultivator however faces no such rent barrier. His objective function is not to obtain profit but to employ his own and family's labour to satisfy consumption requirements, to obtain an adequate livelihood at a customary level. The fundamental difference between a capitalist and a small producer is that labour is a cost alone to the capitalist which he seeks to minimise to obtain profit; while to the small producer his labour itself is simultaneously his source of income, and he would like to find full employment for his labour at an acceptable rate of reward. The small producer, as long as family labour is underemployed and income is inadequate, will therefore invest in improving yields under price-cost conditions which give an addition to the family's income whereas the same price-cost conditions will deter the larger farmer who face the rent barrier, or the farmer hiring labour who can start counting his return only after labour cost is deducted.

Needless to say the small tenant farmer however much he may *wish* to improve his income cannot actually do so as long as rent eats up all surplus above subsistence, and as long as insecurity means that potentially the landlord can evict him and enjoy his efforts to improve. Both security and fair rents are a must, even if the ideal situation of ownership, hence no rent burden, cannot be immediately implemented. The lesson of Operation Barga lies precisely in the fact that it gave owner-like security to the mass of poor tenants by recording them and making eviction difficult. There was no distribution of ownership to the tenant and the title remained with the landowner who could freely transfer the land. But the tenant after recording, acquired a legal existence and did not face the threat of arbitrary eviction as earlier; he could only be evicted if there was due cause (non-payment of rent etc.).

At the same time implementation of fair rents (varying according to extent to which the landowner shared costs) meant that some income remained with the tenant to be used for shifting to a higher-value cropping pattern and for tubewell investment, helped by spread of institutional credit. Doctoral research studies of the early 1990s have shown that in some 80 per cent of leases in the sampled villages the legal rental share was actually paid and in the remainder it was somewhat higher than the legal share, but considerably short of the half-share earlier prevalent.

The results with regard to production have been quite outstanding. From as situation of near stagnation in the 1960s and up to the mid-1970s, West Bengal in the last 20 years has seen a steady spread of HYV-fertiliser use aided by shallow tubewell investment, over the rice areas cultivated by newly recorded and empowered tenants. Additionally large numbers of formerly landless and land-poor have obtained redistributed vested land, and the raped extension of institutional credit has financed input loans to poorer cultivators taking land on seasonal lease, enabling them to employ the new technology. Recent analysis of the output data show that for 18 years starting in 1977-78 and ending in 1995-96, the growth of yields per acre growth for foodgrains has been even higher at 5.7 per cent annually, and therefore, despite some fall in area the foodgrains output has been growing at 4.6 per cent annually, more than double the population growth rate, in sharp contrast to other states. Yet non-foodgrains have not suffered and have grown at 4.7 per cent annually. Analysts have traced a major role for Operation Barga combined with spread of institutional credit and the dynamic role of the revived, democratised *panchayat* system in unleashing the latent production potential of the rural economy.[3]

A problem with Bengal Operation Barga in the past was that the dimension of gender equality was not explicitly addressed but this has been now recently sought to be rectified by amendments to the relevant Acts. The principle of natural justice demands that women should enjoy the same legal rights as men, but it is not enough to amend the legal provisions alone to permit joint pattas or registration in the name of women heirs by bringing agricultural property in line with the provisions of the Sharada Act. The persistence of social attitudes determined by the centuries-old habits of gender discrimination in our patriarchal society imply that extra effort has to be put in by womens' organisations and bodies of local administration to raise the level of informed consciousness regarding womens' rights.

Let me now come to some specific problems that Orissa faces owing to its particular history. First, the agriculturally rich coastal areas of Orissa took part in the decline of rice yields which occurred in the Bengal Presidency between 1912 and 1947. For Greater Bengal the resulting fall in foodgrains output per head of population was quite high, 38 per cent in the inter-War period, and since in Eastern Bengal there was little fall the decline in the rest of the presidency was even larger. To this day neither Bengal nor Orissa have fully recaptured the output per head it enjoyed in 1900 or 1912, although Bengal owing high recent growth has done better than has Orissa in this respect. Many reasons have been put forward for the earlier decline, ranging from the diversion of the best lands to exportable crops to the hypothesis of the 'moribund delta' (viz. the slow, long-term eastward shift of the main channels of the Ganga leaving a dying portion of the delta in W. Bengal); in the case of coastal Orissa the argument has been that yields fell owing additionally to interference with drainage after the construction of the colonial railways, as the embankment runs at right angles to the line of flow of all the major rivers of Orissa. Whatever the validity of these explanations the fact is true that historically there was a legacy of falling yields and stagnant foodgrains production.

Second, in large measure the non-coastal areas remained under highly exploitative and oppressive princely rule. These were also the predominantly tribal areas where princely rule helped to preserve semi-feudal relations and hindered the spread of education, while the incursion of outsider traders led to tribal land alienation and debt bondage. Today it is tribal Orissa which is the poorest part of the state and Orissa's dismal record of the second highest level of poverty in India (second only to Bihar) derives in large part from its concentration of tribal population. At the all-India level the profile of poverty based on the 1987 large NSS sample shows that whereas the rural poor as a proportion of rural general population was 39 per cent the poor among schedules tribes was 63 per cent of the population of ST's and the poor among Scheduled Castes was 53 per cent of the SC population.

Tribals populations usually live at some distance from centres of governance, their levels of illiteracy and destitution are even higher than that of the general rural population, and their grievances and demand are never adequately articulated. Any programme of lowering rural poverty has to be focussed first and foremost on tribal poverty and this in turn is intrinsically bound up with the production relations in which they are enmeshed. *De facto* tenancy is very high among tribals as the lands of large number have been alienated in the past to non-tribals outsiders and traders. Those who are small owners are enmeshed in debt to traders who have first claim on their crops and who charge a high implicit interest rate through paying a very low price purchase for the crop.

A recent research study on Kalahandi's land relations and output performance has given us some interesting facts. Productivity measured by foodgrains output per head of population has been consistently higher in Kalahandi than both the all Orissa average and the all-India average. Even in the worst drought years productivity has fallen to only marginally below the all-India average. Yet the bulk of the (mainly tribal) producers, are perennially on the edge of starvation and get easily pushed over the edge in drought years. The reason was found to be that a large share of their gross output is drained out as a combination of rent, interest and traders' commission by the landowners leasing land and by traders lending money and buying the crop. Sometimes the same person combines both roles. The surplus is drained out of not only the district, but out of the state altogether through the medium of (mainly Marwari) traders. Thus food production per head is more than adequate in Kalahandi but food entitlements for the producers is pushed down owing to the over-exploitative lease and credit relations in which they are enmeshed.

The solution lies ideally in conferring ownership on tenants; but this is a maximal programme which is unlikely to be feasible in the foreseeable future. What is feasible, even while the existing ownership of land is retained (except for tribal land illegally alienated which must be restored), to focus first on conferring owner-like security of tenure on the lessees by registering them through a drive to record *de facto* tenancy in the presence of the village population. This will only succeed if the onus of proving that a piece of land is being cultivated by a tenant does not lie with the tenant, whose declaration that he does so supported by the general body of the cultivators should be deemed sufficient. The onus of proving that a piece of land is not being cultivated by an unrecorded tenant should rather be on the lessor if the latter whishes to contest that tenant's claim to be registered. Second, the implementation of reasonable maximum rents is required to avoid the over exploitation to which the tenants are currently subject; the extension of government procurement directly from the producers at fair minimum support prices will help to loosen the stranglehold of private traders as will the extension of institutional credit. At the same time it is necessary to extend the public distribution system in these areas to enable those who remain food-deficit, to access foodgrains at an affordable price.

Not only Bengal and Kerala but also Karnataka, Tamil Nadu and Andhra Pradesh have been providing for many years, additional subsidy out of their state budgets to supplement the central consumer subsidy on foodgrains and keep the issue price of foodgrains from the fair-price shops reasonable, so that the poor can afford to by. In Orissa the rural coverage of the PDS is poor and it needs to be extended; additional subsidy out of the state budget also should be considered as at present Orissa's consumer issue price is higher than the average.

III
LAND REFORMS AND NEW ECONOMIC POLICY

There is renewed urgency of land reforms in the light of the new economic policy and liberalisation since 1991. At the all-India level the NEP involved a sharp cut-back in State expenditure in rural areas as a part of macroeconomic contraction, and a rise in rural poverty, from 39 per cent of the population in 1987-88 to 44 per cent in 1992 (according to most estimaters, but even higher, to 48 per cent according to the Tendulkar-Jain estimate). Even when poverty was rising at the all-India level some states were continuing to lower poverty throught maintaining public expenditures and giving additional food subsidy.[4]

The states which reduced poverty even during the economic reform period in the 1990s were West Bengal, Kerala, Andhra Pradesh, Karnataka and Tamil Nadu. The states which saw a considerable rise in poverty from already high inital levels were Assam, Bihar and Orissa; the states which saw large order of rise in poverty from initial low levels included Haryana and Punjab. In Orissa rural poverty which had been falling in the 1980s owing to a stepping up of state expenditures, rose in the nineties as state expenditures were cut. Rural poverty rose from 36.5 per cent in 1990-91 to 49.9

per cent in 1993-94 (employing the official Planning Commission poverty line). The infant mortality rate which is a sensitive indicator fortunately continued to fall in Orissa even as overall poverty was rising but little consolation can be derived from this as Orissa had the highest level of IMR in 1993 at 103 per thousand followed by Madhya Pradesh with 99 per thousand; both continue four years later to register IMAR above 90, reflecting the abysmal state of health care among the tribal population in particular. This may be compared to an IMAR of 55 in West Bengal and 16 in Kerala.

The new economic policy also involved cuts in food and fertiliser subsidy and a new thrust towards the export of primary products. At the all-India level since 1990-91 up to 1995-96 about 5 million hectares of foodgrains predicting area has been diverted to mainly exportable crops production, of which nearly 2 m ha. has gone under cotton and another 2 m. ha. to oilseeds, the fastest growing component of the latter being soyabean which is processed into oilcake for export as livestock feed. The output of foodgrains has not fallen despite absolute decline in area owing to the rise in yields; but yield rise has not been sufficient and for the first time in 30 years the annual compound growth rate; it has been 1.7 per cent during the five years following 1990-91 compared to a population growth rate of nearly 2 per cent availability per head has only been maintained by a large decumulation of stocks, (which in turn had built up with the FCI as purchasing power was cut and off take declined during the period of macro-economic contraction). Apart from cotton and oilseeds, some diversion of paddy-growing land has taken place to prawn culture in coastal areas and to horticulture for export. The foreign transnational corporations engaged in agri-business have been given *carte blanche* to enter the agricultural sector. Altogether liberalisation has undermined food security in the country.

Further with the GATT 1994 agreement being implemented under the WTO, under relentless pressure from the advanced countries the Indian government is giving up quantitative restrictions (QRs) on the import of a large range of manufactured and agriculture products. The advanced countries having lost market for their cereals and dairy products following the economic collapse of Eastern Europe and the former Soviet Union, and more recently the collapse of South East Asia, are now targeting the large Indian market in a big way and want it completely opened up and unprotected to imports from them. This involves unfair trade because the advanced countries while attacking the tiny levels of food and fertiliser subsidies India has and pressurising for their removal, continue themselves to pay out very heavy subsidies to their own farmers. The USA pays 28,000 dollars every year per full-time farmer and the European Union pays 22,000 dollars, over seventy times the income of the average Indian farmer. The GATT agreement has been written in such a way that while reducing certain kinds of subsidies to their farmers (called market support) the advanced countries under various green box, viz. environmental clauses, can increase other kinds of subsidies, like direct cash payments (termed budgetary support). India is also amending its patent Act in line with WTO requirements to allow product patents and the patenting of life forms, which will raise the prices of medicines and also of food, as expensive genetically engineered seeds are sought to be popularised.

Orissa will be particularly vulnerable to the impact of all these measures, owing to the fact that it has rich forest, mineral and marine resources apart from sharing the botanic diversity of the Eastern India region. This will attract the greed of foreign TNC's engaged in agri-business and lead to environmental degradation. Fortunately there is already some awareness of the adverse environmental impact of commercial prawn necessary however that vigilance is exercised so that the ongoing mapping of forest resources and of bio-genetic resources in the state is used for the benefit of its people, and not to enrich foreign companies through bio-genetic piracy using the knowlege systems of the simple tribal people. The very large numbers of foreign funded NGOs at present operating in the state need to be monitored with respect to their activities as it has been found in some states that a few of them are used as conduits by foreign interests for obtaining information on forest and bio-genetic resources which are freely pirated with no compensation to local people.

All these developments, while they may appear not to be directly relevant to land reform, in fact have an important bearing on that question. This is because the overall environment of trade liberalisation and primary export thrust is inimical to the economic interests of the majority of rural people even while it may benefit a minority. How does the majority protect itself from immiserisation, then becomes an urgent question. Apart from the adverse effects on food security, opening up to free primary exports also exposes the farmer to the volatility of world prices, and to a new type of debt-bondage to TNC's supplying genetically engineered seed and crop-specific pesticides.

The cotton story, which I would like to recapitulate, shows that high world prices do not necessarily benefit the direct producer. Owing to a sudden rise in the world price combined with trade liberalising new policies, India saw a 10 to 374,000 units compared to an annual average of 35,000 units in the four preceding years. Exports fluctuated after that but averaged 2,000,000 units during the four years after 1990-91. Raw cotton and yarn exports together have grown at over 100 per cent annually during 1990-91 to 1997-98! Domestic raw cotton and yarn prices rose sharply with the unprecedented exports since obviously cotton output could not expand so fast in such a short time; both handlooms and powerlooms were hard hit and there have been hundreds of closures of power-loom units with large lay-offs of workers.

It is clear that the cotton growers did not ultimately benefit either in the hope of profiting from higher world price, lakhs of small farmers took land on lease and borrowed heavily to plant cotton in Andhra, Maharashtra and Karnataka (area under which as earlier noted has grown by 2 million hectares at the expense of foodgrain area). In 1997 with a combination of failure of rains and pest attacks the farmer lost the crop entirely and faced with ruin, hundreds were driven to the extreme and tragic step of suicide. Even the more prosperous farmers of Punjab have suffered. Monsanto, the giant US-based TNC is a vertically integrated company with interests in seeds, pesticides and agri-business; it has seized upon the distress of cotton farmers to promote its genetically engineered cotton plant Btcotton (trademark 'Bollgard') which is claimed to be toxic to pests; the adoption of this will have major adverse environmental effects and enmesh the farmer in a high-tech debt bondage. The risks of export crop production are borne entirely by the grower; the situation is an asymmetric one because the benefit of high world prices are taken by the seed and pesticide companies and moneylenders while crashing world prices are passed on to the grower.

In such an environment of liberalisation and greater risk, the small farmers need protection more than ever before. They need better and more secure tenure of land better access to institutional credit and they need to organise to face the risk of market involvement not individually but collectively. The government needs to take on the responsibility of procuring exportable crops under a scheme of variable export duty to stabilise the price to the grower. The need for tenancy reform in particular and land reforms in general assumes greater urgency when the entire macroeconomic environment itself is rapidly changing towards greater exposure to unstable global forces.

The fact that such a high proportion of farmers in Orissa are of tribal origin and therefore, not so remote from tribal habits of co-operation and community action, can be looked upon as a positive factor. The need for the times is a determined effort to register the insecure tenants so far operating with oral leases; to implement the existing provisions regarding ceilings and the effective distribution of ceiling surplus land; and to do this while recognizing women's rights.

Admittedly none of the measures of tenancy reform and land reform are easy in the context of Orissa and the argument is often heard that the successful West Bengal model cannot be adopted here in this state owing to the vastly different political situation and the absence of political will. At the same time the argument that there is no existing political will can become excuse for not taking the subject of tenancy reform seriously which itself acts against the emergence of political will. We have often referred to the West Bengal experience, but it is worth bearing in mind that Orissa's other neighbour to the south Andhra Pradesh has also been highly successful in reducing rural poverty, in fact at a greater relative extent than even West Bengal or Kerala. It has done this through a determined effort mainly under the N.T. Rama Rao regime to implement existing laws (partly under the constant pressure of militants activities), to extend its rural PDS and ensure the provision of subsidised foodgrains to the poor and to revive democratic decentralization through its mandal and panchayat systems. Andhra Pradesh has reduced the rural poverty level from 40 per cent in 1978 to only 16 per cent by 1993 and continued to reduce poverty in the nineties when it was rising in Bihar and Orissa. Both Tamil Nadu and Karnataka have also reduced rural poverty substantially. Thus it is not only the left Front government led by the communist parties but also the governments formed in the other southern states from the late 1970s which were responsive to popular demands, which have made impressive gains in the fields of land reform, rural poverty reduction, better health and literacy.

Although populism is often used in a pejorative manner, we see nothing wrong in the state being responsive to legitimate demands by the poor for a betterment of their life; indeed in a democracy it is the responsibility of the state to so serve the interests of the many who are politically enfranchised, but remain grossly deprived and economically disenfranchised. As Orissa goes into the new millennium it is time for its leaders too, to make a determined effort to raise the state from its present abysmal level. In this effort, registration and security for tenants and implementation of their distributive elements of land reforms are an essential first step.

REFERENCES

1. These issues are discussed with supporting references and evidence in more detail in my *The Agrarian Question and the Development of Capitalism in India* (First Daniel Thorner Memorial Lecture. Oxford University Press 1986).
2. Our argument, on absolute ground rent as a barrier to investment, is on a different theoretical basis from, and more general, than the argument based on the interlinking of modes of exploitation (often wrongly referred to in the literature as the interlinking of markets). It is not necessary for our argument, for example, that the same economic agent should both lease-out and lend money; it is enough of the lessor uses his money capital in *any other* money, including of course moneylending. Our argument has been presented at greater length in 'Tenancy and Accumulation' in K. Basu (edited) *Agrarian Question* (Oxford University Press, 1994).
3. See 'Institutional Change and Output Growth in West Bengal Agriculture' by Manoj K. Sanyal, Pradip K. Biswas and Samaresh Bardhan in *Economic and Political Weekly,* November 21-28, 1998.
4. These data are taken from a country study on poverty in India undertaken jointly by Abhijit Sen and Utsa Patnaik, Poverty in India (available as DSA, Working paper of same title. December 1997, Centre for Economic Studies and Planning, JNU). See also Abhijit Sen. Economic Reforms, Employment and Poverty: Trends and Options, *Economic and Political Weekly*, Special Number August, 1996, Vol. 31, Nos. 35-37.

Chapter 4

Some Aspects of Tenancy Debate: Implications for Policy Reforms

PUSHPENDRA and B. K. SINHA

I
INTRODUCTION

The tenancy debate is very old. Adam Smith (1776), perhaps for the first time, raised a serious discussion. It continued through J.S..Mill (1848), Ricardo and Karl Marx. The 20th Century has witnessed generation of a fairly rich literature over tenancy, contributions for which has not come from the economists alone but also from academics from other disciplines, like sociology. Yet, one feels that there is a need to revisit some of the earlier debates in light of the changes taking place in the regular course and also under the changed environment of the nineties. The first question that arises in this context is to what extent tenancy continues to be relevant today. The second question is that how does and to what extent tenancy affect the labour market. The reverse position also becomes an issue of inquiry. The third issue is that how does tenancy influence the land market. The fourth issue is that of the resource-use-efficiency under the tenancy arrangements. The credit market has important implications for technological innovations. It, therefore, rightly emerges as the fifth issue. Further, the form of tenancy has a lot to do with the backwardness of agriculture. A relatively new area of investigation is that of reverse tenancy as a form of capitalist farming. These constitute the sixth issue of inquiry. Then comes the range of legal and institutional positions in respect to the state's intervention in the tenancy practices. Then there are the customary practices and rights relating to land that compel us to take the cultural aspects of tenancy into consideration. The politics of tenancy is no less important than its economics. However, for a small section of the academia, interestingly, tenancy remains an issue of politics rather than of economics and the *vice versa*. Not subscribing to any extreme view of this nature we propose to subject the entire discussion within the framework of political economy. These issues provide the fulcrum of the central theme of this article.

Structurally this paper has been arranged into three main sections. In the first section we take an overview of some aspects of theoretical constructs of tenancy in the present day context. In the second section we take an overview of the current debates on tenancy policy of the government and discuss their implications for policy reforms. In the third section we discuss issues related to governance, and legal as well as administrative reforms. At the end, we discuss available policy options in lieu of conclusion, for the objective of this paper is not to conclude debates with recommendations but to throw up issues for discussions in the workshop.

II
TENANCY *VIS-À-VIS* OTHER MARKETS

Labour Market and Tenancy

We begin with rather the most frequently asked question: why tenancy persists? Despite strong state-wise variations in legal provisions regarding tenancy ranging from total ban to permissive or regulated forms of tenancy, it continues to persist in all the major states of India. After registering a progressive decline in leased-in area since the 8th Round of the NSS in 1953-54, interestingly, for the first time during 1981-82 and 1991-92 (from 37th to 48th round of NSS) the percentage share of leased in area to the total area went up, though marginally, from 7.2 per cent to 8.3 per cent.[1]

The continuation of tenancy implies that there exist two parties—those who have land to lease and those who are prepared to take this land on lease. Let us first take up the issue from the lessor's perspective. The lessors will normally include those who have large holdings; the absentee landowners; who have moved out of agriculture, fully or partially due to an occupational shift; those who have a small family size or families with single or disabled persons to preclude effective supervision; poorer sections of rural society who have to lease-out for want of resources to invest; and those who lease-out customarily. The question obviously arises that why the lessors, particularly from the first three categories continue to hold on to land. They have both the options available—that of the market and of capitalist farming. There could be several explanations. In essence, either the landowner finds the land market or investment opportunities in other than agriculture unattractive, or, as Utsa Patnaik (1994) puts it, the landowner finds that he can get more by way of rent and income on capital saved than by investing that capital in direct cultivation. The landowners engage in self-cultivation, under normal conditions, up to the point where the marginal return from their land becomes zero. Beyond that point the economics of return causes a discouragement effect upon self-cultivation. Under conditions of backward agriculture the value-addition comes mostly from the labour. Since non-labour value-addition is lacking for want of modernisation, the self-cultivator relies upon low-wage trap.[2] The reverse tenants would also have their interest in keeping the wages depressed.

Similarly, why is there a supply of lessees? One explanation could be labour-based. Let us presume a condition of backward agriculture where the lessee is a subsistence farmer or an agricultural labourer who has no other source of livelihood (the underlying assumption is that he is free to make a choice and he has the capacity to make a rational choice). He mostly employs his family labour in tenanted farms. Then, he will lease-in only under the conditions when he finds that leasing in will give him greater returns as compared to what he gets from the labour market. Where the wage market is depressed the possibilities of returns from tenancy will be higher making a greater number opt for tenancy in preference to wage labour. This will lead to increase on the supply of tenants (this situation favours the landowners who find their bargaining position, along with their control and authority strengthened). The labour based explanation holds that the tenant will employ the maximum units of his family labour in order to maximise his output.[3] If tenancy goes up it will exercise a contracting effect upon the availability of the local labour. This brings us to a situation where higher incidence of tenancy may lead to a short supply of labour.[4] Whether this would result in pressure for upward revision of wages depends upon prevailing agrarian relations. Demand and supply of labour may not always affect the existing wages. The wage-based explanation will hold that only under the condition that a class of free labour has emerged will the shortage of labour affect the wages. Under the backward agricultural economy the condition for emergence of such a labour force on large scale seems bleak. Then, there are other explanations like productivity-based explanation and consumption-based explanation. They provide explanations for a variety of ways a landowner is likely to adopt in order to preserve the low wage trap. The commonest methods used are frequently changing the tenant, asking for extra loyalty from them, for example, in form of *begar*, usury practice with high interest rate, hiring-in labour from outside the village and so on.

Finally, the option narrows down to twin choices—either work on low wages or become a tenant. Trapped in the option of low wages or tenancy, one explanation of accepting the latter can be that it ensures a minimum number of days of employment. However, it is well argued that the tenant will apply labour to the tenanted land to the point of optimality. Beyond that point the total product curve for his labour will register a downward slide. In order to optimise his family labour and his share in output, the tenant will try to optimise the leased-in area. Consequently, labour utilisation per unit of land will fall down leading to undermining of the value-addition from labour. The output per unit of land definitely suffers though the output per unit of labour i.e. labour efficiency in all likelihood may increase. The ultimate result is that low-wage-subsistence agriculture is tenancy enhancing by nature.

However, the landowner emerges as a net loser in the process. Now the landowner may try to overcome the situation by limiting the tenants to small holdings. For instance, a landowner will avoid leasing-out to a tenant who leases-in from any other landowner. The other set of measures will include enhancing his share in the produce, strict vigil over application of labour, extraction of forced labour, lessening his contribution in inputs, etc. He uses his superior position in the power structure for this end. At this point politics takes over the economics. Thus, the roles of organisation of the tenants and dispensation of the state are both critical for the tenants.

Land Market and Tenancy

The relation between land market and tenancy can be considered in two different paradigms. One is that where the land markets are depressed the incidence of tenancy is high. The other is opposite:

where the incidence of tenancy is high the land markets are depressed. The three categories of landowners, as mentioned at the beginning of the section, namely the absentees, those not interested in cultivation due to occupational shift and those who want to exit from their land to augment resources for alternate occupations are interested parties to this process. Assuming that the land market is depressed they will fail to find a proper exit. An alternate solution is to lease out the land, frequently resorted to by the landowners. However, the market-depression-induced tenancy will have implications of its own. Let us assume further that this section will have a low supervision in respect of the land leased out. Admittedly marginal benefits of lax supervision will accrue to the tenants but there will be a conscious decision on part of the landowner not to invest in the land as such investment will only be partly recoverable. This condition fits into the model of Amit Bhaduri where he treats the landowner as the one who takes decision whether to innovate or not. The specific context here is that the land is for sale and therefore, the proposal to invest in the land on the part of the tenant will translate into a strong disincentive. The tenant will, hence, be content to invest the minimum effort in the land. To further validate this point let us assume that the land gets sold. The new owner will have a number of choices before him; he may opt for self-cultivation; he may allow the old tenant to continue; alternatively he may lease the land out to a new tenant. In the second and the third options he will again have a number of alternatives depending upon his economic and political position. For instance, a landowner in the large category in the process of increasing his concentration of land may even find it convenient to impose a new set of terms and conditions. In the second place the new owner may like to change the form of tenancy from shared to fixed rent tenancy. Under this condition the risk is transferred to the tenant to a greater extent in comparison to the former condition. Now the onus of investment will also pass on entirely to the tenant from the side of the landowner. There are two further possibilities created under these circumstances. The tenant will be compelled to borrow, most likely, from the landowner himself. The tenant may find the condition unfavourable and decide to give up the land. This will be a perforce dispossession. There is no shortage of supply of tenants and some new tenant may step into his shoes. This will add to the existing internal competition for the land which likely to enhance the utilities of the landowner. The landowners who have not been able to exit and/or where the tenancy is legally not allowed and/or weak in power structure will always feel threatened and recourse to frequent changing of their tenants. There is no need to add to the implications of insecurity of tenure to the minds of the tenant, as there is more than abundant literature on the subject.

Now we proceed to take up the reverse side of the matter—the tenancy depressed market. The tenancy arrangements by providing an alternative to the landowner lead to a postponement in the decision to sell the land. Let us assume a situation where no tenancy is permitted and the provisions are rigidly enforced. The landowner will have limited options: he may take up self-cultivation; he may put it to non-agricultural use; may lease out for commercial purposes; may decide to keep the land fallow; or he may sell the land. In the first situation one section may have to resort to self-cultivation. However, for the sections of landowners already discussed above, this is least likely to occur. The second option is dependent upon so many factors—opportunities, infrastructure, investment capacity, entrepreneurship and backward and forward linkages. The possibilities for this to happen are remote in the backward (in many instances, even in the relatively developed) rural areas. All non-agricultural enterprises do not need large areas. Such activities are carried on mostly in the populated, residential or market areas (except perhaps in the case of industries). Even animal husbandry is not feasible under conditions of absenteeism or remote supervision. Horticulture and sericulture are more exacting in terms of investment and supervision as compared to personal cultivation. The opportunities for commercial leasing out are severely restricted and fraught with danger too. This is likely to induce a change in the land use and the nature of the land from where reclamation at a subsequent date will be difficult. We may take the instance of brick kilns where the land is impaired beyond reclamation. Keeping the land fallow has high opportunity costs. The farmer may keep land temporarily fallow for reasons of productivity. Keeping the land fallow, without sufficient economic reasons, is irrational. Even keeping the land fallow has a fixed cost of maintenance and rent. This leaves us with the last option that appears the most feasible. There are many micro-studies that indicate that despite increase in the incidence of tenancy over a period of time market transactions have been relatively low.[5]

Market transactions necessarily require the presence of two or more transacting parties. Considering that considerable volume of land is available for sale, the question arises: from where does one get a buyer. Urban investment in the rural lands is highly unlikely (given the condition of ban on tenancy). The buyer has to come essentially from the rural areas and will normally be the rural rich and upcoming sections of medium and smaller farmers. Such buyers will have the upper hand in the transactions. There are possibilities of distress sale taking place. More importantly, there will be a re-concentration of land in favour of the larger landowners. There is a genuine question in this context that what the rural rich is going to do with the land he purchases. This highlights a problematique within the model of 'tenancy-depressed market'. The options before the rural rich are clear. Either they take up self-cultivation on an extensive scale or they go in for large-scale investment in the non-agricultural use of the land including in the allied sectors or they do not enter the land market at all. The possibility of the first two courses taking place is higher where the rural infrastructure is strong or the depression in the land markets will continue and the ban on tenancy will remain a politically non-feasible option.

Credit Market and Tenancy

The prevalent forms of credit institutions have serious implications for tenancy. Under conditions of backward agriculture the tenants are normally indebted. In many cases he borrows from the landowner who also functions as *Mahajan*. In the model of Amit Bhaduri the landlord has two sources of earning—one, the rental from the tenant which Bhaduri terms as his property income; the other, his usurious income. In the given model the decision to innovate rests upon the landlord. Technological upgradation of the farm implies that the income of the tenant will also go up thereby reducing his requirements for consumption loans. This will also bring down the usurious income of the landlord. This creates the possibility of lowering the net income of the landlord thus making a technological upgradation undesirable to him. The larger the initial indebtedness the greater is the required scale of technological upgradation to give a rise in the net income of the landowner.

In case the landlord decides to innovate, it implies an upward revision in the rental. The rentals, however, can only be stretched to their economic limits from the standpoint of tenant's acceptability. The landlord will decide to invest only to the point of optimality that has to give a rise in his net income. Suppose, the landowner finds such an investment economically viable. Then comes the issue of mobilising the required capital. In most of the cases the cost will have to be borne by the landlord, though in some cases it is to be shared between the landlord and the tenant, or in a few cases it may come entirely from the tenants side—all depending upon the tenancy arrangements, security of tenure and availability of liquidity or credit to either of the parties. It is possible that the cost of innovation may be thrusted upon the tenant alone. In case of poor tenants, it often amounts to indebtedness of the tenant. In case the landlord himself decides to bear the cost of innovation, the status of tenant is virtually reduced to that of an attached labour. At this point the model of Amit Bhaduri provokes certain questions. In case the cost of innovation is to be shared by the landlord and the tenant, it will definitely add to the further indebtedness of the tenant. In this case also the status of the tenant will virtually be of an attached labour. Here Amiya Kumar Bagchi's theory of retarded capitalism comes to our rescue.[6] Bagchi explains a situation where subsistence farming persists alongside the capitalist farming and fully free labour or labour market fails to emerge.

We now take up the issue of availability of credit not only to the tenant but to the landowner as well. In this very context Griffin[7] argues that under conditions of backward agriculture the landlords also find it difficult to access any credit. They are not to be equated, in all practical terms, to the capitalist farmers. Even when they indulge in usury the transactions are usually small, though its importance for the backward rural economy may be disproportionately high. Thus, backwardness of agriculture may be viewed as more a function of credit shortage in the rural areas rather than the reluctance of the landowners to innovate as propounded by Bhaduri. Here we simulate certain situations. The first is that the credit is available uniformly to the landowner and the tenant, but only for productive investment. The question that now arises is that who is going to use this credit. First, the tenant's side, the tenant is likely to under-utilise this opportunity and in no case he is going to make long-term investments for the simple reason that his tenurial security is missing. The next situation we conceive is where the security of tenure is there, but still would the tenant like to make long-term investments in the land. This is likely to happen, but under certain enabling conditions. Initially, if requirements of consumption loans are not met simultaneously with the productive investment, it is likely to lead to fungibility in respect of the latter. Suppose that both consumption and investment loans are accessible. This will be an unwelcome development for the landowner for it will contribute to a decline in the income of the landowner from usury. In order to protect his net income one uneasy option that the landowner has is to co-operate with the tenant for innovation in agriculture. Suppose, the tenant takes loan for productive investment in land. Each credit, however, implies return with interest, no matter how nominal it is. This will affect the net return at least so long as it is not repaid. It is, therefore, a prerequisite that the returns in the credit phase should be higher even after having discounted the repayment. Similar conditions will apply to the landowner. Von Pischke differs to the cheap credit argument. Providing cheap credit undermines the purpose of credit because it does not allow the parties to high return ventures. Cheap credit also implies that the production process will always be subject to a low scale-cheap credit-low production trap. The third situation is that credit is not uniformly and easily available. Here Terry Byres[8] holds that it is only few rich landowners who have greater access to institutional credit and also hold their own resources, are prone to invest in innovations. If the landowning section decides to use the credit for innovations the consequence will be further rise in the iniquities. That is, why Terry Byres holds that growth and equity are antagonistic in backward agriculture.

III
AGRARIAN CONDITIONS AND TENANCY

Resource use Efficiency and Tenancy

We have already discussed that under backward agriculture tenancy is characterised by disincentives to investment. The trap of backwardness operates under sub-optimal use of the inputs. Under conditions of backwardness the small farm size is supposedly efficient, though explanations vary from land based to fertility based. However, under capitalist farming conditions large farms are also efficient. Hypothetically it can be held that where all conditions are the same the small farm size will prove more efficient in economic terms. But despite the allocative efficiency the overall production will remain constrained by resources. Theoretically it is alright to argue in terms of efficiencies of small farms but they give rise to so many problems. One is that when the resources are made available will the small farms continue to retain the same efficiencies. It is also possible that the resource constraints remain unresolved. Hence, despite its superior efficiency the medium and the large farms contribute the bulk of the surplus production, though the role of the small farms in warding off starvation conditions is unmistakable.

Tenancy is admittedly a risk-sharing mechanism, though the extent and the kind of the risk shared may vary with the modes of tenancy. The question is that why a landowner will search for mechanisms of risk sharing? Stiglitz and Newbery[9] explain tenancy arrangements in terms of sharing of uncertainties of cultivation due to unforeseen like weather, flood, drought, fire etc. appears plausible. Then there are risks of wage-contract and other imponderables. Share tenancy remains the commonest form of risk sharing because under conditions of backward agriculture, it is equally acceptable to the tenant and the landowner. To the tenant because it offers a mechanism of sharing liabilities with the landowner. Suppose the tenant decides to switch over to fixed rent tenancy. Then he should be able to bear the entire risk alone. This pre-supposes certain buffer holding by the tenant which is unlikely to be a case under conditions of backward agriculture. Under the same conditions, share tenancy suits to the landowner for the reason that the landowner in real terms does not share the cost of the principal input, the labour. Hence, the landowner is able to pass on the risk substantially to the tenant. Question may further be asked, why the landowner does not insist for fixed rent arrangement in so far as it is even more risk minimising for him than share tenancy? Perhaps the explanation lies in the market-led demand and supply.

The sociologists do not, however, see this phenomenon in terms of risk sharing. They see it in terms of the customary supervisory roles for the landowning castes/classes and the labour-performing roles for the landless and the lower castes. The supervisory act itself acts as a source of power within the rural social structure. Those who are not a position to do self-cultivation and have alternative sources of income will still not part with the same and frequently operate through tenants. For them what is important here is not rent appropriation, but the act of holding land which in itself amounts to power in the rural structure. Amartya Sen takes a synthesised view of the agrarian relations, which is governed by a combination of market forces, custom and power.[10]

Terms and Conditions of Tenancy

The forms of tenancy have deep implications for the above issues, as we have discussed. There is a general consensus that the shared tenancy represents its most inefficient form though the dichotomy is that it is also the most largely practiced. To use a typically Marshallian argument, the tenant will have interest in investing in the land till so long as the cost of innovation is less than the incremental productivity gains accruing to him, or the returns are greater than the capital invested. To the contrary in the fixed rental tenancy the entire gains of the investment accrue to the tenant. (Though we do not deny the link between productivity and the rent implying thereby that with increase in productivity there will be demand for enhanced rents. Even if this happens there will be definitely a time lag.) Hence, innovations are more likely to be accepted by the tenants holding on fixed rent as compared to the shared tenants. Logically, the question arises that why sharecropping persists. We have discussed the explanation provided by Amit Bhaduri that the powers of decision making lies with the landowner whose interests are against innovations for the reasons already discussed.

From the above we can deduce that fixed rent tenancy will be preferred by the farmers who are in position to entirely bear the cost of the inputs and also as discussed above the tenant has the incentive to innovate. The possibilities of fixed rent tenancy will be higher in situations where capitalist farming is practised. The question here is that whether tenants from landless or the marginal farmer groups will be in a position to undertake the cost of fixed rent tenancy. This also pre-supposes the existence of a well-developed credit market. We have already discussed the credit market institutions. In its absence, in all likelihood, the landless and tenants from small marginal groups will find difficult to accept the capital-intensive mode of tenancy. We imagine a situation where this has already happened. The implications of this are manifold: now a section of the erstwhile tenant will have to find place in the labour market. The practice of reverse tenancy, even if under arrangements of share tenancy represents the entry of a section of farmers into entrepreneur class. In any case the farm production will rise, but at the cost of equity.

Investment in Agriculture and Tenancy

In the present day there is an overpowering tendency to view the tenancy debate within the twin context of the need to attract investment into agriculture and to facilitate a smooth process of land transaction without attempting for any major change in the ownership pattern. A dominant view (particularly in the government circles[11]) is that backwardness of agriculture can be cured with enhanced investment flow. Since independence investment in agriculture has come primarily from two sources—the institutional source or the public investment and private investment, mostly through farmers. The public investment has come mainly in the form of subsidies on agricultural inputs like seed, fertilisers, private pumpsets, borings, diesel oil, tractors, agricultural farm equipments, electricity etc. The other form of public investment consists of direct investment to create agricultural infrastructure such as dams, canals, public tubewells, land development, watershed, drainage, extension etc. etc. The public investment, in form of provisions of subsidised credit facilities, creates incentives for private investment. Moreover, the public investment has a greater spread out effect. However, the role of public investment is not always equity promoting, since access to public investment or opportunities created by them are frequently apportioned by those sections who command better social and political endowments. Under certain conditions it may promote inequities, for example, the inequalities between the riparian and the non-riparian farmers, or between the landlosers due to displacement by the major public irrigation schemes and the command area farmers of such schemes. There are instances where the landowners find it remunerative to operate through the Scheduled Caste tenants on account of the subsidies admissible to them. The investment goes into the lands, which in any case, belongs to them.

The private finance consists of the investment made by the farmers out of their own resources (for the time being we keep the institutional borrowings by the farmers out of reckoning). The resource for private investment may be generated out of the surplus accumulations from agriculture. In the agriculturally backward areas the possibilities of generating surplus are meagre while in the developed areas the chances are naturally better. There are, however, strategic options always available even in the backward areas. For instance, a farmer may sell a part of his holdings for investment in the remaining areas and create capitalist agriculture. Likewise in the agriculturally developed areas there may exist constraints that retard private investment in agriculture, e.g. rise in the input cost without an accompanying commensurate procurement prices. Due to the rising incremental costs of production a certain crops may not be a financially gaining proposition. He may like to switch over to other crops for which there may not be developed forward linkages.

Now, we proceed to examine the ways available to attract private investment. The first question to arise in this regard is which of the modes—private or public—has the maximum investment potential. One of the assumptions is that the public investment has reached its plateau. The government is now limiting its investment role while the sectors, hitherto strictly within government domain, are being opened up. To effect individual private investment under conditions of backward agriculture is a difficult proposition and cannot be stepped up overnight. The transformation process involves a substantive incubation period. The private financial companies may not have the resources or the right motive to take up the task of modernisation of agriculture. The counter argument is that the private finances are capable of the task if provided with the necessary enabling conditions and the society is prepared to bear the social costs. The social costs include the assertion of the capitalist forces in the rural power structure, the economic hardships/sufferings that the vast rural masses would be subjected to during the transition phase and the possibility of social unrest. It is impossible to assume the feasibility of such steps in a country that has passed through fifty years of competitive democracy.

It is, nevertheless, possible in the areas of developed agriculture to accelerate the individual private investment considerably. However, for this it is necessary that all impediments—legal or otherwise—are removed and the investors are offered a strong incentive structure. The removal of prohibition or restriction on tenancy is one important (legal) option. The raising of procurement prices of produce is another option but that means gain only for those with net marketable surpluses. For attracting additional private investments, agriculture has to be presented as competitive. The simple assumption is that if the investment in agriculture is financially rewarding then the landowner would not like to live on simple appropriation of rent and usurious income from tenants. Attracting private investment will, thus, have a definite discouragement effect upon subsistence tenancy though at the same time it will also have an encouragement effect upon reverse tenancy. In any case, the eviction of the subsistence tenants is inbuilt into investment approach. Historically, in the wake of the Zamindari abolition, there have been large-scale evictions of the subsistence tenants in respect of the personal lands of the former intermediaries. The danger of a second phase looms large in the capitalist transformation of the Indian agriculture. Those who argue for some institutional safeguards to protect the tenants' interest work will need to advance some solid economic reasons (mere political reasons may not be sufficient). One argument may that the subsistence tenant can transform himself into an 'enterprising tenant' under institutional protectionism. In any case, arguments for safeguards do not reject capitalist transformation of Indian agriculture but simply put condition-precedents to it.

The private institutional finance may enter into agriculture through the availability of private institutional sources of credit, direct leasing in by private companies for development of their captive farms, private investment in the development of agricultural infrastructure such as supply of electricity, irrigation, seed production and so on. Even in future with the privatisation of sectors like petroleum, and with the de-regulation of prices of essential agricultural inputs like fertilisers or diesel the market forces will acquire a greater role. Attractive as it may appear this path is fraught with dangers of its own. In the first place it will not only hinder the utilisation of the available private institutional finances for reasons of rise in the costs of the inputs, but may ultimately result in loss in terms of net investment. This will further trigger off the process of eviction of not only the tenants but of the small and the marginal farmers and a section of the medium farmers as well for the reasons of viability. A process of re-concentration of land will be imminent. The possibility of our getting confounded with such dangers may be just a matter of time. The full implications of such policy initiatives are, however, yet to be studied.

Till so far we have looked at the interface of tenancy with labour, land market, credit market, resource use efficiency and investment in agriculture. We have also discussed, though briefly, the debates over modes of tenancy. While searching for answer to why tenancy persists explored the interplay of different factors and related possibilities. In the following section we will discuss the multivariate nature of the Indian tenancy practices and their implications for future policy reforms.

IV
AGRARIAN RELATIONS AND FEATURES OF TENANCY

We have already established that under the conditions of backward agriculture leasing-in remains relevant both for the lessee and the lessor. It is important to locate the relationship between a lessee and a lessor in the overall context of the agrarian relations. Under the conditions of backward agriculture, the agrarian society finds it difficult to attain the stage that facilitates the emergence of agrarian classes of free wage labourers, self-cultivating peasants and large-scale farmers. Classification of different sections of agrarian society in neat class categories becomes highly problematic if social, economic and political positions are taken together into consideration. For the sake of avoiding the controversies over the determination of agrarian classes, we find it relatively convenient to identify the occupational groups engaged in agriculture, a section of which also practice tenancy. Some of these occupational groups are: free wage labourers, owner-operator, pure tenant, wage labour-cum-tenant, wage-labour-cum-owner operator, tenant-cum-owner operator, and wage labour-cum-tenant-cum-owner operator. The identification of these occupational groups, however, is not sufficient by itself. The owner-operator occupational group is to be further categorised according to size-class and leasing out or leasing in practices. Similarly, tenants will vary as per their size-class of holding (in case they are not landless) and the size-class of their leased in area. Further, categorisation is possible of those occupational groups who are either owner-operator-cum-tenant or who engage in both leasing in and leasing out. Thus, these occupational groups can be categorised into several sub-groups, and their inter-relationship characterises their agrarian relationship. The proportion in which these occupational groups present themselves in any agrarian society is indicative of the extent of tenancy and the level of agricultural development. For instance, a high proportion of free agricultural labourers indicates the higher level of modernisation. In the context of backward agriculture if large number of cultivators are small and marginal holders the greater are the chances of there being a high incidence of tenancy.

Though there are wide regional variations in the experiences, based on the studies made by the Probationers[12] over the years, the following could be seen as the broad features of tenancy:

(a) Leasing-in by the lower size-class from the higher size-class;
(b) In terms of the social groups leasing in by the lower castes from the land-endowed higher class;
(c) Low leasing-in by the landless labourers;
(d) Higher incidence of leasing in by the small and marginal farmers;
(e) Low mechanisation in tenanted farms;
(f) Lack of security of tenure (except where the state has intervened strongly on behalf of the tenants);
(g) Share cropping as the dominant mode of tenancy;
(h) Low leased in area per household signifying the subsistence nature of tenancy;
(i) Low-investment-low-output trap;
(j) High incidence of indebtedness amongst the tenants;
(k) Low volume of transactions in the land market;
(l) Low wages in agriculture;
(m) Use of labour as the principal input;
(n) Use of tenancy as a mode of control over labour; and
(o) Tenancy as a means of reinforcing the supervisory role of superior castes.

Now, it will be interesting to examine the policy options the government is offering. Will they help to break the backwardness trap of agriculture? Will they help the small and marginal farmers to modernise their farm operation without falling into another trap of indebtedness (which has in recent years taken life of so many cotton farmers in some of the states)?

Policy Suggestions: The Official Viewpoint

Two policy papers of the Government of India[13] in the recent times suggest that the government is strongly in the favour of legalising leasing-in, which according to the papers, will facilitate accessibility to land by small and marginal farmers, bring-in massive flow of private investment in agriculture, and boost up production and productivity. These papers also rule out the possibility of rise in the incidence of tenancy or re-emergence of absentee landlords on a large scale. Surprisingly, the policy note of 1999 suggests increasing the upper limit of operating land on lease up to 50 hectares.

To prove their point they cite the findings of the several rounds of the NSS that show a secular decline in the incidence of tenancy. According to the policy paper of 1997, the credit for this is attributed to the new technology which "favours owner-operation, requires personal supervision and compels owner-operators to take quick entrepreneurial decisions". It concludes that "in areas of Green Revolution, where the new technology has taken roots, there is no risk of a drastic increase in the tendency to lease out and revert to the Zamindari culture even if the ban on leasing is lifted". However, there is little ground to hold this argument. In the agriculturally developed areas, for instance in Haryana the percentage of leased-in area to the total operated area rises as we move from the smaller to the larger size-classes of holdings. In the 10.01 ha and above size-class, only 29.45 per cent of operated area fall in the category of owned land whereas 70.55 per cent of land were leased-in. The latter represents around 28 per cent of the total operated area, which is by all means substantial particularly in absolute terms.

Extending the argument of the paper further, the segments of farmers leasing-in in this highest size-class are those who can safely be presumed to engage in mechanised agriculture. The question now arises that if the new technology favours only owner-operator by its nature then how does it account for the phenomenally high incidence of leasing-in in this size-class. This implies that reverse tenants possess the entrepreneurial capacities for quick decision-making and managerially efficient supervision. Reverse tenancy has, thus, emerged as a fact of agrarian relations in Green Revolution areas like Haryana where tenancy is legally permitted. It becomes quite clear why the government is keen to raise the upper limit of leasing-in up to 50 hectares. Obviously, small and marginal farmers will not lease-in to this volume. Then, what has happened to the smaller lessees in rural Haryana? The area leased-in by farmers in the size-classes of up to 1 ha, comes to around 11 per cent of the total operated area in the same size-class (in the size-class of 0.002-0.20 and 0.21-0.50 the figures stand at 1.26 and 1.35 per cent respectively) which, in fact, constitutes only 5.33 per cent of the total estimated operated area in rural Haryana. One frequently cited explanation for the above is that the farmers in the smaller size-classes are, due to the marginalisation of their holdings, gradually opting for non-agricultural occupations. However, the extent of this tendency is yet to be determined fully. The question remains what does the legal process have in stock for the small lessees. The proposal of the Department of Rural Development, one is constrained to observe, has no solace for this class. Legalising tenancy will, in all likelihood, have little impact upon availability of land to the small and marginal tenants. Their accessibility to such land, given the constraints, may already have reached near the plateau. Similarly, it would have negligible impact on the terms and conditions of tenancy. After all, there is little difference in the conditions of the 'legalised' tenant of Bihar and 'illegal' tenant of UP. It may at best have little impact on the status and bargaining strength of the tenant, rather it will secure the position of the landowner who due to various legal restrictions fear losing out their land. The implications for the former have to be considered before making policy interventions.

An argument is frequently advanced that the distribution of operational holding is less inequitable than the ownership pattern due to the prevalence of tenancy. The Concept Paper also argues in the same vein. The common conclusion is that the prevalence of tenancy promotes access to land. In so far as the NSS figures are concerned there has always been lower concentration of inequality in operational holdings in comparison to ownership holdings in a given year (NSS Round). However, while the Gini's coefficient for ownership holdings has remained by and large the same (in fact a slight decrease is witnessed) the Gini's Coefficient for operational holdings has shown a progressive upwards climb. From 0.583 in 1960-61 it has gone up to 0.641 in 1991-92. Thus, at present operational holdings may be comparatively less iniquitous but the time trend is towards inequity.

Table 4.1: Trends in Concentration of Inequality in Holdings

Year	*Gini's Coefficient*	
	Operational Holding	*Ownership Holding*
1960-61	0.583	0.731
1970-71	0.586	0.709
1981-82	0.629	0.712
1991-92	0.641	0.710

Source: Different Rounds of NSS as reported in Sarvekshana, January-March, 1997.

The time trend in concentration of operational holding and the example of Haryana once again prove the point that modernisation of the Indian agriculture may not shower its benefits upon the small and the marginal farmers. In the next section, we return to rather old positions of legalising tenancy with strict provisions for ensuring the rights of the tenants, particularly recording the tenancy rights and making tenancy a heritable right. We will also examine, in brief, the problems of governance in this regard.

Tenancy, as is the case with the larger portfolio of land reforms, cannot be viewed in isolation of the macro-economic policies of the state and the overarching umbrella of political economy. To begin with, it needs be acknowledged that land reforms *per se* no longer occupy the centre stage of the political agenda. The diffused centrist nature of the Indian polity does not allow the lone pursuit of the pro-proletariat policies. Even the Left parties are no exception. This change in orientation arises from the compulsions to share political power bringing about a change in the basic constituency of the hitherto left parties. As such no pressure is being generated for tenancy reforms from within the organised political process. A part of the pressure that would have emerged in the ordinary course of events for land reforms as a whole is being released through the phenomenon of migration of labour to the high wage areas that we have already discussed. To the contrary, within the government ethos, land reforms, by and large, have been overtaken by rural development. The incursion of the foreign capital compulsorily seeks the opening and enlargement of the rural markets for which it is considered necessary to release the lease market from all restrictions.

There are diverse state responses to the tenancy issues articulated through the legislative measures. These responses are discerned in respect of the key areas—whether leasing out is permissible and, if so, on what terms including the share of produce, recording in the state records-of-rights, security of tenure, accrual of full-fledged ownership rights, surrender of tenancy, resumption by the landowner and adjudication of disputes. Using some of the parameters, we have categorised tenancy into three main patterns. In the first are those which do not permit tenancy in any form, e.g. the state of Kerala prohibits tenancy practices altogether. The second pattern allows leasing out only in respect of certain privileged categories like serving defence personnel, widows, minors till they attain majority, disabled persons etc. This includes the states of Uttar Pradesh, Madhya Pradesh, Himachal Pradesh, Maharashtra, Gujarat and the Telangana part of

Andhra Pradesh. Lessors other than the privileged categories may also lease out their lands, but for specified periods alone. Even within this broad classification, state and region-wise diversities persist. In Madhya Pradesh a *Bhumiswami* (landowner), not privileged, may lease out a part of his holdings for a period not exceeding one year during any consecutive period of three years[14]. The lessee may be evicted under orders of the Sub-divisional Officer on the grounds of contravention of any material terms or conditions of lease or on the lease ceasing to be in force [S.169(5)]. In any other case, the occupancy rights shall accrue to the lessee and he shall become entitled to the protection of law. In Maharashtra and Gujarat, leasing out is permitted but, on completion of one year, the tenant acquires title through the right to purchase. This right, however, accrues on application and the tenancy arrangements could continue and infinitum in absence of such an application. In the second category of states leasing is permitted but the conditions of lease are regulated. States of West Bengal, Bihar, Orissa, Rajasthan, Tamil Nadu and the Andhra area of Andhra Pradesh fall in this category. West Bengal permits only sharecropping where the share of the produce is defined and the right of cultivation is heritable but not transferable. In Tamil Nadu, Uttar Pradesh, Karnataka, Rajasthan and Andhra region of Andhra Pradesh provide for registration of tenancy and security of tenure. In Bihar, a settled raiyat or the one who has held land continuously for a period of 12 years in the village acquires occupancy right in respect of the land held by him and can be evicted only under the due process of law. He may also acquire full-fledged raiyati rights on payment of an amount equivalent to twenty-four times the rent [S.48 (c), Bihar Tenancy Act]. The third category includes such states like Punjab, Haryana and Assam wherein tenancy is permitted but which do not provide for compulsory registration of tenancy nor for security of tenure. In Punjab and Haryana, however, the tenant becomes entitled to purchase the land on lease where he holds it continuously for a period of four years. Other classification using the same or similar criteria have been attempted including one by Haque[15] wherein he makes a fourfold classification. There is another more simplistic classification, the satisfying clause being that whether tenancy is allowed without ownership rights accruing or not. In this while West Bengal, Tamil Nadu and Rajasthan stand at one extreme the rest are on the other. All states consider tenancy a pernicious practice and intervene to varying degrees in the lease market with differing effectiveness.

Despite the variegated provisions two features stand out regarding tenancy. In the first place tenancy continues to exist in all states including Kerala where tenanted holdings accounted for 2.9 per cent of the operated area in 1991-92. Haryana has the highest reported incidence of tenancy (33.3%) while Punjab comes next (18.8%). The second feature is that after 10 years (1980-81 to 1990-91) it has shown rising trends from 7.18 (1981-82) to 8.52 (1991-92). We have noted that the bulk of this increase has come in the large size class (16.7 per cent of the tenant holdings and 20.9 per cent of the area leased in).[16] It is also significant to note that the provision of the vesting of title has not been used much except in the states of Kerala and Maharashtra in the initial phases. This presents tenancy as a major issue of governance. The presumption attached to the state intervention through laws is that of reasonable implementation. One implication drawn is that the capacity of the state to implement its edicts against the diktats of market forces has proved inferior. The second of the implications is that the rights have accrued to the tenants with the promulgation of the legislation. Non-implementation of these rights on a scale as large as this amounts to a constitutional violation, particularly in respect of Article 39. Abdication of this vital responsibility to implement the constitutional liability detracts seriously from the basic governance and undermines the rule of law. This, in the third place, brings into question the character of the state, which cannot be expected to implement the laws no matter how radical, or good they appear unless they further the interests of the governing classes. Hence, the emphasis on the instrumentality of law as a cure for malfeasance of the market appears quite misplaced. To the contrary one has to look beyond law as a policy option. In the fourth place, the re-emergence of the Panchayat institution once hailed as the panacea for all ills, has in deeper analysis had a legitimising effect upon the rural power structure. This is likely to further reduce the effectiveness of the state intervention. To the contrary, in the fifth place, where radical movements have taken place the tenants have emerged much stronger in terms of bargaining strength.

The above implications place the tenancy debate in an altogether new perspective. The crucial questions remain: whether tenancy should be permitted uniformly in all states; whether it should be recorded; who should record; whether the share of products and by products should be regulated by law or left to the contracting parties; whether some limits should be prescribed on fixed cash tenancy; who decides the terms of tenancy; whether reverse tenancy be disallowed by law; who adjudicates; and last though not the least who adjudicates. In sum and substance we come back to the debate whether tenancy should be governed by the demands of the market or by law based upon considerations of equity and empowerment. Since tenancy continues to be the only institution that ensures certain flexibility which the land market cannot ensure, there is need for streamlining the tenancy legislation in a manner that will not drive it underground and make it exploitative, and at the same time ensures that it will not jeopardize the equity in landholdings by triggering undue reverse tenancy beyond permissible ceiling limits.

REFERENCES

1. It is well-accepted that due to fears of various kinds of legal provisions, in most of the cases limiting by nature, the incidence of tenancy is often under-reported.
2. This creates another trap of low wage-backward agriculture of which the self-cultivator is himself a victim, a phenomenon we shall discuss in greater detail at the appropriate place.
3. Coincidentally, the same argument is forwarded to validate the inverse relationship between farm size and productivity.
4. It is also possible that due to already depressed employment generation in agriculture still there be abundance of labour force.
5. See, micro-studies in Jan Breman, Peter Kloos and Ashwin Saith (eds.) The *Village in Asia Revisited*, Oxford University Press, New Delhi, 1997.
6. Amiya Kumar Bagchi, *The Political Economy of Underdevelopment*, Oxford University Press, New Delhi, 1987.
7. K. Griffin, *The Political Economy of Agrarian Change*, Macmillan, 1974
8. Terry J. Byres, "The Dialects of India's Green Revolution", *South Asian Review*, 2, 1972.
9. J. E. Stiglitz, "Incentives and Risk Sharing in Sharecropping", *Review of Economic Studies*, 61, 1974. DMG Newbery, Risk Sharing, "Sharecropping and Uncertain Labour Markets", *Reviews of Economic Studies*, 44, 1977.
10. Amartya Sen, *Resources, Values and Development*, Oxford University Press, New Delhi, 1984.
11. See footnote number 13.
12. These are based upon the reports submitted by the IAS Probationers as part of their socio-economic assignments during their district training as well as on the preliminary findings of the survey of tenancy status in UP by the Centre for Rural Studies, LBSNAA, Mussoorie. In addition to the mentioned below, there may be certain additional features of tenancy, but they would

be inconsequential for conceptualisation of the tenancy debate. For instance the leasing out of the distant plots and the leasing in the conveniently located plots or leasing in by a lessee of a particular size class holding from a lessor of the same size class ownership holding.

13. Policy Relating to Sharecropping and Leasing, Department of Rural Development, Government of India, December, 1997; and Concept Note on Legalising Leasing of Agricultural Land, Prime Minister's Office, Government of India, July 1999.
14. Section 168(1), MPLR, 1959.
15. T. Haque, *Impact of Tenancy Reforms on Productivity Improvement and Socio-Economic Status of Poor Tenants*, NCAEPR, 1999, Mimeo.
16. *Sarvekshana*: Vol. XX, No. 3.

Chapter 5

Volatility in Land Markets and Rural Poverty

C. S. MURTY

I
VOLATILITY IN LAND MARKETS

With interest rates prevailing in the organized credit sector reaching ever so low levels[1] and the inflation rate too falling to levels long unknown[2], those involved with rural areas are in a state of flux. The reaction of the rich over the years in such situations has been to buy land, whether or not the immediate revenue from the land warrants its purchase, for the simple reason that there are capital gains to be had from the purchase of land that is inelastic in supply. But with increasing curbs on the acquisition of additional land and because of the deterrent effects of land ceiling laws, one alternative left to the rich is to invest in money lending activity. Some have started to take land on lease and cultivate it along capitalist lines thus giving a renewed emphasis to the so called 'capitalist' tenancy.

Raising Rate of Interest and Rural Poverty

Also, ironically, the prospects of getting high rewards from lending money in rural areas have multiplied. With the small and marginal farmers using up all sources of funds and are being driven to acute debt crises following successive droughts in many parts of the country prior to 2003-04, and the prudential norms of the commercial banks preventing them from lending to the rural sector, at least to the extent they ought to have lent (the 18% credit earmarked for the priority sector has never been supplied), there arose a spurt in the demand for credit in rural areas. This is bound to have pushed up the interest rates charged by the non-institutional sources of finance. For years now, the model rate of interest has not been higher than 36 per cent. But seen in conjunction with low interest rates in the banking sector and the low inflation rate, the very 36 per cent could work out to a very high real interest rate. These conditions ruined the economy of the poor peasant—not only is he to now pay higher rent for the land he might lease-in, for he has to vie with large farmers who entered the lease market in a big way (Murty, 2004), but he also has to shell out more money in the form of interest charges for the demand for rural credit has touched an all time high.

Growing Indebtedness

Whatever be the future that holds for the petty peasant, he cannot abruptly stop relying upon the agricultural sector on the ground that farmers in general and petty cultivators in particular, have of late been not having it good in the sector—have been becoming victims of a crisis that has seized the sector. If crops fail he would more likely to end up debt/deeper debt, besides losing hold over the land he owned or leased-in. Then with one important avenue of employment lost to him, he might have to take recourse to the option of prematurely ending his life, with the hope that at least in his death his family would be better off because a relief package is often provided by the 'democratically' elected governments to provide succor to the families of the diseased. In short, the small and marginal farmers as also tenants are presently left in a lurch. The land market has thus become volatile.

II

TOWARDS PEASANT BASED AGRICULTURE

How best can one mitigate the predicament of the rural poor in this context. It is necessary: (1) to increase the access of land to the poor who wish to cultivate it, (2) to increase the supply of credit to the needy farmers, (3) to ensure a sustainable increase in farm incomes, so that farmers would not be driven into debt, and farming as an occupation becomes something to be cherished and not despised,

(4) to augment the supply of cultivable land, and (5) to change the mindset of the farmer who is on the verge of committing suicide through policy changes that are within the realm of possibility for 'soft' states to implement. The paper sets out to address to these problems, though, in a discursive way.

If we are to rely on the NSS 1991-92 (the latest available data), an estimated 38.15 per cent (or 39.18 lakh hectares) of tenanted holdings were operated by farmers having more than 4 hectares of operational holdings (whom we call the 'large' farmers) and 42.85 per cent (44.39 lakh hectares) of the land operated by them was the tenanted land (GOI, 1997). The surplus land distributed in this country up to September 1991 was 19.48 lakh hectares. Compare this with the tenanted land under the control of large farmers as of 1991-92, which was 44.39 lakh hectares. And what is more, even the NSS estimates of land under lease, though are on a far higher side compared to the leased-in land as per the Agricultural Census, are admittedly underestimates themselves (Sanyal, 1997; Sawant, 1991). Following a peasant based model of development, if all the tenanted holdings and the tenanted area held by large farmers are transferred, by restricting the entry into the lease market to only the landless and marginal peasants, the welfare of the petty cultivating classes (and with linkage effects the interests of the rural people) could be improved enormously. Thus, what we could achieve through redistribution of land for over 40 years, could be surpassed many times over, if the policy of limiting the lease market to the petty peasantry is implemented (Murty, 2004).

The peasant farm economy is not inefficient. There is the apprehension that the small and marginal holdings will not be efficient because they face credit rationing and therefore, will not be able to make adequate investment and because they are risk averse. However, indirect evidence available from both the Agricultural Census and the NSS goes to negate this stand, at least in case of Andhra Pradesh (GOAP, 1997). Agricultural Census data on the intensity of cropping on the irrigated, and un-irrigated lands, and on the proportion of fallow land in cultivated land for different size-classes of farmers shows that in respect of all the three variables the performance of the farmers was inversely related to the size of holding in 1995-96. Evidence from the NSS is not so categorical. Yet it also suggests that size of holding had no relation with the efficiency with which a farm was cultivated (Table 5.1). The Eighth Five Year Plan document also categorically subscribes to the view that given the present state of agricultural technology even a small farmer can be viable both in terms of employment and income of a family. Thus even the limited land reforms of the above type can be seen as an intrinsic part of the anti-poverty strategy.

Table 5.1: Some Indicators of Land Use Efficiency: Andhra Pradesh

(*percentages*)

Indicator	*Marginal*	*Small*	*Semi-medium*	*Medium*	*Large*	*All Classes*
AGRICULTURAL CENSUS: 1995-96						
NSA in operated area	86.80	85.54	83.97	80.01	70.19	82.79
GCA/NSA	131.65	120.49	116.10	112.34	108.42	119.02
Current fallows in NSA	14.10	15.01	16.38	20.60	34.67	17.87
Current and other fallows in NSA	14.70	16.09	17.91	22.95	38.61	19.46
Culturable waste and fallows in NSA	14.85	16.35	18.27	23.51	39.91	19.86
Gross irrigated area/Net irrigated area	126.61	121.62	119.56	116.72	112.87	121.45
Gross un-irrigated area/Net un-irrigated area	138.24	119.67	114.17	110.45	107.07	117.43
NSS: 1991-92						
Current fallows in NSA	1.38	2.31	2.05	3.96	0.43	2.28
Current and other fallows in NSA	1.55	2.94	2.43	4.81	2.72	2.96
GCA/NSA	141.64	136.66	130.85	133.08	140.40	135.50
Gross irrigated area/Net irrigated area	163.92	160.69	151.66	154.33	163.01	157.75
Gross un-irrigated area/Net un-irrigated area	116.13	117.23	113.97	119.56	130.73	118.30

Also, if our foodgrain production is gradually increasing, although not in years of severe natural calamities, it is no less because the poor peasant is putting in his best effort to garner whatever little that he is possibly can from his tiny piece of land. It is not so much because any revolutionary changes have come about on the technological front. It is long time since our scientists have hit upon a technology that could usher in a second Green Revolution. Their time is now taken over by the development of pesticides, fertilizers, herbicides, machines and the like. The peasant based agriculture would increase the rate of growth of employment and income in agriculture and in the allied sectors, and may be in the inter-linked industrial sector as well.

Twin Problems of Peasant Based Agriculture

Crop Losses

The peasant based agriculture is beset with two fundamental problems. One, recurring losses to those engaged in farming. The probability of a farmer incurring huge losses from cultivation seems to have increased enormously in the recent past. In any case, the poor farmer cannot afford to incur losses on account of crop failure even in one year. In any year he should be guaranteed of a certain minimum return. He should be made to feel that agriculture is an occupation to be cherished and not to be detested. It is, therefore, essential that every farmer, more so, the small and marginal farmers, is covered under the farm income insurance scheme. The Farm Income Insurance Scheme initially launched on a pilot basis in Rabi 2003-04 in 18 districts of 12 states covering wheat and paddy is in the right direction (GOI, 2004). The scheme is desirable because it protects the farmer against low yields and low prices for output. As one of the alternatives to this scheme, rainfall insurance scheme is mooted. If pushed through, it will give raise to far too many problems. A normal rainfall need not culminate in normal income to the farmer. The quantum of rainfall and its spread may be good. But there is no guarantee that all farmers will be able to carry out agricultural operations just when rains warrant them to do so, for reasons of non-availability of timely seeds, credit, labour etc. So, even if the extent of rainfall and its spread is appropriate, there is no guarantee that farm income to the cultivator would be reasonable. Two other issues need clarification. One, the premium rates payable by farmers to be eligible to be covered under the insurance schemes should, as far as possible, be progressive, or should involve an element of subsidy for small and marginal farmers in the early years of implementation of the schemes. Second, and more important, for the crop insurance schemes to be sustainable, it is essential that the premium rates are not too low and that as vast an area as is practically possible and viable should be fixed for the operation of the schemes. The insurance schemes confined to small geographical parts, would only add to costs of operation of the scheme, involves enormous amount of time and would not be sustainable. The viability problems of farm insurance, thus, are far too many. But there should be a system that ensures protection of small-marginal farmers against crop losses.

Credit Shortage

The second problem that confronts the small and marginal farmers is the one relating to credit. Farmers, whether they have owned or leased-in land, cannot farm efficiently, without quality credit. And to expect that all credit needs of the farmers could be supplied by the institutional agencies is not wise, for the simple reason, that even today, non-institutional agencies supply a large chunk of the credit of the farmers. Moreover, the quality of credit supplied by the latter agencies is of high quality. Therefore, it is not only necessary to ensure that the institutional credit supply does not get clogged (this is what happens with loan waivers, overdues, undue credit or interest subsidies or restructuring of credit) but the non-institutional agencies supply credit at reasonable rates of interest. It is obvious that for the institutional agencies to supply credit to the petty owners and tenants, it is necessary that record of rights exists, whether they be clear-cut ownership rights or leasehold rights. Without these it is just not possible to consider advancing loans to them.

Regulation of Money Lenders and Interest Rates

Why cannot rural money lenders be allowed to operate? Are they not providing quality credit to the people of rural areas by advancing loans at any time, without undue delay and without following intricate procedures that institutional sources of finance cannot escape from? Can we allow them to operate in the rural scene without unduly interfering in their business, just as industrialists in urban areas are allowed to do, provided they agree to come into the ambit of the government's rules and regulations (which in any case are few in the era of reforms)—provided they get themselves registered with an appropriate agency? Money lenders, registered or otherwise, usually oblige the borrower into signing on two promissory notes—one, assuring him to charge only the government fixed interest rate, but a larger than the amount actually lent (as a hedge against loss of interest in the event of the loan needs to be recovered through court), and the interest rate actually payable by the borrower (in no event will it be less than double the legislated interest rate) for the actual sum lent. Making the needy borrower sign on 'stamped' papers devoid of any conditions being written on them (empty stamped papers) is another practice to put the borrower in a fix. In fact, there could be myriad other ways in which a money lender could extract a higher than legislated interest rate from his borrowers—the ways may differ depending upon the nature of the collateral offered as a security against the loan.

The government is letting this to happen. Now the grouse is not only against the tax paying registered money lender as such but against those who are not registered. We are driven to a situation where any act done under the garb of tax is not a crime and does not call for punishment. Ironically the village credit market offers a great scope to raise tax revenue for the government if it forces all the money lenders of villages to register themselves and make them pay taxes based on their activities. We are not against this, for after all, as said earlier, money lenders cannot be dispensed with, as the quality of credit supplied by them is superior to that provided by the institutional sources. But the catch lies in the government's willingness to use the tax income generated from the new registered money lenders for rural areas and in its ability to bring the rural interest rates under control (of course the government cannot absolve itself of its responsibility of subjecting the industrialists also to some degree of price control). The question arises: Under what conditions do rural money lenders not resent registering the actual amount lent and charging a low real rate of interest on the amount? After all, it is not to their advantage to register because, if they register, they have to pay tax on their activities, besides having to charge only the 'reasonable' interest rate stipulated by the government. A scheme that motivates money lenders registering their lending activities and abide by the conditions stipulated in the law is outlined below.

The solution to the problems facing the agricultural sector today could be found in proper prioritizing of government spending—in crying a halt to the urban bias in development planning. Resources raised through cesses and taxes could as well be used to partly pay-up both institutional and non-institutional loans of farmers and other poor of rural areas to resolve the crisis presently facing rural areas and the agricultural sector. If this is made a routine policy in case of all the loans registered, but, for genuine reasons not repaid by the rural borrowers, it should be possible to induce the non-institutional lenders into accepting to charge a low rate of interest on their loans, for the risk faced by them in carrying out lending operations is now greatly reduced with the involvement of the government.

There is the danger that both the lender and the borrower could collude and claim a sum larger than the amount originally contracted, from the government agency in charge of clearing part of the dues of the defaulting borrowers. But such an act will never be to the benefit of the borrower. The argument that the collusive action will be to the benefit of both the lender and the borrower does not stand to logic, because, (1) the borrower cannot fully absolve himself of repaying the entire sum of the loan at some point in time in future and, therefore, (2) if he has to repay the remaining sum from his own resources, what he gains through the collusion with the lender might be far below the amount he will be compelled to pay later. The more the borrower seeks to gain form the collusive arrangement with the lender, the more he might lose. Not only that: The fact that the government pays up part of the loan when the borrower is in financial distress does not mean that he is totally waived off that part of the loan. Sooner or later, either with incomes arising from crop insurance or with unexpected incomes of a bountiful harvest, that part of the loan the government had paid up to the lender, has now to be repaid to the government in this model by the borrower.

Now that the lenders will be more certain of recovering loans, they may not resent a programme of this kind. This scheme could be shown to be far superior to the alternative of loan waivers and moratorium on debt. Also, why cannot the government undertake to stand as guarantor to loans borrowed from non-institutional sources of finance, subject to the condition that the lenders, as noted, register their loans with it. Let not the onus of declaring the outstanding loans fall on the debt-ridden farmers, lest it hurts their pride and will not go to lessening the suicides. One could perceive some advantages of these steps. Non-institutional lenders stop pestering their debtors for repayment of loans at a time when the whole agricultural sector is facing a crisis and incomes derived by farmers are barely enough for their sustenance. A certain degree of control could be exercised over the non-institutional credit and interest charges on such credit brought down. Institutional sources of finance will now be able to increase recycling of their funds for, part of their dues are paid up. The scheme will not make any great demands on the exchequer. It could also relieve farmers of the impending threat of not finding enough resources for investment in the present kharif season.

It will aid to alter the mindset of those on the verge of committing suicide, without in anyway endangering their self-respect. The peasant will be made to feel that there is still hope, be led to believe that the government machinery is still sensitive to his sufferings and can provide him immediate relief without his having to run from pillar to post in trying to get the benefit of the relief. The more important thing is, it will safeguard his self-respect, better still, help him restore his lost pride. It will infuse confidence in him and make him feel that he shall overcome his troubles in a none too distant future, while holding his head high, with dignity.

The scope for raising the resources needed for rejuvenating the agricultural sector appears bright once we begin appreciating the deep rooted urban bias in our development planning and begin exploring the ways to lessen it. It is important that the government accommodates the Universal PDS, pushes through food-for-work programme with greater commitment, engages personnel to ensure supply of quality fertilizers, pesticides and seeds to farmers and makes sure that the authority and responsibility given to the extension machinery are on par with each other so that it becomes possible to revitalize the machinery. Also important is to entrust the job of the dissemination of information relating to the availability of ground water resources to farmers through qualified technical personnel. This is possible if we can end the urban bias in development planning and design incentive, protection and promotion programmes to suit the specific needs of the small holder peasant farming.

III
LAND LEASE MARKET: TOWARDS A REGULATORY MODEL[3]

Is there a case for fresh initiatives in respect of tenancy legislation? The case for altering the landlord-tenant relations of production exists so long as these relations act as a fetter on the release of the forces of production. There is no reason why the inimical relations should disappear with the passage of time if market forces are allowed to have their sway. Efforts at altering the agrarian system so as to free it from the defects through tenancy reforms should continue. To stop such efforts on the ground that past experience with land reform programmes has not been encouraging is an error. Failure only signifies the need to correct earlier tenancy laws or to evolve new ones based on an understanding of the three aspects of the land lease market—the extent of tenancy, the efficiency and exploitation of tenants. On one extreme there are those who argue that the radical land-to-the-tiller policy should be pursued in right earnest and on the other there are those who voice the need for completely liberalizing tenancy. In between the two extreme postures, there are several variants.

First, on one extreme, liberalisation of tenancy may be interpreted to mean making all tenancy laws null and void. Implicitly it would amount to steadfastly protecting the property rights of landlords. Any one wanting to lease-in or lease-out land is at liberty to do so. There would be no restrictions on the period of lease, and the rent on the tenanted land would be the one determined in the market. The landlord could switch the tenants at will or could take back the land for personal cultivation.

Second, it is possible to think of legalizing tenancy, the West Bengal way. The Left Front government in West Bengal launched the Operation Barga (OB) programme in 1978 and thereby institutionalized tenancy. Under the programme tenants are conferred occupancy rights over the lands leased-in by them. Restrictions are imposed on the rents payable on tenanted lands and the scope for resumption of the lands by the landlords is severely curtailed. Provisions are made to bring the tenants into the fold of institutional financing agencies.

Third, the radical redistributist policy of land-to-the-tiller could be followed. The policy envisages compensation payments to landlords. It is the state which compensates the landlords to begin with and the beneficiaries pay up the amount to the state subsequently. This policy model has been successfully enforced in Kerala and there are demands that the West Bengal government also adopt this model as next step to its 'Operation Barga' programme. However, the thinking in government circles, as evident from the Ninth and Tenth Five Year Plan documents, seems to veer towards making leasing-in of land permissible within the ceiling limits.

Fourth, provide for security of tenure and fix ceilings on rents but let the onus of taking advantage of the laws fall on tenants.

Fifth, legalise tenancy but only in a limited way and fall in line with changing times.

The implications of the above five options will be analysed below from the view point of: (1) equity, (2) feasibility and more importantly, (3) their contribution to sustainable development of the agricultural sector in our attempt to evolve a land reform programme for future implementation in the 'soft state' like that of Andhra Pradesh.

Let us consider why the *first* option does not contribute to sustainable agricultural development and will also be not feasible. It will not contribute to equity either. No political establishment will ever try with the idea of making the existing tenancy laws null and void even if it is perfectly clear that they are serving no definite purpose. To do so is to invite the needless wrath of the people. Since anyone can lease-in land, large farmers might step into the lease market and deprive the small and marginal farmers of tenanted land thus endangering equity. In any case, this option does not enhance equity even if all the tenants are small because the market determined rental charges could be exorbitantly high. Their capacity to invest will be low because of high rental charges. Also, there is no guarantee that the tenants, whether they be large or small, will put in adequate investment in the tenanted land because they can be asked to quit from the land any time by their landlords. Absence of security of tenure and the resultant lack of incentive to put in durable investment in land are considered serious obstacles to tenurial efficiency.

The *second* policy option noted above is the one followed in West Bengal. Subsequent to the launching of the OB programme, that is in the 1980s, the rate of growth of food grain production attained in the state was the highest among the major states of the country (Rawal and Swaminathan, 1998). Whether it is a coincidence or the OB programme actually improved the private investment climate and therefore, led to rapid growth of food grain output is difficult to tell because of two reasons. One, during the period there was an expansion in irrigation facilities in the state and at least part of the increase in the growth rate should be attributed to the expansion of the facilities (Haque, 2003). And two, in the 1990s there was a slackening of growth of food grain production in the state raising doubts about the model's ability to contribute to sustainable development of the agricultural sector. But it is noted that the primary sector's growth rate of (adjusted) SDP in West Bengal during 1990-2000 at 7.09 per cent was higher than the growth rate during 1980-90 at 6.39 per cent (Bhattacharya and Sakthivel, 2004). The West Bengal model may aid the registered tenants to farm efficiently, because the rent payable by them being low, and with greater access to institutional credit, they should have greater capacity to invest. What is intriguing is that one of the important gains that follows from the West Bengal type tenancy reform—security of tenure—does not necessarily work towards increasing investment on land and towards greater land use efficiency

(Place and Otsuka, 2001). Further, the notion that recording of rights of tenants will make tenants draw a large share of their credit from institutional sources also seems to be belied (Haque, 2001). Pal (1995) has shown that the OB programme has had a depressing effect on productivity because bargadars lacked entrepreneurial ability and supporting facilities. This is reported to have given rise to a vicious circle of lower investment, lower productivity and meagre returns for investment and resulted in inefficiency, lower productivity and inequitable income distribution.

It is possible that inefficient cultivators will remain in cultivation when attempts are made to register tenancies. Some landowners may want to lease-out to concentrate on non-farm activities but refrain from doing so, for the fear that once leased-out, the land stands leased-out and they will not get back the land and they get little rent as the tenants' rights are entered in the revenue records and because the legislated rents are far below the market rents. So they remain in cultivation but pay little attention to the cultivation of lands. The West Bengal model no doubt contributes to equity. And to conceive and implement programme of this nature is no doubt credible. It appears that the model also, in general, seems to improve investment climate. But its potential to bring about sustainable development of the agricultural sector is, however, yet to be firmly established, particularly in the context of landholdings which are unequal than West Bengal.

For the political leadership in 'soft' states, this option will not be palatable. Also, in West Bengal it is feared that the protected rights of bargadars might get eroded in the event of the Left Front loses control of the government. Already occupancy tenants of the state are reportedly entering into agreements with their landlords to return a part of the land leased-in by them in return for ownership rights over the rest of the land over which they had been conferred occupancy rights (Rawal, 2001; Hamstad and Nielsen, 2004). It is also contended that the process of providing security of tenure could not be completed and it reached more or less a stalemate. It was found politically unviable, just as it was, sometimes ethically indefensible when 'landlords' were themselves small (Chandra *et al.*, 1999).

The *third* option pertains to the land-to-the-tiller policy. Kerala demonstrated in no uncertain terms that even in a federal democratic set-up such radical policies could be pursued if only there is political will (Herring, 1983). But recent evidence from the state shows that tenancies are re-emerging (Eswaran, 1990). For the fear that they will lose ownership right, landowners who otherwise would like to lease-out, may not wish to lease-out and will remain in cultivation. They may prove inefficient or they may leave the land uncultivated. Kerala model is highly equitous, no doubt. But it is also the most difficult to push through in the era of liberalisation. If Kerala could implement the radical land-to-the-tiller policy, it is because the Communists Parties with strong commitment to 'land to the tiller' have often been in power in the state starting from 1957. It might have been the need to believe in itself, as the first democratically elected communist government anywhere in the world, and because it had the support of a highly conscious peasantry that the Left governments in Kerala might have opted for this radical policy. Even West Bengal with a stable Left Front government since 1977 could not go all out and adopt this radical policy. The model does not guarantee sustainable development of the agricultural sector, because inefficient landowners may be found controlling land.

The *fourth* policy option open to the state is to maintain *status quo*. For instance, in AP there are separate laws governing tenancies in Andhra area and Telangana area. Consider the Telangana Act, 1950 (as amended in 1954). The Act does not end tenancies and gives protected status to some tenants. It was enforced with vigour at one time following threats from extremists. Now few landowners come forward to lease-out their lands in the region because of the impending danger of losing the land altogether and as argued earlier, they will remain in cultivation or hold the land uncultivated even though they have little interest in cultivation. Large proportion of land is left fallow in Telangana area may be because of the above factors. The tenancy law pertaining to the Andhra area of AP in its present form does not seem to serve any purpose but with thought and planning it can be made to serve the objective of bringing about a sustainable development of agriculture. We will turn to it below as a part of discussing a sustainable model.

The *fifth* option noted above is to legalise tenancy in a limited way. It may have the following components. Provide only *limited* security of tenure to the tenant. In any case, security of tenure *per se*—that is, if it fails to increase investment on land—will not lead to greater profits from land to the tenant (Place and Otsuka, 2001) and it may at times even make the tenant recalcitrant and inefficient (Ghatak and Ingersent, 1984). It is necessary to permit landowners to resume land for personal cultivation, however defined, or to switch tenants after the expiry of the period of lease, for the animosity of the landlord is often directed not so much against the tenant as against his protected status (Khusro, 1958). A certain degree of uncertainty of tenure will ensure that tenants will put in their best effort and cultivate the land efficiently, if only to keep the landlords satisfied through prompt payment of rents.

Fix ceilings on rents that are reasonably below the market rents. This will leave sufficient returns to tenants to invest in lands. Provide legislative guarantee to landlords, whether resident or non-resident, to the effect that in no case will the ownership rights over the tenanted lands be conferred on tenants automatically or will the tenanted lands be usurped by the state. From the micro-level studies conducted in the Punjab and Karnataka we learn that absentee landlordism is of a high order—15 to 17 per cent in the former and 25 to 35 per cent in the latter, at least in some parts (Haque, 2001). Registering the rights of tenants should be quite appealing to them. As they are away from the village where the land is located, they will be under the constant apprehension that their lands may be permanently usurped by somebody some day. There is also no guarantee that they will receive rents promptly from their tenants. When they make visits to collect rents from the tenants, it is possible that the tenants may not pay up the rents due, for whatever reason. But with tenants' rights being recorded they can now be rest assured that the land will not come under unlawful occupation and they are also assured of greater certainty in rental receipts. The two important provisions that tenurial security granted to the tenant is restricted and that there will never be any threat to the ownership right on the leased-out land will enhance the feasibility of pushing through the laws. Further, land owners may not totally refrain from investing in their lands, for the reason that they will continue to have unbridled ownership right over the lands.

These provisions can ensure that efficient cultivators will remain in the cultivation of land. This makes sustainable development of agriculture possible. It is desirable, however, to bar the entry of large farmers into the lease market, for the reason that their entry will give a severe jolt to peasant based agriculture (where employment opportunities will be far more and where income distribution will be more equal than in the alternative scenario based in capitalist farming) and will jeopardize the interests of the petty peasants who hope to advance on the agrarian ladder by leasing-in small pieces of land. The tenancy law as it is obtaining in the Andhra area is largely consistent with the one postulated above except that no concerted effort has ever been made to register tenancies and to enforce the legislated rents. If tenancies are not recorded the gains that follow from this liberalized law will not contribute to the development of the agricultural sector.

Additionally, if the landlord is assured of receiving legislated rents with certainty even in years of unfavourable monsoons, there should be little resentment to let the tenant record his rights in land. This can be ensured by covering all cultivators under the crop, income, rainfall, or credit insurance scheme. The present practice is such that when the risk associated with the cultivation of tenanted land is covered under a crop insurance scheme, it is the owner who stands to gain by the scheme and not the tenant as he does not have a record of rights over the land leased-in by him to claim his due share in the insured amount (Murty, 1996). It is known that the liability of the tenant towards his landlord is in practice largely limited (Stiglitz, 2000) because when crops fail landlords are generally considerate towards their tenants and allow them some discount on the rent payable or may even completely waive the rents. The present practice, therefore, is such that both the landlord and his tenant lose when crops fail. Crop insurance schemes as they are being implemented today face the grave problem of not being sustainable as the premium rates are very low. To circumvent this problem several alternatives are being proposed (Sinha, 2004). We have come to a stage in Andhra Pradesh where the immediate implementation of insurance scheme of one form or the other is a must, what with a multitude of farmers committing suicides following crop losses. In this scheme of things, the tenant once registered has to pay the legislated rent but through an institutional agency (Vyas, 1970) which also caters to the credit needs of the tenant, may be through a cooperative set up as well as access to other sources of institutional credit. Long leases are not part of the programme and protected tenancy is out of question, for it can endanger efficiency and will enrage landlords (Appu, 1996).

Compensating the tenant for the unexhausted durable investment made by him is a difficult proposition. Moreover, it is the landlord who should undertake long-term investment. One way of ensuring this is to compel him in a discreet way. If part of the rent paid by the tenant is retained by the intermediate agency and if the tenant is permitted to undertake durable investment on land drawing resources from the portion of the rent accumulated, with the consent of the landlord, land improvements can be effected at fairly regular intervals.

The portion of the rent accumulated at the agency rightfully belongs to the landlord in this model and in the event of the expiry of the lease contract, the accumulated part of the rent may be transferred to the landlord (Murty, 1996).

Since the tenant's right is recorded he can be extended both consumption and production credit. It is quite possible that landlords also continue to take interest in the cultivation of the leased-out plots even after the recording of the rights of tenants because they are not unduly worried about getting the land back from their tenants in case of need as security of tenure is severely restricted. This will put the tenants at an advantage, for tenants lacking entrepreneurial talent can benefit from the landlords' knowledge. Further tenants will continue to have the benefit of drawing credit from their landlords, a facility unthinkable if occupancy rights are conferred on the tenants. Institutional sources of credit, as noted earlier, are incapable of meeting the entire credit needs of tenants and in such a context credit from landlords is a boon. It is shown that inter-linked credit and rental markets need not always work to the disadvantage of tenants. One alternative by which the landlord can ensure efficient use of land by the tenant and thereby guarantee himself of the prompt receipt of rent from the tenant is advance him the needed credit on time (Stiglitz, 2000). The petty owners wanting to lease-out should be prevented from leasing-out to well-off tenants for whatever reason and their consumption credit needs along with the credit needs of their tenants should be met. Since the programme is not radical but only regulatory it should be possible to enforce it. Even if some lease contracts occur outside the purview of the agency despite all the preventive efforts they cannot be sizeable in number because it is not to the advantage of the tenant to transact outside the legal framework with no access to cheap institutional credit and without the benefit of legislated rents.

Once the leasehold rights are recorded it should also be possible to bring in enormous amount of fallow land under cultivation (the upper limit of which could be 17.63% of NSA as of 2002), because it is often argued that one of the reasons for not putting the fallow land to good use or any use is the frictions prevailing in the countryside. As to the question of making the non-institutional sources of finance, like money lenders, to pump in credit to the poor farmer, the present paper comes out with a model. These two models together are expected to reduce the volatility of the rural land markets even as they seek to mitigate the poverty of the poor farmer of the countryside.

END NTOES

1. For instance, the 'bank rate', which was 10.00% per annum in 1990-91 fell substantially to 6.25% in 2002-03 and further to 6.00% in May 2004. Government of India, *Reserve Bank of India Bulletin*, Vol. 58. No.7, July, 2004, New Delhi, p. S564.
2. The annual average inflation based on the WPI of all commodities, which was 10.6% during 1991-91 to 1995-96 slide down to 5.1% during 1996-97 to 2000-01 and further to 4.2% between 2001-02 and 2003-04. Government of India, *Economic Survey, 2003-04*, Ministry of Planning, New Delhi, p. 84
3. This section is primarily a revised version of a paper presented by the author at a 'National Seminar on Institutional Policy Options for Sustainable Agricultural Development' held during 10-11th April, 2004, at Osmania University, Hyderabad and organized jointly by the Department of Economics of the University and the Acharya N.G. Ranga Agricultural University, Andhra Pradesh.

REFERENCES

Appu, P. S. (1996). *Land Reforms in India: A Survey of Policy, Legislation and Implementation*, Vikas Publishing House, New Delhi.

Chandra, B., Mukherjee, M., and Mukherjee, A. (1999). *India After Independence*, Viking, New Delhi, p. 382.

Eswaran, K. K. (1990). 'Re-emergence of Land Leasing in Kerala: The Case of Kuttanad', *Social Scientist*, November-December.

Ghatak, S., and Ingersent, K. (1984). *Agriculture and Economic Development*, The Harvester Press, UK.

Government of Andhra Pradesh, (1997). *Report on Agricultural Census: Andhra Pradesh, 1995-96*, Directorate of Economics and Statistics, Hyderabad.

Government of India, (1997). *Operational Land Holdings in India, 1991-92: Salient Features*, NSS 48th Round, National Sample Survey Organisation, Report No. 407, Department of Statistics, New Delhi.

Government of India, *Economic Survey, 2003-04* (2004). Ministry of Planning, New Delhi, pp. 162-63.

Haque, T. (2001). *Impact of Tenancy Reforms on Productivity Improvement and Socio-Economic Status of Poor Tenants*, National Centre for Agricultural Economics and Policy Research, Policy paper, 13, New Delhi, pp. 93-94, 104.

Haque, T. (2003). 'Land Reforms and Agricultural Development: Retrospect and Prospect', in Suresh Pal *et al.*, (eds.) *Institutional Change in Indian Agriculture*, National Centre for Agricultural Economics and Policy Research, New Delhi, 2003, p. 270.

Herring, R. J. (1983). *Land to the Tiller: The Political Economy of Agrarian Reform in South Asia*, Oxford University Press, Delhi.

Khusro, A. M. (1958). *Economic and Social Effects of Jagirdari Abolition and Land Reforms in Hyderabad*, Atma Ram and Sons, Kashmere Gate, Delhi, 1958. Cited from Haque, T., *Impact of Tenancy Reforms on Productivity Improvement and Socio-Economic Status of Poor Tenants*, Policy paper, 13, National Centre for Agricultural Economics and Policy Research, New Delhi, 2001, p. 9.

Murty, C. S. (1996). 'Intervention in the Land Lease Market: Case for a Regulatory Model', *IASSA Quarterly*, Vol. 15. No. 1.

Murty, C. S. (2004). 'Land Reforms in Lease Market: Are Marginal Farmers Affected?', *Economic and Political Weekly*, Vol. 39, No. 29, July 17, pp. 3270-71.

Pal, S. S. (1995). *Impact of Tenancy Reform on Production and Income Distribution: A Case Study of Operation Barga in West Bengal*, Policy paper 1, National Centre for Agricultural Economics and Policy Research, New Delhi.

Place, F., and Otsuka, K. (2001). 'Tenure, Agricultural Investment and Productivity in the Customary Tenure Sector of Malawi, *Economic Development and Cultural Change*, Vol. 50, No. 1, October, p. 96.

Rawal, V. (2001). 'Agrarian Reform and Land Markets: A Study of Land Transactions in Two villages of West Bengal, 1977-95', *Economic Development and Cultural Change*, Vol. 49, No. 3, 2001, p. 623; Hamstad, T. and Nielsen, R. (2004). 'West Bengal's Bargadars and Landownership', *Economic and Political Weekly*, Vol. 39, No. 8, pp. 853-55.

Rawal, V. and Swaminathan, M. (1998). 'Changing Trajectories: Agricultural Growth in West Bengal, 1950 to 1996', *Economic and Political Weekly*, October 3.

Sanyal, S. K. (1977). 'Trends in Some Characteristics of Landholdings: An Analysis for a Few States', *Sarvekshana*, Vol. 1, No. 1, July-October, 1977; Sawant, S. D. (1991). 'Comparative Analysis of Tenancy Statistics: Implications for Concealed Tenancy', *Artha Vijnana*, Vol. 33, No.1, March 1991.

Sinha, S. (2004). 'Agriculture Insurance in India: Scope for Participation of Private Insurers', *Economic and Political Weekly*, Vol. 39, No. 25, June 19, 2004, pp. 2605-12.

Stiglitz, J. E. (2000). 'The New Development Economics', in Meier, G. M. and Rauch, J. E., (eds.) *Leading Issues in Economic Development*, Seventh Edition, Oxford University Press, New York, p. 352.

Vyas, V. S. (1970). 'Tenancy in a Dynamic Setting', *Economic and Political Weekly*, Vol. 5, No. 26, June 27.

Chapter 6

Changing Tenancy Relations in Rural India

H. R. SHARMA

I
INTRODUCTION

The institution of tenancy has remained one of the most debated rural institutions since the days of Adam Smith. The classical economists debated the relative efficiency of different tenurial systems, namely, fixed rent tenancy and share tenancy (metayage as it was called in French following a 50-50 sharing). The proposition that share tenancy is an inferior contractual system is clearly stated in Alfred Marshal's Principles (1920, 535-536); it is quite often referred to as Marshallian inefficiency or tax equivalent approach to share tenancy. In more recent times, the theoretical debate has branched into two schools. While one school supports the Marshallian inefficiency proposition, the other has sought to demonstrate that resource allocation must be efficient regardless of tenurial contracts[1]. In a somewhat related debate, marxists consider tenancy in general, and share tenancy in particular, as a source of exploitation and surplus appropriation, whereas the neo-classicals explain its emergence and persistence in terms of imperfect rural markets characterised by moral hazards, information asymmetry, high transaction costs, etc.[2]

In the Indian context, a number of empirical studies, based on sample surveys, have looked into various aspects of tenancy relations like magnitude, type, relative efficiency of different land tenure systems, and so on. The studies pertaining to Eastern Indian states, especially of the earlier vintage, have, *inter alia*, shown that tenancy, in particular share tenancy, in conjunction with the exploitative interlinkages in credit and labour markets act as a formidable barrier in the introduction of new agricultural technology (Bhadhuri, 1973, 120-137; Prasad, 1973, 869-872 and 1974, 1305-1308; Bharadwaj and Das 1975, 221-240). More recent studies for these states have, however, reported qualitative changes in diverse aspects of tenancy relations (Chadha and Bhaumik, 1992, 1009-17 and 1089-98; Swain, 1999, 2657-2666 and 2752-2758). Likewise, studies in other states, especially in agriculturally developed regions like Punjab, Haryana and Western Uttar Pradesh, have brought out certain features like increasing incidence of self-cultivation, emergence of fixed rent tenancy, participation of medium and large households in the lease market as lessees (Singh, 1989, A89-A92; Bhalla, 1983, 841-847; Srivastava, 1989, 339-395; Siddiqui, 1999, A143-A145).

How far changes in different aspects of tenancy relations reported by various field studies for different states/regions have gained ground at the macro level? Has the magnitude of tenancy declined continuously since 1953-54? How the incidence of mixed holdings and entirely leased-in holdings have changed overtime? Has share tenancy, considered to be more exploitative, really given way to fixed rent tenancy? Is the lease market now dominated by medium and large households as lessees and marginal and small households as lessors? What is the pattern of these changes across different states? Do the tenancy relations continue to be affected by the traditional factors like the availability of indivisible and non-tradable inputs? Do the recent changes in the rural economy like increase in rural non-farm employment, increase in wages, spread and permeation of new agricultural technology in conjunction with growing mechanisation, make a significant impact on different aspects of tenancy relations? Given the diversity of tenancy relations in different parts of the country, one may not expect a uniform pattern emerge. A critical review of the literature reveals that available studies are limited in coverage both in time and space and do not cover all aspects of tenancy relations (Bardhan, 1976, 1505-11; Laxminaryan and Tyagi, 1977a, A58-A62; 1977b, A77-A82; Swami, 1988, 555-568). The answer to above questions assumes significance in the wake of liberalisation when it is being increasingly argued that since land ceiling is politically more sensitive issue, the easiest way to reform agrarian structure and activating the land market lies in legalising leasing-in and leasing-out.[3] This study attempts to answer some of these questions. The study is organised in seven sections. Section II is devoted to analysing the nature of available data and the adjustments required to weave a consistent temporal story. Sections III and VI analyse changes in the extent and terms of tenancy respectively. While section V examines the extent and changes in reverse tenancy, the effect of different factors on the magnitude, type and direction of tenancy is quantified in section VI. Section VII summarises the major findings.

II
THE DATA

The National Sample Survey reports on landholdings and Agricultural Census are the two major sources of data on tenancy relations. However, as is well known, the agricultural census data are largely a carry forward of less reliable land revenue records at the grassroots level for most of the states. Not only that, the methodology used to tabulate the census data leaves much to be desired. In comparison, the NSS data are based on a more scientific methodology and are broadly temporally comparable. Again, although the data on tenancy, both from NSS and Census, are under estimates, the degree of underestimation tends to be more pronounced in case of census data inasmuch the tenancy contracts are seldom entered in the revenue records[4]. We have, therefore, relied upon the NSS data. Annexure 6.1 shows in detail the conceptual framework underlying data on different aspects of tenancy in different NSS rounds, since 8th round (1953-54). In the 8th round, though separate figures were available on agricultural and operational holdings, the break up of operated area into leased-in and owned area was available for operational holdings alone. The data, therefore, do not give any clue about the incidence of tenancy in relation to agricultural holdings and area leased-in. The gap can effectively be bridged in by dividing total area under each category of holdings into owned and leased-in area in the same proportion as given for same category of operational holdings. The data on terms of tenancy was not available. Further, mid-1950s was still a period during which the process of erstwhile zamindari tenants were being conferred ownership rights. These tenants are not strictly comparable with the tenants in a lease market. The 16th/17th round also did not provide detailed data on the magnitude and terms of tenancy. The detailed data on the magnitude and terms of tenancy was, however, available from 26th round onward. We have made some adjustments in data to ensure temporal comparability. First, the holdings reported under the head 'others' in the 37th round have been included in those that were reported as 'neither owned nor leased-in'. Similarly in the 48th round, holdings reported 'not recorded' have been clubbed with 'neither owned nor leased-in' holdings. The area reported 'not recorded' has been included in the area reported as 'neither owned nor leased-in but otherwise possessed'[5]. However, if such holdings and area had not been included in NSS rounds prior to 37th round, the temporal comparability would be affected. We have no such clarification available in the 26th round report. Second, different tenancy contracts have been clubbed under four major heads like fixed money, fixed produce, share of produce and other terms. Thus for the 26th round, 'other terms' include holdings and area operated under usufructuary mortgage. The new terms of tenancy introduced in the 37th and 48th rounds (Annexure 6.1), including usufructuray mortgage, have been clubbed with other terms to ensure temporal comparability[6].

III
MAGNITUDE OF TENANCY

The incidence of tenancy may be measured either in terms of proportion of area leased-in or area leased-out. While the former is based on the information supplied by tenants, the latter represents the landowners' side of the lease market[7]. Though the tenancy estimates arrived from both the sources are gross underestimates, the degree of underestimation tends to be less if it represents the lessees' viewpoint. This is based on the commonly shared impression that those leasing-out are large holders. The situation may change. However, for the purpose of this paper, we shall measure the magnitude of tenancy in terms of changes in the proportion of operational holdings leasing-in and operated area leased-in. It is further important to know how the incidence of different types of holdings, i.e., entirely owned self-cultivated, mixed (partly owned and partly leased-in) and entirely leased-in holdings has been changing over time. The decomposition of leased-in holdings yields useful insights. For example, those who own land participate in the lease market mainly to equalise differing ratios of the their factor endowment like family labour, bullock, machinery, etc. Also sometimes, they may lease-in a plot of land which is located near their home and lease-out the one that is located at a distance. In comparison, the landless households mainly enter the lease market to make a living because of limited alternative employment opportunities.

Table 6.1: Changing Incidence of Tenancy in Rural India, 1953-54 to 1991-92: Major States (per cent)

State	*Year*	*OH*	*MH*	*ELIH*	*NONLIH*	*OWNED*	*LIA*	*NONLIA*
Andhra Pradesh	1953-54	56.58	26.59	16.83	—	78.79	21.21	—
	1971-72	78.34	20.94	0.72	—	90.98	9.02	—
	1981-82	83.45	15.27	1.04	0.23	92.98	6.23	0.79
	1991-92	79.69	13.32	2.43	4.56	88.49	9.57	1.94
Assam	1953-54	41.2	23.55	35.25	—	57.05	42.95	—
	1971-72	75.27	7.83	18.9	—	80.31	19.69	—
	1981-82	83.93	10.77	3.5	1.8	90.99	6.35	2.66
	1991-92	79.88	5.07	7.35	7.7	85.84	8.87	5.29
Bihar	1953-54	64.83	23.53	11.64	—	87.65	12.35	—
	1971-72	60.24	39.03	0.73	—	85.5	14.5	—
	1981-82	78.03	20.04	1.01	0.56	88.68	10.27	1.05
	1991-92	86.02	1.9	5.56	6.52	92.81	3.91	3.28
Gujarat	1953-54	63.15	22.7	14.15	—	80.63	19.37	—
	1971-72	90.68	8.61	0.71	—	96.09	3.91	—
	1981-82	94.61	3.8	1.34	0.25	97.8	1.95	0.25
	1991-92	92.83	2.36	2.35	2.46	92.7	3.34	3.96
Haryana	1953-54	43.62	36	20.38	—	60.21	39.79	—
	1971-72	62.65	33.73	3.62	—	76.74	23.26	—
	1981-82	72.29	25.51	2.2	—	80.31	18.22	1.65
	1991-92	78.96	12.41	4.83	3.8	66.07	33.74	0.19
Himachal Pradesh	1953-54	—	—	—	—	—	—	—
	1971-72	—	—	—	—	—	—	—
	1981-82	87.24	12.27	0.49	—	94.6	3.2	2.2
	1991-92	84.08	3.8	5.01	0.71	92.18	4.83	2.99
Jammu & Kashmir	1953-54	65.22	20.96	13.82	—	77.93	22.07	—
	1971-72	85.78	13.78	0.44	—	91.81	8.19	—
	1981-82	88.16	11.73	0.11	—	95.19	2.37	2.44
	1991-92	91.2	5.35	0.52	2.93	94.44	3.73	1.83
Karnataka	1953-54	59.03	27.8	13.17	—	79.59	20.41	—
	1971-72	71.18	22.84	5.98	—	84.11	15.89	—
	1981-82	83.14	14.57	1.78	0.51	92.12	6.04	1.84
	1991-92	80.35	6.14	3.73	9.78	84.53	7.43	8.04
Kerala	1953-54	53.89	23.01	23.1	—	79.9	20.1	—
	1971-72	82.67	9.94	7.39	—	91.41	8.59	—
	1981-82	90.89	4.87	2.92	1.32	95.52	2.05	2.43
	1991-92	90.99	2.54	3.21	3.26	95.37	2.88	1.75

(Contd.)

(*Contd.*)

State	Year	OH	MH	ELIH	NONLIH	OWNED	LIA	NONLIA
Madhya Pradesh	1953-54	42.75	40.76	16.49	—	80.55	19.45	—
	1971-72	78.98	15.71	5.31	—	92.54	7.46	—
	1981-82	81.91	14.19	1.13	2.77	92.65	3.56	3.79
	1991-92	80.21	5.06	6.48	8.25	86.53	6.3	7.17
Maharashtra	1953-54	52.6	38.06	9.34	—	80.32	19.6	—
	1971-72	88.03	10.54	1.43	—	93.83	6.17	—
	1981-82	87.15	9.29	2.69	0.87	94.21	5.2	0.59
	1991-92	89.22	5.53	2.4	2.85	90.5	5.48	4.02
Orissa	1953-54	64.81	27.32	7.87	—	87.43	12 57	—
	1971-72	67.76	27.7	4.54	—	86.54	13.46	—
	1981-82	74.27	24.06	1.49	0.18	83.97	9.92	6.12
	1991-92	70.46	17.69	1.7	10.15	84.41	9.48	6.11
Punjab	1953-54	43.62	36	20.38	—	60.21	39.79	—
	1971-72	47.05	48.17	4.78	—	71.99	28.01	—
	1981-82	76.19	21.71	1.64	0.46	82.21	16.07	1.72
	1991-92	80.27	15.6	1.43	2.7	80.82	18.83	0.35
Rajasthan	1953-54	67.69	17.34	14.97	—	79.08	20.92	—
	1971-72	91.08	8.3	0.62	—	94.72	5.28	—
	1981-82	89.53	8.51	1.52	0.44	94.47	4.31	1.22
	1991-92	90.32	6.22	1.55	1.91	92.41	5.19	2.4
Tamil Nadu	1953-54	46.03	27.56	26.41	—	72.99	27.01	—
	1971-72	68.35	27.35	4.3	—	86.94	13.01	—
	1981-82	70.45	19.7	8.56	1.29	87.37	10.92	1.71
	1991-92	74.56	11.02	5.82	8.6	84.91	10.89	4.2
Uttar Pradesh	1953-54	71.14	23.89	4.37	—	88.67	11.33	—
	1971-72	72.18	26.34	1.48	—	86.99	13.01	—
	1981-82	78.53	20.61	0.82	0.04	88.05	10.24	1.7
	1991-92	80.84	14.47	2.64	2.05	88.45	10.49	1.06
West Bengal	1953-54	58.26	24.71	17.13	—	74.66	25.34	—
	1971-72	65.44	31.28	3.28	—	81.26	18.74	—
	1981-82	71.58	19.37	7.02	2.03	86.18	12.34	1.48
	1991-92	75.4	12	5.27	7.33	85.74	10.4	3.86
All-India	1953-54	60.63	26.79	12.58	—	79.48	20.52	—
	1971-72	74.31	21.83	3.86	—	89.43	10.57	—
	1981-82	80.58	16.24	2.37	0.81	91.08	7.18	1.74
	1991-92	81.98	8.87	3.85	5.3	87.91	8.28	3.81

Source: Computed from the following NSS Reports:

(i) Report on Landholdings (4); 8th Round 1953-54, NSS Report No. 66.
(ii) Report on Landholdings (5); 8th Round 1953-54, NSS Report No. 74.
(iii) Report on Landholdings (5); 8th Round 1953-54, NSS Report No. 74.
(iv) Report on Some Aspects of Landholdings; 26th Round 1971-72, NSS Report No. 215.
(v) Report on Landholdings (2); 37th Round 1982, NSS Report No. 331.
(vi) Report on Some Aspects of Operational Holdings; 48th Round 1991-92, Report No. 407

Table 6.1 provides changing percentage of different categories of holdings and the area owned and leased-in. We are critically aware that the tenancy data of 8th Round with the reference period 1953-54 could include considerable tenants under zamindari and hence a step decline in both pure-tenant and mixed-holdings category. While tenancy under zamindari refers to a kind of freezing of tenancy market, the tenancy under the later ryotwari refers to the open tenancy to the extent legally permitted and reported. The following features emanating from the table need to be highlighted. First, the percentage of entirely owned self-cultivated holdings (EOH) increased continuously since 1953-54 in eight states (Bihar, Haryana, Jammu & Kashmir, Kerala, Punjab, Tamil Nadu, Uttar Pradesh and West Bengal). The increase in the entirely owned holdings in these states was accompanied by decrease in the per cent of mixed holdings (MH), especially since 1971-72. In so far as entirely leased-in holdings (ELIH) are concerned, no neat pattern was in evidence; in states like Haryana, Jammu & Kashmir, Kerala and Uttar Pradesh the percentage of such holdings declined up to 1981-82 but increased thereafter; in Bihar they declined up to 1971-72 and increased afterwards and in Punjab they declined continuously. Second, in Andhra Pradesh, Gujarat, Himachal Pradesh, Madhya Pradesh and Orissa, the percentage of entirely owned holdings increased during seventies but declined during eighties. There was no clear pattern in these states in so far as mixed holdings were concerned. However, the per cent of entirely leased-in holdings increased in all these states except Gujarat. The increase in entirely owned self-cultivated holdings in most of the states could, *inter alia*, be attributed to the restrictive tenancy laws, and spread of new agricultural technology making agriculture more remunerative. Third, in most of the states there was a very high increase in neither owned nor leased-in but possessed (NONLIH) holdings. The extent of these holdings indicates the encroachment of government land and also includes holdings which are in the possession of the tenants but whose ownership rights have yet not been vested in them. Fourth, the proportion of leased-in area (LIA) to total operated area declined till 1981-82 in most of the states but increased by varying degrees thereafter in ten major states (Andhra Pradesh, Assam, Gujarat, Haryana, Himachal Pradesh, Jammu & Kashmir, Karnataka, Madhya Pradesh, Punjab and Rajasthan). Among the remaining states, while in Kerala and Tamil Nadu, the proportion of leased-in area declined between 1953-54 and 1981-82 followed by practically no change thereafter, in Uttar Pradesh and Orissa no clear-cut pattern was discernible. Fifth, like neither owned nor leased-in holdings, the proportion of operated area neither owned nor leased-in (NONLIA) increased by varying degrees between 1981-82 and 1991-92 in eleven states, namely, Andhra Pradesh, Assam, Bihar, Gujarat, Himachal Pradesh, Karnataka, Madhya Pradesh, Maharashtra, Rajasthan, Tamil Nadu and West Bengal. In some of the states the increase was quite substantial. In brief, the increase in the incidence of tenancy in most of the states during eighties was marked mainly by an increase in the per cent of entirely leased-in holdings. What explains an increase in such holdings? Whether this increase is the manifestation of deepening poverty and unemployment? Is it a response to rising agricultural wages and productivity witnessed in 1980s? Or the growing desire on the part of the landless households to lease-in land and practice commercial agriculture and earn profits? There are some important empirical questions that we seek to answer in a later section. Another important feature was very high per cent of neither owned nor leased-in holdings.

The trend in the households 'not operating land' also captures the changing incidence of tenancy. It, however, needs to be pointed out that households not operating land consist of two groups: one, who own land but do not operate because of a variety of reasons, and the other who neither own nor operate any land. It also needs to be mentioned that not all households who own but do not operate land are rentiers; some of them, particularly belonging to lower farm size category, may not be cultivating as they do not own enough cultivable land and some may also be keeping their land fallow. The available information on all the three categories of households shows that there has been a continuous decline since 1961-62 in the numerical strength of households owning but not operating land in all the states except Jammu & Kashmir, Punjab and Rajasthan. Nevertheless, a continuous decline in the per cent of such households across the board notwithstanding, in four states, namely, Andhra Pradesh, Maharashtra, Orissa and Punjab more than one-fifth of the rural households owned but did not operate land. The incidence of such households was also very high in states like Gujarat, Haryana and Karnataka.

IV
TERMS OF TENANCY

The proportion of operational holdings leasing-in and area leased-in does not capture all the nuances of tenancy. Even in a narrow economic sense, the proportion of area leased-in under different terms of tenancy has substantially different implications both for allocation of resources and well being of tenants[8]. It is, therefore, essential to study temporal changes in terms of tenancy. The details regarding changes in the per cent of holdings leasing-in and area leased-in under different terms of tenancy have been given in Table 6.2. The table calls for the following comments. First, there had been a significant decline in the per cent of holdings leasing-in under share tenancy (ST) in most of the states. The notable exceptions were Assam, Kerala and Rajasthan where during eighties, the per cent of holdings leasing-in under share tenancy remained practically unchanged and Andhra Pradesh, Karnataka, Madhya Pradesh and Orissa where they increased by varying degrees. Regarding the proportion of operated area leased-in under share tenancy, it declined continuously in about ten major states. In the remaining states, it declined between 1971-72 and 1981-82 but increased by varying degrees between 1981-82 and 1991-92. Second, the proportion of holdings leasing-in under fixed rent tenancy, particularly fixed money (FM), declined between 1971-72 and 1981-82 but increased during the subsequent decade in most of the states except Bihar, Himachal Pradesh and Uttar Pradesh where it declined and Tamil Nadu where it remained practically unchanged. The proportion of operated area leased-in under fixed rent tenancy, again especially under fixed money, also exhibited the similar trend; it declined during seventies but increased thereafter across the board except Bihar where it declined continuously. Third, over the period there has been a continuous decline in the proportion of holdings leasing-in under other terms (OT) which, as mentioned above, include usufructuary mortgage, from relatives, share cropping with other terms, etc. in a majority of the states. However, in some states, most notably, Andhra Pradesh, Gujarat, Tamil Nadu and West Bengal, the proportion of holdings leasing-in under other terms increased between 1971-72 and 1981-82 but declined between 1981-82 and 1991-92. In so far as the proportion of operated area leased-in is concerned, in four states (Andhra Pradesh, Gujarat, Karnataka, and Rajasthan) it increased during seventies but declined afterwards.

In others like Assam, Bihar, Jammu & Kashmir, Kerala and Punjab reverse pattern was in evidence, i.e. it declined during seventies but increased subsequently.

Table 6.2: Changing Incidence of Holdings and Area Leased-in Under Different Terms of Tenancy in Rural India, 1971-72 to 1991-92: Major States

(*Per cent*)

State	Year	Holdings				Area			
		FM	FP	ST	OT	FM	FP	ST	OT
Andhra Pradesh	1971-72	4.32	3.5	8.03	7.6	2.56	1.28	3.19	2
	1981-82	1.18	1.74	0.97	10.04	0.81	0.69	0.55	4.18
	1991-92	4.2	4.35	4.69	2.49	2.47	2.56	2.77	1.76
Assam	1971-72	8.36	4.08	4.14	14.94	3.36	3.06	8.24	5.02
	1981-82	1.73	0.75	3.01	6.81	0.98	0.53	2.24	2.59
	1991-92	2.46	0.58	3.95	5.69	1.51	0.36	2.47	4.54
Bihar	1971-72	1.22	1.93	27.93	9.92	0.18	1.01	11.35	1.97
	1981-82	1.55	0.95	12.25	5.7	0.67	0.37	4.94	1.7
	1991-92	0.75	1	3.45	2.29	0.37	0.39	1.33	1.81
Gujarat	1971-72	2.83	0.63	2.54	3.3	0.89	0.4	1.55	1.08
	1981-82	0.21	0	0.54	4.06	0.1	0	0.19	1.66
	1991-92	2.01	0.08	1.2	1.23	1.33	0.06	0.79	1.16
Haryana	1971-72	6.33	3.64	20.07	12.56	2.89	1.98	12.55	5.84
	1981-82	7.12	4.11	9.73	6.35	4.41	1.87	7.51	4.34
	1991-92	11.71	0.99	3.78	0.93	20.73	1.75	6.7	4.56
Himachal Pradesh	1971-72	—	—	—	—	—	—	—	—
	1981-82	1.83	1.88	2.32	3.22	0.24	0.52	1.06	1.38
	1991-92	1.36	0.9	1.08	5.72	0.66	0.43	0.52	3.21
Jammu & Kashmir	1971-72	0.31	1.6	10.89	1.42	0.06	0.65	6.99	0.35
	1981-82	0.11	0.63	2.5	2.24	0.05	0.29	1.58	0.45
	1991-92	0.56	1.81	0.71	3.3	0.35	1.13	0.43	1.82
Karanataka	1971-72	8.25	6.8	9.71	7.34	4.9	3	6.21	1.77
	1981-82	1.34	0.79	2.11	6.55	0.22	0.27	1.17	3.78
	1991-92	2.25	1.61	3.15	2.7	1.52	1.09	2.12	2.7
Kerala	1971-72	2.54	4.37	1.18	10.71	1.12	3.43	0.63	3.4
	1981-82	0.12	0	0.01	6.45	0.07	0	0.27	1.71
	1991-92	1.08	0	0.14	4.46	0.46	0	0.01	2.36
Madhya Pradesh	1971-72	2.74	1.64	5.56	12.63	1.12	0.64	2.16	3.54
	1981-82	0.36	0.21	1.3	6.32	0.06	0.04	0.99	2.46
	1991-92	1.78	2.5	2.9	3.16	0.96	1.35	1.57	2.42
Maharashtra	1971-72	3.16	1.97	4.47	4.34	1.54	0.85	2.55	1.21
	1981-82	1.37	0.58	2.92	4.85	0.57	0.12	2.53	1.98
	1991-92	2.97	0.53	1.72	2.28	1.98	0.36	1.14	1.99
Orissa	1971-72	3.78	3.51	12.41	13.78	1.01	1.8	5.68	4.96
	1981-82	1.93	2.34	8.79	5.74	0.51	0.8	4.16	4.43
	1991-92	3.78	1.07	9.79	3.73	1.86	0.44	4.82	2.35

(*Contd.*)

(Contd.)

State	Year	Holdings				Area			
		FM	FP	ST	OT	FM	FP	ST	OT
Punjab	1971-72	15.47	6.73	24.71	10.53	7.97	3.27	12.58	4.19
	1981-82	8.32	0.91	9.2	5.05	6.77	0.74	6.41	2.15
	1991-92	9.14	3.39	2.1	8.46	9.26	3.45	2.13	4.01
Rajasthan	1971-72	0.7	1.07	2.13	5.28	0.52	0.56	1.36	2.83
	1981-82	0.3	0.26	1.76	4.68	0.15	0.06	0.93	3.17
	1991-92	1.26	1.61	1.94	3.17	0.79	1.01	1.21	2.18
Tamil Nadu	1971-72	5	7.25	13.27	9.43	1.98	3.74	5.52	1.82
	1981-82	5.68	3.01	5.54	10.48	2.11	2.17	3.99	2.66
	1991-92	5.55	3.5	2.76	4.75	3.53	2.23	1.76	3.37
Uttar Pradesh	1971-72	2.44	1.45	15.12	11.27	0.87	0.76	7.17	4.22
	1981-82	2.48	1.39	9.86	7.61	0.88	0.5	5.13	3.74
	1991-92	1.71	2.81	8.58	4.24	0.97	1.59	4.87	3.05
West Bengal	1971-72	0.66	0.71	30.64	5.08	0.16	0.48	17.34	0.75
	1981-82	0.73	1.95	11.01	10.23	0.35	1.47	6.85	2.54
	1991-92	1.58	2.14	8.51	4.9	0.9	1.21	4.83	3.46
All-India	1971-72	3.26	2.7	13	9.11	1.63	1.23	5.06	2.67
	1981-82	1.86	1.22	6.21	6.97	0.78	0.45	3	2.95
	1991-92	2.55	1.96	4.63	3.41	1.57	1.2	2.85	2.66

Source: Computed from the following NSS Reports:

(i) Report on Some Aspects of Landholdings; 26th Round 1971-72, NSS Report No. 215.

(ii) Report on Landholdings (2); 37th Round 1982, NSS Report No. 331.

(iii) Report on Some Aspects of Operational Holdings; 48th Round 1991-92, Report No. 407

The relative importance of different terms of tenancy can be better understood in terms of per cent of leased-in holdings and area operated leased-in accounted for by different terms of tenancy. Table 6.3 shows that despite decline in the importance of share tenancy in 1991-92 it still accounted for about half of the leased-in holdings and area leased-in in Orissa, Uttar Pradesh and West Bengal; in Bihar its share was around 40 per cent. In three other states (Andhra Pradesh, Assam and Karnataka), share tenancy accounted for about 30 per cent of leased-in holdings and area leased-in. At the all-India level, its share was around one third of the leased-in holdings and leased-in area. The importance of fixed rent tenancy contracts, both in terms of holdings and area, increased practically in all the states. As a result, in 1991-92, the fixed rent tenancy contracts were relatively more important compared to share tenancy in about half of the states like Andhra Pradesh, Gujarat, Haryana, Karnataka, Madhya Pradesh, Maharashtra, Punjab and Tamil Nadu. The tenancy contracts included under other terms accounted for a very high per cent of leased-in holdings and area and were relatively more important compared to both fixed rent tenancy and share tenancy in five states (Assam, Himachal Pradesh, Jammu & Kashmir, Kerala and Rajasthan). In brief, over the period the fixed rent tenancy contracts had tended to become more important in comparison to share tenancy. In some states, tenancy contracts included under other terms had assumed very high importance.

Table 6.3: Changing Distribution of Leased-in Holdings and Leased-in Area by Terms of Tenancy in Rural India, 1971-72 to 1991-92: Major States

(*Per cent*)

State	Year	Holdings				Area			
		FM	FP	ST	OT	FM	FP	ST	OT
Andhra Pradesh	1971-72	18.11	14.98	34.38	32.54	28.29	14.2	35.2	22.31
	1981-82	13	11.07	8.83	67.1	13	11.1	8.8	67.1
	1991-92	26.7	27.65	29.81	15.84	25.9	26.8	28.9	18.4
Assam	1971-72	20.09	9.83	34.09	35.99	17.05	15.6	41.83	25.52
	1981-82	15.43	8.35	35.35	40.87	15.4	8.4	35.3	40.9
	1991-92	19.4	4.57	31.17	44.86	17	4	27.8	51.2
Bihar	1971-72	2.98	4.72	68	24.3	1.24	6.97	78.28	13.51
	1981-82	6.53	3.59	73.32	16.56	6.5	3.6	73.3	16.6
	1991-92	10.02	13.35	46.05	30.58	9.5	12.8	43.5	34.2
Gujarat	1971-72	30.59	6.75	27.24	35.42	22.76	10.22	39.4	27.62
	1981-82	5.15	0.59	9.7	84.56	5.1	0.5	9.7	84.6
	1991-92	44.46	1.79	26.52	27.23	39.9	1.6	23.7	34.8
Haryana	1971-72	14.81	8.51	46.93	29.57	12.42	8.51	53.97	25.1
	1981-82	24.1	10.76	41.13	24.01	24.2	10.8	41.2	23.8
	1991-92	67.26	5.7	21.17	5.33	61.4	5.2	19.9	13.5
Himachal Pradesh	1971-72	—	—	—	—	—	—	—	—
	1981-82	7.43	16.21	33.11	43.25	7.28	16.5	33.01	43.21
	1991-92	14.99	9.91	11.94	63.16	13.64	8.98	10.87	66.51
Jammu & Kashmir	1971-72	2.77	12.4	75.59	9.24	0.78	0.59	87.08	11.55
	1981-82	2.31	12.14	66.47	19.08	2.17	11.96	66.85	19.02
	1991-92	9.75	31.05	12.27	46.93	9.37	30.21	11.81	48.61
Karanataka	1971-72	25.72	21.18	30.27	22.83	30.82	18.87	39.06	11.25
	1981-82	3.61	4.46	29.98	62.65	3.6	4.7	29.3	62.4
	1991-92	23.15	16.58	32.42	27.85	20.4	14.7	28.6	36.3
Kerala	1971-72	13.51	23.24	6.27	56.98	13.03	39.82	7.33	39.82
	1981-82	3.37	—	13.19	83.44	3.4	—	13.2	84.9
	1991-92	19.02	—	2.48	78.5	15.9	—	2.1	82

(*Contd.*)

(*Contd.*)

State	Year	Holdings				Area			
		FM	FP	ST	OT	FM	FP	ST	OT
Madhya Pradesh	1971-72	11.82	7.29	24.76	56.13	15.02	8.57	28.95	47.46
	1981-82	1.71	1.1	27.78	69.41	1.7	1.1	27.8	69.4
	1991-92	17.21	24.17	28.05	30.57	15.3	21.4	24.9	38.4
Maharashtra	1971-72	24.22	13.88	31.42	30.48	28.74	16.46	37.26	17.54
	1981-82	10.94	2.31	48.56	38.19	11	2.3	48.5	38.2
	1991-92	39.59	7.07	22.94	30.4	36.2	6.5	20.9	36.4
Orissa	1971-72	18.63	17.3	61.15	2.92	7.5	13.44	42.2	36.86
	1981-82	5.15	8.06	41.96	44.83	5.1	8.1	42	44.8
	1991-92	20.58	5.83	53.29	20.3	19.7	4.7	50.9	24.7
Punjab	1971-72	26.93	11.71	43	18.36	29.23	12.71	46.66	11.4
	1981-82	42.13	4.6	39.87	13.4	42.1	4.6	39.9	13.4
	1991-92	52.56	19.5	12.07	15.87	49.2	18.2	11.3	21.3
Rajasthan	1971-72	7.62	11.52	23.03	57.83	7.84	11.87	23.74	56.55
	1981-82	3.46	1.4	21.51	73.63	3.5	1.4	21.6	73.5
	1991-92	15.78	20.18	24.31	39.73	15.2	19.4	23.4	42
Tamil Nadu	1971-72	14.3	20.74	37.97	26.99	15.16	28.69	42.31	13.84
	1981-82	19.3	19.86	36.5	24.34	19.2	19.9	36.5	24.4
	1991-92	33.52	21.13	16.67	28.68	32.4	20.5	16.1	31
Uttar Pradesh	1971-72	8.21	4.78	49.87	37.14	6.68	5.84	55.11	32.37
	1981-82	8.6	4.88	50.1	36.42	8.6	4.9	50.1	36.4
	1991-92	9.86	16.21	49.48	24.45	9.2	15.2	46.5	29.1
West Bengal	1971-72	1.78	1.91	12.6	13.71	0.85	2.57	92.58	4
	1981-82	2.84	11.92	55.55	29.69	2.8	11.9	55.6	29.7
	1991-92	9.61	13.02	51.77	25.6	8.6	11.7	46.5	33.2
All-India	1971-72	11.61	9.62	46.31	32.47	15.42	11.64	47.87	25.07
	1981-82	10.88	6.28	41.84	41	10.9	6.3	41.9	40.9
	1991-92	20.32	15.62	36.89	27.17	19	14.5	34.4	32.1

Source: Computed from the following NSS Reports:

(i) Report on Some Aspects of Landholdings; 26th Round 1971-72, NSS Report No. 215.

(ii) Report on Landholdings (2); 37th Round 1982, NSS Report No. 331.

(iii) Report on Some Aspects of Operational Holdings; 48th Round 1991-92, Report No. 407.

V
REVERSE TENANCY

A plethora of micro studies have reported substantial changes in the tenurial relations, especially in those areas where new agricultural technology has made much headway. It is reported that medium and large households dominate land lease market as lessors and that small and marginal households make up the multitudes of lessors[9]. The reversal in the tenurial relations could, *inter alia*, be attributed to a number of factors like the spread of new agricultural technology making agriculture more remunerative, ceilings on ownership holdings and no ceiling on operational holdings, increase in the rural non farm employment opportunities, increase in the real wages, and increased mechanisation of agriculture. Against this background, it is important to ascertain the extent of reverse tenancy and to know whether it has really gained ground or deserves to be treated as small aberration confined to a few localised belts in the usual tenant landlord relationship. With this objective in mind, we analysed the per cent distribution of lessors and lessees along with the distribution of area leased-in and leased-out among different categories of households. The details are provided in Tables 6.4 and 6.5.

From demand perspective, Table 6.4 throws up the following features. First, a preponderant majority of the lessees belonged to landless and marginal households; the proportion of lessees belonging to lower farm size categories still went higher if small households were to be included. Not only that, in most of the states, the per cent share of these households in the lessees increased substantially between 1971-72 and 1991-92. The notable exceptions were Punjab and Uttar Pradesh where their share remained unchanged and Haryana where it declined. At the all-India level, more than three fourth of the lessees were landless and marginal households. Second, in so far as the distribution of leased-in area was concerned, despite some decline in the share of landless and marginal households, they still accounted for more than 70 per cent of the total leased-in area in Assam, Bihar, Himachal Pradesh, Tamil Nadu, Uttar Pradesh and West Bengal. In five other states (Andhra Pradesh, Gujarat, Jammu & Kashmir, Madhya Pradesh and Orissa), the per cent of leased-in area accounted for by them increased significantly and in 1991-92 they accounted for more than 60 per cent of the total leased-in area; in Orissa their share was more than 80 per cent. In the remaining states, the per cent of leased-in area accounted for by households belonging to lower farm size categories remained practically unchanged in Maharashtra but declined in Karnataka, Kerala and Rajasthan. In two agriculturally prosperous states, viz. Haryana and Punjab, the per cent of area leased-in accounted for by these households declined markedly. As a natural corollary, the per cent of area leased-in accounted for by higher category households increased substantially and in the beginning of nineties, they accounted for 70 per cent of the total leased-in area in the former and 57 per cent in the latter state.

Table 6.4: Distribution of Lessees and Area leased-in by Categories of Households, 1971-72 to 1991-92

(*Per cent*)

State	Year	Households Leasing-in Land						Area Leased-in					
		Land-less	Margi-nal	Small	Semi-Medium	Medium	Large	Land-less	Margi-nal	Small	Semi-Medium	Medium	Large
Andhra Pradesh	1971-72	23.48	23.71	21.02	6.22	4.62	1.14	1.8	30.19	10.94	8.99	43.07	5.01
	1991-92	38.92	44.55	10.25	5.12	1.08	0.08	8.82	56.23	17.48	11.08	5.35	1.05
Assam	1971-72	50.17	36.9	9.1	3.45	0.38	—	55.17	29.65	10.44	4.33	0.45	—
	1991-92	43.47	45.64	9.42	0.89	0.58	—	22.76	56.16	16.12	2.38	2.58	—
Bihar	1971-72	11.16	70.43	10.52	6.15	1.65	0.09	1.48	71.34	15.23	8.03	3.4	0.52
	1991-92	13.54	76.38	8.07	1.71	0.3	—	6.28	78.82	9.94	4.08	0.88	—
Gujarat	1971-72	11.11	42.01	19.14	16.67	9.85	1.22	3.89	46.05	15	12.81	20.57	1.68
	1991-92	61.73	25.03	6.22	6.08	0.94	—	19.85	48.37	22.09	6.56	3.13	—
Haryana	1971-72	24.52	42.58	12.27	12.24	7.3	1.09	4.36	44.7	14.15	20.44	12.23	4.12
	1991-92	4.45	28.75	19.86	40.25	6.4	0.29	0.01	13.8	14.95	33.82	37.26	8.16
Himachal Pradesh	1971-72	—	—	—	—	—	—	—	—	—	—	—	—
	1991-92	42.09	50.47	6.27	1.17	—	—	21.28	69.6	6.69	2.43	—	—
Jammu & Kashmir	1971-72	6.47	53.37	24.93	12.94	2.29	—	2.5	42.83	20.67	32.83	1.17	—
	1991-92	24.69	47.84	24.69	0.62	2.16	—	5.81	60.47	30.23	3.49	—	—
Karnataka	1971-72	31.5	32.28	11.21	12.41	10.4	2.2	23.45	30.23	12.06	9.8	17.08	7.38
	1991-92	35.47	30.1	17.92	10.09	5.65	8.77	3.92	33.36	21.18	24.61	14.37	2.56
Kerala	1971-72	52.82	38.94	5.03	2.41	0.67	0.13	26.81	49.95	13.35	6.73	2.65	0.51
	1991-92	57.98	38.26	2.42	0.87	0.47	—	16.61	53.61	11.91	13.48	4.39	—
Madhya Pradesh	1971-72	33.95	31.32	12.25	10.78	9.76	1.94	13.76	30.76	14.29	18.33	19.77	5.09
	1991-92	38.68	36.58	12.91	7.04	3.53	1.26	20.72	41.3	13.84	12.39	8.58	3.17

(*Contd.*)

(*Contd.*)

State	Year	Households Leasing-in Land						Area Leased-in					
		Land-less	Margi-nal	Small	Semi-Medium	Medium	Large	Land-less	Margi-nal	Small	Semi-Medium	Medium	Large
Maharashtra	1971-72	34.77	27.68	13.52	12.29	9.06	2.68	4.31	18.73	5.51	8.66	57.85	4.94
	1991-92	63.6	16.8	9.25	5.82	4.33	0.2	7.75	18.31	33.5	20.02	19.37	1.05
Orissa	1971-72	24.72	52.69	14.99	5.6	1.82	0.18	9.34	55.9	17.05	13.12	4.09	0.5
	1991-92	38.52	50.69	6.42	3.56	0.81	—	3.68	77.49	10.6	7.87	1.16	—
Punjab	1971-72	19.21	36.67	13.5	20.95	8.57	1.1	4.82	45.53	14.07	20.75	10.62	4.21
	1991-92	12.9	42.35	13.03	16.74	14.32	0.66	0.72	23.52	18.17	26.73	29.49	1.37
Rajasthan	1971-72	12.64	32.73	23.17	15.86	11.91	3.69	12.72	30.8	15.65	12.18	17.54	11.11
	1991-92	35.5	31.42	14.88	10.4	7.05	0.75	13.13	25.38	18.86	26.17	13.9	2.56
Tamil Nadu	1971-72	47.95	41.96	5.68	3.56	0.77	0.08	12.53	68.03	10.75	5.38	3.28	0.03
	1991-92	47.14	44.79	5.46	2.17	0.35	0.89	6.04	64.94	15.93	9.02	3.86	0.21
Uttar Pradesh	1971-72	16.18	64.92	12.18	5.05	1.61	0.06	5.12	68.21	15.02	8.65	2.95	0.05
	1991-92	14.71	66.84	14.31	3.01	0.94	0.19	3.98	68.46	18.93	5.7	1.36	1.57
West Bengal	1971-72	27.67	59.39	9.41	3.08	0.45	—	7.83	77.5	9.25	4.18	1.24	—
	1991-92	24.41	69.29	4.26	1.92	0.12	—	8.81	80.67	7.71	2.71	0.1	—
All-India	1971-72	28.32	48.46	11.54	7.2	3.77	0.7	7.88	45.43	13.72	17.37	12.11	3.49
	1991-92	34.62	47.89	9.96	5.26	2.03	0.24	7.87	45.94	17.47	15.6	11.84	1.28

Source: Computed from the following NSS Reports:

(i) Report on Some Aspects of Landholdings; 26th Round 1971-72, NSS Report No. 215.

(ii) Report on Some Aspects of Ownership Holdings; 48th Round 1991-92, Report No. 399.

Table 6.5: Distribution of Lessors and Area leased-out by Categories of Households, 1971-72 to 1991-92

(Per cent)

State	Year	Households Leasing-Out Land					Area Leased-out				
		Marginal	Small	Semi-Medium	Medium	Large	Marginal	Small	Semi-Medium	Medium	Large
Andhra	1971-72	52.7	20.8	15.32	8.3	2.88	12.38	18.54	22.04	27.61	19.43
Pradesh	1991-92	72.71	13.2	11.55	2.26	0.28	41.55	22.62	29.59	5.16	1.08
Assam	1971-72	38.85	29.95	24.66	6.33	0.21	18.23	26.44	40.02	13.04	2.27
	1991-92	64.42	28.12	12.76	2.7	—	36.5	22.19	34.6	6.71	—
Bihar	1971-72	45.03	25.35	19.07	9.84	0.71	24.12	20.12	27	23.69	5.07
	1991-92	46.35	24.29	18.88	8.63	1.85	19.29	22.21	26.99	21.36	10.15
Gujarat	1971-72	31.6	21.85	20.17	21.76	4.62	9.78	16.45	25.45	34.61	13.71
	1991-92	48.32	24.96	10.23	11.52	4.97	23.5	15.18	12.18	21.32	27.82
Haryana	1971-72	48.24	6.6	17.05	22.54	5.57	9.52	5.27	20.58	47.27	17.36
	1991-92	16.32	11.88	44.24	26.67	0.89	59.07	4.99	33.82	0.56	2.36
Himachal	1971-72	—	—	—	—	—	—	—	—	—	—
Pradesh	1991-92	52.98	31.97	11.29	3.76	—	34.49	30.66	14.98	19.87	—
Jammu &	1971-72	19.74	28.48	8.42	43.36	—	18.23	57.65	6.47	17.65	—
Kashmir	1991-92	39.22	50.98	5.88	3.92	—	30.77	40	4.61	—	24.62
Karnataka	1971-72	27.05	30.32	22.83	16.65	3.15	7.13	23.21	25.53	36.81	7.32
	1991-92	29.25	18.04	39.75	11.5	1.46	5.92	13.57	53.29	23.48	3.74
Kerala	1971-72	75.6	13.44	7.39	3.34	0.23	45.51	20.12	18,58	15.79	—
	1991-92	80.57	14.29	4.91	8.23	—	—	—	—	—	—
Madhya	1971-72	18.55	22.67	28.32	21.24	9.22	4.72	14.48	31.67	34.88	14.25
Pradesh	1991-92	29.45	26.86	29.29	12.03	2.37	8.42	20.52	34.65	30	6.41

(Contd.)

(*Contd.*)

State	Year	Households Leasing-Out Land					Area Leased-out				
		Marginal	Small	Semi-Medium	Medium	Large	Marginal	Small	Semi-Medium	Medium	Large
Maharashtra	1971-72	23.3	23.68	37.72	10.35	3.95	3.92	12.18	30.44	40.91	12.55
	1991-92	38.35	22.36	24.06	13.01	2.22	8.27	16.22	32.44	33.98	9.09
Orissa	1971-72	64.8	15.77	13.8	4.5	1.13	43.22	15.85	28.05	9.68	3.2
	1991-92	63.51	26.28	7.09	2.43	0.69	31.76	43.26	18.37	5.4	1.21
Punjab	1971-72	31.08	15.63	25.4	21.93	5.96	7.34	9.22	28.59	31.52	23.33
	1991-92	35.85	22.94	28.74	10.79	1.68	12.39	19.98	38.68	21.33	7.63
Rajasthan	1971-72	8.56	20.53	18.01	39.76	13.1	1.01	6.8	5.86	39.32	46.97
	1991-92	18.98	22.87	29.56	20.55	8.04	2.68	8.31	23.84	34.87	30.38
Tamil Nadu	1971-72	50.53	23.7	14.22	9.23	2.32	15.12	10.02	21.72	19.18	33.94
	1991-92	71.39	17.02	9.05	2.05	0.49	45.79	18.78	25.39	7.13	2.99
Uttar Pradesh	1971-72	54.99	20.12	14.67	8.83	1.39	27.48	19.35	28.15	19.73	5.29
	1991-92	58.1	20.27	15.81	5.51	0.31	26.28	23.03	35.4	14.16	1.13
West Bengal	1971-72	57.56	21.6	11.02	9.82	—	24.07	27.5	24.36	24.07	—
	1991-92	67.36	19.35	11	2.09	—	41.5	18.95	31.52	8.03	—
All-India	1971-72	47.83	21	17.55	11.1	2.52	18.52	16.02	23.42	29.96	15.07
	1991-92	51.37	28.34	19.11	7.84	1.34	14.25	18.19	34.17	25.56	6.83

Source: Computed from the following NSS Reports:

(i) Report on Some Aspects of Landholdings; 26th Round 1971-72, NSS Report No. 215.

(ii) Report on Some Aspects of Ownership Holdings; 48th Round 1991-92, Report No. 399.

In sum, the evidence pertaining to the demand side of the lease market clearly brings out the dominance of lower category households in the lease market, both in terms of lessees and the amount of area leased-in, in most of the states. The only notable exceptions were Punjab and Haryana where households from higher category accounted for most of the area leased-in.

This is, however, half of the story. And before passing any judgement on the strength of reverse tenancy, it is important to know whether households from lower categories also dominate the lease market as lessors. Table 6.5 provides information about the supply side of the lease market. The following comments are in order. First, there had been a significant increase in the per cent of lessors who belonged to marginal and small households between 1971-72 and 1991-92. Consequently, in the later year, they accounted for more than 90 per cent of the total lessors in Assam, Jammu & Kashmir and Kerala; between 85 to 90 per cent in Andhra Pradesh, Orissa, Tamil Nadu and West Bengal and between 70 to 80 per cent in Bihar, Gujarat and Uttar Pradesh. In some other states like Madhya Pradesh, Maharashtra and Punjab the per cent share of these households in all lessors declined which was around 30 per cent in 1991-92. Second, regarding the per cent share of marginal and small households in the total area supplied in the lease market, Table 6.5 shows that it was around 70 per cent in Jammu & Kashmir and Orissa; between 60 and 65 per cent in Andhra Pradesh, Tamil Nadu and West Bengal and between 50 to 60 per cent in Assam and Uttar Pradesh. In the remaining states, the per cent share of marginal and small households was around 25 per cent or even less. In Punjab it was 32 per cent. At the All India level, they accounted for around one-third of the total leased-out area[10].

In brief, combining the evidence from both the demand and supply side of the lease market, NSS data suggests that the households belonging to lower farm size categories dominated the lease market both as lessees and lessors in a majority of the states including Punjab. In Haryana, lease market was dominated by semi-medium, medium and large households both as lessees and lessors. The traditional variety of tenancy, where majority of the lessees comes from lower farm size categories and the lessors from higher farm size categories was noticed only in two states (Karnataka and Rajasthan). In terms of the acreage transacted, three distinct patterns emerged. First, in about half the states (Andhra Pradesh, Assam, Jammu & Kashmir, Orissa, Tamil Nadu, Uttar Pradesh and West Bengal) households belonging to lower farm categories accounted for more than half of the total leased-in and also contributed more than half of the leased-out area. Second, in six states, namely, Bihar, Gujarat, Karnataka, Madhya Pradesh, Maharashtra and Rajasthan tenancy relations conformed to traditional variety with most of the leased-in area being accounted for by lower category households and leased-out by those belonging to higher categories. Third, in two agriculturally developed states while semi-medium, medium and large households accounted for most of the leased-in and leased-out area in Punjab, the extent of reverse tenancy was more pronounced in Haryana. In the ultimate analysis, tenurial relations in most of the states conformed neither to the traditional variety characterised by the hegemony of medium and large households as lessors and lower category households as lessees nor to the much talked about reverse tenancy marked by the preponderance of lower category households as lessors and higher category households as lessees. The evidence at our disposal reveals that the lessors and lessees belonging to not very different farm size categories dominate the lease market in most of the states.[11]

VI
DETERMINANTS OF TENANCY

The households with land and those without land participate in the lease market with different motives. While the former enter the lease market to utilise their factor endowment like family labour, bullocks, farm machinery like tractors, tube wells, optimally, the latter do so to earn livelihood in the absence of alternative employment opportunities. Sometimes, the landless households, particularly in agriculturally developed regions, may also lease-in land to practice commercial agriculture and make profits. Further, about types of tenancy, as postulated by neo-classical economists, households are likely to choose tenancy contracts according to their risk bearing ability; those who are economically better off and risk takers may opt for fixed rent tenancy. And those who are economically impoverished and vulnerable are more risk averse and opt for share tenancy (Hallangan, 1978, 344-354; Ray, 1998, 475-478). In empirical literature, factors such as indivisible and non-tradable inputs, nature of crops grown, area under irrigation, and so on have been reported important determinants of tenancy and its types (Bliss and Stern, 1982, chapter 5; Bardhan, 1976, *op cit.*; Laxminarayan and Tyagi, 1977a, and 1977b, *op cit.*). However, as mentioned above, rural areas in recent times (particularly during the eighties) have witnessed substantial changes in non-farm employment opportunities, real wages and extent of mechanisation. These changes have profound implications for different aspects of tenancy relations. For example, with the increase in rural non-farm employment and wages, the dependency of rural households on lease market is expected to diminish. In a similar vein, with the permeation of new agricultural technology in conjunction with the growing mechanisation of agriculture, households belonging to higher farm size categories are expected to lease in more land to reap scale economies. To what extent these and other factors impinge on different aspects of tenancy relations is an empirical question that we seek to answer in this section.

To examine the effect of different factors on the magnitude of tenancy, a regression analysis was done with proportion of leased-in area and entirely leased-in holdings as dependent variables, and poverty, unemployment, landlessness, number of bullocks, household size, proportion of irrigated area, fertiliser consumption, extent of mechanisation, non-farm employment and wages, as independent variables.[12] The results (Table 6.6) reveal that factors like unemployment, poverty, bullocks, household size and landlessness, did not affect the proportion of leased-in area; the regression coefficients associated with these variables neither had expected signs nor were statistically significant. In comparison, factors surrogating spread of new agricultural technology like proportion of irrigated area, fertiliser consumption and extent of mechanisation affected the proportion of leased-in area positively and significantly. The entirely leased-in holdings were, however, affected positively and significantly by factors like unemployment and poverty. The factors facilitating the commercialisation of agriculture like irrigation, fertiliser consumption and extent of mechanisation did not have any significant effect on the incidence of these holdings. These findings suggest that the landless households enter the lease market to earn livelihood rather than making profits. Regarding types of tenancy, Table 6.7 shows that while the factors like poverty and irrigated area affected the holdings under share tenancy positively and significantly, the effect of rural non-farm employment and incidence of landlessness was negative and significant. The effect of wages was also negative though it was statistically insignificant. In terms of proportion of area leased-in under share tenancy, the effect of incidence of landlessness was negative whereas proportion of irrigated area had a positive and significant effect. The effect of level of wages and rural non-farm employment was negative but statistically insignificant. Further, Table 6.8 shows that factors like irrigation, fertiliser consumption and the extent of mechanisation had a positive and significant effect in inducing the households of higher farm size category to lease-in land. The regression coefficients associated with these variables had expected signs and were statistically significant. However, in respect of per cent of area leased-in accounted for by higher category households, though the regression coefficients had plausible signs, the effect of mechanisation alone was statistically significant.

Table 6.6: Determinants of Tenancy: Results of Regression Analysis (Pooled Data)

Dependent Variable	*Independent Variables*					R^2
	Constant	*Irrigation*	*Fertilizers*	*Machinery*	*RNF*	
Leased-in Area	0.90	0.22** (6.22)	—	—	—	0.60
Leased-in Area	3.91	—	0.06* (4.20)	—	—	0.40
Leased-in Area	2.81	—	—	0.09* (3.56)	—	0.33
Leased-in Area	8.07	—	—	—	0.05 (0.29)	0.00

Note: (i) * and ** denote levels of significance at one and five per cent respectively.
(ii) Figures in parantheses are 't' values.
(iii) Number of observations are 28 and 14 each for 1981-82 and 1991-92.

Table 6.7: Determinants of Share Tenancy (ST): Results of Regression Analysis (Pooled Data)

Dependent Variable	*Constant*	*LL*	*Irrigation*	*Fertilizers*	*RNF*	R^2
% area under ST	4.75	-0.16** (-2.02)	—	—	—	0.14
% area under ST	0.83	—	0.06* (3.49)	—	—	0.40
% area under ST	2.17	—	—	0.01 (1.40)	—	0.33
% area under ST	3.86	—	—	—	-0.04 (-0.75)	0.00

Note: (i) * and ** denote levels of significance at one, five and ten per cent respectively.

(ii) Figures in parantheses are 't' values.
(iii) Number of observations are 28 and 14 each for 1981-82 and 1991-92.

Table 6.8: Determinants of Reverse Tenancy: Results of Regression Analysis, 1991-92

Dependent Variables	*Independent Variables*				
	Constant	*Irri.*	*Fert.*	*Mach.*	r^2
% of households owning above 2 hectares in total lessees	0.91	0.28** (2.03)	—	—	0.26
% of households owning above 2 hectares in total lessees	2.68	—	0.09*** (1.85)	—	0.22
% of households owning above 2 hectares in total lessees	-8.85	—	—	0.26* (7.09)	0.81

Note: (i) *, ** and *** denote levels of significance at one, five and ten per cent respectively.
(ii) Figures in parantheses are 't' values.
(iii) Number of observations = 14.

In brief, the results of the regression analysis show that the factors associated with new agricultural technology were more important in determining diverse aspects of tenancy relations. The level of rural non-farm employment and wages did not have significant effect and, in some cases, even the signs were not plausible. The results also lend support to the hypothesis that landless households were obliged to participate in the lease market because of poverty and unemployment.

VI
SUMMING UP

The evidence from NSS data shows significant decline in the incidence of tenancy during the forty years period since 1953-54; the proportion of leased-in area in the beginning of nineties was much less in all the states compared to that in the-mid fifties. In so far as time trend was concerned, while there was a continuous decline in the incidence of tenancy practically in all the states up to 1981-82, the trend was reversed between 1981-82 and 1991-92, when the proportion of area leased-in increased by varying degrees in ten states, namely, Andhra Pradesh, Assam, Gujarat, Haryana, Himachal Pradesh, Jammu & Kashmir, Karnataka, Madhya Pradesh, Punjab and Rajasthan. The increase in the proportion of leased-in area during eighties was accompanied by an increase in the entirely leased-in holdings in nine states (Andhra Pradesh, Gujarat, Haryana, Himachal Pradesh, Jammu & Kashmir, Kerala, Madhya Pradesh, Orissa and Uttar Pradesh). The decline in the incidence of tenancy over the period was also corroborated by continuous decrease in the incidence of households owning but not operating land in most of the states. Another important feature was increase in the proportion of neither owned nor leased-in area between 1981-82 and 1991-92 in as many as eleven states like Andhra Pradesh, Assam, Bihar, Gujarat, Himachal Pradesh, Karnataka, Madhya Pradesh, Maharashtra, Rajasthan, Tamil Nadu and West Bengal. The terms of tenancy have also recorded significant change over the period. The importance of share tenancy, both in terms of holdings and area leased-in, has declined significantly. It is evident from the fact in 1991-92, share tenancy accounted for more than half of the leased-in holdings and area leased-in only in three states, namely, Orissa, Uttar Pradesh and West Bengal; in Bihar its share was around 40 per cent. In eight states (Andhra Pradesh, Gujarat, Haryana, Karnataka, Madhya Pradesh, Maharashtra, Punjab and Tamil Nadu) fixed rent tenancy was relatively more important and accounted for most of the leased-in holdings and area leased-in. In five other states (Assam, Himachal Pradesh, Jammu & Kashmir, Kerala and Rajasthan) other terms, which included usufructuary mortgage, from relatives, share tenancy with other terms, etc., were relatively more important.

At the national level there are no clear trends either towards the traditional variety of the tenancy relations or towards the much talked about phenomenon of reverse tenancy. The NSS data reveal that in a majority of the states households belonging to not very different farm size categories dominate the lease market. The traditional variety of tenancy relations where majority of the lessees are landless or smaller holders and lessors are medium or large holders was in evidence only in two states (Karnataka and Rajasthan). In terms of acreage transacted, three distinct patterns emerged. First, in seven states, namely, Andhra Pradesh, Assam, Jammu & Kashmir, Orissa, Tamil Nadu, Uttar Pradesh and West Bengal most of the leased-in and leased-out area was accounted for by households belonging to lower categories. Second, traditional variety of tenancy relations, where most of the leased-in area is accounted for by lower category households and leased out by those coming from higher categories, was found in six states (Bihar, Gujarat, Karnataka, Madhya Pradesh, Maharashtra and Rajasthan). Third, in two agriculturally most prosperous states while semi-medium, medium and large households accounted for most of the area leased-in and area leased out in Punjab, the extent of reverse tenancy was more pronounced in Haryana. The results of the regression analysis further show that factors surrogating spread of new agricultural technology like irrigation, fertiliser consumption and the extent of mechanisation were relatively more important in determining various aspects of tenancy relations. The factors representing indivisible and non-tradable inputs like bullocks and household size did not have significant effect. The extent of poverty and unemployment had a significant effect on entirely leased-in holdings lending support to the hypothesis that landless households lease-in land to earn livelihood. Further, while factors like rural non-farm employment and wages did not have significant effect on the extent of tenancy, they had a negative effect on share tenancy.

ANNEXURE 6.1

Data on Diverse Aspects of Tenancy Relations in Different NSS Rounds, 8th Round to 48th Round

Aspects	8th Round	17th Round	26th Round	37th Round	48th Round
1. Incidence of Tenancy	The data on owned and leased-in holdings and owned and leased-in area are available for operational holdings. The definition of these holdings in the 8th round included non-agricultural holdings like water tanks, temple, mosque, etc. However, the data for agricultural holdings were provided separately. Assuming that non-agricultural holdings are not transacted in the lease market, the break up given for operational holdings can be applied to agricultural holdings (Report No. 66. Table 1.5. 2.5).	The statewise data on tenancy are not available in the 17th round.	The data on leased-in area are available both for ownership and operational holdings have been classified into two categories i.e. owned and leased-in holdings. Likewise, operated area has also been divided into owned and leased-in area (Report No. 215, Table 19).	The operational holdings have been classified into following categories: (i) Entirely owned (ii) Entirely leased-in (iii) Both owned and leased-in (iv) Neither owned nor leased-in (v) Others The operated area has been reported under the three heads: - Owned - Leased-in - Neither owned nor leased-in but possessed (Report No. 331, Table 5)	The operational holdings have been classified into the following types: (i) Owned holdings (ii) Leased-in holdings (iii) Otherwise possessed (iv) Not recorded The leased-in area has been reported under: (i) Owned holdings (ii) Leased-in holdings (iii) Otherwise possessed (iv) Not recorded (Report No. 407, Tables 3R and 4R)

(Contd.)

(*Contd.*)

Aspects	*8th Round*	*17th Round*	*26th Round*	*37th Round*	*48th Round*
2. House-holds not operating land	The data for such households are not available.	The data on households not operating land and their classification into those who own but do not operate and those who neither own nor operate land are available (Report No. 144, Table 8).	The data on all the three categories of households, viz. Households not operating land, households owning but not operating and those who neither own nor operate any land are available (Table 5).	The data on the households not operating land alone are available. However, the data can be decomposed into those who own but do not operate and those who neither own nor operate by using information available in report on household ownership holdings. By finding out the number of landless households who lease-in land and subtracting them from total number of landless households we arrive at those landless households who neither own nor operate any land. Finally, subtracting these households from those who do not operate land we get the number of households who own but do not operate (Report No. 338, Table 1 and Report No. 399, Table 7).	The data on the households not operating land alone are available. However, the data can be decomposed into those who own but do not operate and those who neither own nor operate by using information available in report on household ownership holdings. By finding out the number of landless households who lease-in land and subtracting them from total number of landless households we arrive at those landless households who neither own nor operate any land. Finally, subtracting these households from those who do not operate land we get the number of households who own but do not operate (Report No. 408, Table 1R and Report No. 399, Table 4R).

(*Contd.*)

(*Contd.*)

Aspects	*8th Round*	*17th Round*	*26th Round*	*37th Round*	*48th Round*
3. Terms of Tenancy	The data on the terms of tenancy are not available in the 8th round.	The data on the terms of tenancy are not available in the 17th round.	The data on the leasing-out in case of ownership holdings are available on the following terms: (i) Under usufructuary mortgage (ii) On crop sharing basis (iii) On other terms In comparison, the data on the ownership holdings leasing-in are available on the following terms: (i) Fixed money Fixed produce (ii) Share of produce (iii) Usufructuary mortgage (iv) Other terms (Tables 3 and 4) In case of operational holdings and operated area leased-in, the data are available onth following terms: - Fixed money - Fixed produce - Share of produce - Usufructuary mortgage - Other terms (Table 19)	The data on per cent of ownership holdings leasing-in and per cent of owned area leased-in and leased-out are available on the following terms: (i) Fixed money (ii) Fixed produce (iii) Share of produce (iv) Share of produce with terms (v) Usufructuary mortgage (vi) Other terms (Tables 4.1 and 4.2) Likewise, the data on operational holdings leasing-in and area operated leased-in are given on the following terms: - Fixed money - Fixed produce - Share of produce - Share of produce with other terms - Usufructuary mortgage - Other terms - Not recorded terms (Tables 6 and 7)	While reporting on per cent of ownership holdings leasing-in, and area leased-in new terms have been introduced. The terms of tenancy are: (i) Fixed money (ii) Fixed produce (iii) Share of produce (iv) Service Contract (v) Share of produce with other terms (vi) Usufructuary mortgage (vii) From relatives under no specified terms (viii) Under other terms In respect of operational holdings and area operated, the data on following terms of tenancy are reported: (i) Fixed money (ii) Fixed produce (iii) Share of produce (iv) Service Contract (v) Share of produce with other terms (vi) Usufructuary mortgage (vii) From relatives under no specified terms (viii) Under other terms (ix) Not recorded terms

(*Contd.*)

(*Contd.*)

Aspects	*8th Round*	*17th Round*	*26th Round*	*37th Round*	*48th Round*
4. Reverse Tenancy	The information on the per cent of different categories of households leasing-in and leasing-out and area leased-in and leased-out by them is not available in the 8th round.	Information on per cent of different categories of households leasing-in and leasing-out and area leased-in and leased-out by them is not available in the 17th round.	The extent of reverse tenancy can be estimated by using information available in Tables 3 and 4, Report No. 215.	In the 37th round, the amount of land leased-in by the landless households is not reported. Thereore, the true extent of reverse tenancy can not be estimated (Tables 6 and 7).	The extent of reverse tenancy can be estimated as the Report No. 399 (Table 4R) provide data on the different categories of households leasing-in and the amount of land leased-in by them.

Source: (i) Report on Landholdings (4); 8th Round 1953-54, NSS Report No. 66.

(ii) Report on Some Aspects of Landholdings; 17th Round, 1961-62, NSS Report No.144.

(iii) Report on Some Aspects of Landholdings; 26th Round 1971-72, NSS Report No. 215.

(iv) Report on Landholdings (1); 37th Round 1982, NSS Report No. 330.

(v) Report on Landholdings (2); 37th Round 1982, NSS Report No. 331.

(vi) Report on Landholdings; 37th Round 1982, NSS Report No. 338.

(vii) Report on Some Aspects of Household Ownership Holdings (1); 48th Round, NSS Report No. 399.

(viii) Report on Some Aspects of Operational Holdings; 48th Round 1991-92, NSS Report No. 407.

(ix) Report on Livestock and Implements in Household Operational Holdings; 48th Round, 1991-92, NSS Report No. 408.

APPENDICES

Table 1: Data on Independent Variables, 1981-82

States	Une.	Pov.	Bull.	HS	LL	Irr.	Fert.	Mach.	Wage	RNF
Andhra Pradesh	5.6	26.5	65	4.76	11.93	35.43	58.2	29.54	4.57	19.7
Bihar	4.2	64.4	82	5.68	4.11	33.67	27.46	13.03	4.59	13.6
Gujarat	3	29.8	95	5.77	16.83	22.93	40.38	91.84	5.25	19.6
Haryana	3.4	20.6	66	6.81	6.14	62.21	68.99	109.56	6.13	24.4
Karnataka	4.7	36.3	97	5.66	13.7	15.95	37.15	97.97	3.68	16.4
Kerala	13.4	39	9	5.24	12.77	13.36	45.66	13.29	10.06	43
Madhya Pradesh	1.6	48.19	154	5.56	14.39	11.79	11.78	67.25	3.47	12.7
Maharashtra	4	45.2	95	5.2	21.24	12.66	26.83	100.23	4.08	19.9
Orissa	5.1	67.5	110	5.3	7.66	22.9	13.78	36.26	3.81	16
Punjab	4.1	13.2	60	5.66	6.41	86.84	192.07	134.35	9.11	22.1
Rajasthan	3.1	33.5	102	5.75	8.13	21.27	9.25	60.21	5.02	16.7
Tamil Nadu	12	54	47	4.56	19.13	48.7	92.17	17.57	5	22.5
Uttar Pradesh	2.2	46.5	93	5.69	4.85	47.42	75.36	64.58	3.96	13.7
West Bengal	8.8	63.1	85	5.47	17.2	24.57	48.02	44.31	4.85	22.2

2: Data on Independent Variables, 1991-92

States	*Une.*	*Pov.*	*Bull.*	*HS*	*LL*	*% Irr.*	*Fert.*	*Mach.*	*Wage*	*RNF*
Andhra Pradesh	2.5	22.1	48	4.4	11.25	39.87	149.74	60.74	18.99	20.9
Bihar	1.9	46.3	76	5.6	8.58	43.18	85.36	48.79	16.95	12.9
Gujarat	2.4	21.6	54	5.4	16.33	29.33	76.66	82	20.03	23.3
Haryana	2.0	19.5	38	5.8	3.69	77.14	191.19	174.73	28.98	27.7
Karnataka	2.0	34.9	66	5.7	9.98	22.58	74.4	103.19	19.01	18.3
Kerala	5.1	30.3	4	5	8.41	12.34	85.79	14.91	43.23	44
Madhya Pradesh	1.1	42.4	119	5.5	15.19	20.66	42.01	73.33	16.99	13.3
Maharashtra	1.9	35.9	65	5.1	19.56	15.38	68.63	108.16	19.41	27.1
Orissa	2.5	36.5	94	5.1	13.83	26.24	33.35	42.91	16.3	18.4
Punjab	0.9	9.3	21	5.5	5.86	94.58	296.68	180.07	41.94	25.2
Rajasthan	0.5	25.9	47	5.7	6.43	27.2	31.39	83.8	28.36	18.6
Tamil Nadu	5.8	37.5	25	4.3	17.93	47.9	140.78	43.56	25.08	24.6
Uttar Pradesh	1.0	34.8	57	5.7	4.9	62.29	134.27	74.38	21.43	15.9
West Bengal	3.0	49.5	60	5.2	10.97	54.27	139.36	65.88	23.64	26.4

END NOTES

1. For a summary of theoretical debates see Cheung, 1969; Otsuka and Hayami, 1988, pp. 31-68 and Otsuka, *et al.*, 1992, pp. 1965-2018.

2. The neo-classicals' views about tenancy in general and share tenancy in particular, have been summarised in above- mentioned studies. In addition, also see Stiglitz, 1989, chapter, 3, pp. 18-29: Braverman and Stiglitz 1982, pp. 695-715 and Ray, 1998, ch. 12. The marxists' views have been discussed, among others, by Pearce 1983, pp.42-70, Bharadwaj, 1975, pp. 221-240; Prasad, 1973, pp. 869-872 and 1974, pp.1305-1308 and Bhadhuri, 1983.
3. The freeing of lease market has been advocated at different intellectual fora. The annual conference of Indian Society of Agricultural Economic recommended the freeing of lease market way back in December 1994. Similarly in a seminar on 'Wither Tenancy' organised by Lal Bahadur Shastri National Academy of Administration on September 24-25, 1999, a majority of the participants favoured deregulation of lease market. The legalisation of tenancy has also been favoured by many scholars like Rao and Gulati, 1994, pp. A167-168, among others. Also see Appu, 1996.
4. The conceptual and definitional framework employed in tabulating census data and their implications for temporal comparability have been discussed in Sharma, 1995, chapter IV.
5. The operational holdings for the 8th and 26th rounds have been decomposed in to entirely owned self-cultivated holdings, mixed holdings and entirely leased-in holdings by using the following procedure.
   All holdings = Proportion of owned holdings + proportion of leased-holdings
   Mixed holdings = All holdings-100.
   Purely leased-in holdings = Proportion of leased-in holdings-mixed holdings.
   Entirely owned self-cultivated holdings = 100—proportion of mixed holdings-proportion of purely leased-in holdings.
6. Because of re-organisation of the states in 1956, statewise comparability of the 8th round data with that of later rounds was affected seriously. As many as seven major states, namely, Kerala, Karnataka, Madhya Prádesh, Maharashtra and Tamil Nadu were affected. Some adjustments were made to make 8th round data for these states comparable with later rounds. For details, see Sharma, 1995, chapter IV.
7. The amount of leased-in land should ideally be equal to the amount of leased-out land. However, the amount of leased-in area is more than the leased-out area. The difference can be attributed to the reporting bias. The difference also arises because rural households lease-in land from urban households, panchayats, temples, etc. Since these institutions are not covered in the NSS, some discrepancy could be attributed to their exclusion.
8. According to classical economists fixed rent tenancy is superior and ensures efficient allocation of resources as compared to share tenancy. Marxists view the share tenancy more exploitative compared to fixed rent tenancy. However, according to neo-classicals fixed rent tenancy contracts are often not optimal in a second best world where rural markets are not perfect. For details see Ray, 1998, chapter 12.

9. The studies which have reported reversal in the tenurial relations are Vyas, 1970, pp. A73-A80; Nadkarni, 1976, pp. A137-A146; Jodha, 1981, pp. A118-A128; Singh, 1989, *op cit.*; Srivastva, 1989, *op cit.* and Siddiqui, 1999, *op cit.*
10. We assume that the degree of under estimation in the leased-out area because of reporting bias is equally spread among different categories of households. Nevertheless, the conclusions are not going to be affected significantly even if the reporting bias is more pronounced among higher category households.
11. Some micro studies have also reported that a majority of lessors and lessees belong not to very different farm size classes. See Bhalla, 1983, *op cit.*; Ray, 1978, pp. A119-A124 and Swain, 1999, *op cit.*
12. The regression analysis was done separately for 1981-82 and 1991-92 and also after pooling the data for both the years. However, because the results for both years were broadly similar, the results for the pooled data alone are reported. Further, since most of the independent variables are expected to have high degree of correlation, these were entered into the analysis one by one.

REFERENCES

Appu, P. S. (1996). *Land Reforms in India: A Survey of Policy, Legislation and Implementation*, Vikas Publishing House Pvt. Ltd., New Delhi.

Bardhan, Pranab K. (1976). 'Variations in Extent and Forms of Agricultural Tenancy: Analysis of Indian Data Across Regions and Overtime', *Economic and Political Weekly*, Vol. XI, Nos. 37-38.

Bhadhuri, Amit (1973). 'A Study of Agricultural Backwardness Under Semi-fedualism', *Economic Journal*, Vol. 83, No. 329, March.

Bhadhuri, Amit (1983). *Economic Structure of Backward Agriculture*, Academic Press, London.

Bhalla, Sheila (1983). 'Tenancy Today: New Factors in Determination of Mode and Level of Rent Payment for Agricultural Land', *Economic and Political Weekly*, Vol. XVIII, Nos. 19, 20 and 21.

Bliss, C. T. and N. H. Stern (1982). *Palanpur: The Economy of an Indian Village*, Clarendon Press, London.

Braverman, A. and Joseph E. Stiglitz (1982). 'Share Cropping and Interlinking of Agrarian Markets', *American Economic Review*, Vol. 72, No. 4.

Chadha, G. K. and S. K. Bhaumik (1992). 'Changing Tenancy Relations in West Bengal: Popular Notions, Grass Root Realities', *Economic and Political Weekly*, Vol. XXVII, Nos. 19 & 20.

Cheung, S. N. S. (1969). *The Theory of Share Tenancy*, Chicago University Press, Chicago.

Jodha, N. S. (1981). 'Agricultural Tenancy: Fresh Evidence from Dryland Areas in India', *Economic and Political Weekly*, Vol. XVI, No. 52.

Laxminarayan, L. and S. S. Tyagi (1977a). 'Tenancy: Extent and Interstate Variations', *Economic and Political Weekly*, Vol. XII, No. 22.

Laxminarayan, L. and S. S. Tyagi (1977b). 'Interstate Variations in Types of Tenancy', *Economic and Political Weekly*, Vol. XII, No. 39.

Marshal, Alfred (1920). *Principles of Economics*, Macmillan, London.

Nadkarni, M. V. (1976). 'Tenants from Dominant Class: A Developing Contradiction in Land Reforms', *Economic and Political Weekly*, Vol. XI, No. 52.

Otsuka, Keijiro and Yujiro Hayami (1988). 'Theories of Share Tenancy: A Critical Survey', *Economic Development and Cultural Change*, Vol. 37, No. 1.

Otsuka, Keijiro, Hiroyuki Chuma and Yujiro Hayami (1992). 'Land and Labour Contracts in Agrarian Economies', *Journal of Economic Literature*, Vol. XXX, December.

Pearce, R. (1983). 'Sharecropping: Towards and Marxist View', *The Journal of Peasant Studies*, Vol. 10, Nos. 2-3.

Prasad, Pardhan H. (1973), 'Production Relations: Achilles' Heel of Indian Planning', *Economic and Political Weekly*, Vol. VIII, No. 19.

Prasad, Pardhan H. (1974), 'Reactionary Role of Usurer's Capital', *Economic and Political Weekly*, Vol. IX, Nos. 32-34.

Rao, Hanumantha C. H. and Ashok Gulati (1994), 'Indian Agriculture: Emerging Perspective and Policy Issues', *Economic and Political Weekly*, Vol. XXIX, No. 53.

Ray, Debidas (1977). 'The Small Lessor and Big Lessee: Evidence from West Bengal', *Economic and Political Weekly*, Vol. IX, Nos. 32-34.

Ray, Debraj (1998). *Development Economics*, Oxford University Press, New Delhi.

Siddiqui, Kalim (1999). 'New Technology and Process of Differentiation: Two Sugarcane Cultivating Villages in UP', *Economic and Political Weekly*, Vol. XXXIV, No. 52.

Singh, Iqbal (1989). 'Reverse Tenancy in Punjab Agriculrture: Impact of Technological Change', *Economic and Political Weekly*, Vol. XXIV, No. 25.

Sharma, H. R. (1995). *Agrarian Relations in India: Patterns and Implications*, Har Anand Publications, New Delhi.

Srivastva, Ravi (1989). 'Tenancy Transactions During Transition: A Study Based on Field Work in Uttar Pradesh (India)', *The Journal of Peasant Studies*, Vol. 16, No. 3.

Stiglitz, Joseph J. (1989). 'Rational Peasants, Efficient Institutions and a Theory of Rural Organisation: Methodological Remarks for Development Economics', in *The Theory of Agrarian Institutions*, Pranab Bardhan (ed.), Oxford University Press, New Delhi.

Swain, Mamta (1999). 'Agricultural Tenancy and Interlinked Transactions-I: Neo-classical and Marxist Approaches', *Economic and Political Weekly*, Vol. XXXIV, Nos. 37 & 38.

Swamy, Dalip (1988). 'Agricultural Tenancy in the 1970s', *Indian Journal of Agricultural Economics*, Vol. XLIII, No. 4.

William, Hallagan (1978). 'Self Selection by Contractual Choice and Theory of Sharecropping', *Bell Journal of Economics*, Vol. 9, Autumn.

Vyas, V. S. (1970). 'Tenancy in a Dynamic Setting', *Economic and Political Weekly*, Vol. V, No. 26.

NOTES TO APPENDIX 1

Description and source of variables: (i) *Une*: Unemployment rate (male); Vaidhyanathan, A (1986), 'Labour Use in Rural India: A Study of Spatial and Temporal Variations', *Economic and Political Weekly*, Vol. XXI, No. 52, Table 6.8, p. A135.

(ii) *Pov*: Per cent of households below poverty line; Sen, Abhijit (1996), 'Economic Reforms, Employment and Poverty: Trends and Options', *Economic and Political Weekly*, Vol. XXXI, Nos. 35,36 & 37, Table 6.7, p. 2466.

(iii) *Bull*: Bullocks per 100 households and Mach: Number of modern capital equipment like sprayer, duster, tube wells, tractor, trolley, etc. per 100 households, Estimates of Livestock and Agricultural Implements Classified by Household Operational Holdings; 37th Round, NSS Report No. 338, Table 6.3.

(iv) *HS*: Average household size; LL: Per cent of landless households, Report on Landholding (1), 37th Round, NSS Report No. 330, Table 6.1.

(v) *Irr*: Per cent gross cropped area irrigated; Fert: Fertiliser consumption (kg./hec); Bhalla, G. S. and Gurmail Singh (1997), 'Recent Developments in Indian Agriculture: A State Level Analysis', *Economic and Political Weekly*, Vol. XXXII, No. 13, Table 6.5, p. A8.

(vi) *Wage*: Average wage earnings for agricultural labourer (male) in agricultural occupations, Rural Labour Enquiry, 1983: Report on Wages and Earnings; Table 6.3.1 (a) 1.

(vii) *RNF*: Rural non-farm employment (male), Mitra Arup (1993), 'Rural Non Farm Employment, Poverty and Women', *The Indian Journal of Labour Economics*, Vol. 36, No. 4, Table 6.1, p. 45.

NOTES TO APPENDIX 2

Description and source of variables: (i) *Une*: Unemployment rate (persons), Parthasarthy, G. *et al*, (1998), 'Determinants of Rural Non-Agricultural Employment: The Indian Case', *Indian Journal of Agricultural Economics*, Vol. 53, No. 2, Table 6.9, p. 151.

(ii) *Pov*: Per cent of households below poverty line; Sen, Abhijit (1996), 'Economic Reforms, Employment and Poverty: Trends and Options', *Economic and Political Weekly*, Vol. XXXI, Nos. 35,36 & 37, Table 6.7, p. 2466.

(iii) *Bull*: Bullocks per 100 households; HS: Average household size and Mach: Number of modern capital equipment like sprayer, duster, tube wells, tractor, trolley, etc. per 100 households, Livestock and Agricultural Implements in Household Operational Holding; 48th Round, NSS Report No. 408, Tables (3R), 4(R) and 7(R).

(iv) *LL*: Per cent of landless households, Report on Landholding (1), 48th Round, NSS Report No. 399, Table 6.1.

(v) *Irr*: Per cent gross cropped area irrigated; Fert: Fertiliser consumption (kg.\hec); Bhalla, G. S and Gurmail Singh (1997), 'Recent Developments in Indian Agriculture. A State Level Analysis', *Economic and Political Weekly*, Vol. XXXII, No. 13, Table 6.5, p. A8.

(vi) *Wage*: Average wage earnings for agricultural labourers (male) in agricultural occupations, Rural Labour Enquiry, 1993-94: Report on Wages and Earnings; Table3.1 (a) 1.

(vii) *RNF*: Rural non-farm employment (male), Mitra Arup (1993), 'Rural Non Farm Employment, Poverty and Women', *The Indian Journal of Labour Economics*, Vol. 36, No. 4, Table 6.1, p. 45.

Chapter 7

Tenancy and Rural Poor: Some Important Issues

R. P. SINGH

I
INCOME INEQUALITY

The country is passing through the era of planned economy and every sector of the economy is expected to contribute according to its mite to the overall improvement in the quality of life of every citizen of the country. It is recognized fact that despite five decades of planning and overall growth in the economy there has not been much improvement in the quality of rural life. Poverty still continues to be a formidable challenge before the nation. The growth in the economy has remained concentrated in a few sectors and in certain regions of the country. This has created wide regional disparities and inequalities among different sections of the society.

Income inequality and resource inequality are positively associated with poverty. Evidence indicates that even at the global level the income gap between the poor and the rich is widening. The share of the poorest 20 per cent of the households in total income has remained almost stagnant, i.e. 2.5 per cent during 1960 and 1991, while the share of 20 per cent richest in total income has increased from 50.1 to 61.1 per cent during the same period.

In India, though there has been a general perception of growing income inequalities, there is no clear evidence of the same. Some impressionistic estimates, however, bring out the nature of the disparities. Reading these income groups along with consumption expenditure data give some crude indication of disparities in levels of living. Table 7.1 shows that there seems to be upward mobility in income in rural areas during 1985 to 1995 but, in general, income inequality has worsened over time as the income share of people in the middle and higher income groups has increased considerably. Table 7.1 clearly indicates that the share of all the groups of households in total income, except lower income group, increased over time. In fact, the share of lower income groups of households in total income sharply declined from 73.6 per cent in 1984-85 to 57.2 per cent in 1995-96 while the share of top income group of households increased almost 7 times from 0.3 per cent to 3 per cent during the same period. This shows that still more than half of the people have very low income while merely 2 per cent people enjoy substantially higher income. This indicates that poor have become poorer and rich have become richer.

Table 7.1: Share of Different Household Income Groups in Rural India: 1985-86 to 1995-96

(*Per cent Share*)

Income group (%)	*1984-85*	*1989-90*	*1995-96*
Lower 20%	73.6	67.3	57.2
Lower Middle 20%	21.4	23.9	29.0
Middle 20%	4.0	7.1	8.6
Upper Middle 20%	0.7	1.2	3.1
High 20%	0.3	0.5	2.0
All	100.0	100.0	100.0

Source: India, Aha!, Rama Bijapurkar, *Business World*, 22 January to 6 February 1999, pp. 70-72.

This is further confirmed by the fact that lower income group of households account for 57.2 per cent in total population but their share in total expenditure is only 44 per cent. In contrast, only 2 to 3 per cent of upper middle income and higher income group of household account for 5 to 6 per cent in the total expenditure. The middle income group and higher income group of households account for almost double the share in total expenditure compared to their share in total population (Table 7.2). This indicates that lower income group of people not only have lower share in the income but also do not get minimum basic needs.

Table 7.2: Percentage Share of Different Income Group in Population and Expenditure in Rural India

(Percentage Share)

	Income Group (%)				
		Lower Middle	*Middle*	*Upper Middle*	*High*
Population	57.2	29.0	8.6	3.1	2.0
Expenditure	44.0	31.4	13.1	6.3	5.2

Source: India, Aha!, Rama Bijapurkar, *Business World*, 22 January to 6 February 1999, pp. 70-72.

Besides, there are sharp regional disparities in income distribution in the country. Though, there has been some improvement in the income distribution after economic reform process but the condition of lower income group of households has not improved much. In the pre-economic reform period the proportion of lower income group of households in different regions was already quite high, i.e. 59 to 78 per cent but after the economic reform process declined sharply to 44 to 57 per cent (Table 7.3).

Table 7.3: Regional Income Disparities in Rural India during Pre- and Post-Economic Reform Period

(Percentage Share)

	Income Group (%)				
Region		*Lower Middle*	*Middle*	*Upper Middle*	*High*
NORTH					
Pre-Reform	67.1	22.6	8.2	1.4	0.7
Post-Reform	57.3	27.2	9.4	3.2	2.9
SOUTH					
Pre-Reform	78.4	17.4	3.4	0.5	0.2
Post-Reform	61.4	27.1	7.5	2.7	1.3
EAST					
Pre-Reform	62.6	26.5	8.8	1.4	0.7
Post-Reform	61.9	27.4	6.9	2.3	1.3
WEST					
Pre-Reform	59.2	31.9	7.4	1.3	0.4
Post-Reform	44.5	36.8	11.3	4.7	2.7

Source: India, Aha!, Rama Bijapurkar, *Business World*, 22 January to 6 February 1999, pp. 70-72.

Regional comparison of income distribution clearly shows that in the pre-reform period income inequality in Southern region was quite high compared to other regions. In southern region, more than 78 per cent of the households were in the lower income group while the corresponding figures for northern, eastern and western region was 67, 63 and 59 per cent respectively. Similarly in southern region, the proportion of rich households (upper middle income and higher income group) was only 0.7 per cent compared to 2.1 per cent in northern and eastern region and 1.7 per cent in western region. The proportion of people in higher and upper middle income group in western region increased from 1.7 in the pre-reform period to 7.4 per cent after the economic reform. While in other regions, the increase in the higher income group was marginal. However, after economic reform, the income distribution became much more skewed in all the regions, specifically in the western region. In the eastern region, the proportion of households in the lower income group reduced marginally compared to other regions (Table 7.3).

II
RESOURCE INEQUALITY

Land is the main productive resource in rural areas and supports more than three-fourths of the population. Inequality in income is mainly due to inequality in productive resources, especially land. It is clear from Table 7.4 that during 1990-91, about 70 per cent of the farmers owned holdings of less than 1 hectare accounting for merely 17 per cent of the total area. In contrast, only less than 1 per cent of the households owned land holdings of more than 10 hectares and accounted for about 14 per cent of the total land. During last 30 years, there has been considered increase (75 per cent in 1960-61 to 91 per cent in 1990-91) in the number of marginal and small landholdings owning less than 1 to 2 hectares of land. Also, their share in total land has increased considerably from 20 per cent to 51 per cent. This has happened mainly because reduction in the number and area of other categories of farmers i.e. semi-medium, medium and large farmers due to splitting of families. However, the ground reality indicates much more inequality than reflected in the official record.

This shows that land as the basic productive resource is highly inequitably distributed. During the last 50 years there has been some polarisation of land holdings but still the status of land distribution in all states continues to be broadly the same as it had been in 1952-53, except that in the numeric terms. But the land base of these farmers has hardly increased. Average land holding size, both owned and operational, is shrinking and factor productivity shows declining trend. Evidence also indicates that relative landlessness is increasing and there is broadening of equality. Contrary to common belief concentration of holdings has not increased appreciably. Inequality in distribution of owned holdings is relatively high compared to operational holdings. Gini co-efficient of ownership holdings shows that the inequality increased marginally from 0.710 in 1971 to 0.713 in 1981 and 0.716 in 1991. While the inequality in operational holdings, which was less skewed, increased considerably from 0.586 in 1971 to 0.672 in 1991. There is decline in the number as well area of large farmers during last 30 years but their holding size declined in physical unit, not in terms of quality. These farmers still command large (qualitatively better) production unit of land. However, these large farmers have not expanded at the expense of the small farms. Smaller farmers have also disproportionately brought more land than large holdings. The percentage decline in the average size of the marginal holdings is much higher than the percentage decline in the average size of the large holding.

Table 7.4: Distribution of Owned Land Holdings

Size of Holding	*1960-61*	*1970-71*	*1981-82*	*1991-92*
Marginal (less than 1 ha)				
Holding	60.06	62.62	66.64	69.38
	7.59	9.76	12.22	16.93
Small (1-2 ha)				
Holding	15.16	15.49	14.70	21.75
Area	12.40	14.68	16.49	33.97
Semi-Medium (2-4 ha)				
Holding	12.86	11.40	10.78	5.06
Area	20.54	21.92	23.38	17.63
Medium (4-10 ha)				
Holding	9.07	7.83	6.45	2.84
Area	31.23	30.75	29.83	17.64
Large (above 10 ha)				
Holding	2.85	2.12	1.42	0.95
Area	28.24	22.91	18.07	13.83

Source: National Sample Survey, 17th, 26th, 37th and 48th rounds.

Land Reform has been partially successful in providing "land to the tiller" and reducing the skewed distribution of land. Various issues of land reform have been discussed at different forums and repeatedly it has been pointed out that for the success of any economic reform or structural adjustment programme, basic change in the structure of economy and land base is necessary (Tarlok Singh *et al.*, 1992). Despite the fact that the structural changes in land ownership (land reforms) is the precondition for economic development and eradication of poverty in any country, it has not received adequate attention of policy makers and academicians in India.

Experience of many Asian countries indicates that these countries did not have poverty eradication programme but could reduce the poverty considerably through strategies of redistribution of assets, particularly land; empowerment of women; decentralisation; and employment oriented growth, etc. Some of these countries could implement land reform in a much more effective way and created a strong institutional base of productive resource. In India, a number of legislative measures have been taken up in various states and the constitution has been amended almost 13 times to ensure property rights. But, except a few of the measures such as abolition of Zamindari/Ryotwari system, limited distribution of surplus land acquired from Land Ceiling Act and consolidation of holdings in a few states other effective measures could not be taken up in most parts of the country.

Table 7.5: Proportion of Landless Households during 1960-61 to 1991-92

	Landless (Households owning less than 0.002 ha)	*Near Landless (households owning land between 0.002 and 0.200 ha)*	*Total*
1960-61	11.68	26.22	37.90
1970-71	9.64	27.28	37.42
1981-82	11.33	28.60	39.93
1991-92	11.25	31.15	42.40

Source: National Sample Survey, 17th, 26th, 37th and 48th rounds.

An outstanding development of Indian agrarian structure has been the rapid growth of landless agricultural labourers. They constitute about 10 per cent of the agricultural population and make up about 25 per cent of the labour force. This has led to the marginalisation and pauperization of peasantry resulting into abnormal increase in agricultural labour work force in the rural areas (Haque, 1997). Besides, it has created social tension in many parts of the country. The landless and near landless households constitute the bulk (nearly 40%) of farming community and are marginalised in the development process (Table 7.5). These are the people who heavily rely on tenancy for their survival.

III
LAND LEASE MARKETS AND TENANCY REFORMS

Tenancy is complex arrangement between landowner and tenants to share the risks in farming and ensure timely availability of labour during peak farming operations. The types and form of lease arrangement vary from cash renting to crop sharing in different forms. Leasing arrangements is conditioned by the individual owner tenant circumstances. Tenancy contracts are often flexible enough to incorporate information from mid-season production contingencies. Besides, linked transactions between land and other factors of production and product market are not that prevalent but still do represent a sizeable share of tenancy transactions (12%). Many tenancy arrangements improve risk-bearing capacity of the landowner as risk is transferred to or shared by the tenant. In general, the quality of leased-out plots is inferior. The share cropped plots compared to owner operated plots when evaluated from perspective of crop failure indicates that there is positive and statistically significant differences in the resource stability indices between owned and share cropped plots (Singh and Walker, 1982). However, tenancy is often with mutual consent and not by coercion.

There are many reasons for leasing-in and leasing-out land. But most common is resource adjustment (Jodha, 1981). Intertemporal adjustment to risk of resource losses, particularly depleted bullock stocks, especially during drought, is a common phenomenon in dryland areas. Tenancy transactions tend to equalise land and bullock ratio. Alternative employment opportunities in preference to cultivate land and demand for timely loans is another consideration in the lease contracts (Walker and Ryan, 1990). Tenancy contracts allow people to make better use of individual endowments and to arrive at combination of income, efforts, and risk that reflect their endowment and tastes (Binswanger and Rosenzweig, 1981). Tenancy contracts are often made between partners to ensure labour availability during peak period and meet the requirement of credit.

NSS data shows that there is decline in tenancy with increase in the proportion of owner cultivation from 9.6 per cent in 1971-72 to 11.3 per cent in 1991-92. There are about 5.6 million households who lease-out land while 17.1 million reported to be leasing-in land. About 9 per cent of land is under tenancy. The official record indicates definite trend in declining tenancy but ground realities show opposite trend and in fact tenancy is on the increase (Parthasarathy, 1990). Often due to fear of loosing the ownership rights tenancy is not recorded and leads to large scale concealed tenancy.

There is indication that absolute rent has also increased over time. In a recent study (Murthy, 1999) it was found that there is a sharp difference in the rent during kharif and rabi season. During rabi season per acre rent has considerably increased from 4.6 quintal in 1978-79 to 7.5 quintal in 1991-92 to 9.8 quintal in 1998-99. This increase in rent was mainly because of substantial increase in yield of rabi crops. However, the production cost has also increased and the tenants were able to get on average 3.8 quintals net of total costs (including imputed value of cost of labour). However, the share of tenants has remained stable during 1978-79 to 1996-97, despite substantial increase in the yield. This shows that the tenants have not equally shared the production gains. Many landlords provide interest-free credit both cash and kind to the tenants. But due to change in the production relations this has been distorted against the tenants. Besides, the landowners also provide necessary inputs, of course, they adjust in the share of produce. It has also been observed that in a few cases, landlords take share in only main produce and by-products like fodder, stalk of pigeonpeas, etc., used as a fuel, is fully given to the tenants. However, all these complex arrangements largely depend upon the traditional linkage with the tenants.

Since the use of commercial inputs like fertiliser use has increased over time it has become a major component of the total cost of production. Fertiliser coast as per cent of tenants' produce net of rent is about 75 per cent and is now met mostly by fertiliser dealers. Hence, the tenants have become much more dependent on fertiliser dealers for credit to purchase new inputs. Therefore, these dealers have also become indirect partner in the lease arrangement and have a major claim on the produce of the tenants (Murthy, 1999).

It is often debated that tenants, especially small and marginal farmers do not invest enough in land and have, in general, low productivity. Binswanger and Rosenzweig (1986) examined the differential consequences for land productivity in owned and operational holdings and found that operated area is negatively correlated with land productivity. Besides, time of lease, production environment and personal characteristics of farmers significantly affect leasing mechanism and land productivity. However, managerial skill and commitments to farming translates into higher land productivity. But evidence indicates that landowners, who lease-out land normally play managerial role while the role of tenants is often supervisory. This also makes difference in the productivity of owned and lease-in land.

As has been mentioned that production efficiency is related to the form of tenancy. In general, there are two types of tenancy, i.e. cash renting and sharecropping. However, the sharecropping arrangements vary to large extent across regions and even within the region. It largely depend upon the local environment, irrigation facilities, types of land, personal characteristics, etc. Sharecropping and fixed renting co-exist in each village but sharecropping is clearly more prevalent in dryland villages. Sharecropping does result in a loss in production efficiency compared to owner operation or fixed renting. Wage relations, characteristics of owner operation, do not appear to be displacing tenancy.

In general, tenants and landowner often belong to the same farm size class. But there are some tenants who belong to other farm size classes also. In some of the dryland villages it was found that nearly half (47%) of the partners coming from the same farm size group were common. Reverse tenancy was also noted in 32 per cent of the cases, where small farmers leased-out land to large farmers. However, 22 per cent of the large farmers leased-out their land to medium and small farmers. Tenancy market is quite active in the villages and in fact increasing over time but it does not appear to be a means to acquire land or accumulate wealth (Walker and Ryan, 1990).

There is often debate to relax tenancy or put more restriction. But experience shows that despite laudable concern by the policymakers to ensure tenurial rights through restriction on or regulation of tenancy, it has gone mostly against tenants and small farm households, who own small pieces of land. There is considerable increase in the concealed tenancy. A large number of salaries class people and migrants still own a large part of the land in the villages but do not cultivate on their own. They either keep land fallow or lease-out to landless households for a short period, preferably one season. In general, they lease-out to those families who are close to them or had taken loan from them. Their main interest is to maintain the ownership of land and do not make any investment for land improvement. The tenants, especially the sharecroppers, as usual also do not make any investment in land because of short-term lease. In the process land is being overexploited and become degraded. Such degradation of land has a high environmental and social cost.

Tenancy has another dimension. It is also related to concentration of holdings as well as subdivision and fragmentation of holdings. The land ceiling laws has to be seen in relation to tenancy also. The land ceiling laws has not been very effective in providing land to landless people and whatever land has been given to them is of poor quality. Many of the land allottees even after getting the sanction order has not been able to take physical possession even after a long period. However, in some places the distribution of land has been effective and even irrigated land has been distributed to landless. This has helped them in improving their economic condition. Besides, it has reduced their dependency on tenancy.

Subdivision and fragmentation of holdings is another major problem. Evidence clearly indicates demographic pressure on land, and disintegration of family institutions, splitting of families and preference for staying separately have led to excessive subdivision and fragmentation of landholdings. The small size of farm alone is not the problem but excessive subdivision and fragmentation of their holdings in smaller pieces creates more problem in farming operations and proper management of inputs, etc. A large number of marginal and small farmers own very small pieces of land, i.e. less than 0.2 hectare, which make farming operations difficult even by bullocks and leads to inefficiency and low productivity.

The input costs have increased over time and farming has become more capital intensive. The subsistence marginal and small farmers find it difficult to continue farming because of low profitability. Hence, they prefer to lease-out their land, preferably to fellow farmers and join the labour market.

Tenancy legislation has led to the demise of longer-term contractual arrangement such as "*Rehan*" tenancy in some part of the country. It has been found that more than 60 per cent of the tenancy is only for one season. This sort-term lease discourages the use of inputs such as farmyard manure that farmers (rightly) believe have residual or more lasting effect (larger than one year) on crop yield. If tenancy legislation substantially reduces the periodicity of leasing, increasing cost of acquiring and acting on information for both partners, then the static inefficiency costs of sharecropping cannot be broken down to measure the separate contribution of tenancy *per se* and periodicity effect induced by tenancy legislation (Walker and Ryan, 1990).

IV
TENANCY: TOWARDS FLEXIBILITY WITH REGULATION

In many states there is a ban on agricultural tenancy, except for certain categories of disabled people. But concealed tenancy exists almost everywhere. The blanket ban on tenancy has neither helped the landless poor households nor the rich landowners, who lease-out their land. Hence, there seems to be no justification to put restriction on tenancy. In fact, if agricultural tenancy is permitted, at least within the ceiling limits it may activise the land lease market for rapid rural growth and enhance the poor people's access to land. Several studies have indicated that in the relatively backward areas, marginal farmers and landless labourers earn a substantial part of their income through lease in land. In the relatively developed areas, however, there is growing tendency towards reverse tenancy, also known as commercial tenancy. While this tends to increase concentration of operational holdings, there are certain advantages of commercial tenancy, most notably its favourable impact on productivity growth. This commercial tenancy should be encouraged at least within ceiling limits, so that commercial tenants do not increase the size of landholding beyond the ceiling. What is more important in this regard is the protection of land rights of small farmers, who lease out land (Planning Commission, 1992).

There are divergent views about the effectiveness of tenancy legislation. A group of people feels that tenancy legislation has outlived its utility. Land hunger, the imperatives of viable agriculture, the unavoidable search for not-farm economic activities for a living have given rise to fairly extensive clandestine tenancy in quite a few areas of the country. Legally created tenancy serve to improve the viability of many operational holdings and create opportunities for more labour absorption and remove the existing fitters from the hands of those owners of miniscule farm holdings who can seek wage or self-employment for fear of losing of their land. Empirical evidence shows the leasing-in by small and marginal farmers in considerably more widespread than leasing-out by them, although the phenomenon of so-called reverse tenancy in certain areas is also not practical (NIRD 1996).

Even if the economic logic of land-man relationship may justify the restoration of tenancy as a legally valid institution, many practical considerations weight against it. The legal prohibition against tenancy has served to moderate the tendency for creation of clandestine tenancy. There is apprehension that removal of legal restrictions on tenancy might open the floodgate and innumerable petty farmers will be swept away by the tide of the land market and they will swell the ranks of the urban proletariat. It is conceded that a certain measure of clandestine tenancy will have the broad umbrella of protection for small and marginal farmers implicit in the present dispensation. The profitability of small and marginal farm is another dimension, which needs special attention because in the absence of remunerative cultivation, small and marginal farmers may lease out their land to the resource-rich larger farmers or multinationals. This may further accentuate land inequality and leads to increasing landlessness and marginalisation of peasantry (NIRD, 1996). Hence, this aspect required special consideration.

The basic question arises that how to ensure access of better quality land to poor people and more specifically land rights to women. A large number of rural women (20%) are engaged in farming and most of them are poor. There is unequal intra-household distribution of basic necessities such as food, health care, etc. There can be many poor women even in non-poor households also. Hence, they require special attention to empower them through land tenurial rights. In fact, its is necessary to improve the productive capacity of land through effective land management system by which even the smaller and marginal holdings can be made economically viable and profitable.

It is a known fact that most of the small and marginal farmers especially the tenants don't have adequate access to quality inputs in time. Besides, in the absence of ownership rights and their small size they don't have access to credit, which is crucial for development of farming. It is often debated that technology is neural to scale and there is no need to develop separate technology for small and large farmers. But in reality, technologies are scale-neutral but not resource-neutral. In India, most of the technologies used are land-saving and production system continues to be labour-intensive. There seems to be no evidence of increasing return to scale in agriculture. Hence, size class argument is not very relevant. The peasant farms are still more efficient in allocating their resources than the capitalist large farms. Hence, there is need to strengthen the peasant base and ensure appropriate

Despite several efforts made in the past to ensuing tenurial rights to tenants, it has not been very effective in many states. Tenancy has been abolished in many states but there is a need to open up tenancy for increasing investment in agriculture and upward mobility of various sections of rural population. However, this needs to be taken up carefully to protect the interest of the landowners as land is not only a productive unit but has a great sentimental attachment. The tenancy contracts many be relaxed to encourage long-term lease arrangement so that tenants can invest in land. This will improve the productivity, which will be beneficial for both—the owner and the tenant in maintaining soil fertility and avoiding land degradation.

Though every state has a land reform law but unfortunately it is not fully and properly implemented mainly due to lack of systematic land records at the village level. The Tenancy Acts have greater relevance and teeth (of course, subject to availability of proper land records). In fact, the very small and marginal land owners should be kept out side the scope of tenancy laws that give a right to the tenant of such land to become owner of the land by paying a nominal price. The tenancy on such lands should be allowed to continue, with freedom to the owner to resume it for self-cultivation. This is necessary to facilitate the poor landowners to become mobile in order to gradually get out of farming. The strict tenancy law giving right to the tenant purchase the land should be applied to the lands of the other type of landowners. If a state chooses, it can opt for the less radical tenancy law now in operation in West Bengal, provided the state can properly enforce it (Rath, 1996).

There are many absentee landlords, who due to fear of loosing land ownership rights, keep their land fallow. Leaving such a large area uncultivated adversely affects the production and poses a great food security risks, which any country can not afford. Also, it is not in the interest of landless families and marginal farmers, who are deprived of cultivating land due to strict regulations and restrictions. The tenancy has to be seen in the light of larger interest of large number of landless and marginal farmers and it can be regulated and made flexible enough so that landowner who lease-out land do not loose their rights. Tenancy is an age-old practice and has been able to maintain social harmony and production relations, it needs to be considered more in social context rather purely economic considerations.

REFERENCES

Binswanger, H. P. and Rosenzweig, M. R., (1981). *Contractual Arrangements, Employment, and Wages in Rural Labour Market: A Critical Review*, New York, Agricultural Development Council.

Binswanger, H. P. and Rosenzweig, M. R., (1986). "Behavioural and Material Determinants of Production Relations in Agriculture", *Journal of Development Studies* 22 (3): 503-539.

Bijapurkar, Rama (1999). "India, Aha!", *Business World*, 22 January-6 February 1999, pp. 70-72.

Haque, T. (1997). "Relevance of Land Reform in the Wake of Economic Liberalisation" a Paper presented in the Workshop on Land Reforms: Agenda for Ninth Plan, help at NIRD, during January 18-19, 1997

Jodha, N. S. (1981). "Agricultural Tenancy: Fresh Evidence from Dryland Areas in India". *Economic and Political Weekly* 16 (52): A 118-A128.

Murthy, C. S. (1999). "Has Rural Prosperity Benefited the Poor?", Paper presented in the Seminar on Rural Prosperity and Agriculture: Strategies and Policies for the Next Millenium, at NIRD, Hyderabad, November 5-6, 1999.

NSS. National Sample Survey, 17th, 26th, 37th and 48th rounds.

NIRD (1996). *Proceedings of the Workshop on Responsive Administration*, National Institute of Rural Development, Hyderabad.

Parthasarathy, G. (1990). "Changing Agrarian Structure and Directions for Land Reforms in Andhra Pradesh in 1990s", in T. Singh, Haque and A. V. S. Reddy (Ed.), *Impact of Land Reforms on Agriculture and Rural Development*, NIRD, Hyderabad and IASSI, New Delhi, 1992.

Parthasarathy, G. (1991). "Lease Market, Poverty Alleviation and Policy Options", *Economic and Political Weekly*, March 30, 1991.

Planning Commission, (1997). "Report of the Sub-group on Land Reform, Land Use and Land Management", presented at the Workshop on Land Reforms: An Agenda for the Ninth Plan, organised by LBSNAA, Mussoorie at NIRD, Hyderabad, January 1997 (mimeo).

Rath, N. (1996). "Approach to Rural Development in the Coming Years: A Note", presented in the Seminar on "Strategies for Rural Development in the Ninth Plan, organised at National Institute of Rural Development, Hyderabad.

Singh, R. P. and Walker. T. S. (1982). "Determinants and Implications of Crop Failure in the Semi-Arid Tropics of India", Economics Programme Progress Report No. 40 Patancheru: ICRISAT.

Singh, Tarlok, Haque, T. and Reddy, A. V. S. (1992). "*Impact of Land Reforms on Agriculture and Rural Development*", NIRD, Hyderabad and IASSI, New Delhi.

Walker, T. S. and Ryan, J. G. (1990). *Village and Household Economics in India's Semi-arid Tropics*, The Johns Hopkins University Press, Baltimore and London.

Chapter 8

Operation Barga and Rural Poverty: West Bengal Experience

SANKAR KUMAR BHAUMIK

I
INTRODUCTION

In spite of the beneficial effects of land reforms measures, the Indian record in this respect has been dismal. As is well known, right from the beginning of planning era, the importance of land reforms has been duly recognised at the time of plan formulation. However, at the level of implementation, the programme has largely gone by default (See Bandyopadhyay, 1988; Appu, 1996). Reviewing the progress of land reforms in the country so far, the Ninth Five Year Plan notes:

> Despite attempts at land reforms over successive Plan periods, the basic character of the agrarian economy has not undergone any structural change. The pattern of land distribution is highly skewed, with a high concentration of land in the hands of a few land owners on the one hand and the growing number of marginal and sub-marginal farmers on the other...(Govt. of India, 1999, p. 24).
>
> ...in the area of tenancy reforms very little progress has been made, after the initial abolition of 'zamindari' and transfer of title to owner-cultivators in the immediate post-

> Independence period. The successful implementation of tenancy laws has been confined to West Bengal, Karnataka and Kerala...in the Eighth Plan, there was no progress in respect of conferment of rights on tenants and therefore the issue of tenancy reforms is still illusory...(*Ibid.*, p. 25).

The past failures of land reforms programmes notwithstanding, the Ninth Five Year Plan renews the call for a proper implementation of land reforms programmes in the future. The Plan sets out its agenda thus:

> While the ingredients of land reform policy would continue to be the same, as before, the focus would shift to a few critical areas. All efforts would be made to detect and redistribute the ceiling surplus land and to enforce the ceiling laws stringently. Given the small and marginal farms are viable, both from the efficiency and equity points of view, it is desirable that the existing ceiling limits are strictly enforced. More importantly, tenancy reforms would have to be taken up especially in States characterised by semi-feudal modes of production. The rights of tenants and sharecroppers need to be recorded and security of tenure provided to them...(*Ibid.*, p. 27).

Given the above context, in the following part of this note, we briefly present the West Bengal story of implementation of tenancy reforms measures particularly, after coming into power of the present Left Front Government (LFG) in the state. In particular, we discuss the conditions that facilitated much better implementation of such measures in West Bengal. We also briefly touch upon the impact of tenancy reforms measures in changing traditional (exploitative) tenancy relations and subsequently setting its agrarian economy on the road for better performance—both in terms of achieving higher growth as also establishing more equitable agrarian regimes. Having understood this, we would note some of the lessons emerging from West Bengal experience for implementation, in other (non-performing) states, of tenancy reform programme as set out in the Ninth Plan document.

II
OPERATION BARGA

The fact that there has been relatively better implementation of tenancy reforms measures in the state of West Bengal does not necessarily mean that all was well there historically. To keep the record straight, as in other eastern Indian states, the colonial intervention in Bengal led to the establishment of *zamindari* system. Under this system, the peasants (the actual tillers of land and now to be designated as the 'tenants') lost their customary rights over land while the *zamindars* (the erstwhile revenue collectors) became the proprietors of land. The historical literature is replete with the stories of misery of the tenants at the hands of the *zamindars* (see Dasgupta, 1984; Cooper, 1988; Bhaumik, 1993). To mention briefly, instead of providing leadership towards development of agriculture, the *zamindars* in Bengal (as elsewhere) embarked on sub-infeudation and rack-renting. Alongside the zamindars, there emerged a new category of large landowners in colonial Bengal, commonly called the *jotedars*. The *jotedars* too were engaged in subletting of land and extracting heavy rent from the tenants. In fact, the tenants were subjected to various forms of exploitation and oppression (rent-exploitation, debt-burden, semi-feudal bondage and so on) by the *zamindars/jotedars*. What is more, there was hardly any initiative on the part of the colonial rulers to safeguard the interest of the tenants.

During the post-independence period, carrying forward the spirit of the Congress Agrarian Reforms Committee (1949), West Bengal went in for several measures including the one for abolishing 'semi-feudal' landlordism. Intermediaries in land were abolished and subletting of land prohibited through various reform measures. A series of tenancy reform laws also were enacted during the fifties, sixties and early seventies with the aim of protecting the rights of the tenants (particularly, the share tenants) [see, for details, Dasgupta, 1987; Bhaumik, 1993, Ch. III]. However, West Bengal has been no exception among the states of India in its unsatisfactory implementation of many of the tenancy reform laws until about the mid-seventies.

The coming into power of the Left Front Government in West Bengal in 1977 is to be marked as a significant event in the context of subsequent implementation of land reforms measures (including tenancy reforms) in the state. The LFG came to power with vigorous support of the weaker sections (particularly in rural areas) and with the promise of protecting their interest. Consequently, it had *no dearth of 'political will'—the most important prerequisite for successful implementation of any reform measure for the most vulnerable sections of the society.* As for tenancy reforms, the LFG realised that not much legislative work is left undone by the previous Governments. The LFG thus concentrated on plugging the loopholes in the existing legislation and strengthen its implementation.

The most significant tenancy reform programme of the LFG has been launching of the programme of Operation Barga (O.B.). The O.B. programme was launched for the quick recording of the names of bargadars (share tenants) in order to provide them legal security against eviction by the landowners and enforcement of their crop-sharing rights. What is novel about O.B. is that the drive to register the names of bargadars was undertaken with the collaboration of the groups of beneficiaries and with the active assistance of rural workers' organisations and self-governing institutions (the panchayats). Typically bureaucratic methods of recording the bargadars had failed in the past mostly because of hesitation on the part of bargadars to come forward individually under eviction threat by the landowners. The LFG thus adopted the strategy of developing "group action among potential beneficiaries to enable them to overcome the fear psychosis by creating a mutual support system" (Bandyopadhyay, 1980, p. 4). In other words, the O.B. programme was implemented through an *organised movement of the class of bargadars under the facilitating condition created with the restoration of the panchayati raj system.* The government also realised that mere registering the title of cultivation of the bargadars would not be very effective in improving their conditions unless meaningful steps are taken to break the ties of bondage this group might have with the landowners and local moneylenders. The government thus implemented in collaboration with commercial banks, *gramin* banks and co-operatives the scheme of extending credit facility to the bargadars (on a limited scale from the *kharif* season of 1978 and more vigorously since 1979).

The immediate impact of such an organised movement by the tenants to record their names with whole-hearted support from the LFG could be realised from the figures available on the number of registered bargadars in the state. While up to early 1979 about 5.20 lakh bargadars had recorded their names in West Bengal (Bhaumik, 1993, p. 68), the number of registered bargadars increased rapidly to about 14.39 lakh by December 1991 and to 14.86 lakh in September 1998 (Table 8.1). A significant proportion of these bargadars belonged to the category of scheduled castes/scheduled tribes. Of the bargadars recorded till September 1998, while nearly 30 per cent of them belonged to scheduled castes, 11 per cent are drawn from the scheduled tribes. Another noteworthy point is that amount of land per recorded bargadar (0.74 acre in September 1998) has not been insignificant particularly when compared with the average size of operated area in the state. As per 1991-92 N.S.S. data, the marginal holdings (less than 2.50 acre) constituted 80 per cent of all holdings in the state and the average size of such holdings has been 0.74 acre. However, the average size of all operational holdings for the state in 1991-92 stood out to be 1.47 acre.

Table 8.1: Recording of Bargadars in West Bengal

Time Point	*Number of Bargadars*				*Area of barga land (in acre)*	*Average area per bargadar (in acre)*
	SC	*ST*	*Others*	*Total*		
Dec. 1991	431199 (29.96)	171272 (11.90)	836779 (58.14)	1439250 (100)	1103463	0.77
June 1994	443382 (30.39)	169747 (11.64)	845781 (57.97)	1458910 (100)	1115413	0.76
Sept. 1998	451848 (30.41)	164039 (11.04)	869773 (58.54)	1485660 (100)	1098703	0.74

Note: Figures in the brackets are percentages.
Source: GOWB, *Economic Review*, 1991-92, 1994-95 and 1998-99.

III
RESTRUCTURING TENANCY, AGRICULTURAL GROWTH AND RURAL POVERTY

The importance of recent tenancy reforms measures in the state of West Bengal could not be understood properly in terms of the figures on number of recorded bargadars alone. Any objective evaluation of such programmes must look into the patterns of changes in terms and conditions of tenancy following their organised struggle through the O.B. programme. This issue has been dealt with by several scholars (see, for example, Bhaumik, 1993; Banerjee and Ghatak, 1996). We mention below some of the findings emerging in this context:

(1) Following the implementation of the programme of O.B., the recorded bargadars could exercise their legally stipulated crop-sharing rights. This becomes more glaring through comparison of crop-sharing patterns of recorded and unrecorded bargadars;

(2) The bargadars who do not record their names (though few cases) are found to be involved mostly in seasonal tenancy arrangements. Sometimes the desire on the part of the bargadars to maintain good relation with the landowners may also prevent them in going in for recording their names. Under the circumstances prevailing in West Bengal, there is no more any significant trace of semi-feudal vested interests obstructing the tenants to record their names so as to deprive them of their tenancy rights;

(3) Following the implementation of O.B. programme, the transactions between the landlords (lessors) and the bargadars (lessees) have tended to be confined to the land-lease market alone. Consequently, there is no evidence of bargadars being exploited by the landlords through a tie-up between land lease and credit contracts (land-credit interlinkage) (also see Bhaumik and Rahim, 1999);

(4) Compared with the unrecorded bargadars, the recorded ones are much better served by the institutional credit agencies as a higher proportion of them now receive institutional credit. This contributed in reducing their dependence on the landlords for credit support;

(5) The economic performance of the recorded bargadars has been much better as compared to the unrecorded bargadars. This becomes clear from the fact that the former apply higher quantities of inputs (material inputs, human labour etc.) and reap higher levels of output per acre of tenanted land in comparison to latter; and

(6) The O.B. programme helped in establishing more impartial distribution of returns from cultivation between the bargadars and the landlords. Such a conclusion follows from the fact that the recorded bargadars have been able to extract a larger share of total returns compared to the unrecorded ones.

The above observations convey some of the gains enjoyed by the tenants following their recording of names. It, however, needs to be noted that tenancy reforms as through the O.B. programme has been only one segment of whole agrarian policies being implemented by the LFG. The other associated programme has been recovery of ceiling surplus lands and their distribution to the landless and land-poor. Another priority area of the LFG has been promoting the interests of the agricultural labourers through, *inter alia*, periodic revisions of minimum wages and their enforcement with the intervention of the organisations of rural labourers (for details, see Dasgupta, 1987). As the LFG restored the panchayati raj system in the state, it enabled more active participation of the people in planning and implementation of various rural developmental programmes. Greater and greater proportion of state budget have started to be allotted to the panchayats so as to further strengthen the decentralised system of governance as has been established by the LFG.

The agriculture in West Bengal as a whole progressed remarkably during the period following implementation of institutional reform measures (of which tenancy reforms is a part). Thus while the annual compound growth rate of agricultural output in the state for the period 1949 to 1980 is estimated at 1.74 per cent (Boyce, 1987), the same for the period 1980-81 to 1994-95 is calculated to be 4.98 per cent (Rashid, 1996). The performance of the state appears to be specifically impressive in the sphere of foodgrains production (see Table 8.2). This single performance has led the state to the topmost position among major states of India in recent years. For the period 1981-82 to 1991-92, the annual compound growth rate of foodgrains production in West Bengal is found to be 6.5 per cent. This is significantly higher than Haryana (4.3%), Punjab (4.0%) and Uttar Pradesh (3.5%)—the three important Green Revolution states of the country (see CMIE, 1993, p.10). Considering a larger time span (1980-95), however, the growth rate of foodgrains production is found to be 4.56 per cent which still appears to be impressive as compared to other states of India. What is more important is that such a boost in foodgrains production has come about through significant expansion in yield (particularly, in respect to yield of Aman paddy) rather than area (Rawal and Swaminathan, 1998).

Table 8.2: Rate of Growth of Foodgrains Production in West Bengal

Period	Compound Annual Rate of Growth		
	Production	Area	Productivity
1950-60	0.79	0.44	0.32
1960-70	3.32	1.13	2.06
1970-80	0.96	0.07	1.06
1980-90	5.81	0.96	5.18
1990-95	2.13	0.44	1.68
1950-80	2.56	0.76	1.78
1960-80	2.54	0.74	0.08
1980-95	4.56	0.72	3.85

Source: Rawal and Swaminathan (1998).

Table 8.3: Rate of Growth of Rice Production by Season in West Bengal: 1960-95

Period	Aus			Aman			Boro		
	Production	Area	Yield	Production	Area	Yield	Production	Area	Yield
1960-70	6.24	3.95	1.75	0.43	0.27	0.32	26.98	17.50	9.86
1970-80	-5.40	-2.76	-2.48	1.99	0.25	1.79	2.29	2.65	-0.68
1980-90	4.81	-0.42	5.20	4.90	0.29	4.57	12.76	10.80	1.98
1990-95	-1.27	-2.50	1.77	1.39	-0.18	1.57	4.46	5.20	-0.70
1960-80	1.45	0.38	0.56	0.62	0.23	0.52	17.80	13.90	4.40
1980-95	3.26	-1.60	4.78	4.03	0.34	3.67	9.80	8.60	1.25

Source: Rawal and Swaminathan (1998).

Another important feature that is often not recognised in the literature is that the unprecedented production gains in West Bengal agriculture has been brought primarily by its marginal and small farming categories (they together constituted 92 per cent of all holdings and controlled about 71 per cent of total operated area in 1991-92). This is contrary to the experience of the green revolution states where the farmers from higher categories played greater role in bringing production increases following adoption of new agricultural inputs. Furthermore, there has been rapid decline in rural poverty in the state following the implementation of agrarian reform programmes over past couple of decades or so. Table 8.4 below shows that during the period since 1972-73 or 1977-78, West Bengal recorded the highest decline in poverty in percentage point terms among the major states in India.

Table 8.4: Estimates of Rural Headcount Poverty by the Expert Group Method

States	1973-74	1977-78	1983	1986-87	1987-88	1989-90	1990-91	1992	1993-94	Change in 1993-94 over 1983	Change in 1993-94 over 1977-78
Andhra Pradesh	48.40	38.10	25.60	14.60	20.90	19.50	22.10	27.40	16.00	-9.60	-22.10
Assam	52.70	59.80	42.60	39.70	39.40	35.20	33.70	51.70	45.00	2.40	-14.80
Bihar	63.00	63.30	64.40	50.10	52.60	52.40	46.30	61.10	58.00	-6.40	-5.30
Gujarat	46.40	41.80	29.80	30.30	28.70	14.80	21.60	33.70	22.20	-7.60	-19.60
Haryana	34.20	27.70	20.60	19.50	16.20	13.30	19.50	17.70	28.70	8.10	1.00
Karnataka	55.10	48.20	36.30	36.60	32.80	45.40	34.90	45.50	28.20	-8.10	-20.00
Kerala	59.20	51.50	39.00	33.50	29.20	34.40	30.30	26.00	25.90	-13.10	-25.60
Madhya Pradesh	62.70	62.50	48.90	47.80	41.90	39.50	42.40	47.90	40.80	-8.10	-21.70
Maharashtra	57.70	64.00	45.20	44.60	40.80	34.80	35.90	53.60	38.60	-6.60	-25.40
Orissa	67.30	72.40	67.50	55.20	57.60	52.90	36.50	49.00	49.90	-17.60	-22.50
Punjab	28.20	16.40	13.20	13.00	12.60	3.20	9.30	10.20	12.50	-0.70	-3.90
Rajasthan	44.80	35.90	33.50	29.20	33.20	26.10	25.90	31.70	27.50	-6.00	-8.40
Tamil Nadu	57.40	57.70	54.00	41.20	45.80	38.40	37.50	44.30	32.60	-21.40	-25.10
Uttar Pradesh	56.50	47.60	46.50	36.60	41.10	30.50	34.80	47.90	42.60	-3.90	-5.00
West Bengal	73.20	68.30	63.10	47.30	48.30	37.20	49.50	44.00	40.30	-22.80	-28.00
India	56.40	53.10	45.60	38.30	39.10	34.40	35.00	44.00	37.50	-8.10	-15.60

Source: Sen (1996).

Nevertheless, there have serious discussions among the scholars over the issue of connection between agricultural progress and institutional changes in the context of West Bengal. Some good reviews on the literature is available elsewhere (see, in particular, Lieten, 1992; Sengupta and Gazdar, 1996; Rawal and Swaminathan, 1998; Rogaly, Harriss-White and Bose, 1999). We reproduce below a few comments made by the scholars in this context.

As the only state in India; West Bengal has registered more vesting and distribution of land than was originally predicted...the barga registration programme has accorded to most of the sharecroppers a guaranteed and heritable access to their plots, and has largely done away with the interlocking structure of dependence (Lieten, 1992, 275-76).

The process of agrarian reform in West Bengal...did affect a substantial proportion of population. Taken together, the 1.44 million beneficiary households of Operation Barga, and the 2.15 million of beneficiary households of ceiling laws, constitute around half of all rural households in West Bengal...the Left Front reforms...changed balance of power...by instituting redistribution of claims to land affecting millions of people. This...is not an insignificant development (Sengupta and Gazdar, 1996, 196).

Institutional changes (*in West Bengal*) affected production in a myriad ways, both directly such as through a reduction of rents, changes in security of tenure, redistribution of land, and public investment, and indirectly such as through changes in land markets and increased agricultural wages. Institutional reforms in rural West Bengal led to important changes in incentive structures and in the functioning of markets, for example, in the capacity of different agents to participate in a market (Rawal and Swaminathan, 1998, 2601, italics added).

IV
INSTITUTIONAL REFORMS AND DEVELOPMENT : THE LESSONS

Thus West Bengal experience clearly underlines the potential of institutional reforms not only for achieving better agricultural growth but also to establish distributive justice thereby obtaining some solution to the problem of poverty in backward agrarian economies.

Some of the lessons emerging from West Bengal experience of tenancy reforms are the following:

- *First*, it is to be noted that *the most important prerequisite for successful* implementation of land reforms programmes (including tenancy reforms) is the *political will on the part of the parties in state power*. To reiterate, the relatively better performance of West Bengal in this regard could be attributed to sincerity on the part of the ruling LFG to strike at rural vested interest. Unless the parties in state power acquire the will to protect the tenants' lot, the scheme of tenancy reforms would continue to remain as mere paper exercise.
- *Second*, even when the government in power is not unwilling to implement some degree of reforms so as to protect the interest of weaker sections, it may not be possible to achieve desired results in the face of stiff opposition from vested interest groups. In this context, *the West Bengal experience suggests for launching organised movement of the tenants in collaboration with other weaker sections* (agricultural labourers, petty farmers and so on) for protecting their interests. For successful recording of the tenants' names in other states to protect their rights (non-eviction by the landowners, allowance of legally stipulated share of crop etc.), mass mobilisation along that direction could be a useful strategy. In any case, *the recording of tenants' names should not be viewed as a purely juridical-cum-beauracratic exercise*. In the event of organisational weaknesses of weaker sections in most areas, the restoration and strengthening of panchayati raj institutions appear to be a workable strategy for tenants' mobilisation for struggles against vested rural interests.

Further, the West Bengal experience of tenancy reforms also suggests that in the matter of implementation of any programme favouring the weaker sections, there is no room for adopting a dilly-dally approach. Since the tenants mostly belong to the weaker socio-economic category, there always remains the possibility of such programmes being foiled by their superior masters. Thus *any scheme drawn for protecting tenants' interest need to be enforced with a sense of urgency.*

Appropriate detection of tenancy and the tenants in rural areas has been always a difficult problem. To the extent that tenancies represent informal arrangements between the lessors and the lessees, the possibility of tenancies remaining undetected becomes even higher for the official surveys. Thus it is not surprising to find that in a state such as Bihar, which is known for continuing semi-feudal production relations in agriculture, only 3.9 per cent of operated area is reported to be under tenancy in 1991-92 as per N.S.S.O. surveys. *The problem of concealment of tenancy could perhaps be overcome to some extent through involvement of local self-governing institutions (the panchayats) along with the usual official machinery at the time of recording of tenants' names.*

Finally, the issue of 'reverse tenancy' assumes significance in the context of implementation of tenancy reforms measures in the future. As is well known, in many areas of India, there have been a gradual tendency of cultivators from higher farm size categories leasing in huge areas from those belonging to lower categories in order to reap greater benefits of new production technology. Clearly, protecting interests of these tenants implies serving the economically better off tenants in rural areas. In this context, it might be argued that *the course of tenancy reforms could not be uniform across different regions of India.* In states that still continue to remain agriculturally backward, perhaps a tenancy reform policy of West Bengal-type would be the one to emulate. However, in those regions/states where incidence of 'reverse tenancy' appears to be high/increasing, only those tenants whose operated area does not exceed a given limit could be chosen for recording and extending other facilities (credit etc.). In the matter of implementation of differential schemes of tenancy reforms, we foresee no difficulty—constitutional or otherwise. Land reforms (including tenancy reforms) being the state subject, each state of India could devise its own course of action keeping in view the regional specificity. However, there should be a national consensus for implementing the programmes devised for protecting interests of poor tenants. It may be necessary to emphasize that under the current constitutional framework, it may not be possible to implement the policy of 'land to the tiller'. Further, the resource endowments of the rural households (as may be indexed by their land-labour ratios) differ markedly. Consequently, tenancy could not be withered away from the countryside. Tenancy would persist in either form—concealed or open. However, it makes good and responsible governing sense for the state governments to record them and provide necessary protection to their interests.

REFERENCES

Ahluwalia, Montek Singh (1996). "New Economic Policy and Agriculture: Some Reflections", *Indian Journal of Agricultural Economics,* Vol. 51, No. 3.

Appu, P. S. (1996). *Land Reforms in India: A Survey of Policy, Legislation and Implementation*, Vikas Publishing House, New Delhi.

Bandyopadhyay, D. (1980). *Land Reforms in West Bengal*, Calcutta, June.

Bandyopadhyay, Nripen (1988). "The Story of Land Reforms in Indian Planning", in Amiya Kumar Bagchi (Ed.), *Economy Society and Polity: Essays in the Political Economy of Indian Planning*, Oxford University Press, Delhi.

Banerjee, A. V. and M. Ghatak (1996). "Operation Barga: A Study in the Economics of Tenancy Reform" (mimeo), Department of Economics, Chicago University.

Bardhan, Pranab and Christopher, Udry (1999). *Development Microeconomics,* Oxford University Press, New York, Ch. 11.

Bhaumik, Sankar Kumar (1993). *Tenancy Relations and Agrarian Development: A Study of West Bengal*, Sage Publications, New Delhi.

Bhaumik, Sankar Kumar and Abdur, *Rahim* (1999). "Interlinked Credit Transactions in Rural West Bengal", *Indian Journal of Agricultural Economics,* Vol. 54, No. 2.

Boyce, James K. (1987). *Agrarian Impasse in Bengal*, Oxford University Press, Delhi.

CMIE (1993). *Performance of Agriculture in Major States: 1967-68 to 1991-92*, Bombay.

Cooper, Adrienne (1988).*Sharecropping and Sharecropper' Struggle in Bengal, 1930-1950*, K. P. Bagchi & Co., Calcutta.

Dasgupta, Biplab (1984). "Mode of Production and the Extent of Differntiation in Pre-British Bengal," *Social Scientist*, Vol. 12, No. 8.

Dasgupta, Biplab (1987). *Monitoring and Evaluation of the Agrarian Reform Programme of West Bengal* (mimeo), Calcutta, December.

Government of India (1999). *Ninth Five year Plan 1997-2002*, Vol. 2, Planning Commission, New Delhi.

Johl, S. S. (1995). "Agriculture Sector and New Economic Policy", *Indian Journal of Agricultural Economics,* Vol. 50, No. 3.

Lieten, G. K. (1992). *Continuity and Change in Rural West Bengal*, Sage Publications, New Delhi.

Rashid, Abdul (1996). *Growth and Instability in West Bengal Agriculture Since Independence*, M. Phil. Dissertation (unpublished), Department of Economics, Calcutta University.

Rawal, Vikas and Madhura, Swaminathan (1998). "Changing Trajectories: Agricultural Growth in West Bengal", *Economic and Political Weekly*, Vol. 33, No. 40.

Ray, Debraj (1998). *Development Economics*, Oxford University Press, Delhi, Ch. 12.

Rogaly, Ben, Barbara Harriss-White and Sugata, Bose (1999). *Sonar Bangla? Agricultural Growth and Agrarian Change in West Bengal and Bangladesh*, Sage Publications, New Delhi.

Sen, Abhijit (1996). "Economic Reforms, Employment and Poverty: Trends and Options", *Economic and Political Weekly*, Vol. 31, Nos. 35-37, September.

Sengupta, Sunil and Haris, Gazdar (1996). "Agrarian Politics and Rural Development in West Bengal", in Jean Dreze and Amartya Sen (Eds.), *Indian Development: Selected Regional Perspectives*, Oxford University Press, Delhi.

Timmer, C. Peter (1991). "The Role of the State in Agricultural Development" in C Peter Timmer (Ed.), *Agriculture and the State: Growth Employment and Poverty in Developing Countries*, Cornell University Press, Ithaca.

Chapter 9

Emerging Land Lease Market in Haryana

P. C. BANSIL

I
AN OVERVIEW

The picture regarding leasing-in and leasing-out of land is discernible all along the farm size continuum. A phenomenon of reverse tenancy no doubt existed even in the pre-green revolution era and it only got magnified with the introduction of the new farm technology. Undoubtedly, the incidence of tenancy had declined considerably during the preceding three decades or so, yet contrary to the picture revealed by published reports, including agricultural census and the National Sample Survey data, concealed tenancy operates on a considerable scale and form, which varies from region to region. The reported decline in the incidence of tenancy, however, is generally accepted to reflect the reality and can be attributed to three main factors:

(i) The legislation of protection of tenants' rights, compounded perhaps by fears that greater political assertiveness of tenants would result in stricter enforcement of the laws. This may have led to eviction of tenants and resumption of leased land for self-cultivations.

(ii) The tendency gets reinforced by technological progress in the form of high-yielding varieties-irrigation-fertilisers. As long as it increases the returns to cultivation, the owners have incentive to shift from tenancy to self-cultivation, involving failure to renew leases or eviction of tenants. This phenomenon is stated to have occurred on a significant scale in the states of Punjab and Haryana, the heart land of the green revolution.

(iii) In so far as the larger farmers are better placed to exploit the potential of the new technology, whether because they have the resources needed to have access to complementary inputs or because of scale economies, the small and marginal landowners may have an incentive to lease-out land to the larger and better endowed cultivators. This phenomenon has also been documented in various research studies in the case of Punjab and Haryana. The decline in conventional tenancy and the growth of reverse tenancy would lead to an increase in the proportion of agricultural households not operating any land, and greater concentration of operational holdings.

All said and done, a concern has been expressed in the Ninth Plan (1997-2002) document that in the wake of liberalisation there is now a move to make certain changes in tenancy regulations to attract private corporate investment in agriculture. Hence, it has been suggested to reconsider the issue of land reforms, particularly from the point of view of the poor as access to land is still a major source of livelihood in rural India. In point of fact, the experience of several countries in East Asia shows that land reforms, leading to structural equity in the distribution of land, are an essential prerequisite for economic development through agricultural transformation. Keeping the above canvass in view where the tenancy situation in the country has been depicted in a nutshell, we may now examine the main features of tenancy system in Haryana State.

II
TENANCY REFORMS IN HARYANA

In so far as Haryana is concerned, all land legislations enacted by the erstwhile State of Pepsu and the pre-1956 Punjab, of which Haryana remained part till October 1966, automatically became applicable to the State when it was formed on 1st November, 1966. Areas in the State where Pepsu laws were applicable were the districts of Jind and Mohindergarh and tehsil, Charki, Dadri of Bhiwani district. Elsewhere Punjab laws became applicable.

In so far as the abolition of intermediary rights in the state was concerned, there were three Acts applicable to the State, viz. (i) The Punjab Occupancy Tenants (Vesting of Proprietary Rights) Act, 1953; (ii) The Punjab Abolition of Ala Malkiyat and Talukdari Rights Act, 1952; and (iii) the Pepsu Abolition of Ala Malkiyat and Talukdari Rights Act, 1954. Intermediary tenures like Zamindari, Jagirdari, Inamdary have been abolished practically in all the States including Haryana as a result of which about 21 million cultivators have been brought into direct contact with the State.

Prevalence of intermediary tenancy in the state was confined to a comparatively small area, which once formed part of the then PEPSU and these too were completely abolished in the State. This was also confirmed by the National Commission on Agriculture, 1976. In so far as tenancy reforms are concerned, it was reported that after the tenancy legislations were enacted in Haryana, then part of Punjab, large-scale eviction took place mostly under the pretext of self-cultivation by landlords and voluntary surrender by tenants. Peasants who were then tenants were reduced to the status of sharecroppers on the same land. Further, though there was no bar on leasing-out land according to tenancy legislations in the State, the nature of tenancy had undergone change in such a manner so as to keep the land of the land owner free from any kind of encumbrance which gave scope for further legislation.

Tenancies in Haryana are regulated by the Pepsu Tenancy and Agricultural Land Act, 1955, in the Pepsu area and by the Punjab Security of Tenure Act, 1953, as amended from time to time, in other areas of the State. Both these Acts are broadly similar so far as provisions relating to tenancy are concerned. The main provisions relating to tenancy reforms are as under:

(i) The maximum rent was fixed at one-third of the gross produce or value thereof;
(ii) Security of tenure was conferred on tenants holding land which was within the permissible limit of 30 standard acres allowed in respect of the landlord;
(iii) A tenant could be ejected on grounds of personal cultivation by the landowner;[1]

(iv) A tenant was not to be ejected from a minimum area of five standard acres within the permissible limit, until he was provided with an alternative piece of land by the State Government;

(v) The right of resumption had to be exercised within a period of one year from the commencement of the Act by landowners belonging to the Armed Forces of the Union and within a period of six months by other landowners;

(vi) In Pepsu area, tenants in continuous possession of land for 12 years were to get complete security of tenure in an area not exceeding 15 standard acres; and

(vii) Besides, optional right of purchase of ownership was given to tenants in respect of non-resumble area. In Pepsu area, the compensation fixed was 90 times the land revenue or Rs. 200 per acre whichever was lower. In other areas a tenant in continuous possession of land for six years could purchase the non-resumable area at a price which would be three-fourths of the average value of similar land prevailing during the previous 10 years.

After the tenancy legislation was enacted in Haryana, then a part of Punjab, large scale eviction took place under the pretext of self-cultivation. The National Commission on Agriculture has reported that upto March 31, 1973 about 144 thousand hectares of land was resumed for self-cultivation, involving 78 thousand tenants. After the resumption of land, the tenants became sharecroppers on the same land. The post-legislation period is characterised by increasing number of sharecroppers in Haryana. Tenancy legislation in Haryana as well as in many other parts of the country thus resulted in only changing the status of tenants to share croppers. There has, however been a sea change in the land system scenario in the recent past.

III
THE STUDY

Keeping the above in view and the overall progress in the implementation of land reforms in the state, we undertook an indepth study (sponsored by the Ministry of Rural Development) in Gurgaon, Karnal and Bhiwani districts of Haryana to find out the present status of tenancy and growth of land market in the state.

Three districts were selected purposively from three different agro-economic regions of the state. The districts were Gurgaon in the southern region, Karnal in the north and Bhiwani in the west. From each district, two blocks were selected by adopting stratified random sampling technique. From each block 5 villages were selected again adopting stratified random sampling technique. Finally, from each village 10 farmers were selected at random for intensive study. Important findings of the study are discussed here.

Terms of Tenancy

Though the minimum rent prescribed in tenancy legislation in the State is one-third of the gross produce, many tenants were paying as much as half of the gross produce as rent. In Karnal and Bhiwani districts, the terms of tenancy was generally in cash. About 92 to 100 per cent of the respondents who leased-in land in these districts settled for payment in cash. In fact, in Karnal district, the terms of tenancy in all cases was in cash, and mostly the tenants made payment from the sale proceeds of wheat only. This further established prevalence of land market in the State. However, in Gurgaon district, majority of the respondents leased-in land on crop sharing basis. In fact, in this district those respondents who leased-out land also settled for sharing of crops. In Bhiwani Block of Bhiwani district, terms of leasing-out land was in cash in all the cases. No inference, however, can be drawn on the prevailing system of leasing-out land as only a few of the respondents actually leased-out land (Table 9.1)

Table 9.1: Nature and Terms of Tenancy (%)

District	Block	No. of Respondents			Nature of Tenancy		Terms			
							Cash		Kind	
		Leased-in	Leased-out	Both	At will	Occu-pancy	Leased-in	Leased-out	Leased-in	Leased-out
Gurgaon	1	92.0	6.0	2.0	100.0	0.00	6.5	0.0	93.5	100.0
	2	84.0	12.0	4.0	100.0	0.00	29.8	0.0	70.2	100.0
Karnal	1	96.0	4.0	0.0	100.0	0.00	100.0	100.0	0.0	0.0
	2	98.0	2.0	0.0	100.0	0.00	100.0	100.0	0.0	0.0
Bhiwani	1	90.0	8.0	2.0	100.0	0.00	92.2	100.0	7.8	0.0
	2	94.0	4.0	2.0	100.0	0.00	95.7	50.0	4.3	50.0
All District		92.3	6.0	1.7	100.0	0.00	67.3	41.7	32.7	58.31

Yield Differences

Another very interesting finding of the study is that no conspicuous difference in yield of various crops cultivated by the respondents in owned and leased-in land was observed in the selected blocks. This would be revealed from the figures shown in Table 9.3. Since lease period in majority of cases was only one year, most of the respondents did not apply any organic manure on leased-in lands, but compensated the same by inorganic fertilisers. This certainly bridged the yield gap between leased-in and owned lands, but deprived the leased-in land of its rich humus (Table 9.2).

Table 9.2: Differences in Yield (In Quintals Per Hectare between Owned and Leased-In Land)

Crops	*Status of land*	*Gurgaon*		*Karnal*		*Bhiwani*	
		Block 1	*Block 2*	*Block 1*	*Block 2*	*Block 1*	*Block 2*
Wheat	Owned	28.9	29.6	55.5	55.8	33.3	39.4
	Lease	28.5	29.0	55.5	55.5	33.0	39.0
Bajra	Owned	6.6	6.0	0.00	0.00	4.8	4.5
	Lease	6.5	6.5	0.00	0.00	4.5	4.5
Rice	Owned	30.0	29.0	32.0	34.0	0.00	0.00
	Lease	29.0	28.8	32.9	34.0	0.00	0.00
Gram	Owned	0.00	8.6	0.00	0.00	0.00	0.00
	Lease	0.00	8.5	0.00	0.00	0.00	0.00
Sugarcane	Owned	0.00	0.00	64.2	64.0	0.00	0.00
	Lease	0.00	0.00	64.0	63.0	0.00	0.00
Cotton	Owned	0.00	0.00	0.00	0.00	1.40	1.50
	Lease	0.00	0.00	0.00	0.00	1.32	1.50
Potato	Owned	0.00	0.00	182.80	180.00	0.00	0.00
	Lease	0.00	0.00	180.0	180.00	0.00	0.00

Percentage of Area Leased-in by Different Categories of Farmers

It has been observed that the area leased-in constituted nearly 42.4, 56.6 and 34.3 per cent of the total operational holdings of the sample households in Gurgaon, Karnal and Bhiwani districts respectively. Further, the highest percentage of leased-in land in each district was in the size class of 4-6 hectares followed by the size-class of 6 hectares and above (Table 9.3). This phenomenon itself amply substantiates our hypothesis that the big farmers are now leasing-in land and there exists a system of reverse tenancy. However, in the emerging land market, even the marginal land owning class (0-2 ha) has also been taking land on rent and nearly 34 to 39 per cent of the operational land was leased-in by the farmers belonging to this class.

Table 9.3: Area Leased-in (Ha) and Percentage Share of the Total Operational Holdings in each Size Class of Holdings

District	*Size Class (ha)*	*Area leased (ha)*	*% share of leased-in land in the total operational holdings*
Gurgaon	0-2	69	39.0
	2-4	35	30.0
	4-6	72	60.0
	6 & above	22	42.0
	Total	198	42.0
Karnal	0-2	28	39.0
	2-4	78	52.0
	4-6	170	62.5
	6 & above	126	58.3
	Total	402	56.6
Bhiwani	0-2	45	34.0
	2-4	55	26.0
	4-6	163	47.0
	6 & above	72	26.0
	Total	335	43.0

Categories of Farmers Leasing-out Land

It was observed that farmers belonging to all categories, viz. marginal, small, middle and big were leasing-in and most of the cases, the marginal and small farmers leased-out their land due to their uneconomic size of holdings, high investment cost, high wage rate and non-availability of the required credit. Even many of the middle and big categories of land owners leased-out their land for reasons like employment outside, labour shortage or non-availability of water for irrigation. All the same, no positive relationship could be established between the different categories of farmers—those who leased-in and those who leased-out land (Table 9.4).

Reasons for Leasing-in and Leasing-out Land

More than half of the respondents (57.18%) reported that they had leased-in land to make their holdings economic. The next most important driving force behind leasing-in land was increased profitability in agriculture. In fact, as high as 38.52 per cent respondents admitted that agriculture in the state had over the years graduated from subsistence level to a business proposition following availability and application of productivity raising technologies. Thus increased profitability also led to a system of reverse tenancy leaving behind the age-old system of exploitative tenancy despite plethora of tenancy regulation and land ceiling laws enacted in the state (Table 9.5).

Table 9.4: Percentage of Farmers Leasing-out Land

District	*Size Class (hect.)*	*No of respon-dents*	*Status of those who leased-out land to the respondents (per cent)*			
			Marginal	*Small*	*Middle*	*Big*
Gurgaon	0-2	46	39.0	22.0	26.0	13.0
	2-4	23	61.0	26.0	9.0	4.0
	4-6	16	25.0	19.0	37.0	19.0
	6 & above	3	67.0	0.0	33.0	0.0
Karnal	0-2	21	33.0	19.0	29.0	19.0
	2-4	24	25.0	42.0	25.0	8.0
	4-6	34	41.0	35.0	6.0	18.0
	6 & above	16	56.0	19.0	12.5	12.5
Bhiwani	0-2	29	24.0	45.0	21.0	10.0
	2-4	17	47.0	23.0	12.0	18.0
	4-6	34	44.0	32.0	18.0	6.0
	6 & above	21	29.0	19.0	29.0	23.0

Table 9.5: Reasons for Leasing-in (%)

District	*Block*	*Make the holding economic*	*Increased profitability*	*Availability of pump set*	*Other unspecified reasons*	*Total*
Gurgaon	1	10.87	82.60	4.35	2.18	100.00
	2	71.43	25.0	3.57	0.00	100.00
Karnal	1	50.00	50.00	0.00	0.00	100.00
	2	73.46	21.74	0.00	4.80	100.00
Bhiwani	1	77.78	17.78	4.64	0.00	100.00
	2	59.57	34.04	6.39	0.00	100.00
All Districts		57.18	38.52	3.15	1.15	100.00

Further, in Gurgaon and Bhiwani districts a small percentage of respondents (3.15%) leased-in mainly the adjacent lands of their own in view of the availability of pumpsets on the lessors land. There were a few other reasons for leasing-in land like improved accessibility to own land, lessors not being interested in cultivation and lessor remaining away from the village.

Out of 300 respondents, only 18 respondents (6%) had leased-out land and majority of them (41.72%) did so as the respondents were engaged in non-farm employment. Labour shortage (29.17%), uneconomic holding (11.12%), high investment cost (11.05) and high wage rate (4.17%) were also the reasons for leasing-out land (Table 9.6).

Table 9.6: Reasons for Leasing-out Land (%)

District	Block	Uneconomic holding	High invest cost	High wage rate	Labour short age	Employment out side	Credit crunch	Other Misc. Reasons	Total
Gurgoan	1	0.00	33.00	0.00	0.00	67.00	0.00	0.00	100.00
	2	16.7	33.3	0.00	0.00	33.3	0.00	16.7	100.00
Karnal	1	50.00	0.00	0.00	50.00	0.00	0.00	0.00	100.00
	2	0.00	0.00	0.00	100.00	0.00	0.00	0.00	100.00
Bhiwani	1	0.00	0.00	25.00	25.00	50.00	0.00	0.00	100.00
	2	0.00	0.00	20.00	30.00	50.00	0.00	0.00	100.00
All District		11.12	11.05	4.17	29.17	41.72	0.00	2.78	100.00

IV
CONCLUDING OBSERVATIONS

We observed that tenancy was prevailing in all the districts irrespective of the size of holdings establishing the prevalence of much talked about reverse tenancy, i.e. bigger land owners were leasing-in land from the small and marginal farmers as well as from the absentee landowners. While the bigger farmers leased-in land mainly due to increased profitability in agriculture following adoption of green revolution technologies, the smaller and marginal farmer leased-in land mainly due to increased profitability in agriculture following adoption of green revolution technologies, the smaller and marginal farmers leased-in to make their holdings economic thereby increasing their farm income.

Further, we found that in all cases tenancy was at will and there was no evidence of occupancy tenancy. As against the earlier system of exploitative tenancy, a system of land market has developed where there was competition for leasing-in land. Under this competitive economy, there is no tenant in real sense of the term. Whether a person leases in or leases out, it is purely an economic proposition. Further, under the existing situation lease period was generally very short, 1-2 years in expectation of higher rent when fresh lease contracts were made.

Thus under the situation as it exists in Haryana today, land is just like any other commodity, of course, a scarce one and there is an open competition among those who want to take on rent whether a small or a big land owner. Even a few landless farmers also were leasing-in land. Further unlike the age-old system of perpetual tenancy, presently, in most cases, the leasing-in period has been for one or two years. This phenomenon is to a great extent, similar to that of urban areas where the owner of a house usually lets out to a reliable tenant for a very short period of eleven months or so. Moreover, instead of crop sharing, the land owners leasing-out land prefer, in majority cases, *cash as rent which is invariably taken as advance.* Another very conspicuous feature of the changed tenancy system in the State is that there is now no evidence of occupancy tenancy.

Some new trends emerged with the spread of green revolution. Big farmers started leasing-in land mainly from absentee landlords or small and marginal farmers to undertake large scale farming for larger profit. In fact, farming gained a new aura of respectability. It is not that the big farmers alone are the gainers and have assumed the reins of farm management, the small and marginal farmers as well have now been competing for land on rent in the present land market.

From our study in Haryana State it is observed that the old concept of tenancy is no longer valid. Not all those who lease-out are big landowners, as petty farmers owning small parcels of land also often lease-out owning to their poor resource position. Even the village artisans and agricultural labourers possessing tiny plots of land lease-out. The petty landholder who has leased-out his land, is as per traditional concept, a landlord but if there is a choice he could as well be engaged in some other work, leasing-out his tiny plot.

We have observed that in our study districts, among all size class of operational holdings, over quite a substantial area, one may assume that tenancy system does not prevail at all in the state. In fact, the most poignant feature in agricultural tenancy is that though it has been abolished in most of the states through various enactments, it is still existing in some form or other and is largely concealed.

However, in Haryana State, the existing tenancy scenario is quite different. The reverse tenancy seems to have become an irreversible phenomenon and apparently a healthy sign as well, as the lessees are having economy of scale by leasing-in land in a competitive land market. Even if the small and marginal farmers lease-out their lands, they are gainers in the existing lease conditions, as often they become the equal sharers of the gains in production without anything being invested by them. In fact, landlord-tenant relationship in agricultural land has now become a concept of bygone days in the state.

Chapter 10

Changes in Land Holding Structure, Farm Size, Productivity and Tenancy in Punjab

RAMESH CHAND

I
LAND HOLDING STRUCTURE IN PUNJAB

Punjab State has remained in the forefront of agricultural development in the country since the adoption for green revolution technology during late 1960s. The state presents a fine example of technology led economic transformation. There is considerable interest to know how the green revolution technology has affected land tenure, farm size-productivity relationship and tenancy, as these are important from growth as well as social welfare point of view. The present paper is an attempt in this direction. The paper examines the changes in farm size distribution in the state during different phases of green revolution technology using data from agricultural census. The relationship between farm size and productivity and the recent pattern of tenancy are analysed using micro level data from four village in Ludhiana district which is agriculturally most progressive district in the state. The possibility of reeducating number of tiny holdings and increasing farm size to viable level through removal of land ceilings in the Indian context is also discussed.

Number of land holdings in the state dropped from 13.75 lakh in 1971 to 10.27 lakh in 1981. The latest agricultural census for the year 1990-91 places the figure at 11.17 lakh. Sharp decline in the number of operational holdings between 1971 and 1981 and relatively small increase in the subsequent decade is observed in all the district (see Table 10.1). Accordingly, size of operational holdings increased from 2.95 hectare in 1971 to 4.10 hectare in 1981 and then came down to 3.79 hectare in 1991.

Distribution of land holdings according to size classes show that the number of marginal farms in the state declined from over 5 lakh in 1971 to about 2 lakh in 1981 and then rose to about 3 lakh in 1991. Similarly, the share of marginal size category in total holdings declined from 38 per cent in 1971 to 19 per cent in 1981, and then increased to 26.5 per cent in 1991. Semi-medium holdings which accounted for about 18 per cent of the total holdings in 1971 decreased by about one-fourth by 1981, and increased marginally in the following decade. Semi-medium farmers, constituting 26 per cent of total holdings at present, showed remarkable stability in their number which remained around 2.86 lakh. Population of medium farmers in the size category 2-4 hectares was slightly higher than their population during 1971, while large farmers showed a marginal decline in the same period.

Table 10.1: District-wise Trend in Number and Size of Operational Holdings in Punjab, 1971, 1981 and 1991

Region/District	*Total Holdings '000*			*Average Size (Hec.)*		
Sub mountain Region:	*1971*	*1981*	*1991*	*1971*	*1981*	*1991*
Rupnagar	65	49	54	1.84	2.61	2.09
Hoshiarpur	148	94	98	1.65	2.69	2.64
Gurdaspur	123	100	113	2.11	2.60	2.64
Sub-total	336	243	265	1.85	2.63	2.53
Central Region						
Patiala	84	79	96	4.63	4.95	4.05
Ludhiana	91	74	83	3.46	4.44	3.91
Jallandhar	116	75	86	2.44	3.99	3.41
Kapurthala	53	35	39	2.49	4.19	3.63
Amritsar	187	115	124	2.08	3.64	3.52
Sub-total	531	378	428	2.84	4.19	3.70
South West Region						
Sangrur	108	90	102	4.16	5.13	4.49
Bhatinda	107	91	102	4.79	5.53	4.80
Faridkot	136	114	107	3.67	4.60	4.83
Ferozepur	158	111	112	2.94	4.46	4.51
Sub-total	508	406	424	3.78	4.89	4.66
Punjab	1375	1027	1117	2.95	4.10	3.79

Note: After 1994 some more districts have been created in the State.

Sources: 1. Agricultural Census of Punjab, 1971, 1981 and 1991.

2. Statistical Abstract of Punjab. Various Issues.

The distribution of holdings according to size category reveals that during the first decade succeeding adoption of green revolution technology 60 per cent marginal and one-fourth small holdings vanished, whereas, the number of holdings at upper tail showed modest increase. During the eighties, which is the second decade of post-green revolution period, marginal and small holdings showed small increase and large holdings slightly decreased. The reasons for this type of trend are: *First*, with the onset of adoption of green revolution technology crop production activity became economically highly attractive which created an active land market for sale and purchase and for lease of cultivable land. *Second*, agricultural progress in the initial years following green revolution generated large employment avenues in non-farm activities which prompted many farmers with sub-marginal holdings to either sell their land or lease it out and earn higher income in non-farm jobs compared to the farming. *Third*, initially, new technology was found to be more favourable to large size farms mainly because the mechanical inputs like pumpsets, tractors, threshers etc., associated with new technology, were lumpy units which are indivisible and thus uneconomic for use at smaller sized farms.

Over time, product innovations resulted in development of smaller sized machines and capital assets which, along with the emergence of hire-in and hire-out market for farm machinery and implements, eased the constraints in adoption of new technology by lower sized holdings. Also, the green revolution has had its full impact by 1980-81 and the change process initiated by it slowdown in subsequent period. Employment in all non-farm rural occupations except public services slowed down which reduced the pace of shift from farm to non-farm occupations. Another factor which contributed to reversal in 1980s, of the process of elimination of lower sized land holdings experienced in 1970s, is emergence of commercial dairying. Promotion of commercial dairying in the state has complementary relationship with crop production and its improved viability of uneconomic smaller sized holdings.

It is also worth noting the number of holdings increased by less then 9 per cent during 1981 to 1991 compared to 21 per cent growth in population. This shows that most of the owners of the newly fragmented holdings due to law of inheritance did not go for self-cultivation as they might have either sold out or leased-out their land.

Size class distribution of holdings in various districts reveals that concentration of marginal and small farmers is highest in Sub-Mountain region while concentration of large and medium farmers is highest in South-West region. Central districts are at the top in respect of concentration of semi-medium holdings.

Inequality in Land Distribution

According to the agricultural census date for the year 1990-91 average size of land holdings in marginal farm size category (below 1.00 hectare) was 0.55 hectare while an average operational holding in large size category operate on 16.07 hectare area (Table 10.2).

Table 10.2: Farm size category wise distribution of Land Holdings and Operational Area in Punjab, during 1990-91

Size Class	*Area*		*Holdings*		*Average size hec*
	'000 hec	*Per cent*	*'000 hec*	*Per cent*	
Marginal less than 1 hec	164	2.3	296	26.5	0.55
Small: 1-2 Hec	328	4.7	204	18.3	1.61
Semi-medium: 2-4 hec	841	12.0	289	25.9	2.91
Medium: 4-10 Hec	1622	23.1	261	23.4	6.21
Large: More than 10 hec	1077	15.3	67	6.0	16.07
Total	4032	100.0	1117	100.0	3.79

Source: Same as in Table 10.1.

Marginal farmers constitute 26.5 per cent of total holdings but operate only on 2.3 per cent area. On the other hand, large farmers account for 6.0 per cent holdings and operate more than 15.3 per cent area. Semi-medium holdings of the size 2 to 4 hectares comprise one-fifth share in both total holdings as well as total area.

II
THE FIELD STUDY

The sample for the study was drawn from four C.D. blocks representing different levezls of agricultural development. Subsequently, one village from each of the selected blocks was selected at random for detailed study which includes village Lalton from Ludhiana block, Bullowal from Pakhowal block, Khanjarwal from Sidhwan Bet and Toose from Subhar block were selected. In the final stage a sample of 75 cultivating households was selected randomly from each of the sample villages. In village Khanjarwal there were not sufficient cultivating households, therefore, the balance (34) households were selected at random from the contiguous village Bassian Bet (see Ramesh Chand 1999 details).

The randomly selected cultivator households were divided in four size categories namely marginal, small, medium and large having size ranges 0-2.50 acre or 0-1 hectare, 2.50 to 5.00 acres or 1 to 2 hectares, 5.00 to 10.00 acres or 2 to 4 hectares and above 10 acres or 4 hectares respectively. The distribution of sample households over various size categories is shown in Table 10.3. The information pertain to agricultural year 1993-94.

Table 10.3: Size-Specific Distribution of Sample Households

Size Category	*Village*				*Aggregate*
	Bullowal	*Toose*	*Khanjarwal**	*Lalton*	
Marginal	24	19	21	17	81
Small	23	29	16	19	77
Medium	15	20	23	24	82
Large	12	17	15	15	59
Total	74	75	75	75	299

* Includes 43 households from Bassian Bet Village.

Pattern of Land Distribution

Distribution of land across size categories can be significantly different depending upon whether size of own holding is used for size classification or size of operational holding is used for the classification. This is particularly time when lease-in or lease-out is a common practice. Accordingly, the size classification based on own and the one based on operated area can result in contrary conclusion about nature of land tenancy.

Incidence of leasing-in land according to size classes based on ownership land holding and operational land holding is presented in Table 10.4. When own area is used for size classification ratio of leased-in land to own land and share of leased-in land in operated area shows strong negative association with the size of holding. As against 59 and 44 per cent share of lease-in land in operated area in marginal and small size categories medium and large farmers leased-in 31 and 28 per cent of operated area. For every acre of their own land marginal farmers lease-in 1.44 acre of land and small farmers lease-in 0.73 acre of land. Compared to this, large and medium farmer lease-in only 0.36 and 0.33 acres of land for every acre of their own land (Table 10.4).

Now instead of ownership holding when we used size of operational holding for size classification entirely different picture emerges. Ratio of lease-in land to own land and share of lease-in land in operated area showed sharp increase with the increase in farm size. Small and marginal farmers lease-in 11 per cent of area operated by them as against 31 and 48 per cent leased-in by medium and large farmers. Similarly, ratio of own land to operated land increased from 6 per cent in the case of marginal holdings to 92 per cent at large size holdings.

Similarly, when the phenomenon of lease-in of land is studied using number of lease holders, the classification based on operated area shows sharp increase in per cent of farmers leasing-in land as the farm size increase. On the other hand, size classification based on own area shows that the incidence of leasing-in land is at least as common among lower sized categories as among the upper size categories.

The reason for the two types of classifications showing entirely different result is quite simple. As the operated area also includes leased-in land it results in movement of some of the farmers with leased-in land to upper size categories, while there is no such addition to bottom size category. More so, any farmer in top size category increasing size of land holding by leasing-in land remains in that category only. Thus, the frequency of farmers leasing-in land gets reduced in the bottom category and increases in the top category resulting in a bias in favour of large size category and against bottom size category. Opposite holds true for lease-out phenomenon which results in movement of some farmers from upper size category to lower size category which would exaggerate incidence of lease-out of land in bottom category and underestimate it in top size category, when size classes are formed based on operational area of holdings.

Unless inter-class movement due to leased-in and leased-out land exactly cancel each other there are bound to be variations in results based on size of ownership holdings and operational holdings. This raises the question that which of the two, out of ownership and operational holdings, is appropriate, for making size classes to study the phenomenon of lease-in and lease-out of land in relation to farm size.

Table 10.4: Pattern of Land Ownership of Sample Farms, Ludhiana District

Village/ Farm Size Category	*Average size acre*	*Area per person acre*	*Distribution of area (%)*	*Per cent farmers leasing in land*	*Category share in lease in area (%)*	*Land rent per acre (Rs.)*	*Average size acre*	*Distribution of area (%)*	*Operated area leased in (%)*	*Per cent farmers leasing in land*	*Category share in lease in area (%)*	*Share of leased in land in operated area*
Bullowal												
Marginal	1.51	0.29	8	50s	38	5438	1.75	9	8.57	8	3	9
Small	3.87	0.55	17	26	18	5436	3.63	15	13.22	22	9	13
Medium	7.18	0.91	31	16	23	5000	7.40	30	32.97	53	29	33
Large	16.42	1.84	44	50	20	5327	19.20	49	32.97	92	60	33
Average	5.99	0.86	100	35	100	5316	6.31	100	27.26	35	100	27
Toose												
Marginal	0.92	0.16	5	71	24	6577	1.51	5	38.41	42	4	38
Small	3.96	0.61	17	35	12	7079	3.91	11	12.28	14	3	12
Medium	7.27	0.94	33	43	31	6393	7.39	23	30.04	60	17	30
Large	20.60	1.57	45	50	33	6716	25.50	37	47.06	82	76	47
Average	6.13	0.82	100	51	100	6624	9.13	100	39.21	51	100	39
Khanjarwal												
Marginal	1.60	0.25	5	27	6	4109	1.57	4	1.27	5	0	1
Small	3.90	0.54	18	48	55	5740	3.78	15	6.61	13	2	7
Medium	7.58	0.94	37	17	12	4083	7.84	32	24.36	39	22	24
Large	14.96	1.46	40	38	28	6004	21.10	47	48.34	80	76	48
Average	6.54	0.83	100	32	100	5523	7.86	100	34.10	32	100	34
Lalton												
Marginal	1.73	0.26	11	38	19	4630	1.85	7	0.00	0	0	0
Small	3.88	0.51	29	46	32	5628	3.97	17	11.84	21	3	12
Medium	7.42	0.90	36	50	30	5979	7.80	22	36.79	67	25	37
Large	18.00	1.80	24	40	19	6426	22.98	18	58.75	87	72	59
Average	4.98	0.65	100	44	100	5698	8.52	100	43.90	44	100	44
Ludhiana												
Marginal	1.42	0.24	7	48	20	5528	1.68	6	11.31	14	2	11
Small	3.90	0.55	20	40	29	5839	3.81	14	11.29	19	4	11
Medium	7.37	0.92	34	30	25	5802	7.64	26	30.89	55	22	31
Large	17.19	1.63	39	45	25	6307	22.46	38	47.95	85	72	48
Average	5.91	0.79	100	40	100	5886	7.96	100	36.81	40	100	37

In our opinion, the size classification based on own area, rather than operated area, is more appropriate to know the relationship between farm size and incidence of land tenancy, because of following reasons: One, own area is stable whereas operated area keeps on varying depending upon the area leased-in and leased-out. Two, compared to operated area, own area is considered better indicator of socio-economic status of household. Three, various policies like land ceiling and development of weaker sections take own area into consideration. Four, when the purpose is to study the incidence of lease-in or lease-out of land in relations to the size status it is appropriate to use only own area because it is independent of the phenomenon being studied whereas operated area is not an independent variable.

The next issue concerning the relation between farm size and land lease is the selection of indicators. For instance, land lease can be studied using any of the following indicators:

(i) Proportion of farmers in various size categories undertaking land lease.
(ii) Share of different categories in leased land *vis-à-vis* their share in own land.
(iii) Area leased per farm household.

The share of various size classes in leased-in land has already been discussed in detail in the previous section. per cent of farmers leasing-in land in different size groups in our sample shows a mixed pattern in various villages while aggregate sample of all the villages indicates that 48 per cent marginal, 45 per cent large, 40 per cent medium and 30 per cent small cultivators for go for leasing-in land (Table 10.4, i.e. size classification based on own area). As expected, when size classification is done according to operated area, proportion of farmers leasing-in land, in bottom categories, declined sharply to below 20 per cent and that in medium and large categories rose to 55 and 80 per cent. But, as discussed above land lease-incidence in relation to size of holding based on area of ownership holding is better indicator compared to the holding classification based on these results it can be inferred that when area is used as an indicator, marginal and small farmers are found to be leasing-in considerably higher area compared to upper size categories and when the number is used as the indicator, relation between leasing-in of land and farm size is U-shaped. We are not commenting on the relationship between incidence of lease-out of land and farm size, as our sample consists only of cultivating households, and those households who leased-out their entire cultivable land are not represented in the sample.

Distribution of sample households according to size categories of operational holdings indicate that about 20 per cent household operate on large size holdings above 10 acres and 27 per cent marginal size holdings below 2 acres. Small and medium farmer constitute about 26 and 27 per cent of the total cultivating households.

Village-wise, concentration of marginal farmers is highest in Bullowal, followed by Khanjarwal. Pooling of small and marginal size categories show that Bullowal and Toose villages have the highest concentration of this category. Concentration of large farmers is highest in Toose village and lowest in Bullowal village.

Average size of holding in different villages varies between 1.50 to 1.75 acre for marginal category 3.63 to 3.99 for small, 7.40 to 7.84 for medium and 19.20 to 25.50 for large size category. Aggregate of all categories show that the average farm size is highest in Tosse (9.13 acre) and lowest in Bullowal (6.31 acre).

Farm Size and Crop Performance

Farm size related variation and differences in net return per unit area and use of major inputs can be seen from Tables 10.5 and 10.6. Aggregate data of all the four sample villages indicate that value of output per acre of net area under cultivation was Rs. 11506 at marginal farms, Rs. 12436 at small and Rs. 12682 at large farms. Medium sized farms obtained highest productivity per unit of land.

Table 10.5: Productivity and Return from Aggregate Crop Production According to Farm Size Categories 1993-94

Particulars	*Village*	*Marginal*	*Small*	*Medium*	*Large*	*Aggregate*
Total values productivity	Bullowal	11159	12258	13443	12091	12344
	Toose	11577	12240	13026	12456	12491
	Khanjarwa	11678	12760	14147	12892	13201
	Lalton	12197	12625	15187	13189	13644
	Ludhiana	11506	12436	14011	12682	12970
Net return over cost all	Bullowal	6816	7535	7409	7255	7319
	Toose	6975	6785	7957	7363	7422
	Khanjarwa	7295	8145	9245	8118	8424
	Lalton	7877	7971	10499	8214	8826
	Ludhiana	6983	7573	8887	7703	7991

In all the villages, output per unit area increased with farm size upto medium size holding and declined thereafter. Lowest productivity is recorded at the farm having size below 2.5 acres. It can be inferred from these results that the relationship between farm size and productivity is of inverted U-type.

The large size farm category in our case consists of all the farms having holding size above 10 acres. This could conceal the fact that some farm size within this broad category is more productive compared to medium size holdings. To explore this possibility large sized holdings were further divided into four categories having farm size 10-15 acres, 15-20 acres, 20 to 25 acres and more than 25 acres. Land productivity at these categories is shown below:

Table 10.6

Size of Large Holding	*Output per Acre (Rs.)*
10-15	11932
15-20	12998
20-25	12483
More than 25 Acres	12947

These figures show that land productivity at all the large holding size categories is lower than the medium size category and there is no definite size related pattern in land productivity among the holdings above 10 acres. Net return over cost A1 as well as over other types of costs like A2, B1, B2, C1 and C2 is also is also highest at medium size holdings while marginal farmers remained at the bottom (Table 10.5).

III
LAND CEILINGS AND LAND LEASE MARKETS

Indian agriculture is dominated by small holders. Average size of holding during 1990-91 was 1.55 hectare and it is decreasing with the division of holding under population pressure. About 78 per cent farmers operate on less than 2 hectare land and 60 per cent own less than 1 hectare holding. Proportion of farmers operating more than 10 hectare farm size is below 1.6 per cent, and they operate about 17 per cent land area.

A case has been made during the last few years for removal of land ceilings on ownership holding and for corporatisation of farming.

This is based on the logic that to take advantage of scale economies and to promote export oriented agriculture farm size must be very large. It is also felt that smaller size holdings cannot go for production of high value crops due to diseconomies in marketing small lot of surplus. It is also argued that small and marginal holdings are not viable and removal of land ceiling would provide much needed impetus to growth and development (Johl, 1995). Similarly, Dandekar (1994) is of the view that continuation of ceiling on holding area and existing law on lease market inhibits fullest exploitation of technology and denies opportunity for growth to dynamic farmers. Based on this Dandekar strongly pleaded for upward relaxation in land ceilings.

On the other hand some researchers do not agree with the logic of economies of scale and do not find justification in removing land ceiling and consider agriculture as a safety net in the process of economic reforms (Rao, 1995 and Vyas, 1994). However, Vyas (1991) acknowledges problem of sustaining tiny holding how so ever efficient they are.

Another alternative to encourage non-viable small farmers to move out of agriculture and to expand size of operational holding is "freeing the lease market for land". This requires change in land lease laws. The existing land lease laws are such that they create fear in the mind of land owners that it would be difficult to get the land back if it is once leased-out. There are many rural households who are not genuinely interested in farming but they are not willing to sell land for social reason and also due to economic reason because land value generally appreciates faster than deposits. However, these households are willing to lease-out land to earn rent income. Creation of active lease market with full security to get the land back would increase availability of land for cultivation by reducing fallow land, results in reduction in number of cultivator and expand size of operational holdings.

It seems that liberalization of land lease would be more helpful than removal of land ceiling in expanding farm size. In our opinion relaxation or removal of land ceiling would not enable genuine farmers to significantly increase farm size. Establishing big farm at one place assumes that several farmers having contiguous land or land in the same area would be willing to dispose of their land. This assumption would be rarely met. The only place where land for establishing large farms would be available is wasteland which do not belong to private individuals. There is justification for allowing relaxation in land ceiling for those type of land because reclaiming such land require huge resources and capital. Thus large sized farms can come up in such areas as it has happened in Terai area of Western Uttar Pradesh.

Inability of relaxation in land ceiling to give rise to large size holdings is also evident from another fact. The existing ceiling limits permit holding up to 18 acre (7.28 hectare) of irrigated land with two crops, 27 acres (10.93 hectare) of irrigated land with one crop and about 50 acres for dry land in majority of the states. This simply mean that if land for purchase was available in the market and if there was sufficient interest and attractive economic returns available on expanding and establishing farms upto these limits, then country would have witnessed increase in farm size as well as proportion of farmers in the upper land holding size category. In reality what has happened is reverse of this. The reason for this is that not many farmers even in marginal size category are willing to sell their land because they have no alternative source to get employment and earn livelihood. *We strongly feel that removal of ceiling on land would neither help in reducing number of un-viable tiny holdings nor it would help in expanding farm size.* The only way to reduce the number of tiny and un-viable holdings is to provide alternative employment to workers from cultivator class outside agriculture, while farm size can be expanded by liberalizing land lease, protecting security of ownership.

REFERENCES

Dandekar, V. M. (1994). *The Indian Economy 1947-92*, Volume 1, Agriculture, Ch.6, Sage Publications, New Delhi.

Johl, S. S., (1995). "Agriculture Sector and New Economic Policy", *Indian Journal of Agricultural Economics*, Conference No. 50 (3) July-September.

Rao, C. H. Hanumantha (1994). "Reforming Agriculture in the New Context". *Economic and Political Weekly*, 29(16/17): 1005-1010, April 16/23.

Rao C. H. Hanumantha (1995) "Liberalization of Agriculture in India: Some Major Issues", *Indian Journal of Agricultural Economics*, 50(3), July-September.

Ramesh Chand (1999). *Agricultural Diversification in India*, Mittal Publication, New Delhi, Ch. 5.

Vyas, V. S. (1999). "Efficiency and Equity in Indian Agriculture—Can the Twins Meet?" in Ramesh Chand and V. P. S. Arora (ed.) *Agricultural Inputs and Output Market Reforms in India*, Agricultural Economic Research Association (India), New Delhi.

Chapter 11

Sharecropping Tenancy and Terms of Access to Land to the Poor: A Comparative Study

A. P. SINGH

I
INTRODUCTION

The purpose of land reforms is two-fold. On the one hand, "it aims to make more rational reordering of the limited and useful land resources by affecting conditions of holdings, imposing ceiling that cultivation can be done in most economical and efficient manner without any waste of labour and capital. At the same time it also explores the possibility of utilising the wasteland". On the other hand, land reforms serves as a means of redistributing agricultural land to the underprivileged classes, and of improving the terms and conditions on which the lands are tenanted to the actual tillers.

The entire concept of land reforms aims at the abolition of intermediaries and endeavours to benefit the actual cultivator. Tenancy reform is one of the main aspects of land reforms. The provisions for the security of tenancy and rent regulation are intended to provide a congenial atmosphere ensuring that the tenant feels secure of reaping the fruits of his labour. This paper is an attempt to compare the status of the sharecropping tenancy in Tamil Nadu and Uttar Pradesh.

It is widely felt that if production has to be raised, cultivation should be properly organised and supported by various inputs. If the tenant suffers insecurities of different sorts, production is bound to fall. And if the State ensures, full protection against eviction, with various programmes for rural development the production turns out to be better. Ultimately both the tenant and the landlord is in advantageous position. Therefore, attempts should be made for the identification, registration and protection of informal, oral or any other type of tenancy. This is the most important and a difficult task of tenancy reforms. Tamil Nadu government took steps for as early as in 1955 to sort out this issue. The Tamil Nadu Cultivating Tenants Protection Act, 1955 is intended to protect the cultivating tenants from the threat of being evicted. This act specifies various grounds under which eviction can be made by the landowner. The Tamil Nadu Cultivating Tenants (Payment of Fair Rent) Act, 1956, seeks to ensure the payment of fair rent by the tenants. This Act fixes the liability of the tenant to pay and the right of the landowner to collect the fair rent payable under this Act. This also fixes the respective liabilities of the tenants and the landlords to meet the various costs of cultivation. Section 4 of this Act attempts to quantify the fair rent payable to the tenants. The fair rent can be in cash or kind as per the contract between the landowner and the tenant or at the option of the tenant. In 1972, the Tamil Nadu Cultivating Tenants Arrears of Rent (Relief) Act was passed to provide protection to the tenants against eviction on grounds of arrears of rent. Under Section 3 of this Act, if the current rent (rent of the *Fasli* year from 1 July, 1971 to 30 June, 1972) was deposited then all the previous arrears are deemed to have been discharged. The Tamil Nadu Agricultural Lands Record of Tenancy Rights Act, 1969 provides for the registration of the names of the persons cultivating the agricultural land of private landowners and of public trusts in the State. Under this Act, Records of Tenancy Rights have been prepared by entering full details of the registered tenants therein for safeguarding the interests of the tenants. As far as tenancy legislation is concerned Tamil Nadu did well. Referring to the achievement of Tamil Nadu's achievement under recording of tenancy, B. K. Sinha observes "Tamil Nadu has achieved, very similar to what West Bengal has done through 'Operation Barga' but in the regular course of administration sans the fanfare. It bespeaks of the inner strength of governance in the state (Sinha, 1999). The progress of recording of tenancy in Tamil Nadu is captured in the Annexure I. The acts can secure the tenure but security is not sufficient to the tenants. In contest of Uttar Pradesh, the State government did nothing directly to the tenancy reform but in spite of that the condition of tenants in the State is not worse than Tamil Nadu. This clearly indicates that only tenancy reforms are not enough to improve the condition of the tenants. The local situation and agricultural practices should also be linked with the tenancy reforms. There may be many reasons for that situation. To clarify this problem it is necessary to study various aspects of the problem like differences in ownership and operational patterns, differences in input and output sharing and in leasing pattern.

Structural Distribution of Holdings

The main objectives of this part are: (i) to study the changes, if any, in the distribution of ownership and operational holdings in the States of Tamil Nadu and Uttar Pradesh, and (ii) to see the extent to which the farmers and farms still suffer from size disincentive and tenurial disabilities. The principal tool of analysis used in this exercise is Ginni Coefficient. Concentration of ownership and operational holdings as revealed from the NSS 37th round and 48th round may be seen from Table 11.1.

Table 11.1: Concentration of Ownership Holdings in Tamil Nadu and Uttar Pradesh (37th and 48th Rounds)

Broad Classes	*Tamil Nadu*				*Uttar Pradesh*			
	% of households		*% of area*		*% of households*		*% of area*	
	1982	*1992*	*1982*	*1992*	*1982*	*1992*	*1982*	*1992*
Marginal	81.85	87.13	23.57	33.28	67.95	74.40	20.36	27.42
Small	10.89	8.01	27.24	26.24	17.38	14.73	24.08	24.88
Semi-Medium	4.95	3.81	23.53	24.15	10.23	7.92	28.11	25.82
Medium	2.16	0.92	20.94	12.15	4.06	2.76	22.25	18.14
Large	0.16	1.11	4.71	4.18	0.37	0.21	5.18	3.73
Ginni Coefficient	0.6244	0.5429			0.5542	0.523		

Source: Sarvekshana, Vol. XIX, No. 2, 65th issue October-December 1995.

Table 11.1 indicates that inequality in the distribution of ownership holdings is more in Tamil Nadu than in Uttar Pradesh in 1982 as well as 1992. Uttar Pradesh showed further decline in inequality in 1992. However, during 1982-1992, the rate of decline in concentration of ownership holdings was much steeper in Tamil

Nadu than in Uttar Pradesh. However, the share of landless households is greater in Tamil Nadu (17.9%), as compared to India (11.3%) and Uttar Pradesh (4.9%).

Now we shall 'urn to the pattern of operational holdings in both the States, based on the data of the NSS of 37th and 48th round. Table 11.2 shows that in the case of operational holdings too, the concentration ratio or inequality is higher in Tamil Nadu than in Uttar Pradesh. And this difference persists from 1982 to 1992 as well. However, for operational holdings, the Ginni ratio for Tamil Nadu shows a decline from 0.56 in 1982 to 0.53 in 1992, where as in Uttar Pradesh the Ginni ratio for the same period shows an increase from a relatively low of 0.43 to a high of almost 0.50. If these trends continue, one can read that operation of the lease markets moving in two directions. While in Tamil Nadu the lease markets appear to be moving towards loosening of the land concentration in agricultural operations, in Uttar Pradesh it appears to move towards concentration.

A comparative reading of Tables 11.1 and 11.2, also reveal certain interesting aspects of operation of lease markets and the question of inequality in access to land. In both Tamil Nadu and Uttar Pradesh, in both 1982 and 1992 the share of the area operated by marginal farmers was less than the share in the area of ownership. In Tamil Nadu, in 1982 the semi-medium holdings appear to be net-gainers of operational holdings, but by 1992 the operational land gain seems to be in favour of medium and large holders. This doesn't appear to alter the declining land concentration probably because of the land gain by way of ownership by the marginal farmers appear to be high enough. In Uttar Pradesh, the semi-medium and medium holdings show net additions to land operated.

Table 11.2: Concentration of Operational Holdings in Tamil Nadu and Uttar Pradesh (37th and 48th Rounds)

Broad Classes	*Tamil Nadu*				*Uttar Pradesh*			
	% of households		*% of area*		*% of households*		*% of area*	
	1982	*1992*	*1982*	*1992*	*1982*	*1992*	*1982*	*1992*
Marginal	71.37	77.17	22.39	28.94	59.60	68.01	18.09	24.96
Small	16.72	14.14	26.72	28.06	21.58	18.52	23.76	26.31
Semi-Medium	8.28	6.62	25.37	24.72	12.88	9.85	28.04	26.30
Medium	3.35	1.80	20.68	13.22	5.40	3.33	23.62	18.18
Large	0.28	0.27	4.84	5.06	0.54	0.29	6.49	4.25
Ginni Coefficient	0.5561	0.5263			0.432	0.4988		

Source: Sarvekshana, Vol. XX, No 3, 70th issue January-March 1997.

Land Lease Markets

Though the measures of land reform undertaken since Independence appear to have deterred the growth of exploitative tenancy, there is still a high proportion of tenanted land in total operated area. The NSS data of 37th and 48th rounds show that in Tamil Nadu the percentage share of leased-in area is the same for both the rounds. There may be various reasons for constant leasing in the State. An important reason is non-profitable agriculture under tenancy. Another reason could be the implementation of registration of tenancy in the State. Landlords do not want to give their land on lease because they have fear of loosing their land. On the other hand in Uttar Pradesh the leasing is increasing as per the NSS data. It clearly shows that tenancy is profitable here. Landlords do not have any fear to give their land on leasing due to acceptance of informal tenancy in the State. Registered tenancy ensures security and identity to the tenant but it appears to induce fear of loss of land among owners of the land.

Terms of Land Lease Markets in Tamil Nadu

To examine the arrangement of sharing of inputs and output, we used the data collected by the IAS Probationers during the year 1991 and 1994. The Probationers surveyed 18 villages in 6 districts of 5 sub-zones of Tamil Nadu. There are three types of tenancy prevalent in the State. Here, the terms of lease under sharecropping are being examined, since the sharing of inputs between landlord and tenant is a phenomenon associated with sharecropping but not with other forms of tenancy like fixed kind rent and fixed cash rent. According to Bardhan (1984) pure tenant is likely to prefer share tenancy where rental share is collected at the time of harvest. Similarly, the landlord under share tenancy has also a special incentive to give production loan since he shares in outcome of its use. The Bardhan (1984) also points out that the tenanted area under sharecropping will be higher in the case of more labour intensive crops where harvest wages are higher and where employment is larger. Laxminaryan and Tyagi (1982) on the other hand, argue that inferior bargaining power and paucity of cash resources compel the small tenants to accept crop sharing arrangements and sharecropping arrangement is also influenced by historical factors. Both sharecropping and fixed kind rent have historical pattern in different areas of the State. The fixed kind rent in particular was the most important form of tenancy in areas with canal irrigation and in other areas sharecropping was the major form. Sharecropping continues to persist in areas where it was historically prevalent as also where concealed tenancy is very high. Further the study of Bardhan (1984) also maintains that when the landlord does not share in the cost, crop share to the tenant is generally higher, and when the landlord shares in the costs, the tenant's crop share is lower. The arrangement of crop share between sharecropper and the landlord is being examined in this light. Table 11.3 shows the share in produce of the tenants.

Table 11.3: Distribution of Tenants by Share of Gross Produce in Tamil Nadu

Sub-zone	*Tenant's*	*Crop Share of Tenant*							
		Nil	*1/4*	*1/3*	*1/2*	*2/3*	*3/4*	*1*	*Total*
North	%	0	2.5	15	82.5	0	0	0	100
Eastern	Number	0	1	6	33	0	0	0	40
Cauvery	%	2.86	0	28.57	40	28.57	0	0	100
Delta	Number	1	0	10	14	10	0	0	35
Western	%	0	0	0	27.27	72.73	0	0	100
	Number	0	0	0	3	8	0	0	11
Southern	%	0	14.28	28.56	48.57	2.86	0	5.72	100
	Number	0	5	10	17	1	0	2	35
Total	%	0.83	4.96	21.49	55.37	15.70	0	1.65	100
	Number	1	6	26	67	19	0	2	121

Source: IAS Probationers' District Assignment Reports on Land Reforms, 1991-1994, LBSNAA.

Table 11.3 shows that 55.37 per cent of the sharecroppers get half the gross produce, 15.70 per cent get two-third of the produce and 26.45 per cent get one-third of the gross produce. There is considerable variation sub-zone wise in the share of produce to the sharecroppers. In North Eastern Zone 82.50 per cent of the sharecroppers get half the share of gross produce, in Cauvery Delta Zone, 40 per cent of them get half the share of gross produce, 28.57 per cent get two-third share of the gross produce and rest get much lower share. In western Zone 27.27 per cent get half the share of the produce and 72.72 per cent get two-third share of the produce, in Southern Zone 48.57 per cent get half the share of gross produce, 2.86 per cent get two-third share of gross produce and rest get much lower share of the gross produce. The terms of sharing of input cost between landowners and sharecroppers can be seen in Table 11.4.

Table 11.4: Distribution of Tenants by Share of Input in Tamil Nadu

Sub-zone	Tenant's	Cost Share of Tenant							
		Nil	*1/4*	*1/3*	*1/2*	*2/3*	*3/4*	*1*	*Total*
North	%	00	0	0	12.5	0	0	87.50	100
Eastern	Number	00	0	0	5	0	0	35	40
Cauvery	%	11.43	0	11.43	0	0	0	77.14	100
Delta	Number	04	0	4	0	0	0	27	35
Western	%	00	0	72.73	9.09	0	0	18.18	100
	Number	00	0	8	1	0	0	02	11
Southern	%	00	0	0	0	0	0	100	100
	Number	00	0	0	0	0	0	35	35
Total	%	03.31	0	9.92	4.96	0	0	81.82	100
	Number	04	0	12	6	0	0	99	121

Source: IAS Probationers' District Assignment Reports on Land Reforms, 1991-1994, LBSNAA.

It is seen that at the State level, 81.82 per cent of the sharecroppers meet the entire cost of inputs and labour charges, in 3.31 per cent of the cases the landowners meet the entire cost and only in 14.88 per cent of the cases the input cost is shared between the landowners and the tenants. There is also considerable variation sub-zone-wise in the share of inputs of the sharecroppers. In North Eastern Zone, 12.50 per cent of the cases shared equally and 87.50 per cent of the tenants meet entire cost. In Cauvery Delta Zone, 11.43 per cent landowners meet entire cost themselves, but in 77.14 per cent of the cases, entire cost is paid by the tenants. In Western Zone, 72.73 per cent of the tenants shared one-third in the inputs, 9.09 per cent shared equally and in 18.18 per cent cases entire cost is meet by the tenants. In Southern Zone, the pattern in the input sharing is very much surprising. In this Zone all tenants bearing all the cost of the cultivation. It would be appropriate to examine the cost and crop sharing simultaneously as given in Table 11.5.

Table 11.5 reveals that 112 (92.56 %) out of the 121 cases of tenancy are on the produce share ranging from one third to two-thirds gained to the land owner. But the most frequent common is 50 per cent produce sharing in almost 60 per cent of the cases. Regarding the sharing of the input cost, in almost 85 per cent of the cases the tenants bear the entire cost. The form of tenancy where the tenant bears the entire cost of inputs and shares half the produce terms out to be the most common in practice. The extreme form of exploitation where entire costs are borne by the tenants and at the same time offering two-thirds produce share to the owner, also exists in 10 per cent of the cases. A very meagre proportion of about 4 per cent tenants, also appear to get away with sharing just 25 per cent of the produce, in some cases the owners sharing a part of the costs too. But that is exceptional.

Table 11.5: Distribution of Tenants by Share of Gross Produce to Input Share in Tamil Nadu

Input Share	*Gross Produce Share*							
	Nil	*1/4*	*1/3*	*1/2*	*2/3*	*3/4*	*1*	*Total*
Nil	0	0	3	1	0	0	0	4
1/4	0	0	0	0	0	0	0	0
1/3	0	2	2	0	8	0	0	12
1/2	0	0	0	6	0	0	0	6
2/3	0	0	0	0	0	0	0	0
3/4	0	0	0	0	0	0	0	0
1	1	4	18	63	11	0	2	99
Total	1	6	23	70	19	0	2	121

Source: IAS Probationers' District Assignment Reports on Land Reforms, 1991-1994, LBSNAA.

As per the statutory provisions of tenancy reforms legislation in the State, the tenant should get 75 per cent of the share of the gross produce. As per this statutory norm all the sharecroppers get less than the prescribed fair rent. Thus all the sharecroppers are placed in an exploitative situation with respect to the payment of fair payment and bulk of them are placed in highly exploitative terms because the gap between the prescribed statutory norms and what they are actually getting is quite big.

Uttar Pradesh, in contrast to Tamil Nadu, hardly did anything to bring tenancy into legal fold. IAS probationers also surveyed the 11 districts of 6 different sub-zones of Uttar Pradesh during 1991 to 1994. They surveyed 20 villages of the State. Some of their reports are analysed here.

II
TERMS OF LAND LEASE MARKETS IN UTTAR PRADESH

Srivastava (1989), studied two villages of Eastern U.P. where the predominant share between landlord and tenant was 50 : 50. In the sharing of by-products two trends were observed. It was either equally shared or wholly belonged to the tenants. A higher rent (2/3rd and 3/4th) was also found in small number of transactions, which was prominent in the agriculturally advanced area of the Western U.P., where the by-products were also shared in proportion to the crop share. These higher rents are confined to the poor and lower middle peasants. The study by Sharma and Dreze (1990) points out that the standard contracts are *aadah batai*; *tihai* and *chauthai*, which entail three specific profiles of input and output shares. It would be extremely rare, for the landlord and tenant to design a tenancy contract with non-standard terms. However, there is no standardization of the fixed rate contract. The amount of rent paid is a matter of mutual agreement between the partners.

Sharma and Dreze (1990) adduced some important reasons for the prevalence of the 50 : 50 crop share between the tenant and landowner. They argue that the persistence of this pattern of sharing is usually when credit is a major constraint and when the tenants and landlords have similar endowments and prices. In such a case, the cost sharing of 50 : 50 assumes the minimization of joint costs. The second reason adduced by them is the advantage of equal sharing of costs, along with the general case of having similar output and input share on efficiency grounds. The 50 : 50 rule has proved so resilient that cost sharing has emerged as an adaptation to the requirement of modern agriculture. Relating to the sharing of cost, Srivastava (1989) observed in the study that landlords in one Eastern U.P. village did not at all share the input cost. On the other hand, the cost of certain inputs are shared in proportion to output, in one village of Eastern U.P. and in the village of Western U.P. the traditional cost sharing arrangements involved only the sharing of seed and fertilizers and the tenants had to bear the responsibility of supplying the inputs. The introduction of canal irrigation has been instrumental in including irrigation charges as a part of the terms of lease. The input cost generally shared included seed, fertilizers and irrigation charges. In the agriculturally advanced village of Western U.P., Srivastava (1989) found that the traditional cost sharing arrangements have been overridden by a new scheme of the landlord contributing three-fourths of the cost in over 60 per cent cases. The traditional cost shares have been adjusted to include new inputs and the tenancy situation is in a dynamic flux. This has facilitated productivity gains, but the major changes are towards not only sharing the cost of some input but also towards the increase of the share for landlords of both input and output. The study by Sharma and Dreze (1990) shows that the cost sharing is a part of sharecropping contract. Input and output shares according to them, are conducive to productivity efficiency. The basic principle of equal sharing of output and non-labour input is very widespread. In this background we have to analyze the trends in the cost and produce sharing. In Uttar Pradesh also, three types of tenancy are prevalent, i.e. Sharecropping, fixed kind rent and fixed cash rent. Sharecropping is the major form of the tenancy, and 137 out of 161 have leased-in land on this basis. The following table shows the pattern of sharing gross produce between tenant and landowner in all the sub-zones.

Table 11.6: Distribution of Tenants by Share of Gross Produce in Uttar Pradesh

Sub-zone	*Tenant's*	*Crop Share of Tenant*						
		Nil	*1/4*	*1/3*	*1/2*	*2/3*	*3/4*	*1*
North Eastern	%	0	0	68.42	31.58	0	0	0
Plains	Number	0	0	13	06	0	0	0
Eastern UP	%	0	0	0	100	0	0	0
Plains	Number	0	0	0	8	0	0	0
Central UP	%	0	0	0	100	0	0	0
Plains	Number	0	0	0	11	0	0	0
North Western	%	0	0	0	100	0	0	0
Plains	Number	0	0	0	39	0	0	0
South Western	%	0	6.25	2.08	91.67	0	0	0
UP Plains	Number	0	3	1	45	0	0	0
Bundelkhand	%	0	0	18.18	81.82	0	0	0
	Number	0	0	2	9	0	0	0
Total	%	0	2.19	11	86.13	0	0	0
	Number	0	3	16	118	0	0	0

Source: IAS Probationers' District Assignment Reports on Land Reforms, 1991-1994, LBSNAA.

Table 11.6 shows that predominant pattern in all the sub-zones is equal sharing of gross produce between tenant and landowner.

This is also broadly consistent with other studies, which have 50 : 50 share of the produce as the standard norms. However, there is considerable variation with respect to the sharing of inputs, which could be seen from Table 11.7.

Table 11.7: Distribution of Tenants by Share of Inputs in Uttar Pradesh

Sub-zone	*Tenant's*	*Cost Share of Tenant*						
		Nil	*1/4*	*1/3*	*1/2*	*2/3*	*3/4*	*1*
North Eastern	%	0	0	0	26.32	5.26	0	36.84
Plains	Number	0	0	0	5	1	0	13
Eastern UP	%	0	0	0	100	0	0	0
Plains	Number	0	0	0	8	0	0	0
Central UP	%	0	0	0	100	0	0	0
Plains	Number	0	0	0	11	0	0	0
North Western	%	0	0	0	71.79	25.64	0	2.56
Plains	Number	0	0	0	28	10	0	1
South Western	%	8.16	0	2.04	85.71	0	0	4.08
UP Plains	Number	4	0	1	42	0	0	2
Bundelkhand	%	0	0	18.18	81.82	0	0	0
	Number	0	0	2	9	0	0	0
Total	%	2.92	0	2.19	69.34	13.87	0	11.68
	Number	4	0	3	95	19	0	16

Source: IAS Probationers' District Assignment Reports on Land Reforms, 1991-1994, LBSNAA.

There are three distinct patterns of cost sharing which emerge in Uttar Pradesh. First sharing of cost equally between the landowner and the tenant. This accounts for 95 cases i.e. 69.34 per cent of the total cases. Second, where two-thirds of the cost borne by the tenant and one-third by landowner and this accounts for 19 cases, i.e. 13.87 per cent of the total cases. The third pattern is one where the entire cost is borne by the tenant and this accounts for 16 cases, i.e. 11.68 per cent of the total cases.

The first pattern has been noticed overwhelmingly in Central UP Plains (100%), South Western UP Plains (85.71%), Bundelkhand (81.82%), North Western Plains (71.79%) and North Eastern Plains (26.32%). The second pattern in Eastern UP Plains (100%), North Western Plains (25.64 %) and North Eastern Plains (5.26%). The third pattern prevalent in North Eastern Plain (68.42%), South Western UP Plain (4.08%) and North Western Plain (2.56%). The combined picture of relationship between the crop and the cost sharing is presented in Table 11.8.

Table 11.8: Distribution of Tenants by Share of Gross Produce and Input Share in Uttar Pradesh

Input Share	*Gross Produce Share*							
	Nil	*1/4*	*1/3*	*1/2*	*2/3*	*3/4*	*1*	*Total*
Nil	0	3	1	0	0	0	0	4
1/4	0	0	0	0	0	0	0	0
1/3	0	0	2	1	0	0	0	3
1/2	0	0	0	88	0	0	0	88
2/3	0	0	0	19	0	0	0	19
3/4	0	0	0	0	0	0	0	0
1	0	0	13	10	0	0	0	23
Total	0	3	16	118	0	0	0	137

We divide the whole pattern of input and output sharing into four broad categories. The description of the different category is as follows:

- *First*, 'highly favourable' to tenants where the tenant bears the entire cost and retains two-thirds of the produce. There is no case in UP of any tenant getting more than 50 per cent of the produce share, even if the cost share is 100 per cent.
- *Second*, the cost and crop share is equally shared between the landlord and tenant. This practice is very much prevalent in the Uttar Pradesh. Probationers' field studies found 88 (64.23 %) cases of this practice. This category is 'moderately favourable' to tenants.
- *Third*, the tenants bear the entire cost of cultivation and receive half the share of the gross produce. The State has ten cases of this type. This category is 'exploitative' to the tenants.
- *Fourth*, the tenants bear the entire cost of cultivation and receive one-third to one-fourth of the gross produce. This category is 'highly exploitative' and Uttar Pradesh has thirteen instances of this type of practice. There could be other variations but the above four-way classification captures the nature of the terms of tenancy prevailing in Tamil Nadu and Uttar Pradesh.

III
CONCLUDING OBSERVATIONS

Here we compare the existing practices in two States on the basis of the categories defined above. Table 11.9 indicates that 70.20 per cent of the sharecroppers in Tamil Nadu are in more vulnerable situation as compared to only 31 per cent of the sharecroppers of Uttar Pradesh. They receive less payment displaying high degree of exploitation. Thus the status of the sharecroppers in Tamil Nadu is quite pathetic. At this juncture a strong administrative and legal intervention is necessary to ensure their right to fair rent. The high performance of Tamil Nadu in tenancy above, as observed earlier, may not ensure fair deal to the tenants.

Table 11.9: Terms of Tenancy in Tamil Nadu and U.P.

Category	*Percentage of Tenants*	
	Tamil Nadu	*Uttar Pradesh*
Highly Exploitative	18.18	9.49
Exploitative	52.06	21.90
Moderately Favourable	20.67	68.61
Highly Favourable	9.09	0

On the other hand, Uttar Pradesh, which has highest incidence of tenurial insecurity, have some better position in terms of sharing. Security of tenants is a most important element in any tenancy reform programme. The sharecroppers in Uttar Pradesh are not regarded as a tenants because of the fact that tenancy is yet to be legitimated by the government. But in Tamil Nadu Sharecroppers are treated as partners in cultivation and are kept under the ambit of legal protection. This has resulted into a "sweet" relationship between the partners, as per repercussion agriculture does not suffer. Therefore, recording of the tenancy is the positive point of the Tamil Nadu. The issue of fair rent is inter-linked with the problem of security of tenure. So far the security of tenants in Tamil Nadu is concern, it is having fair amount of recorded tenants. In spite of this our findings says that the condition of the tenants is not very good in terms of input and output sharing.

West Bengal has tackled the problem of sharecroppers in a unique way. The State has passed laws giving heritable right of cultivation to sharecroppers. Share was fixed on 25-75 per cent basis (75% to sharecroppers). Tamil Nadu should also go like West Bengal. Taking an overview of the situation a fair conclusion w.r.t Tamil Nadu should be that too much of attempts were made through legislation to control various abuses in tenancy system, but their implementation had been unsatisfactory and tardy. Apart from inherent defects in law, too much reliance on not so sympathetic bureaucracy has invited resistance from the landowners. Failure to develop institutional support system to serve as links between clients and patrons, and inability or unwillingness to foster support from the organisations of beneficiaries were main reasons for partial success of all these legislative attempts towards tenancy reform.

ANNEXURE I

TENANTS REGISTERED UNDER TAMIL NADU RECORD OF TENANCY RIGHT ACT 1969

	Tenants Registered		*Registered Area*	
Year	*Number*	*% age*	*Extent*	*% age*
1972-73	388483	78.01	590164	84.92
1973-74	2253	0.45	2519	0.36
1974-75	8614	1.73	11215	1.61
1975-76	3163	0.64	1977	0.28
1976-77	4275	0.86	7595	1.09
1977-78	2358	0.47	2301	0.33
1978-80	25985	5.22	7969	1.15
1980-81	1100	0.22	2271	0.33
1981-82	1866	0.37	8529	1.23
1982-83	977	0.20	1462	0.21
1983-84	417	0.08	563	0.08
1984-85	91	0.02	111	0.02
1985-86	14	0.00	33	0.00
1986-87	16	0.00	46	0.01
1987-97	58388	11.72	58245	8.38
1997-98	0	0.00	0	0.00
Total	498000	100	695000	100

Source: Sinha, B. K. (1999) "Tenancy in Tamil Nadu: Evidence from the field" paper presented of National Workshop on "Whither Tenancy", LBSNAA, 24-25, September, 1999.

REFRENCES

Athreya, B., Djurfeldt, G. and Lindberg, S. (1990). *Barriers Broken: Production*

Relation and Agrarian Change in Tamil Nadu; Sage Publication, New Delhi.

Bardhan, Pranab K. (1984). *Land, Labour, and Rural Poverty: Essays in Development Economics*; Oxford University Press, Delhi.

Gough, Kathleen (1981). *Rural Society in South-East Asia*; Cambridge University Press, Cambridge.

Jafri, S. N. A. (1985). *The History and Status of Landlords and Tenants in the United Provinces*; Usha Publication, New Delhi.

Ledejinsky, Wolf (1965). *Study on Tenurial Conditions in Package Districts, Report of Ford Foundation Consultant*; Planning Commission, New Delhi.

Mencher, Joan (1978). *Agriculture and Social Structure in Tamil Nadu*; Carolina Academic Press, Durham.

Roy, S. C. (1988). *Land Revenue Administration in India*; Reliance Publishing House; New Delhi.

Shanker, Kripa (1980). *Concealed Tenancy and its Implications for Equity and Economic Growth: A Study of Uttar Pradesh*; Concept Publication; New Delhi.

Sharma, N. and Dreze, J. (1990). *Sharecropping in Palanpur*; London School of Economics, London.

Sinha, B. K. (1999). "Tenancy in Tamil Nadu: Evidence from the field" paper presented of National Workshop on "Whither Tenancy", LBSNAA, 24-25, September, 1999.

Singh, B. and Mishra, S. D. (1962). *A Study of Land Reforms in Uttar Pradesh*; Oxford University Publication; New Delhi.

Srivastava, Ravi (1989). "Tenancy Contracts during Transitions: A Study based on Field Work in Uttar Pradesh"; *Journal of Peasant Studies;* 16 (3); April 1989, pp 339-395.

Tripathy, R. N. (1985). *Tenancy and Efficiency of Farming in a Developing Economy*; Mittal Publication, Delhi.

IAS Probationers' *District Assignment Reports on Land Reforms*, 1991-1994, LBSNAA.

Chapter 12

Poverty Alleviation: Relative Roles of Land Lease and Sales Markets in a Prosperous Part of UP

GYANENDRA MANI and V. K. PANDEY

I
LAND AND THE POOR

With millions of farmers engaged in it, agriculture constitutes the largest, riskiest and most uncertain economic activity in the country. Land being the basis of production system and symbol of status particularly in rural India, the first State intervention during the post-independence era came in the form of legislative measures for land reforms which were aimed at eliminating feudal relations in the agrarian society, encouraging owners tillers and reducing tenancy to almost inability conditions. The legislation was based not only on the canons of justice and equity but also on the need to herald the advent of an agrarian revolution with benefits to cross-section of the different segments of rural farmers in particular and the rural economy in general. Apart from the tenancy aspect, consolidation of holdings with a view to making a fundamental change in the character of agriculture from 'subsistence' farming to 'economic' farming was another aspect of land reform measures where fragmented holdings were aimed to be brought together for consolidation. As far as enactment of legislation is concerned, nearly all the states except a few like Nagaland, Meghalaya, and Mizoram, which have predominantly communitarian land relation, have enacted the legislation by now which is aimed at the consolidation of each tiller's landholdings into one contiguous plot. However, the implementation has been found to be patchy and sporadic as the work has been completed only in states like Punjab, Haryana, and Western Uttar Pradesh and is in progress in some states like Orissa and Bihar. Although farms in India are typically small (average size of holding 1.5 hectare) throughout the country, the average size of land holding by state ranges from about 0.33 hectares in Kerala and 0.89 hectares in UP to 3.61 hectares in Punjab, 4.11 hectares in Rajasthan and 6.82 hectares in Nagaland.

The land reform measures concentrated mainly on abolition of intermediaries, security of tenancy and regulation of rents, consolidation of holdings, imposition of ceiling and redistribution of surplus land beyond ceiling among the landless. However, these institutional arrangements could not provide a solution to restrict the further fragmentation and regrouping of land holders into various size classes on account of inheritance and sale operations.

Despite the distribution of considerable extent of surplus land (nearly 1.9 million hectares by the end of Seventh Five Year Plan out of 2.9 million hectares of land declared surplus) amongst the landless farmers, the number of landless in rural areas has multiplied over the past few decades from 27.9 million in 1951 to over 50 million in the 1990s. It is understood that over two million small and marginal farmers now lose their land or are alienated from it each year. The latest report on the State of Food Insecurity in the World (SOFI, 2003) published by the Food and Agriculture Organization (FAO) of the United Nations has estimated that out of a total of 842 millions undernourished people in the world in 1999-2001, 214 millions, i.e. over 25 per cent, were in India alone (India has about 17 per cent of the world population). In India, the number of undernourished increased by the biggest magnitude of nearly 20 millions (compared to all other countries of the world) during the period 1995-97 to 1999-01.

The land being the prime factor, its ownership and distribution pattern not only directly influences its use pattern but also the investment and production decisions in agriculture. Although it appears that the policy objectives have served fairly well in transforming the traditional Indian famine-affected agriculture to the modern technology based self-sufficient production system. However, a large number of landless, some of whom were dispossessed of their entire land holdings could not be absorbed in the other sectors of the economy which require some skill either of technical nature (manufacturing sector) or of professional nature (service sector) and therefore, most of these landless have been working as wage earners.

Further, in a developing country like India, facing an ever increasing pressure on agricultural production due to population rise as well as economic development, the operations of both the land sale and land lease transactions in market for agricultural land are to be viewed seriously in the light of the State's social objectives of distributing agricultural land amongst the landless farmers which leads to the creation a number of non-viable marginal farms. There have been suggestions for a review on some of these land reforms and particularly for relaxation of restrictions on tenancy in agriculture. Rao and Gulati (1994) argued that freeing the lease market for land might contribute to equity as well as efficiency of resource use. Vyas (1994) suggested that the basic approach to land reforms should be to create as many viable land holdings as possible, by expansion of the land holdings of the small farmers, by encouraging them to lease-in land from other small land owners and by enabling them to have larger value added from agriculture. Krishnaswamy (1994) observed that the operative forces today are quite different. They tend to treat small holdings as uneconomic, and convert the small farmers into a tenant farmer or an agricultural labourer.

The operations of land market, in both the segments of sale and lease transactions, reveal the underlying dynamics of agricultural transformation and its implication towards the state policy on agricultural lands. Therefore, a close scrutiny of land sale and lease transactions may well reflect the direction and magnitude of the underlying changes taking place in the agrarian structure and the desirability of such changes under the new economic environment. This paper attempts to examine the pattern and implications of sale and lease transactions in agricultural lands in a highly developed and progressive area. The land market being highly localized, no generalization can be drawn from such a case study of an area as this, yet the emerging observations would definitely be a pointer towards a more generalized approach required in this direction.

Land Markets: A Sample Survey

The study was carried out in Meerut district, which is situated in the most fertile and highly developed Western region of Uttar Pradesh

State. A two-stage stratified random sampling was followed, where each of the total four tehsils of the districts was treated as separate strata. From each tehsil, ten patwari circles were selected randomly at the first stage. Then, at the second stage, ten cases of land sales and six cases of land lease were selected randomly from each patwari circle. Each sale case consisted of one seller and the respective buyer, and each lease case consisted of one lessor and the respective lessee. Thus, a total of 400 sellers, 400 buyers, 240 lessors and 240 lessees were randomly sampled and interviewed for the collection of data relating to their sale/lease transactions in agricultural lands made during the year 1991 (Mani, 1993). All the lease transactions which took place during the reference period of the study in the villages selected for studying the land sale market were listed and one transaction per village (maximum six transaction per patwari circle) was selected randomly.

II
LAND SALES MARKET

It may be observed from Table 12.1 that the marginal and small size-groups together constituted 75.8 per cent of the total sellers, and together sold 61.4 per cent of the total land transacted. But these two groups together constituted only 50.5 per cent of the total buyers and together bought only 39.2 per cent of the total land transacted. On the other hand, the medium and large size-groups together constituted 24.2 per cent of the total sellers, and together sold 38.6 per cent of the total land transacted. But both these latter groups together constituted 35 per cent of the total buyers, and together bought 49.6 per cent of the total land transacted. Apparently these transactions indicate a tendency towards an increasing concentration of land among the medium and large size-groups, and a decreasing share of the marginal and small size-groups. However, this observation is erroneous and does not hold true of the total sample of 800 units both sellers and buyers together and comparing the size group-wise distribution in the pre- and post-transaction situation.

From Table 12.1, it can be well inferred that land sale operations have favoured small and large farmers, which could be on account of viability, and resource use optimizations considerations respectively as far as numbers of farmers and total land owned by these groups are concerned.

Table 12.1: Land Sales Pattern in Meerut District (UP), 1991

Land holding class	Sample				Distribution of total sample			
	Total number of		Total land transacted (ha)		Number of owned holdings		Total land owned (ha)	
	Sellers	Buyers	Sellers	Buyers	Pre-sale transaction	Post-sale transaction	Pre-sale transaction	Post-sale transaction
Landless	0	58 (14.5)	0.000	21.34 (11.2%)	58 (7.3)	131 (16.4)	0.00	0.00
Marginal >0-1 ha	203 (50.8)	118 (29.5)	53.94 (28.3)	40.19 (21.1%)	321 (40.1)	248 (31.0)	179.99 (13.3)	127.01 (9.5)
Small >1-2 ha	100 (25.0)	84 (21.0)	63.06 (33.1)	34.51 (18.1%)	184 (23.0)	193 (24.1)	272.69 (20.2)	274.4 (20.5)
Medium >2-5 ha	85 (21.2)	118 (29.5)	61.40 (32.2)	80.70 (43.3%)	203 (25.4)	179 (22.4)	602.55 (44.7)	533.18 (40.0)
Large >5 ha	12 (3.0)	22 (5.5)	12.22 (6.4)	13.88 (7.3%)	34 (4.2)	49 (6.1)	294.43 (21.8)	399.94 (30.0)
Total Sample	400 (100.0%)	400 (100.0%)	190.62 (100.0%)	190.62 (100.0%)	800 (100.0)	800 (100.0)	1349.66 (100.0)	1334.53$ (100.0)

Note: (i) Figures in parentheses are the percentage of the respective total.

(ii) $ The valne deviates form the corresponding row of the previous column because of land transfers to non-agricultural uses.

The marginal farmers are the biggest losers as their number, total land owned by them as well as average size of land holding during post-transaction period have come down. The average size of land holding of marginal farmers has decreased from 0.561 ha to 0.512 ha during post-transaction period. The small farmers although have gained in terms of numbers as well as total land owned by the groups but the average size of land holding has come down from 1.482 ha during pre-transaction period to 1.422 ha during post-transaction period. Table 12.1, however, reveals a static picture. But in a dynamic context, it is possible that some of the marginal farmers could have ended up as landless as much as some would have moved upto become small farmers. But there is a clear indication that through the sales market in an agriculturally prosperous district like Meerut, it is the large farmer group which is being strengthened in terms of rise in the number as well as share in the land owned.

Table 12.2: Reasons for Sale/Purchase of Agricultural Land

Particulars	*Landless*	*Marginal*	*Small*	*Medium*	*Large*	*Total*
A: Reasons for Sale						
Impulsive (gambling, addiction, etc.)	—	15 (7.4)	7 (7.0)	4 (4.7)	0 (0.0)	26 (6.5)
Social ceremonies and other family consumption needs	—	53 (26.0)	28 (28.0)	26 (30.6)	4 (33.3)	111 (27.8)
Loan payments	—	42 (20.7)	16 (16.0)	110 (20.2)	2 (16.7)	70 (17.5)
Price speculation motive	—	28 (13.8)	5 (5.0)	18 (21.2)	4 (33.3)	55 (13.8)
Investment needs	—	46 (22.7)	21 (21.0)	15 (17.6)	2 (16.7)	84 (21.8)
Land supervision problem	—	19 (9.4)	23 (23.0)	12 (14.1)	0 (0.0)	54 (13.5)
Total	—	203 (100.0)	100 (100.0)	85 (100.0)	12 (100.0)	400 (100.0)
B: Purpose of Buying						
Cultivation	27 (46.6)	103 (87.3)	70 (83.3)	104 (88.1)	20 (90.9)	324 (81.0)
Housing	22 (37.9)	11 (9.4)	10 (11.9)	12 (10.2)	2 (9.1)	57 (14.2)
Industry	9 (15.5)	4 (3.4)	4 (4.8)	2 (1.7)	0 (0.0)	19 (4.8)
Total	58 (100.0)	118 (100.0)	84 (100.0)	118 (100.0)	22 (100.0)	400 (100.0)

Note: Figures in parentheses are the percentage of the respective total.

The sample distribution of sellers and buyers by reasons for sale/ purchase (Table 12.2) shows that the most dominant reason for land sale in all the size groups (overall in 27.8 per cent of cases) was the financial needs for social ceremonies and family consumption. Repayment of old debts was observed as another important reason (overall in 17.5%) forcing land sales in almost all the size-groups, except the small size-groups. Both these financial distress conditions together accounted for 45.3 per cent of the total sale cases. A deeper probe into caste-occupational aspects of buyers and sellers would have captured larger social dynamics involved in the changing agrarian structure.

The analysis of land sale market indicates that absentee sellers and buyers accounted for 18 and 22.2 per cent on their respective samples, giving an impression about the increase in absentee landlordism. However, on detailed enquiry from all the 89 absentee buyers, it was found that 47 of them purchased small parcels of agricultural land for non-agricultural uses and the remaining 42 purchased agricultural land for cultivation.

The Lorenz Curve and Gini Concentration Ratio was used to see the effect on equality in the distribution of land holding ownership. The measures indicate only a slight increase in the inequality of land ownership. The Gini Coefficient increases from 0.4395 to 0.4589. Though, the data do not indicate a very high change in the inequality through the land sale transactions, what is clear is that as of now sales market as such is not likely to lead to distribute land in favour of the poor, especially the marginal and the landless.

The above observations indicate the poor economic base of farmers even in such a progressive and developed area. Such financial needs are inevitable in any society, and the plight of marginal and small farmers in the context is quite understandable on account of small holdings. But that this financial distress accounts for more than half of the cases of land sales by medium and small farmers speaks of the poor economic base of the farmers in general, even in a period considered to be a progressive area.

The technology and capital formation do assume the prime role in raising productivity and income, but this rise must be adequate enough to pay-off the associated debt and leave some margin to the farm family. If farm product do not compare well with the rate of inflation and wage employment over time, the land sale dynamics would keep oscillating around farm-family debts, which might prove an unending burden on the economy in the long run. Despite emergence of some farm lobbies, the farmers, in general, do not enjoy the monopolistic powers like those of traders and industrialists. Hence, the agricultural price policy must strictly ensure a parity among the input and output prices on a regional basis.

Such regional adjustments are allowed to industries and trade. Next, the concept of diversification being currently emphasized upon in agriculture is mostly in the context of liberalization and globalization of the economy and is far from the realm of the general farming community. Only a small section of the most enterprising farmers would really benefit from the catchy notions of export oriented floriculture, aquaculture, pearl culture and horticulture. A more workable and sustainable concept of diversification for the general mass of average farmers of specific agro-çlimatic zones has to be evolved for raising their economic base.

Further, as may be seen from Table 12.2, land sold on account of distress needs (to meet expenditures on social ceremonies and for loan repayments) and impulsive sales accounting for 51.8 per cent of total number of sellers (54.1 per cent in case of marginal and 51.0 per cent in case of small farmers) and 54.3 per cent of total land transacted are not going to yield any benefit as the proceeds of such sales are not utilized for investment in alternative income generating activities and, therefore, this may be treated as loss to the sellers for ever in terms of income and employment opportunities. However, sale of agricultural land on account of investment needs must be able to generate a sustainable income stream higher than the average annual income from crop cultivation on the land being sold out. For example, if a marginal farmer decides to sell out his entire land (say one hectare), the annuity from sale of one hectare of land should be able to cover net income per annum plus average appreciation value of land per unit. It may be well argued here that one hectare of agricultural land, on an average, is not able to generate a net income of Rs. 24,000 or more per annum means that a marginal farmer will always be a poor farmer if consider the present income criteria of poverty line of Rs. 24,200 per annum as minimum requirement for survival of a family. This income criterion of Rs. 24,200 per annum needs revision and many are now demanding the same. The average size of holding of small farmers is around 1.5 ha and therefore, fixing up any amount over and above Rs. 36,000, as a new criteria of poverty line will automatically bring the small farmers too in the category of poor farmers. Therefore, land sale operations do not appear helping to the cause of poor people.

Further, the land sale transactions that involve only a part of total land holdings sold, results in further fragmentation of holdings earlier consolidated at a substantial social cost. It may be noted that 217 out of total sample of 400 sale transactions (i.e. 54.3%) caused fragmentation of holdings through a part of land holdings. This fragmentation on marginal and small holdings makes them non-viable from both the points of view of family sustenance as well as resource use. It was found that a very large number of land sale transactions (more than 20,000 per year in the district) are being made every year for the past several years. Hence, the intensity of the resulting fragmentation can be easily visualized. Blarel *et al.* (1972) observed that the cost of fragmentation includes increased travel time between fields. Hence lower labour productivity, higher transport costs for inputs and outputs, negative externalities (such as reduced scope for irrigation and soil conservation investments), loss of land on boundaries and access routes, and greater potential for disputes between neighbours. Thus, land sale transactions are found to be negative the very objective of consolidation of holdings. Though it would be undesirable and infeasible to exercise a ban on agricultural land sales, yet the incidence of such sales can be reduced by minimization of distress land sales on account of financial needs. It would be better to allocate funds for the financial needs of the farmers (including consumption needs) fulfilled against land mortgage than to waste huge funds in recurrent consolidation works and the associated litigations, etc. Further, the sale of agricultural lands in very small parcels may easily be restricted through suitable regulations. For example, the UP Zamindari and Land Reforms Act, 1950 (substituted by UP Act No. 20 of 1982, with effect from 3 June 1981, under Section 157-A) restricts the transfer of land by the Bhumidhar or Asami Scheduled Caste to Non-Scheduled Caste by any means, except with the previous approval of the Collector, and even then the land after transfer must not fall below 1.26 ha in any case. Such a limit could be worked out on regional basis and made applicable in general sale of agricultural lands.

III
LAND LEASE MARKET

The frequency distribution of lessors and lessees by the size of holding and the reasons for leasing in/out are shown in Table 12.4. It is observed that while leasing-out of land was done almost in equal proportions by the marginal, smal! and medium farmers, leasing-in of agricultural land was largely concentrated among the marginal farmers. Those marginal farmers who have better outside employment opportunities, and, hence constitute absentee owners' group (see Table 12.4) prefer to lease out their tiny holdings, and those not having outside employment opportunities resort to leasing-in more land to make their operated holdings adequate for family sustenance. Similarly, the landless agricultural workers also lease-in land for family sustenance. The small, medium and large farmers having adequate land holdings for family sustenance normally do not participate in lease market except for the reasons of being absentee owners, disabled or having management problems in the case of leasing-out and resource use optimization (family labour or tractor-power) in the case of leasing-in (Table 12.4).

The frequency distribution of lessors by two major occupational groups of absentee and peasant cultivator indicated that little over 40 per cent of lease market comprised the absentee owners all of which lease-out all of their land to tenant cultivators. Among the peasant cultivators, 58.3 per cent leased-out either total or parts of their total land which accounted for 54.3 per cent of the total leased-out lands. The cash rental and crop sharing were found to be almost in equal proportion when the sample was analyzed in terms of leasing. The absentee lessors were generally those who were either having some business or employed somewhere away from their respective residences. These absentee farmers were not able to monitor their land holding properly.

The net effect of leasing on the pattern of operated holdings is shown in Table 12.3. It is from lease market as their number as well as area operated both declined in the post-lease distribution since most of them became small farm operators (based on new operational holdings) after leasing-in of more land while some became non-operators after leasing out (due to being absentee owners or disabled).

The overall impact of lease operations on equity of the distribution was analyzed through Lorenz Curve and Gini Concentration Ratio. The results indicated a considerable improvement in the equity, the Gini falling from 0.3689 to 0.2851 after the lease operations. Thus the results of study indicate that whereas the sale market may somewhat worsen the land equity on permanent basis, the lease market seems to considerable improve the equity for the operational land holding.

Table 12.3: Land Lease Pattern in Meerut District, 1991

Land Holding Class	Sample				Distribution of Total Sample			
	Total Number		Total Land Leased (ha)		Number of Operated Holdings		Total Land Operated (ha)	
	Lessor	Lessee	Lessor	Lessee	Pre-lease Transaction	Post-lease Transaction	Pre-lease Transaction	Post-lease Transaction
Landless	0	41	0.000	51.47	41	113	0.00	0.00
		(17.1)		(25.2)	(8.5)	(23.5)		
Marginal	84	148	53.64	100.53	232	93	150.73	72.22
>0-1 ha	(35.0)	(61.7)	(26.3)	(49.2)	(50.4)	(19.4)	(23.5)	(11.4)
Small	80	28	61.51	18.75	108	183	153.28	259.98
>1-2 ha	(33.3)	(11.7)	(30.1)	(9.2)	(22.5)	(38.1)	(24.2)	(41.0)
Medium	72	21	79.09	28.24	93ss	83	295.55	248.54
>2-5 ha	(30.0)	(8.7)	(38.7)	(13.8%)	(19.4)	(17.3)	(46.7)	(39.4)
Large	4	2	10.06	5.31	6	8	33.92	52.83
>5 ha	(1.7)	(0.8)	(4.9)	(2.6)	(1.3)	(1.7)	(5.4)	(8.3)
Total Sample	240	240	204.3	204.3	480	480	633.48	633.48
	(100.0%)	(100.0%)	(100.0%)	(100.0%)	(100.0)	(100.0)	(100.0)	(100.0)

Table 12.4: Reasons for Leasing of Agricultural Land

Particulars	*Landless*	*Marginal*	*Small*	*Medium*	*Large*	*Total*
A: Reasons for Leasing-out						
Absenteeness	—	62	22	15	1	100
		(73.8)	(27.5)	(20.8)	(25.0)	(41.7)
Disabled	—	12	14	11	0	37
		(14.2)	(17.5)	(15.3)	(0.0)	(15.4)
Addiction,	—	5	8	0	0	13
gambling etc.		(6.0)	(10.0)	(0.0)	(0.00)	(5.4)
Management	—	3	28	38	3	72
problem		(3.6)	(35.0)	(52.7)	(75.0)	(30.0)
Casual attitude	—	2	8	8	0	18
		(2.4)	(10.0)	(11.1)	(0.0)	(7.5)
Total	—	84	80	72	4	240
		(100.0)	(100.0)	(100.0)	(100.0)	(100.0)
B: Reasons for Leasing-in						
Subsistence	39	113	0	0	0	152
	(95.1)	(76.4)	(0.0)	(0.0)	(0.0)	(63.3)
Utilisation of	0	28	22	3	0	53
Family	(0.00)	(18.9)	(78.6)	(14.3)	(0.0)	(22.1)
Utilisation of	0	2	2	16	2	22
Tractor Power	(0.00)	(1.4)	(7.1	(76.2)	(100.0)	(9.2)
Vegetable farming	2	5	4	2	0	13
	(4.9)	(3.3)	(14.3)	(9.5)	(0.0)	(5.4)
Total	41	148	28	21	2	240
	(100.0)	(100.0)	(100.0)	(100.0)	(100.0)	(100.0)

Note: Figures in parentheses are the percentage of the respective total.

The earlier land reforms permit tenancy in agricultural holdings only under inability conditions of the landowners, such as of widows, disabled persons, jailed person, military personnel, etc. But *de facto* tenancy is widely prevalent through largely in concealed forms as reported in several studies (Bardhan, 1976; Laxminarayan and Tyagi, 1977; Kumar, 1991; Singh *et al.* 1991). The present study also attempted to investigate into the reasons for leasing-out and leasing-in of agricultural lands. The results on this account are presented in Table 12.3. It is observed from table that the disability served as the reason for leasing-out only in 15 per cent cases, while the absentee owners and management problems on lands accounted for 70 per cent cases. Similarly, subsistence and family labour use were the major reasons for leasing-in land. As already discussed earlier, the results also indicate that marginal farmers tried to become small and the medium farmers tried to become large through land-lease out of viability considerations. That non-viable tiny holdings are converted into viable small holdings at the lower end and the capital resources are better utilized at the higher end, must be viewed as progressive developments and need to be encouraged. Both these processes can be expected to contribute to resource use efficiency in agriculture. Further, the productivity differentials between the lessors and the lessees, as shown in Table 12.5, indicate better resource management and productivity gains by the lessees. The lease market is also able to absorb some of the landless and is able to provide income and employment opportunities to the poorest of the poor class.

Table 12.5: Productivity of Major Crops on the Farms of Lessors and Lessees

Crop	Yield (qtl/ha)			Column (3) as percentage of column (2)
	Lessor Farm	Lessee farm	Difference	
(1)	(2)	(3)	(4)	(5)
Wheat	30.18	39.69	9.51	131.5
Maize	13.63	14.12	0.49	103.6
Rice	21.41	24.03	2.62	112.2
Sugarcane	644.23	735.17	90.94	114.1
Potato	208.27	280.50	72.23	134.7

The reality is that land lease markets exist to a considerable extent in agriculture, and its beneficial effects on productivity and growth suggest that these markets should be accorded full legal status to tenancy as a general class of land tenure by protecting the interests of both the owners and the tenants. This will help replace a wide range of inability in agriculture by the willing ability to cultivate lands. This will help reduce unnecessary fragmentation of agricultural holdings since lease rent, as an annuity will serve as an alternative to wealth sharing through land sales. In developed areas, where population pressure on agricultural land is less and wages are high, the marginal farmers may gain doubly by leasing-out their lands on rent and taking up wage employment.

REFERENCES

Bardhan, Pranab (1976). "Variation in the Extent and Forms of Agricultural Tenancy", *Economic and Political Weekly,* Vol.11, Nos. 37 and 38, September 11 and 18.

Blarel, B.; P. Hazell; Place and J. Quiggin (1992). "The Economics of Farm Fragmentation: Evidence from Ghana and Rwanda", *World Bank Economic Review,* Vol. 6, No. 2.

Krishnaswami, K. S. (1994). "Agricultural Development under the New Economic Regime", *Economic and Political Weekly,* Vol. 29, No. 26, June 25.

Kumar, S. Hari (1991). "Informal Leasing in Kerala: A study of Kuttanad", *Indian Journal of Agricultural Economics,* Vol. 46, No.3, July-September.

Laxminarayan, H. and S. S. Tyagi (1997). "Inter-State Variations in Types of Tenancy", *Economic and Political Weekly,* Vol. 12. No. 39, September 24.

Mani, Gyanendra Mani (1993). *Study of Sale and Lease Markets in Agricultural Land in Western Uttar Pradesh,* Ph.D. Thesis submitted to G. B. Pant University of Agriculture and Technology, Pantnagar, Udham Singh Nagar (Uttarakhand State).

Rao, C. H. Hanumantha and Ashok Gulati (1994). "Indian Agriculture: Emerging Perspectives and Policy Issues", *Economic and Political Weekly,* Vol. 29, No. 53, December 31.

Vyas, V. S. (1994). "Agricultural Policies for the Nineties: Issues and Approach", *Economic and Political Weekly,* Vol. 29, No. 26, June 25.

Chapter 13

Access to Land, Land Markets and Poverty: The Orissa Experience

BASANTA K. SAHU

I
ACCESS TO LAND, POVERTY AND INSTITUTIONS

This paper, based on a review of literature on different aspects of land markets in relation to their potential as a policy option towards poverty alleviation, provides a comprehensive view of the issues involved. This paper is divided into five sections. The first section, beginning with a brief reference to the importance of land reforms and observing its failure in many developing countries, goes on to explain the links between access to land and reduction of poverty of rural households. The second section refers to constraints on the land markets, to an extent imposed by imperfections in the other markets. The third section discusses the land-lease markets and the fourth the land sales markets. The fourth concludes with certain policy suggestions. The last section presents the Orissa experience. After failure of land reforms in many countries in the past decades, land policy reforms have reemerged as one of the development policies in developing economies. Issue of optimum access to land by the land-poor but efficient users has been taken seriously at different levels for enhancing growth and rapid reduction of poverty. From equity and efficiency point of view, it is believed that land market can play crucial role in agrarian economy. Land reform and/or a pre-existing equitable land distribution are seen as key ingredients of dynamic agricultural sector, and in turn of the overall growth with poverty reduction. But success of land reforms has been uneven and less than desirable in many regions. While it is successful in countries like Japan, Republic of Korea and Taiwan with positive impacts, land reform has failed and remained incomplete in many respects in many developing countries with limited impact on poverty. As a result, extreme inequality in land distribution and under-utilization of productive land co-exists with high poverty in these regions.

In this context, redistributive measures to increase access to land by the poor and development of land markets to effect land transfer to the potential users remain one of the key policy options. But, land markets are constrained by the presence of multiple market imperfections and institutional gaps in many countries. While markets and institutions are the key factors that determine optimum utilization of resources (including land) and increase in welfare gains, available evidence shows that under the situation of market failures and institutional gaps, conventional means of land access fails to create optimum efficiency gains and rapid poverty reduction. Then, it becomes very crucial to understand for whom and under what conditions gaining access to land is effective for faster poverty reduction and where and how government should address these issues for different groups under different socio-economic set up.

An attempt is made in this paper to consolidate the vast literature on access to land, land markets and poverty in developing countries to draw some important lessons and unresolved issues in the context of developing countries like ours. Organisation of the paper is as follows. In the next section we highlight about access to land poverty and institutions. Third section is devoted to discussion on land transactions, access to land through land rental and sales markets, market imperfections and factors affecting land markets. The last section concludes with appropriate policy suggestions.

Given the key role of land as a determinant of access to economic opportunities, access to land will have far-reaching social and economic effects. Access to land by poor will improve their ability to make effective use of their assets—the key to reducing poverty and empowering poor. Implications of access to land not only influence the structure of markets and institutions, but also determine households' ability to produce for their subsistence and to generate a marketable surplus. It also influences households' social and economic status, incentive to invest, sustainable land use, ability to self-insure and access to financial markets. It is argued that land transfers to poor are more effective and socially desirable than income and food transfer. Therefore, access to land has cumulative effects on poverty and growth. Reviewing the experience of Asia, Quibria and Srinivasan (1993) conclude that: it would appear that among those who cultivate land, poverty arises more from an unequal distribution of operational holdings rather than from lack of access to new technology, irrigation, fertilizers, etc. on the part of small farmers and tenants.

Access to land help in mobilizing idle household resources (e.g. family labour, draft animals, labour supervision capacity and managerial skills) and give value to households' assets with zero or low opportunity cost outside the land. It expands direct use of productive factors held by households at relatively lower cost than those who buy these factors. Even, access to small plot of land can prove to be extremely useful for land poor households, particularly female headed family (Agarwal, 1994). Hence there are very high reservation prices for land on small farms (Carter and Barham, 1996). Irrespective of its form, access to land is crucial where farming is expected to be the only sources of income. Access to land provides security against price shocks on the food and labour markets uncertainties. With access to land poor households can insure themselves against food price risks by directly producing some of their needs and can secure access to better quality food. Similarly, risk of unemployment can be compensated by self-employment on the farm. Rural labour households would prefer self-employment of his family labour on owned or on rented land than to wage labour on other's fields. Households will work more intensively on their own land as a coping strategy if they perceive employment and wage are risky.

Access to land provides an assured source of livelihood, when land is combined with variable input and other assets. Evidences show that access to land not only paves the way out of poverty but it increases households' income. While having access to land has a positive effect on household income (Hoddinott, Haddad and Mukherjee, 2000) it also determines per capita income of farming households (Lopez and Valdes, 1997). A study by Besley and Burges (1998) find that 10 per cent decline of the poverty gap in India is attributed to tenancy reforms and abolition of intermediaries.

Although land is more than an asset, it is most unequally distributed in the peasant economy leading to reproduction of poverty and inequality. This further adds to inefficiency in resource use through disincentive effects and negative externalities (Bardhan *et al.* 1998, Kanbur and Lusting, 1999). So from policy point of view, it is important to understand the association between land distribution and efficiency. Difference in performance between two countries having similar situations can be ascribed to differences in barriers to access to land, as with more equitable land distribution indicating easier access to land in India than in Pakistan (Sims, 1988).

Similarly, control of land is particularly important for women as they have a crucial role in land management. Evidence show that the gender dimension of land rights is important for efficiency (Udry, 1995). Their asset ownership can influence gender related spending, for instance, on girls' education. But women have been disadvantaged in terms of land access. Studies show that control over land by women empower them within household and in labor market (Agarwal, 1994) and it improves child welfare in terms of nutrition, heal and education (Haddad, Hoddinott and Alderman, 1997).

Rights on Land

Relating to access to land the most important point to discuss is property rights over land so far as production relations and income distribution are concerned. There is reasonable belief that insecure title to land or lack of security of tenure will affect production and investment incentives. Using district-level data, Banerijee and Ghatak (1996) show that a program of voluntary tenant registration, with registration giving the tenant certain rights, had dramatic effects on productivity in West Bengal from the late 1970s onwards. Major reasons why insecure land rights should affect investment incentives are: fear of expropriation, credit access and collateral and lack of trading opportunities (Besley, 1994). Land market transactions are frequently affected by nature of land rights as improved land rights make it easier to sell or rent land. Since investment in land raises the value of land upon sale or rental, a farmer with better land rights and anticipating the possibility of sale or rental will be more likely to invest in improvements to land. This argument would apply equally well to the functioning of the land market given land rights.

Different rights over a particular land—access to land, appropriation of land, provision of management, exclusion of others and alienation by selling and leasing, are held by different economic agents have different objective functions and they influence the development of markets accordingly. However, it is the ownership of the land that conveys the cumulation of all these rights. Hence, nature of property rights and its implications on households' behaviour that can, in turn, be influenced by government policy are crucial to make optimum use of land. Farmers will make require investments in land if land rights are secured. In the absence of complete property rights, secure access to land can be achieved without implement of all these rights associated with private ownership but it need more policy attention. Communal land rights systems also often function quite well in providing effective security of tenure without having a formal system of land titles. Importance of property rights are argued for:

- Secure property rights increase the incentives of households to invest, provide better credit access and provide an insurance substitute in the event of shocks,
- Well-defined land rights are key factor market functioning. In its absence, households will be compelled to spend valuable resources on defending their land,
- Secure land tenure facilitates land transfers at low cost, improves allocation of land and supports development of financial markets,
- Without secure land rights, landowners will be less willing to rent out their land, which may impede their ability and willingness to engage in non-agricultural employment, and
- By allowing poor to make productive use of their labour, land ownership makes them less reliant on wage labour, thereby reducing their vulnerability to shocks.

Path to access to land can be intra-family transfer, intra-community access, land reform measures and land markets. Here we will mainly focus on land access through land markets and land reforms, which have been key to the current debate and carry much policy importance. Experiences of some Latin American and Asian countries in recent years have successfully drawn attention of policy makers and researchers to back on issues relating to land access.

Otsuka and Quisumbing (2001) find that, even when property rights remain informal, active land rental and land sales markets can exist. This finding confirms observations made by earlier studies (Katz

1999; Procuradoria Agraria, 1998) that where communities with high endowments in social capital are observed to sustain active land markets without formal titling. In contrast, where social capital is insufficient to deter moral hazards in land transactions and informal land markets cannot operate, formal titling is necessary to provide the legal basis for the recognition of property rights and to sustain the emergence of land markets. In their study in Ghana Otsuka and Quisumbing (2001) find that land purchases serve to compensate for low levels of land received through lineage or community transfers. In Sumatra, they find that those who own more paddy land can purchase more land for agro-forestry. In Rwanda, Andre and Platteau (1998) observed that operation of the (illegal) land market led to increasingly unequal land distribution and rapid dispossession of many households.

As regard to social or strong community relations, intensification of land use can, occur without formal property rights. In Africa, trees are frequently planted in land accessed through informal family and community mechanisms as a way of strengthening individual property rights (Sjaastad and Bromley, 1997). Braselle, Gaspart and Platteau (1998) found that the traditional village order in Burkina Faso provides enough security of access to land to induce small-scale investments. These results may be important for policy point of view as they challenge the conventional wisdom, e.g. land titling programmes are *sine qua non* to induce investment in agriculture because they offer security of continued access to land and collateral to qualify for formal credit.

However, formal titling may worsen the security of access to land and constrain land market transactions: titling may increase transactions costs in the circulation of land, create new sources of conflicts, and not add anything to efficiency in resource use (Jansen and Roquas, 1998).

Mainstream economists assume that the introduction of private property rights in land will lead to elimination of risks and uncertainty and it will lead to an active land market. This will bring social benefits by facilitating efficient use of land as a factor of production. Further, the security in land price will have a positive effect on land price, the intensity of cultivation and use of formal credit (Johnson, 1972; Feeder and Feeny, 1991). This will enhance the capacity of farmers since an active credit (formal) market will develop as soon as land acquires collateral value (Hicks, 1969). With an active land market land tends to be transferred to less efficient to more efficient farmers and ultimately land transactions will improve resources allocation. However, real world situations in many agrarian backward economies do not follow the above expectations due to their over simplistic analysis.

Basically, in agrarian economies land markets play following major roles:

- Provide land access to those who are productive, but who own no or little land;
- Allow exchange of land as the off-farm economy develops;
- Facilitate use of land as collateral to access credit markets where possible;
- Enhance ability to transfer land, which increases incentive to undertake land related investments; and
- Facilitate other markets especially financial markets.

II
FUNCTIONING OF LAND MARKETS AND ACCESS TO LAND

Functioning of land markets is the fundamental to achieve resource use efficiency through providing access to land to the potential users. If there are differences in individuals' skills and endowments of different factors of production, markets should help in optimizing factor proportions employed and thus increase overall efficiency of resource allocation. It is evident that regions having similarity in many respects yet have different land market activities. Since there are market failures and institutions dealing with land fail to deliver, it is important to understand the conditions under which land markets can be made to perform efficiently or socially desirable. Here, we have elaborated functioning of different markets and their impact on poverty, equity and efficiency. A modest effort has been made to review evidence on functioning of land markets under different settings.

In theory, if all markets worked perfectly, land sales and land rental markets would be equally effective in providing access to land to potential users. But, this is not the real world situation. as market failures and missing institutions happen to be there for several times. This may jeopardize the competitiveness of beneficiaries, compromising their economic viability, even if access to land in ownership is achieved. Thus, in practice, the context and condition under which land reforms are implemented are highly diverse and complex with missing markets, institutional gaps and government failure. In many occasions, land markets are suppressed by legislation and there is lack of enforcement of property right.

Similarly, all transactions in the land markets do not necessarily contribute to improve productivity and equity as argued in theory. In many developing countries like India, land markets are encountered by multiple market imperfections and policy distortions. There are fundamental structural reasons why formal land sales markets tend not to be 'level playing fields' (Carter and Barham, 1996) for the rural poor. As a consequence, they have a hard time in using these markets to access land. Since permanent transfer of ownership through land sales is not very easy due to market imperfections and other social economic factors, dynamics of these markets tends to play regressively on small holders, leading to the concentration of land ownership. Therefore, it is important to understand the factors affecting the operations of land markets and their potential for pro-poor land transfer. In subsequent sections we have discussed land rental market and sale market and factors affecting them in different settings to draw some policy implications.

Reallocation of access to land across households can have both efficiency and welfare gains, in spite of market failures and high transaction costs on land markets, but there is ample evidence that only access to land is not sufficient to guarantee escaping poverty. Other complementary assets, targeted households hardly have control over it, are necessary to get benefit from access to land. In developing economies, where competitiveness is undermined by lack of supportive institutions, expected investment is deterred by insecurity regarding the conditions for access. Where all these constraints work together, mere access to land may not be the best way out of poverty for all rural households. Although, lower income is met by higher security (in terms of food and fodder security) through access to land mere small piece of land may not be sufficient for poverty reduction (Cornio, 1985; Lopez and Vades, 1997). In this regard poor labour household would expected be better off abandoning farming for the labour market and households with insufficient complementary assets may be better off renting off their land to others who can use it more productively (Sadoulet, Murgai and Janvry, 2001).

A recent World Bank Report (2003) concludes that undesirable outcomes observed in land markets can be due to imperfections in other markets.

First, in settings where the production process is not capital intensive and where access to credit and capital is broadly similar across farm sizes, labour market imperfections result in the productive superiority of family farms.

Second, imperfections in input, product, credit, and insurance markets will affect the functioning of land markets, and will lead outcomes to deviate from what one would expect in a hypothetical situation of perfectly functioning markets. Even well-intentioned regulatory interventions or administrative restrictions on land markets that do not address the underlying causes may end up worsening the situation rather than improving it.

A number of studies across the countries, support the fact that rural factor markets are interlinked (Basu, 1986, 1992; Sarap, 1991; Swain, 2000; Mohapatra, 1997) and ultimately determine the functioning of rural land markets. As rural markets, particularly credit markets, are highly imperfect. Adjusting to imperfections in these markets varies depending on whether land transfers are temporary or permanent. However, issue of labour and credit market imperfections has received considerable attention in the literature (Calvo and Wellisz, 1978; Eswaran and Kotwal, 1985a, b).

III
LAND RENTAL MARKETS

Nature and functioning of land rental markets in different contexts are given more importance in policy discussion due to obvious reasons—rental markets are unequally active in different regions. In developed countries, land rentals mainly serve to consolidate ownership units into larger operational units leading to 'reverse tenancy' (Lastarria-Cornhiel and Melmed-Sanjak, 1998), where both fixed rent and share rent are very active. Here a fairly high per centage of land was rented ranging from 71 per cent in Belgium, 48 per cent Netherlands to 47 per cent in France (Swinnen, 1998). Land rental market is made active to correct for the dispersed land ownership pattern and to achieve economies of scale in use. On the other hand Carter and Salgado (2001) find that the market failures and institutional gaps, inherent in the peasant economy, are more detrimental to participation of small holders in the land market. They observed that land rental markets play pro-poor role by helping land-scarce households gain access to land but it is weakness of property rights, either because titles are insecure or because rights are not enforced in case of conflict, is a major factor in reducing supply of land in rental.

Rental markets have been suppressed by the weakness of property rights that creates fears for landlords that land will not be returned and by land reform legislation that has often made rentals illegal and given possession rights to tenants. In a few cases, such as Operation Barga in West Bengal, comprehensive interventions have improved sharecroppers' rights through tenancy regulation such as imposition of ceilings on rents and not allowing landlords to dismiss tenants who can transfer rental contract to their heirs and public support to tenants (Saha and Saha, 2001). However, in other parts of the country, restoring the dynamics of land rental markets to help poor households gain access to land remains a potentially effective area for intervention in the struggle against rural poverty.

Low level of tenancy exists with relatively high level of rural poverty is another feature of some developing countries. Studies found that the reason for low tenancy rates in India is likely to be related to land reform regulations that prohibit tenancy (Radhakrishnan, 1990; Ray, 1996; Thimmaiah, 2001; Thorat, 1997). Even if some tenancy has moved into informality, this could have important welfare effects (Deshpande, 2002). Indeed, broader economic development provides considerable potential for the development of land rental markets that in many instances has not yet been fully tapped. Pro-poor arguments in favour of rental markets are as follows:

(1) Transaction costs is lower in land rental than in land sales markets because rentals can be verbal, informal, anchored in face-to-face agreements or in local social capital. Even if formally registered, land transactions do not require the costly procedures of title verification and registration, and of contracting for mortgage finance.

(2) Overpricing of the land relative to its use in production, which blocks entry of the poor as owners, does not carry to rents paid on land rental markets. Rents charged usually within the tenant's ability. Even when land sales markets are

seriously distorted, land rental markets can provide access to land to poor.

(3) Tenant-specific land rental contracts can be designed to mitigate the market failures to which the poor are exposed, specifically to make them benefit from the market failures.

(4) Land rental transactions do not require availability of long-term mortgage credit. Neither do they require tying up into the land large amounts of equity capital that can be used as working capital, or to rent land from others.

(5) Rental markets provide choice of contracts, which may allow the rural poor to gain access to land.

Rental markets, however, not necessarily act pro-poor in all cases. As agriculture becomes more capital and management intensive, landlords prefer to select tenants from among the non-poor, especially who can share in capital costs, leading to 'assortative matching' and reducing the promise of vertical mobility offered by sharecropping to the rural poor (Sharma and Drèze, 1996). For small holders, the rising intensity of agriculture in capital and management leads to increased 'reverse tenancy', where land gravitates away from the rural poor towards those with better access to credit, insurance, machinery, information, and contract farming opportunities (Lastarria-Cornhiel and Melmed-Sanjak, 1998). In this context, opportunities for vertical mobility through sharecropping are reduced. Though fixed rent contracts give full incentives to the tenant, high risks and liquidity constraints also reduce demand for the contract (Hayami and Otsuka, 1993).

However, the extent to which land rental will affect the welfare of participating households will depend on the size of the surplus achieved from engaging in rental and on its distribution between landowners and tenants. Recent studies demonstrate that the number and types of outside options available to tenants, such as wage labour and non-farm opportunity, will affect the outcome of the bargaining between landlords and tenants as well as the efficiency of the production outcome obtained (Conning and Robinson, 2002; Mookherjee, 1997). Thus, regulation of the operation of rental markets are unlikely to improve welfare outcomes unless they change the bargaining power of one of the contracting parties. Where this is not the case, by limiting the set of contractual options available, they may decrease overall welfare.

Since land rental markets are characterized by low transaction costs, and require only a limited initial capital outlay it is more flexible and versatile means of transferring land from less to more productive producers than sales markets. Renting is thus more likely to improve overall productivity and can provide a steppingstone for tenants to accumulate experience may be the transition to land ownership at a later stage. But where land tenure is perceived to be insecure, long-term contracts are unlikely to be entered into. Though fixed rent arrangements are more likely to maximize productivity than share rents, poor producers may, however, not be offered fixed rent contracts because of the risk of default. Hence, sharecropping has emerged as a second-best option, even though, sharecropping contracts could be associated with sizeable inefficiencies.

In India, it is observed that more experienced individuals receive tenancy or fixed term contracts and less experienced ones receive wage contracts (Chaudhuri and Maitra, 2001). Recent studies show that landlords are indeed aware of tenants' level of ability (Lanjouw 1999) and that they adjust the terms of contracts to provide higher incentives for more efficient operators and those with better capital endowments (DeSilva, 2000). Sadoulet, Fukui, and de Janvry (1994) confirm that close social relationships can increase the incentive for tenants. Their study compares the attributes of sharecropping contracts with kin and with non-kin and found that non-kin sharecroppers use significantly fewer inputs and obtain less output, whereas for close kin there was neither a disincentive effect nor any reduction in output. This suggests that embedding contractual arrangements in a long-term, personal relationship offers considerable potential to attenuate the disincentives and productivity losses that are otherwise associated with sharecropping contracts. If landlords are absentee or inexperienced in farming, they tend to choose fixed rent contracts (Jodha, 1984; McCarthy, Sadoulet, and de Janvry, 2001; Sharma and Dreze, 1996).

IV
LAND SALES MARKETS

Major arguments in favour of land sales market are that it provides option for permanent access/use of land, which is normally associated with higher investment incentives than short-term rental; making land marketable provides a basis for using it as collateral in credit markets and that land sales markets can provide the basis for financial market development. However, expectations, risk preferences, and the shadow price of capital affect land prices. Land sales markets often fail to guide land allocation towards the socially efficient users largely due to policy distortions, biases in the definition of public goods, and missing institutions. In order to land market transactions replace coercive land reforms in helping the rural poor to gain access to land, they need to be 'assisted' by regulatory or benevolent interventions to enhance the competitiveness of the poor. It is also possible that with increasing land scarcity and formalization of property rights, land sales market may become hostile to poor. A study by Sarap (1995) shows that poor households hardly participate in the land sales markets. It is the rich households dominate in the land sales markets to consolidate their unfavourably located holdings and substitute for better quality and nearer land. Hence, while land sales markets are rarely level playing fields for the poor (Carter and Barham, 1996) it needs much policy attention to locate where these markets can work progressively.

Factors Affecting Participation in Sales Markets

Land Prices

Land price is a key determinant of land sales markets. In agrarian economies where risk of production is high and purchasers' savings are the main source of funds for land acquisition, land prices tend to fluctuate significantly over time depending upon returns from agricultural production. There are factors other than the present value of profits from agriculture tend to fluctuate land price. For instance, where financial markets do not work well, land may be an important store of wealth and may be acquired for speculative purposes. In this context, for poor but efficient producers to gain access to land through sale market may be difficult and land sales markets are likely to lead to undesirable outcomes under credit market imperfections. In addition, policy distortions tend to increase the wedge between the price of land and the capitalized value of the income from agricultural production. Hence distortions in other markets could give rise to the emergence of efficiency-reducing outcomes, such as speculative purchases, distress sales, and artificially inflated land values that reduce access to land by low-income and landless buyers. It is the participants' expectations regarding future price movements considerably determine the activity in land sales markets.

However, survey data on land transactions from India indicate that purchases of land are almost all undertaken by individuals with access to sources of income which are not correlated with agricultural production and that borrowing to finance agricultural land acquisition is virtually non-existent (Sarap, 1995).

Credit Constraints

Despite their greater apparent efficiency, small farmers face great difficulty in expanding their size of holding and profit due to credit constraints—such as access to formal financial markets even in a credit market operating without institutional or government failures. It is evident that the inability of small holders to diversify risk is manifested in the choice of non-profit maximizing portfolios; in this sense, small holders are less efficient than large farmers. An increase in the assets (e.g. land) would enhance ability of small holders to absorb risk, and would improve their efficiency. Compared with rental markets, where contracts can be adjusted to overcome the impact of credit market imperfections, land sales markets will be more affected by these constraints.

Lack of access to credit can be compounded by imperfections in other factor markets such as inactive land market. Any distortions that increase the returns to land, such as subsidies, will be capitalized in land prices putting it beyond the reach of the small holders. This has important implications for the possibility of land acquisition by the poor. Therefore, credit market imperfections followed by policy distortions prevent land sales markets from contributing to increased levels of productivity. However, credit market imperfections can be overcome by interlinked transactions, particular in transactions between a farmer and the trader or commission agent to whom he sells his product. Bell and Srinivasan (1989) found this is an important characteristic of agriculture even in commercialized agriculture but the nature and extent of these transactions warrants further study.

High Transaction Costs and Segmented Sales Markets

High transaction cost is a major impediment to the functioning of land markets. A high transaction costs reduce the ability of the poor to participate in the market. In such situations land sales across farm size classes are virtually absent, although land transactions occur within farm size groups. Since transfers of land rights are complicated in land markets by lack of explicit title to land, and customary rights, re-distributive potential of land sales markets is limited due to high land transaction costs. Transaction costs related to land sales normally include notary fees, registration fees, and survey costs, as well as any transfer fees.

Similarly, land sales markets may tend to be segmented by farm size due to overpricing of land contributed by high transactions costs. As a result, large farmers tend to sell to large farmers, smallholders tend to buy from other smallholders and mostly sell to large farmers under distress conditions, whereas buyers of small farms rarely acquire land from large sellers. The result leads to concentration of the land away from small holders. Therefore, high transaction costs associated with land sales indicates that land acquisition by the poor through the land sales market will be difficult, as a consequence, the potential for productivity-enhancing land redistribution through sales markets is likely to be very limited. So, transfer of land through sale markets can go a long way toward improving productivity and welfare in rural economies.

Distress Sale

Exposure to undiversifiable residual risk causes farmers to resort to liquidation of their assets during periods of severe crisis, a phenomenon commonly referred to as distress sales. Regions with poorly developed insurance and capital markets land sales will likely be few and limited mainly to distress sales. Studies in Bangladesh and India confirm this hypothesis. Rosenzweig and Wolpin (1985) found that farmers in India who experienced two consecutive drought years were more likely than other farmers to sell their land. Historically, distress sales have played a major role in the accumulation of land by large manorial estates in China (Shih, 1992) and in early Japan (Takekoshi, 1967) and by large landlord estates in Punjab (Hamid, 1983). Furthermore, individuals who had to sell off land during crises may not be able to repurchase land during subsequent periods of recovery (Bidinger and others, 1991; Kranton and Swamy, 1999). On the other hand high positive correlation between agricultural profits and land prices also do not benefit much to the poor as result, land prices fall for them precisely when they would like to sell land and *vice versa*. Hence participation of small holders in land sales markets more or less limited to distress sales. Empirical analyses of land sales markets in Chile, Honduras, and Paraguay by Carter and Salgado (2001) show that these markets act regressively, concentrating the land away from small holders.

Cain (1981), who compares land transactions in Bangladeshi and Indian villages with different access to risk-coping mechanisms during 1960–80, illustrates that possibility of transactions in the land sales market being driven by lack of access to credit and insurance rather than by cultivators' productive inefficiency. In villages that had access to a safety net programme, the poor were able to use the land market to augment their landholdings by buying from richer farmers who sold land to undertake productivity enhancing investments such as digging wells, purchasing pump sets, or paying for their children's education and marriages. By contrast, where such consumption smoothing devices were absent, distress sales to obtain food and medicine accounted for most activity in the land sales market.

Public Interventions

Evidence on limited effectiveness of government intervention in land sales markets indicates that poorly designed land market interventions and the regulation of land markets continue to hamper rural growth. Such interventions not only limit access to land by the landless and poor, but also discourage rent out by landlords who are unable to make productive use of their land. It reduces productivity and investment in relation to land.

V
FAILURE OF LAND MARKETS

Rural land markets are not formed or reported sluggish and not developed in many parts of the world, especially in backward peasant economy making land acquisition difficult for the poor. Existence of heterogeneity in terms of multiplicity of contracts, variations in interest rates and differentiated objective functions of different economic agents in the markets are major constraints of land markets formation. A recent World Bank Report (2003) concludes that undesirable outcomes observed in land markets can be due to imperfections in other markets.

First, in settings where the production process is not capital intensive and where access to credit and capital is broadly similar across farm sizes, labor market imperfections result in the productive superiority of family farms.

Second, imperfections in input, product, credit, and insurance markets will affect the functioning of land markets, and will lead outcomes to deviate from what one would expect in a hypothetical situation of perfectly functioning markets. Even well-intentioned regulatory interventions or administrative restrictions on land markets that do not address the underlying causes may end up worsening the situation rather than improving it.

In Indian context there are number of studies support the fact that rural factor markets are interlinked (Basu, 1986, 1992; Sarap, 1991; Swain, 2000; Mohapatra, 1997) which largely determine the functioning of rural land markets. As rural markets, particularly credit markets, are highly imperfect, adjusting to imperfections in these markets varies depending on whether land transfers are temporary or permanent. However, issue of labour and credit market imperfections has received considerable attention in the literature (Calvo and Wellisz, 1978; Eswaran and Kotwal, 1985a, b). Some major factors for failure of land market are discussed below.

Labour Market Imperfections

Under imperfect rural labour markets land-scarce households sell their labour in the market will face some transaction costs, which will imply underemployment and a marginal value of labour time below the market wage. Assuming absence of transaction costs and imperfect supervision capacity, land-abundant households would contract labour to cultivate their land and will have a marginal cost of labour well above the market wage. Under this condition, absence of land markets would force households to cultivate the land they happen to own, implying that land-abundant households would need to cultivate their land with expensive labor and land-scarce households would be trapped by underemployment in low-return, own-farm activity. The latter would be particularly disadvantageous if opportunities existed for off-farm labor market is limited. Assuming that other factors such as ability and access to capital and technology were equal between the two types of households, the ability to obtain additional land would improve the livelihood of land-scarce, labour-abundant households by allowing them to employ their underutilized labor more effectively Indeed, such inefficiency, especially in the employment of labour, is of considerable relevance for China, where the functioning of land markets is significantly restricted.

Credit Market Imperfections

Functioning of capital or credit market has immense impact on land transaction. The positive impact of rental market activation on land access by the poor is diminished if access to capital depends on initial wealth, because of the need for up-front working capital to acquire inputs in addition to land and labour. Such quantity rationing in credit markets arises from the presence of asymmetric information and moral hazard (Stiglitz and Weiss, 1981). In informal credit markets, credit providers use close familiarity and social control to select promising clients. This implies, however, that the scope for diversifying risks across space and different types of clients is limited and means that lending entails high levels of risk, resulting in high interest rates and relatively short-term credits. Formal credit markets can overcome problems of asymmetric information by using collateral, mostly in the form of land. However, the costs of foreclosing on smallholders' land are often quite significant, implying that the transaction costs associated with providing credit to small producers may be so high as to exclude small farmers. Consequently, in the presence of credit market imperfections the supply of working capital depends on the amount of land owned. The optimal size of the operational holding determines access to credit. However, working capital constraints could, therefore, have significant impacts on land sales, and even on rental markets. Interventions in credit markets to overcome these shortcomings are difficult and often have not had the desired effect (Brummer and Loy, 2000; Kochar, 1997).

On the other hand differential credit market access can generate a relationship between farm size and productivity. The relationship can be reverse where credit access is more important than the ability to overcome labour market imperfections. A study of Sudan, shows that yields for virtually all crops are lower for smaller farmers and are higher for larger farmers because ability of the later to access capital and other inputs. In this situation and rental market leads to land transfers from poor and labour-abundant small holders to rich and relatively labour-scarce households (Kevane, 1996). The reason is that capital market imperfections combined with reasonably functioning land and labour markets and a less supervise intensive technology can make renting out land by the small credit-constrained households engaging in owner cultivation and working for a wage employment.

Few Economies of Scale in Agricultural Production

Literature has demonstrated that a large number of agricultural activities do not exhibit true economies of scale in agricultural production. Given the countervailing factors of credit and labour market imperfections, the optimum farm size is very much an empirical question. In the situations where other markets function reasonably well, optimal farm sizes often do not exceed the scale at which family labour is fully occupied. Existence of an inverse relationship between farm size and output per unit area is well documented in literature and the source of this relationship appears to lie in land-labour interactions. The key to the size-efficiency relationship is generally believed to lie in hired labor. In the absence of perfect monitoring, hired labour will have a tendency to reduce work effort. The employer cannot respond to this by reducing the wage, as a minimum reservation wage, which the employer must provide. Thus farmers will prefer to rely on family labour, which can be supervised at low cost. So small family farms will be most efficient.

Though inverse relationship between farm size and productivity can be explained by differences in land quality (Benjamin, 1995; Bhalla and Roy, 1988; Verma and Bromley, 1987), some empirical studies still find a significant negative correlation even after controlling for land quality and other differences associated with farm size. However, this inverse relationship is much weaker in Southeast Asia (David and Cordova, 1994). Acute capital constraints lead to the emergence of a positive relationship between farm size and productivity in Malawi, where both land and labour are extremely scarce (Dorward, 1999).

Failure of Land Reforms

The apparent failure of past land reforms is indicative of the fact that large-scale land redistributions are often politically not feasible. In many cases land redistribution has typically not been effective and tenancy reform was poorly designed. The general experience about land reform efforts have had limited success. Land reforms, where tenancy has persisted, tended to be share tenancy. It creates a bias towards wage contracts as it may be easier to fire a farm worker for poor performance than it is to evict a tenant for the same reason. Many employment contracts may in fact be share tenancy relationships, where the labourer is paid in kind from crop output.

Similarly, an important constraint on land-abundant households leasing their land to small holders is actual or anticipated legal problems. Where legal restrictions make eviction difficult, landlords may rotate sharecroppers to a different plot each year, to prevent them from establishing rights to a particular plot of land. Under this situation the inefficiency of sharecropping is likely to be manifested in the absence efficient fixed rent contracts. This is a major concern from both equity and efficiency perspectives. Thus land reforms have not improved the position of small and landless by discouraging tenancy. For large farm holders the advantages they enjoyed in the pre-reform agriculture sector could persist and translate into more pronounced land concentration in the post reform era. Thus gaining access to land by the poor through land reforms and its anti-poverty impacts remains uncertain. Hence the dynamics of the post-reform land market merit special attention.

VI
ACCESS TO LAND, LAND MARKET AND POVERTY IN ORISSA

Some Features of Land Transaction in Orissa

In India land markets are incomplete, imperfect and interlinked with other markets. Similar trend is found in Orissa (Sarap, 1998; Swain, 1998; Mearns, 1998). Sarap (1998) found that only about 7 per cent of farm land was transacted over a period of thirty years during 1955-95 in a village in Sambalpur district. Thin and wide fluctuating nature of land markets in Orissa was reported by Swain (1998). Early about 5-7 per cent of village land was bought and sold over period 1965-95 in Cuttak and Dhenkanal districts. Sale/purchase transactions constitute about four-fifth of land transactions. Data on other type of land transactions are not available.

However, various processes in executing land sale transactions limit land transfers—transaction cost of land is very high in Orissa, which limit access to land by poor. Charges relating to registration of land transaction are high. In Orissa it includes stamp duty (4.2% of land value), stamp duty surcharge (6-15 %), registration fee (2%), mutation fee, writing of sale deed, demarcation fee, search fee, endorsement fee, incidental fee etc. Interestingly stamp duty and registration fees are important sources of state revenue constituting about 6 per cent of state revenue which has declined from 10 per cent in 1958-59, may be due to widespread under valuation of land in order to reduce stamp duty and registration fee. Actual state income from land registration was Rs. 483.3 million against likely amount of Rs. 612.9 million in 1994-95 and it increased to actual income of Rs. 598 million against the likely Rs.1029.9 million in 1997-98. (*Source*: I.G., Registration, Board of Revenue, Cuttack, Orissa).

Similarly, post-land registration difficulty and inefficiency in land record management add to transaction cost. This not only depresses land market, but also affects poor in terms of their access to arable land. As regards to practice of land record it is poor or miserable in Orissa, which contributes to the failure of land reforms in the state. In fact, large part of the state was under Zamindari system, where rent collection but not land record was given importance. Poor land record and non-revision of record of rights lead to many problems like difficulty in protecting land rights, targeting land development initiative, rising rural conflicts, encroachment of public land, difficulty in access to credit. However, the progress in computerization of land record in Orissa has been tardy.

Functioning of rural land market in Orissa is different from the conventional type—demand for land far exceeds its supply. Land being principal livelihood security in rural area, land sales are mostly distress in nature. Sarap (1998) found about 70 per cent of land sale in Sambalpur area were distress sales in nature and highly inelastic. He found that land sale for investment purpose was very less (20-33%) among marginal groups while it was as high as 50 per cent among large land holders, mainly for purchasing vehicles, building construction, higher education and arrangement for government jobs. His study also highlights that average area per each transaction is relatively larger for large farmers than marginal and small farmers. Large farmers buy land from many groups and also try to exchange for better quality land nearer to their farms. Land transactions more or less remain confined to the same community or caste in the same village among marginal and small groups.

Another study (Swain, 1998) found similar trend of land market operation in Orissa. Distress land sale for consumption, marriage and other social functions, repayment of old loans, medical expenses dominate in total land sales. Though large farmers are the dominant players in the land markets with the aim of buying better quality and better located land to consolidate their holding, land market in Orissa is underdeveloped, sluggish and characterised by distress.

Land Distribution

Reduction of glaring inequalities in land distribution has been one of the objectives of land reforms policy in 1950s and continues to be so in recently launched comprehensive agrarian reform measures. It is important to understand the extent of land concentration, especially among different social groups, and at what level of the land ownership hierarchy, concentration has tended to become more pronounced. While changes in the per centage share of land accounted for by households in different groups tell us about their overall access to land, the proportion of landless household indicates the distribution of available land among particular social group. Though the gains to backward groups (SC & ST) in total land are evident at national and the state level, there is hardly any change in the incidence of overall landlessness in Orissa. Interestingly, in early 1990s the share of ST households in total land has increased appreciably higher than their share in total population, yet incidence of landlessness among tribals has increased in the state.

Table 13.1: Distribution of Holding and Area in Rural Areas 1971-72 to 1991-92 (*in per cent*)

Land Class Size	Orissa				India			
	1971-72		1991-92		1971-72		1991-92	
	Holding	Area	Holding	Area	Holding	Area	Holding	Area
Sub-marginal	22.17	1.81	27.91	3.83	21.25	1.69	37.32	3.32
Marginal	32.35	15.79	32.08	18.27	24.52	7.53	25.09	12.28
Small	25.78	27.32	24.33	30.15	22.32	14.80	17.79	18.70
Medium	17.47	39.37	14.42	37.83	24.13	36.81	15.77	37.54
Large	2.23	14.72	1.26	9.92	7.72	39.17	3.65	28.16

Source: Chadha, G. K., *et al.* (2004).

Does it mean that there is growing concentration of tribal land among the tribals? The evidence in Table 13.2 goes to support it. While the overall trend for all India as well as for Orissa shows decline in the share of large farms in the area cultivated, the ST and SC large farms show an increase in their share. This needs further study.

Table 13.2: Distribution of Holding and Area by Different Social Groups 1982 and 1992

(in per cent)

Land Class Size	Orissa				India			
	1982		1992		1982		1992	
	Holding	Area	Holding	Area	Holding	Area	Holding	Area
Schedule Caste (medium concentration)								
Marginal	75.46	33.28	76.77	38.02	72.40	26.69	72.92	30.16
Small	11.38	31.19	8.09	27.47	8.40	22.71	7.85	22.18
Medium	4.44	20.08	2.87	18.35	4.52	24.17	3.85	20.42
Large	1.48	15.45	1.08	16.16	2.06	26.83	2.04	27.24
Schedule Tribe (high concentration)								
Marginal	51.21	19.37	58.24	23.82	43.22	12.00	54.91	18.70
Small	22.16	27.76	17.27	26.63	17.36	18.75	17.53	22.72
Medium	13.02	32.01	10.02	27.92	14.28	29.21	11.39	27.67
Large	3.56	20.86	3.43	21.63	8.07	40.04	4.67	30.91
Other Caste (low concentration)								
Marginal	55.87	18.09	58.16	25.88	52.20	10.88	57.63	14.91
Small	23.34	30.30	15.27	27.45	16.09	15.62	14.51	17.50
Medium	9.34	22.97	7.58	26.13	12.05	22.59	10.66	24.66
Large	4.65	28.64	2.58	20.54	9.48	50.91	6.66	42.93

Note: Percentage of land less household during 1982 and 1992 was 7.22 and 11.19 for SC, 10.05 and 11.04 for ST and 6.80 and 16.41 for other castes respectively.

Source: Chadha, G. K. *et al.*, 2004.

Land Fragmentation, Ceiling on Land Holding and Distribution of Surplus Land

Orissa has experienced widespread land fragmentation and there is hardly any serious effort to control it. Progress in land consolidation is far from satisfactory. Out of 51,349 villages in the state, only 9,922 villages have been brought under the fold of consolidation operation. Out of this only in 7,730 villages consolidation covering an area of 11,73,394 hectare was completed by the end of 2001-02 (Economic Survey 2003-04, Government of Orissa) which is only 17 per cent of total operated area in the state, out of which 11.5 completed during 1995-98, at a cost of an average of Rs. 6000 per hectare. Protest against consolidation of holdings, lack of confidence, of people in the entire process and inadequate consideration to variation in land quality and location seem to be major reasons for poor progress. From land market point of view, small and scattered land may be preferred by poor farmer because it gives options for sale/mortgage during distress which may not possible under consolidated holdings.

Table 13.3: Land Fragmentation and Distribution of Surplus Land

		Orissa	*India*
Extent of Fragmentation (nos, of parcels)	1982	5.02	4.04
	1992	3.10	2.70
Per centage of Consolidated area to Cultivable Area	1974	0.0	22.28
	1980	22.57	30.20
	2000	15.95	39.81
Declared Surplus Area (upto March 2001) as per cent of Net Operated Area		1.16	2.09
Per cent of Surplus Area for Distribution involved in Litigation (2000)		52.55	50.07
Actual Distributed Area as per cent of Net Operated Area		1.02	1.50

Source: Chadha, G. K. *et al.*, 2004.

Table 13.3 shows a decline in the extent of fragmentation in Orissa but it still remains high among small-marginal farmers. As in many parts of the country, in Orissa too land ceiling measures failed due to lack political patronage and non-radical form and content of ceiling laws. Declared surplus land till recently was negligible at 1.16 per cent of net operated area. While surplus land actually distributed in neighbouring West Bengal has improved the land base of marginal farmers, it failed in Orissa. Large proportion of area declared as surplus has not been distributed due to litigation. Access to land through ceiling surplus land distribution programme in Orissa is only a partial success because it has not improved the economic condition of many beneficiaries (XIM, Bhubaneswar, 1994).

Tenancy and Access to Land in Orissa

There are a numbers of studies on tenancy in Eastern India. It is evident from these studies that tenancy, in particular share tenancy, in conjunctions with the exploitative interlinkages in credit and labour markets, act as most serious threat to the new investment in farm activity. Some qualitative changes in diverse aspects of tenancy relation have been reported in Eastern India (Chadha and Bhowmic, 1992; Swain, 1999).

In spite of widespread perception that land tenancy is inefficient and tenant-landlord relationship is necessarily exploitative, access to land through tenancy remain substantial in backward agriculture like Orissa. In fact, where markets for land, credit, labour, information, insurance and management are missing, tenancy plays an important role in managing productive factors like land, labour and capital. Orissa provides unique picture of tenancy where nature and extent of lease market and terms of tenancy vary across different parts of the state and social groups. About 20 per cent of farm households and one-fourth of total operated area in the state are under tenancy. There is widespread under-estimation of land transaction in lease markets in the state. The best available estimates suggest over 80 per cent of leasing activity are carried out by small and marginal farmers. Though share cropping is predominant in the state there is wide inter and intra-regional variations in leasing activities and terms of tenancy contracts.

Orissa Estate Abolition Act, 1952, initially permitted landowners to retain 33 standard acres of land for personal cultivation which led large scale eviction of tenants. No parallel legislation was there to protect tenants. It was Orissa Land Reform Act, 1960 (amended in 1972) which banned leasing of land except where lessees fell into some excluded groups. Similarly, the Act had provision that permanent occupancy right may legally pass on to the tenants who continuously cultivate a land for 12 years. In sum, the Orissa Land Reforms Act prohibits subletting of land, regulates rent to a maximum of one-quarter of gross produce and grants occupancy right to long-standing tenants.

The abolition of tenancy with the objective to provide land ownership to the tiller was core of most land reforms efforts in India, which expanded access to land by the poor landless. It was believed that tillers of land were locked in exploitative relationship with intermediaries who had little interest in the land but for the extraction of rent. In the context of Orissa, the institution of tenancy has proved to be resilient and attempts to regulate tenancy by legislative means have been counterproductive. Tenancy is as widespread as it is illegal in the state in different forms.

Available data on area under tenancy and number of tenants are highly underestimated. Tenancy contracts are often in oral or concealed form to avoid official laws. In fact, land reform legislation prohibits subletting, regulates rent, confers security of tenure but these provisions have given many landlords and tenant (these sublettings) a common interest in concealing agreement which may be deemed illegal. What is shown in official records, like what is reported in Table 13.4, forms only a fraction of the actual tenancy.

Table 13.4: Changing Incidence of Tenancy in Rural Orissa and India

(*in per cent*)

Particulars	*Orissa*			*India*		
Type of Holding	*1971-72*	*1981-82*	*1991-92*	*1971-72*	*1981-82*	*1991-92*
Owned self-cultivated	67.7	74.27	70.46	74.31	80.58	81.98
Mixed holding	27.7	24.06	17.69	21.83	16.24	8.87
Leased in holding	4.45	1.49	1.7	3.86	2.37	3.85
Neither owned nor leased in but possessed holding	—	0.18	10.15	—	0.81	5.3
Type of Area						
Owned area	86.54	83.97	84.41	89.43	91.08	87.91
Leased in area	13.46	9.92	9.48	10.57	7.18	8.28
Neither owned nor leased in area	—	6.12	6.11	—	1.74	3.81
Changing Distribution of Leased-in Holdings and Area under different terms of Tenancy (in percentage)						
Holdings						
Fixed Money	18.63	5.15	20.58	11.61	10.88	20.32
Fixed Produce	17.30	8.06	5.83	9.62	6.28	15.62
Share Crop Tenancy	61.15	41.96	53.29	46.31	41.84	36.89
Other terms	2.92	44.83	20.30	32.47	41.00	27.17
Area						
Fixed Money	7.50	5.10	19.70	15.42	10.90	19.00
Fixed Produce	13.44	8.10	4.70	11.64	6.30	4.50
Share Crop Tenancy	42.20	42.00	50.90	47.87	41.90	34.40
Other terms	36.86	44.80	24.70	25.07	40.90	31.10

Source: Chadha, G. K. *et al.*, 2004.

Table 13.5: Distribution of Lessees and Area Leased-in

(in per cent)

Particulars	Orissa		India	
Holding	*1971-72*	*1991-92*	*1971-72*	*1991-92*
Land less	24.72	38.52	28.32	34.62
Marginal	52.69	50.69	48.46	47.89
Small	14.99	6.42	11.54	9.96
Semi-medium	5.6	3.56	7.20	5.26
Medium	1.82	0.81	3.77	2.03
Large	0.18	—	0.70	0.24
Area				
Land less	9.34	3.68	7.88	7.87
Marginal	55.9	77.49	45.43	45.94
Small	17.05	10.60	13.72	17.47
Semi-medium	13.12	7.87	17.37	15.60
Medium	4.09	1.16	12.11	11.84
Large	0.50	—	3.49	1.28

Source: Chadha, G. K. *et al.*, 2004.

Table 13.6: Distribution of Lessors and Area Leased-out

(in per cent)

Particulars	Orissa		India	
Holding	*1971-72*	*1991-92*	*1971-72*	*1991-92*
Marginal	64.80	63.51	47.83	51.37
Small	15.77	26.28	21.00	28.34
Semi-medium	13.80	7.09	17.55	19.11
Medium	4.50	2.43	11.10	7.84
Large	1.13	0.69	2.52	1.34
Area				
Marginal	43.22	31.76	18.52	14.25
Small	15.85	43.26	16.02	18.19
Semi –medium	28.05	18.37	23.42	34.17
Medium	6.68	5.40	29.96	25.56
Large	3.20	1.21	15.07	6.83

Source: Chadha, G. K. *et al.*, 2004.

Though these are severe underestimates, the data in Table 13.4 to 13.6 help in understanding changes in the agrarian structure and access to land over time for land poor farmers in Orissa and India. It is argued that though land reform is more of a political issue, activating land market may be easier by liberalizing land rental market. There are some notable differences in different aspects of tenancy between Orissa and the country as a whole.

First, the proportion of owned self-cultivated holdings increased in the country as a whole but it declined during 1991-92 in Orissa. There is a progressive decline in the share of and mixed holdings in the state as well as the rest of the country. The entirely leased-in holdings decline in Orissa but no such trend for the rest of the country.

Second, like at the national level, Orissa experienced very high increase in neither leased nor owned but possessed holding. This may be due to increase in encroachment of government land over a period and poor performance of land administration resulting incomplete transfer of ownership rights of holdings under tenants possession.

Third, proportion of leased-in area to total operated area declined in Orissa during 1970s but no remarkable change thereafter. Change in the share of neither owned nor leased holding was sharp but the area under this category remained unchanged during 1980s in Orissa where as it increased by varying degrees in other states.

Fourth, while there was significant decline in per cent of holdings and area under share crop tenancy at national level during 1970s and 1980s, both area and holdings under share cropping increased in Orissa during 1981-82 to 1991-92. This makes Orissa different from other states as far as terms of tenancy is concerned and it indicates tenancy under more uncertain and exploitative environment in Orissa.

Fifth, share tenancy accounts more than half of total area and holding under tenancy in Orissa, even though it is steadily declining at the national level. While contract under fixed rent tenancy has become more important in the country, Orissa experienced very high rate of share crop tenancy and decline in fixed-produce tenancy. Some field based studies suggest that share tenancy is more prevalent in dry/arid areas and it shows its greater potential to for risk sharing between tenants and land owner. This is an important issue of access to arable land by the poor and needs in the context of dry regions.

Village Studies

Village level studies on tenancy relations are few in Orissa. The two recent studies (Sarap, 1998; Swain, 1998), as mentioned earlier provide more precise estimates of tenancy. It is estimated that about 10-20 per cent of total operational holdings and 10-12 per cent of operational area are under tenancy arrangement. More than 80 per cent of leased-in area is in the size class of less than 10 acres. While

85 per cent of total leased-out area is by farmers having less than 10 acres, the proportion of leased-in area to operated area decreases with increase in size of operational holding. This substantiates the fact that substantial leasing activities are by small and marginal farmers in Orissa. As regard to tennurial arrangement in the state, share cropping is predominant particularly in dry areas accounting for more than 42 per cent of total leased-in area against 14 per cent and 8 per cent under fixed produce and fixed rent contract respectively (Swain, 1998). On the other hand fixed tenancy with payments in cash and kind is common in irrigated area (Sarap, 1998). Different terms of tenancy contract in dry and irrigated areas and wide range rents payable in the state shows the heterogeneity in tenancy contract in the state and this seems to confirm the persistence of potential for risk-sharing under share cropping contract.

While major reasons for leasing-out land reported by these two field studies are problem of labour supervision, lack of bullock power, small and uneconomic holding, poor quality of land and disadvantageous location of land, main factors for leasing-in land are limited non-farm employment, low land labour ratio, availability of bullock and to increase operational holding. However, both landowners and tenants have their own reasons to conceal tenancy arrangements. Irrespective of reasons for tenancy, land lease market remains important means by which rural poor gain access to land. More important is land lease market and other factor markets are interlinked. These interlinkages explain why tenants conceal tenancies and why there is weak position of tenants in determination of rent and right of occupancy. Therefore, liberalizing rental market with certain upper limit on leasing-in, may be important means in enhancing access to land by the poor with possibility of access to institutional credit. Concealing of tenancy affects tenants adversely by denying them security of tenure and consequently limiting their access to credit. From the above discussion it is clear that in the context of Orissa tenancy is a response to missing other markets, especially for labour.

Regarding rent determination prevailing social-cultural norms seem more important than state legislation, and land transactions between similar groups, caste and class are relatively non-exploitative. Hence, from policy point of view effective mechanism for deregulating tenancy is important in order to protect tenants, user right without threatening ownership right of landowners. A written contract with protection under the law can provide tennurial security to the tenants in short run enabling them to access institutional credit and thereby improving agricultural productivity. This will release more land into lease market without making landowners fear the loss of their land.

In sum, the picture of access to land, especially by the poor households is different in Orissa as compared to other states or at the national level. Glaring inequality in land distribution is evident in the state. Land distribution programme in state has failed in improving overall situation marginal groups. Though landlessness among weaker section (SC & ST) households marginally declined during 1980s, may be due to many of them are allotted surplus land, but their economic condition has deteriorated during recent years. On the other hand, sharp rise in landlessness among other castes in the state was marked during 1980s. This indicates that in spite of increase in the land base of marginal groups, it has not been very helpful in improving their well-being. The improvement to access to land needs to be backed up by other support structures like credit and extension, if the poor should reap the benefit of productive asset.

Also, market based mechanism to increase access of land to rural poor may be considered at policy level as high incidence tenancy and encroachment are reported in the state. Deregulation of tenancy may encourage large landowner to participate in land lease-out which will enhance land access of poor and increase government revenue. Improvement in land administration and settlement, computerized land record, quick land-dispute mitigation mechanism, reduction of land transaction cost would improve poor household's access to land.

VII
POLICY SUGGESTIONS

Land markets appropriate regulatory mechanism, can play vital role in efficient land allocation and, hence can enhance growth and reduce poverty and inequality as socially desired. However, permanent transfer of ownership through land sales is not very easy due to market imperfections and other factors, similar benefits can accrue from informal transactions in land rental markets that are less likely to be affected by these problems. Land rental markets, may be more friendly to the poor and access to land via personalized contracts can serve to mitigate many market failures and institutional gaps, making competitiveness of those who use the land more likely. Via land rental, poor households can eventually progress toward the desirable goal of land ownership. This occurs when the income generated through rental is gradually capitalized into land ownership. However, land contracts may be easy entry point for the poor in accessing to land, if the contracts are drawn to compensate for the market failure. Policy initiatives that focus on access to land for the poor seek to assist tenants in obtaining favourable contracts and promote access to contracts where land rent markets are not well functioning. In spite of having competitive advantage of cheap family labour, rural poor could not escape poverty because the present functioning of land markets in general do not provide them with a mechanism of easy access to the land. Weak bargaining power in rural class differentiation, limit poor to get benefit from land market transactions. For them 'class competitiveness' schedule reflects many market failures than their comparative labour advantage. Therefore, land sales markets are not 'level playing fields' for many weaker sections.

Since poor households are frequently exposed to random shocks as well as find with new opportunity from both farm and non-farm sectors, simple gaining access to land is neither adequate for poverty reduction nor ensuring efficiency gains. Rather flexible access to land with low transaction costs is important to allow maximum efficiency in land use. It is household's asset endowment, functioning of markets and institutions are crucial for providing low cost channels of access to land by the poor. On the other hand, over time labour has to be shifted away from agricultural to more productive non-agricultural occupations. Where active labour market and non-farm opportunity exist, access to sub family farms may be socially efficient and effective to reduce rural poverty and landless households may prefer to it over full-scale family farms. Therefore, poverty reduction and labour mobility require skill accumulation, and efficient entry and exit from agriculture requires an active and efficient land market. In effect, the land market should solve a land-labour matching problem, coupling the labour of landless labourers and tenants with land that they can operate to generate remunerative economic opportunities.

From the above discussion on access to land and functioning of land markets in different contexts, it appears that land acquisition for poor households will not be easy with existing land polices and therefore, have a clear implication for the extent to which land markets can serve re-distributive purposes. Although land markets' ability to transfer land from inefficient enterprises to productive users will still not only be beneficial in terms of equity, efficiency and growth, but will also be conducive to the emergence of a reliable and robust financial system, it requires a comprehensive land policy reforms.

Land sales markets alone will not necessarily lead to an optimal allocation of land in the presence of credit and insurance market imperfections. As regard to gaining access to land by the poor land reallocation need to be achieved keeping both efficiency and equity in mind, it may be through land rental markets or through other contracts. Efforts to expand the range of options available to tenants, for instance, via access to infrastructure and non-agricultural labour markets, are likely to have a more beneficial impact on land rental market outcomes and rural productivity than prohibiting certain options.

Conventional government interventions, however, may not improve access to land by the poor in all situations. The possibility of growth-enhancing and poverty-reducing outcomes discussed in this paper can be achieved through selective public intervention by improving the functioning of rural land markets—to eliminate distortions that might bias land market outcomes; to help reduce transaction costs that would increase the barriers to participation, especially by the poor; and to improve the functioning of financial markets. Attention should be paid to outcomes of the measures that have proved difficult to enforce, and their main effect has often been to increase transaction costs for participants or to drive land transactions underground, reducing the welfare of all participants.

REFERENCES

Agarwal, Bina (1994a). *A Field of One's Own: Gender and Land Rights in South Asia*. Cambridge: Cambridge University Press.

—— (1994b). Gender and command over property: a critical gap in economic analysis and policy in South Asia. *World Development* 22(10): 1455-1478.

Baland, Jean-Marie, and Jean Philippe Platteau (1998). 'Division of the Commons: A Partial Assessment of the New Institutional Economics of Rights'. *American Journal of Agricultural Economics*, 80 (3): 644-50.

Bardhan P. (1984). Land Labour and Rural Poverty: Essay in Development Economics. New York. Columbia University Press.

Bardhan P., Samuel Bowles, and Herberd Gintis (1998). "Wealth Inequality Wealth Constant and Eco-Performance. Working Paper: 08-97, CIDER, University of California.

Bardhan, P. S. Bowles and H. Gintis (2000). "Wealth Constraints, and Economic Performance" In A. B. Arkinson and F. B. Bourguignon, eds., *Hand-Book of Income Distribution*. Amsterdam: North Holland.

Basu, K. (1986). 'Market for Land: Analysis of Interim Transactions', *Journal of Development Studies*.

Besley, Robin Burgess (2000). "Land Reforms, Poverty Reduction and Growth: Evidences from India." The Development Economic Discussion Paper no. 13. London School of Economics, London.

Besley, T. and Burges (2000). "Land Reform Poverty Reduction, and Growth: Evidence from India." *Quarterly Journal of Economics* 115(2): 389-430.

Bidinger. P. D., T. S. Walker, B. Sarkar, A. R. Murry, and P. Babu (1991). "Consequences of Mid-1980s Drought: Longitudinal Evidence from Mahubnagar." *Economic and Political Weekly* 26: 105-14.

Binswanger, Hans and Klaus, Deininger and Gershon Feder (1995). "Power, Distortions, Revolt and Reform in Agricultural Land Relations", in J. Behrman and T. N. Srinivasan (eds), *Handbook of Development Economics*, Volume 3B. Amsterdam: North Holland.

Braselle, Anne-Sophie, Frederic, Gaspart and Jean-Philippe Platteau (1998). "Land Tenure Security and Investment Incentives: Further Puzzling Evidence from Burkina Faso", Faculty of Economics, Social, and Management Sciences, University of Namur. (Mimeograph).

Brummer, B. and J. P. Loy (2000). "The Technical Efficiency Impact of Farm Credit programmes: A Case Study of Northern Germany." *Journal of Agricultural Economics* 51(3): 405-18.

Cain, M. (1981). "Risk and Insurance Perspectives on Fertility and Agrarian change in India and Bangladesh." *Population and Development Review* 7(3): 435-74.

Calvo, G. A., and S. Welliz (1978). "Supervision, Loss of Control, and the Optimum Size of the Firm." Journal of Political Economy 86(5): 943-52.

Carter, Michael and Brad Barham (1996). "Level Playing Fields and Laissez-Faire: Post Liberal Development Strategy in Inegalitarian Agrarian Economies". *World Development,* 21(7): 1133-49.

Carter, Michael and D., Mesbah (1997). "Can Land Market Reform Mitigate the Exclusionary Aspects of Rapid Agro-Export Growth?" *World Development*, 21(7): 1085-100.

Chadha, G. K., Suchitra Sen and H.R., Sharma (2004). *State of Indian Farmer: A millennium Study: Land Resources*, Academic Foundation, New Delhi.

Chaduri, A. and P. Maitra (2001). "Tenant Characteristics and the Choice of Tenurial Contracts in Rural India." *Journal of International Development* 13(2): 169-81.

Conning, J. and J. A Robinson (2002). "Land Reform and the Political Organization of Agriculture." Working Paper no. 3204. Centre for Economic Policy Research, London.

Cornio, Andrea (1995). "Farm Size, Land Yields and Agricultural Production Function Analysis of Fifteen Countries", *World Development* 13(4).

de Janvry, A., G. Gordillo, J. P. Platteau, and E. Sadoulet (2001). *Access to Land, Rural Poverty, and Public Action*. Oxford, U.K.: Oxford University Press.

de Janvry, Alain and Elisabeth, Sadoulet (2000). "Property Rights and Land Conflicts in Nicargua: A Synthesis". Berkley: University of California at Berkley. Mimeo.

De Silva, S. (2000). "Skills, Partnerships, and Tenancy in Sri Lankan Rice Farms." Discussion Paper No. 819. Yale University, Economic Growth Center, New Haven, Conn.

Eswaran, M. and A. Kotwal (1985b). "A Theory of Two-Tier Labour-Markets in Agrarian Economies." *American Economic Review* 75(1): 162-77.

Feeder, G. and D. Feeny (1991). "The Land Tenure and Property Rights: Theory and Implications for Development Policy", *The World Bank Economic Review*, Vol. 5, No. 1.

Haddad, Lawerence, John Haddinot and Heral Alderman (1997). *Intra household resources allocation in developing countries: models, methods and policy* Baltimore, MD. John Hopkins University Press.

Hamid, N. (1983). "Growth of Small-Scale Industry in Pakistan"; *Pakistan Economic and Social Review* 21(1-2): 37-36.

Hayami, Yujiro and Keijiro, Otsuka (1993). *The Economics of Contract Choice*. Oxford: Clarendon Press.

Hoddinott, John, Lawerence Haddad and Sanjukta Mukherjee (2000). "Asset and Rural Poverty", Working Paper IFRRI, Wasington DC.

Jansen, Kees and Esther Roquas (1998). "Modernizing Insecurity: The Land Titling Project in Honduras". *Development and Change*, 29(1): 81-106.

Kanbur, Rabi and Nora Lusting (1999). "Why is inequality back on the agenda"? in Annual Conference on Development Economics (1999) Washington DC, World Bank.

Kevane, M. (1996). "Agrarian Structure and Agricultural Practise. Typology and Application to Western Sudan", *American Journal of Agricultural Economics* 78(1):236-45.

Kochar, A. (1997). "Does Lack of Access to Formal Credit Agricultural Production? Evidence from the Land Tenancy Market in Rural India." *American Journal*.

Kranton, R. E. and A. V. Swamy (1999). "The Hazards of Piecemeal Reform: British Civil Courts and the Credit Market in Colonial India." *Journal of Development Economics* 58(1): 1-24.

Lanjouw, J. O. (1999). "Information and the Operation of Markets: Tests Based on a General Equilibrium Model of Land Leasing in India." *Journal of Development Economics* 60(2): 497-527.

Lastarria-Cornhiel, Susana and Jolyne, Melmed-Sanjak (1998). "Land Tenancy in Asia, Africa, and Latin America: A Look at the Past and a View to the Future". Madison: Land Tenure Center, University of Wisconsin.

Lopez, R. and A. Valdez (2000). *Rural Poverty in Latin America.* New York and London: St. Maritn's Press and Macmillan Press.

Mookherjee, D. (1997). "Informational Rents and Property Rights in Land." In J. Roemer, ed., *Property Relations, Incentives, and Welfare.* New York: Macmillan Press.

Platteau, Jean-Philippe (1992). Land Reform and Structural Adjustment in Sub-Saharan Africa: Controversies and Guidelines. *Economic and Social Development Paper No. 107.* Rome: FAO.

Procuradoria, Agraria (1998). *Los Tratos en Ejidos Certificados.* Mexico City: Procuradaoria Agraria.

Quisumbing, A. R. (2001). "Women's Land Rights in the Transition to Individualized Ownership: Implications for Tree-Resource Management in Western Ghana." *Economic Development and Cultural Change* 50(1): 157-81.

Radhakrishnan, P. (1990). "Land Reforms: Rhetoric and Reality." *Economic and Political Weekly* 25(47): 2617-21.

Rosenzweig, M. R. and K. I. Wolpin (1985). "Specific Experience. Household Structure, and Intergenerational Transfers: Farm Family and Labour Arrangements in Developing Countries." *Quarterly Journal of Economics* 100(5): 961-87.

Sajaastad, E. and Daniel Bromely (1997). "Indigenous Land Rights in Sub-Saharan Africa: Appropriation Security and Investment Demand", *World Development* 25(4).

Sarap, K. (1998). "On the Operation of the Land Market in Backward Agriculture: Evidence form a Village in Orissa, Eastern India." *Journal of Peasant Studies* 25(2): 102-30.

Sarap, K. (1996). "Land Market Transactions in Rural Haryana, India", *Economic and Political Weekly*, Vol. 31, No. 29.

Sarap, K. (1991). *Interlinked Agrarian Markets in Rural India*, New Delhi, Sage Publication.

Sharma, N. and J. Dreze (1996). "Sharecropping in a North Indian Village." *Journal of Development Studies* 33(1): 1-39.

Sherry, S. (1998). "Limited Liability. Wealth Differences, and Tenancy Contracts in Agrarian Economies." *Journal of Development Economics* 29(1): 1-22.

Shit, H. (1992). *Chinese Rural Society in Transition: A case study of the Lake Tai Area.* Berkeley: University of California Press.

Sjaastad, E. and Daniel Bromley (1997). "Indigenous Land Rights in Sub-Saharan Africa: Appropriation, Security and Investment Demand". *World Development*, 25(4): 549-62.

Swamy, D. S. (1988). "Agricultural Tenancy in the 1970s." *Indian Journal of Agricultural Economics* 43(4): 555-68.

Swinnen, Johan (1998). "Land Leasing in Western Europe: A Historical Perspective". Policy Research Working Group Paper. Leuven, Belgium: Katholieke Universiteit.

Takekoshi, Y. (1967). *The Economic Aspects of the History of the Civilization of Japan.* London: MacMillan.

Thimmaiah, G. (2001). "New Perspectives on Land Reform in India." *Journal of Social and Economic Development* 3(2): 179-97.

Thorat, S. (1997). "Trends in Land Ownership, Tenancy, and Land Reform." In M. D. Bhupur, ed., *Agricultural Development Paradigm for the Ninth Plan under the New Economic Environment.* New Delhi: Oxford and IBH Publishing.

Udry, Christopher (1996). "Gender, Agricultural Production, and the Theory of the Household". *Journal of Political Economy*, 104(5):1010-46.

World Bank, (2003). *Land Policies for Growth and Poverty Reduction*, Oxford University Press.

Chapter 14

Land Markets, Agrarian Structure and Poverty in Andhra Pradesh

R. VIJAY

I
INTRODUCTION

Discussions regarding the market for land in developing countries is usually centred around tenurial transactions, which seem to dominate the transactions in land. In terms of sale and purchase, the market is described as being inactive. Purely in terms of mainstream Neoclassical Economics, there are a number of explanations proposed in the literature, for this inertia in the market for sale and purchase of land. They range from issues relating to ill-defined property rights structures to inadequacy of the price mechanism in capturing the benefits derived from land and a model of interim transactions in land (Basu, 1986). If there are differences in individuals' skill and endowment of different factors of production, markets should help in optimizing factor proportions employed and thus increase overall efficiency of resource allocation. Inactivity in land market would hinder this smooth reallocation of resources, undermining efficiency of resource allocation[1]. An inefficient allocation of resources would imply that at least one agent can be made better off by a re-allocation. Any pereto inferior allocation would imply that a re-distribution of resource between agents leads to efficiency. This re-distribution could be done either by the market or by the state in terms of land reform policy (Vijay, 1992).

Another important issue in agriculture is the persistence of poverty in the rural areas. This poverty is said to be concentrated in the landless labour and marginal farmers. An issue that is raised in this context is: can formation of market solve the problem of poverty in this segment. By markets one means the market for land, labour and credit markets. Before one can address this issue one needs to analyse the nature and interrelationship between all the three markets. If the land market is incomplete one needs to address whether this affects the formation of the other rural markets.

This paper is divided into six parts. In the second part we present the relationship between the market and structure of the economy. The third section analysis the literature related to the land market. The emphasis is the present the reasons for the low turnover in the market with an emphasis on presentation of a micro model for low turnover in the market. The fourth section presents the villages selected for analysis. The fifth section presents the nature and functioning of the market in the surveyed villages. The last section presents the relation of markets and poverty.

II

LAND MARKETS AND EXOGENOUS STIMULUS

The literature on land markets is dominated by the 'Property Rights School' or the pareto of optimality framework but it would be somewhat tedious here to relate the ground realities of the Indian agricultural land markets. At the empirical, there are quite a few studies on the Land market. An early article on the land market was by V. M. Rao (1972) who studied the land market transaction in villages in the ryotwari regions in Maharashtra. The main conclusion of was that "...sale of land by cultivators, would imply a price-inelastic supply curve" with fixed amount of land entering the market each year which is not a function of the price. The later studies attempt to study the condition of sales and by implication analyze the nature of the land market. The dominant opinion is that the sale of land is under distress condition, which are referred to as distress sales. Kailas Sarap (1990, 1995) in his study of land market in Sambalpur district of Orissa maintains that " the behaviour of land sale and purchase transactions showed the sluggish nature of land market but distress sale is an important phenomenon in the villages". There are other studies also which maintain that sale of land is under distress condition. Deininger and Fader say that undiversifiable residual risk causes farmers to resort to liquidation of their asset during periods of severe crisis (provided the market for credit and insurance is missing), a phenomenon commonly referred to as distress sales.

There are few studies analyze the funds to purchase of the purchases. The "...purchases of land are almost all undertaken by individuals with access to sources of income which are not correlated with agricultural production and that borrowing to finance land acquisition is virtually non-existent (Sarap, 1990). The demand for land are by households who have access to non-agricultural income implying that may be the purchases are non-cultivating households. The literature maintains that the sale of land is due to a shock (temporary) on to the agent and the lack of insurance mechanism to handle this shock. If this is a temporary shock, agents would like to purchase the land back after the shock, which is termed interim sales. What is more important is the external structure which also activates land markets. The outcomes do depend on the nature of external interventions.

An examination of the literature on land transactions suggests that activity in the land market is dictated by exogenous stimuli or changes. Land being a productive asset, i.e. an asset necessary for agricultural production, sale of land would clearly be affected by alternatives in investment and employment available, i.e. by the alternative income streams available. This suggests that the impact of a change in the functioning of the economy, on the land market, can be judged by evaluating the alternative scenarios available. In this section, we propose to examine a few such changes, some of, which affect agricultural sector directly, while some others work through the rest of the economy. Since the existence or emergence of alternatives outside agriculture, comes out as a major determinant for sale of land, we will start by looking at the impact of setting up an industry. The impact of changes in technology in agriculture, which raise the output per acre of land, are discussed next. In the general context of interim transactions and specifically, with reference to technological progress in agriculture, credit markets emerge as a solution to the problem faced by the agent. We examine the impact of such credit markets on the land market. Finally, the impacts of interventions in the labour market are taken up for assessment, given the close link between land and labour markets.

A. Expansion of Investment and/or Employment Opportunities outside Agriculture

Expansion of employment opportunities outside agriculture, such that such opportunities assure a higher wage than in agriculture, would attract labour from agriculture. Similarly, an expansion of investment opportunities outside agriculture would induce a flow of investible resources in such directions. The mopping up of such resources would take the form of sale of land in agriculture, the seller directing the proceeds of the sale to investment in non-agriculture.

The former, by inducing outward migration of labour, would make labour scarce in agriculture. This would have obvious wage raising implications, altering the costs of production. In the process, some hitherto viable units of production in agriculture may become unprofitable. The agent here is left with no option but to sell of land. The continuous expanding set of opportunities, however, can ensure that the transaction is desirable by agents. In other words, agents selling land in this context would take the decision in favour of a regular sale and one would observe the functioning of an active land market. Where transactions would change the composition of the set of agents owning land. This is in contrast to a market characterized predominantly by interim sales, where the set of agents remains unchanged in spite of transactions.

Here, expansion of investment opportunities contributes to hastening such a process, both through the direct stimulus and through its impact on the generation of labour scarcity. An expanding industrial sector provides precisely these two stimuli, encouraging growth of both land and labour markets, which are closely linked, as is evident form earlier discussion.

B. Changes in the Production Function of Agriculture

Consider public investment in the form of a major irrigation project—A dam. The introduction of a dam, i.e. of irrigation facilities, by expanding the production potential of land, would suggest that output per acre of land increases. Further, this is likely to contribute to stabilizing the fluctuations in outputs and incomes from agriculture. These two together would suggest that the need for interim transactions is reduced. On the other hand, since the opportunities in the rest of the economy, are assumed to remain unchanged, the incentive for regular sales too do not exist. In other words, the introduction of technological progress, which is scale neutral and does not involve any costs of adoption, would only contribute to strengthening the rigidity of the land market.

Any change in technology, however, normally involves some costs of adaptation to the technology. For instance, introduction of irrigation calls for investments for levelling the land. In the presence of such costs, the marginal households/savings deficit agents would be out priced. Such agents cannot afford the costs and could well be left with no option but to sell out. Here, the desire for an "interim sale" may well consolidate into a "regular sale"[2]. The case of introduction of HYV technology (high yielding varieties of seeds and the production techniques) too would have similar impact, i.e. such technologies would involve some scale economies in costs, or perhaps, one can view the costs of adoption as some entry price for adoption of technology[3]. In such instances, while some interim transactions could be observed when the economy is adjusting to the introduction of new technology, once the adjustment is complete, the land market would become inert, once again.

C. Interventions in the Credit Market

Our discussion on the basis for interim sales suggests the need for some source of credit to take care of the exigencies created by various shocks faced by the agents. In sharp contrast to interim sales, with credit institutions, even those based on land mortgages, the agent retains use of his land. This very feature enhances the repaying capacity of the agent. The needs for interim transactions, therefore, get considerably reduced. This suggests that the land market becomes more rigid, i.e. the economy settles into a *status quo*.

Further, if one visualizes the role of credit institutions in the context of technological improvements or public investment in agriculture, as discussed in the earlier sub-section, the existence of such institutions would clearly facilitate the adoption of the new technology. In the process, given the assured supplies of credit and liquidity, the need for interim transactions and the basis for regular sales are reduced. In other words, this would further enhance the inactivity in the land market.

D. Interventions in the Labour Market

As discussed in the context of the first subsection here, generation of scarcity in the labour market provides a good stimulus to the land market. Generation of alternative means of employment, providing some steady streams of income and/or by raising the wages, would render some marginal cultivation units unviable, leading to the sale (regular sale, in this case) of such land. Further, the emergence of such alternatives would have a further adverse impact, on costs of production, encouraging the viable units to adopt various productivity enhancing and even labour saving techniques, both of which would require investment in agricultural production. The introduction of such technology, by altering the rates of return to land, might contribute further to either investments in land or regular sale of land, in favour of becoming labourers. Thus, activity in the land market receives a positive fillip. Any interventions in the labour market, which can successfully alter the relative scarcity of land *vis-à-vis* labour would set in motion such a process. A necessary condition, however, is the generation of a belief of the availability of consistent employment opportunities. The employment generation and employment guarantee schemes could provide one such stimulus.

III
THE VILLAGES AND MARKETS: A STUDY OF ANDHRA PRADESH

Agrarian institutions, including the market institutions, have a tendency to undergo changes and transformation, and these changes are associated with the level of development of the regions and sub regions. This is more so when the total economy is not well integrated within itself. For instance, in Andhra Pradesh, it is common to note the existence of the regions, namely, Telangana, Rayalaseema and Coastal Andhra, which can be seen as an illustration of non-integrated regions. However, taking the levels of development, the state is sometimes grouped into five regions. In the scale of development, South Coastal Andhra comprising the Krishna-Godavari-Penna delta region, namely the districts of East Godavari, West Godavari, Krishna, Guntur, Prakasam and Nellore occupies the top place, with a high index of output per hectare. Next in importance comes the region of North Telangana, comprising the districts of Nizamabad, Adilabad,

Karimnagar and Khammam. North Coastal Andhra comprising Srikakulam, Vijayanagaram and Visakhapatnam occupies the third place. Rayalaseema has the fourth place, comprising Cuddapah, Kurnool, Ananthpur and Chittoor and South Telangana comprising Rangareddy, Hyderabad, Mahaboobnagar, Medak and Nalgonda, the fifth place. The regional differences are partly historical and partly due to differential public investments and complimentary private investments. As the institutions are likely to undergo changes with level of investments and consequent level of development, the nine sample villages are chosen from across the regions, except Rayalaseema.

It is usual to present data on farm households on the basis of land classification, either land owned or operated. The agricultural census for example presents data on the basis of land classification. Consolidates of such data is made into Marginal, Small, Semi-Medium, Medium and Large holdings on the basis of size of area held. Given that labour is the predominant factor of production relative to capital, which includes the technology-embodied in it, the use of labour plays an important role in determining inter-farm differences. The farm sector uses not only the physical labour but also the mental labour, that is the knowledge of production process. This is important in the Indian contest, where by tradition; certain caste groups are not permitted to do cultivation themselves but to have ownership and control over the land. While at the other extreme we have cultivation castes who have knowledge on the process of production and whose labour cannot be fully productively employed on agriculture, as they do not have access to land. To mitigate the difficulty that arises due to inherent disjunction in distribution of the land and distribution of labour, the system develops institutions such as tenancy, permanent farm servants, and wage labour to produce output from the mental and manual labour of the peasantry for the households who have only land, but do not cultivate. This is one segment of the agrarian sector with landholders on the one side and labour holders on the other. Another segment of the agrarian sector is the households who have lands and have also necessary labour. These two segments differ significantly in the use of resources, both land and labour, and have different objective function. To capture the inter-farm difference it is essential to classify the households on the basis of resource and the use of labour on the farms. For this purpose we have adopted a five-fold classification. At one end of the spectrum we have households who owned land but not do participate in production.

They may either lease-out land, employ farm servants to organize production or keep the land fallow. These we are calling 'Non-cultivating Households'. These non-cultivating households can be landlords in the conventional sense, can be a government servant, school teacher in the nearby town, can be from non-cultivating caste groups or can be disabled households. The major interest of these households in agriculture is to draw a rental income from land.

The second category is 'Rich Peasant Group', the distinguishing factor of these groups is that they actively participate in the various agricultural operations on their farm. The households may employ permanent farm servants; casual labour and contract labour as the need arises to supplement the deficiencies in supply of labour. The households may or may not own land and may operate on leased-in land either completely or partially. As the households draws on the labour from other households to meet its shortage, logically the household does not supply labour to the other household and by its nature this group holds land not as a rent-yielding asset, but as productive asset, has information on production processes, operates in the labour market, can operate in lease market. The group is market dependent and also has a capacity to generate markets.

The third category 'Middle Peasant Group' distinguishes itself from rich peasant group by its exclusive dependence on family labour to the exclusion of any dependency on labour market for its own farm production. Further it also, like rich peasants, do not contribute to the supply of labour to the labour market. Given the nature of agriculture operations and its timeliness, it does take labour from other families on the basis of exchange labour, and at times, may draw on the labour market also. By its nature the group has self-consumption as an objective of production and has least market orientation and market dependency.

The fourth category is the 'Poor Peasant Group'. The households belonging to this group use their family labour to there own farms but also supply labour to the labour market and thus work on other farm. They derive income from farming as well as from wages, thus forming a major segment of labour supply in the village. The group may either own land or participate in the tenancy market, may produce for market or produce for self-consumption, may opt for non-farm activities, may resort to migration if the agriculture does not provide sufficient income. The strength of this group to sustain within the village or reproduce themselves within the village depends crucially on the strength and operation of its counterpart—the 'Rich Peasant Group' and this is dependent on that group's dynamism and activity.

The fifth category is the group of households who are entirely dependent on sale of labour and this category is called 'Agriculture Labour Group'. Devoid of any ownership of land, the group derives its sustenance from selling labour either as permanent farm servant (sometimes as an inter-generational bonded labour) or as a casual labour, or migrate to agricultural works in neighbouring villages or migrate to the urban areas as manual workers in the informal sector. Depending on the structure of the economy in which they operate, their households try to become cultivators by leasing-in land. But basically they are the suppliers of labour.

The Nature of Functioning of Markets

Based on the above labour-use based classification of rural households, we discuss the functioning of rural land, labour and credit markets. The total number of households in the nine villages are 1737 (Table 14.1) and the total land owned is 3740.35 acres. The average size of land holding works out to be 2.15 acres. In terms of number of families, 'Poor Peasantry' forms a large part of the rural economy and also is the main holders of land in the village. They form 43.29 per cent of the total households in the villages and own nearly 35 per cent of the total cultivated land in the village. If one adds the number of agricultural labourer households to the number of poor peasant household one sees that these two groups form 71 per cent of the total households but own only 36 per cent of the cultivated land.

Table 14.1: Distribution of Households and Land According to Labour Use Classification

(*land in acres*)

Classification	*No. of households*	*% of total households*	*Land owned*	*% of total area*	*Avg. Size*
Agriculture labour	490	28.21	44.13	1.18	0.09
Poor peasant	752	43.29	1333.98	35.66	1.77
Middle Peasant	323	18.60	1014.55	27.12	3.14
Rich Peasant	77	4.43	601.50	16.08	7.81
Non-Cultivating households	95	5.47	746.20	19.95	7.85
All households	1737	100.00	3740.35	100.00	2.15

Source: Field Survey.

The next important group is the 'Middle Peasants' who form 18 per cent of the households and own 27 per cent of the land. The market friendly 'Rich Peasants' form 4 per cent of the households and own 16 per cent of the total cultivated land. The other group is the 'Non-cultivating Households' who form 5 per cent of the households in the village and own nearly 20 per cent of the land.[4]

The Land Market

The nine villages have witnessed 115 sales transactions in the last five years (1998-2003). The total land sold in these transactions is 169.84 acres. The number of purchases in the last five years is 105.98 acres and this is spread in 65 transactions. This discrepancy between sales and purchase transactions are due to underreporting of purchased by some households. Table 14.2 provides information on the number and extent of land sold and purchased in the different size groups. Here one is interested to see who is the main player in the market, i.e. in the demand as well as the supply side. Are the rich peasants main players as buyers or are the non-cultivating households? Where do the poor and middle peasants stand in the market? This would provide information on the evolving structure of the agrarian economy. Net sales define the differences between the sales and the purchases of land in the market. If one has a negative sign for this variable it means sales are less than purchases and the opposite holds if the sign of the variable is positive. We are calculating this variable for each size group in the village. A positive sign for the variable implies that the size-group is on the average a seller of land while a negative sign for the variable implies households in this size group are on the average buyers of land.

At a aggregate level, one sees that the net sales is a negative number which implies that extent of land sold is greater than the extent of land purchased. There may be two reasons for the discrepancy. One potential reason for this difference is that households are systematically under reporting purchase but not sales. Another reason could be the methodology of the survey. The survey was a complete enumeration of all households in the village and not of all households who own land in the village. If there exists households who own land in the village but stay outside the village, these households are not part of the survey. If there exist a large number of purchases of land by households who do not reside in the village one is not able to capture these households. The positive sign for the net sales variable reflects that residents from outside the village are buying land. If non-residents are purchasing land majority of these households are not directly involved in cultivation and so these households are non-cultivating households. So one inference that one can draw is that not only 'Non-cultivators' in the village but also 'Non-cultivators' from outside could be the net buyers of land.

Table 14.2: Distribution of Sales and Purchase of Land According to Labour Use Classification of Households

(land in acres)

Classification	Sales		Purchases		Net Sales
	No. of transactions	*Area*	*No. of transactions*	*Area*	
Agriculture labour	0	0	0	0	0
Poor Peasant	43	41.84	23	19.79	22.05
Middle Peasant	46	58.70	26	27.55	31.16
Rich Peasant	15	23.48	3	6.40	17.08
Non-Cultivating households	11	45.83	13	52.25	-6.43
All households	115	169.84	65	105.98	63.86

Source: Field Survey.

Does this trend hold true for all the different size groups? An expanding economy, either in terms of output market or for returns to factors of production, would imply the rich peasant being the purchasers of land and other groups being the sellers of land. One sees from Table 14.2 that rich peasants are net sellers of land in the village. In terms of size groups the only segment, which are net purchases of land, are the non-cultivating households all other size groups have net sales only. The middle peasant and the poor peasant are also net sellers of land in the village. This would imply two things. One, the outside economy is not growing at a fast rate and two the uncertainty related to the output market are also large and so households are not purchasing the land. This is also corroborated with the evidence that the non-cultivators are net purchasers of land and total sales exceed the total purchase of land in the village. However, land market transactions could not be seen to reflect the stagnation of the outside economy resulting in non-cultivators being the main purchasers of land, while all other class groups including rich peasants being the net sellers of land. The fact that those from outside the village too are buying land, could also reflect the growing importance of land as a store of value, and more often with a speculative motive. This would make access to land by the poor through the land market route much more restricted.

Land Lease Market

A land lease market can be seen to have two different roles. In one case the rich peasants in the economy, who are market friendly, want to expand their operated land but not the owned land, can depend on the land lease market to facilitate the temporary land transfer in their favour. The second process is where agricultural labourers and poor peasantry want access to land so that they can care of their food needs and not depend on the vagaries of the market. In popular literature these segments are called the 'land hunger' segment. In one process one is adjusting to produce for the market while in the second process agents adjust so as to meet their consumption directly by producing what they consume. Here we would like to see the nature of adjustment in the study villages.

Here we present the extent and number of leasing-out contracts and then following it with the extent and number of leasing-in contracts. The total number of households who have reported leasing-out land in the village are 123 and the extent of land leased-out is 477.91 acres. The average land leased-out per contract is 1.45. The dominant leasing-out agents in the villages are the non-cultivating households and they contribute nearly 72 per cent of the land leased-out in the market. The other size groups have negligible extent of land leased-out, with rich and middle peasants accounting for about 10 per cent of the total land leased-out, poor peasantry accounting for about 15 per cent of the land leased-out.

Table 14.3: Distribution of land Leased-out by Households According to Labour Use Classification of Households

(*land in acres*)

Classification	*Number*	*Area*	*Share in total land leased-out*
Agriculture labour	7	8.75	1.83
Poor Peasant	32	70.41	14.73
Middle Peasant	7	28.20	5.90
Rich Peasant	5	23.00	4.81
Non-Cultivating households	72	347.55	72.72
All households	123	477.91	100.00

Source: Field Survey.

In case of leasing-in land, the total number of mostly oral or informal contracts, which are rarely recorded, are 261 and the land reported leased-in is 638 acres, i.e. nearly 17.2 per cent of the land cultivated. There is a difference between the extent of land leased-in and the extent of land leased-out. As was specified in the analysis of the land sales market, here also one needs to explain the difference. One of the reason could be underreporting by the households while the second could be leasing-out of land is by non-residents of the village and so was not reported in the questionnaire. Which are the class groups who are leasing-in land? Are they rich peasants or are they poor peasants? Nearly 50 per cent of the land leased-in is by poor peasantry and their share in the number of contracts is 60 per cent. These together with the other non-market oriented classes in the village account for nearly 80 per cent of the leased-in land. The rich peasant, the market friendly segment, leases-in only 14 per cent of leased-in land. This would imply that the poor peasants are the main demand points of land in the lease market. It suggests that there is not yet any significant extent of reverse tenancy in Andhra Pradesh. And more significantly, the non-cultivating households, who could be described as 'landlords', with no direct productive involvement agriculture, are the ones who are leasing-out. However, this observation is subject to the condition that labour use based classification also echo land based classification of households.

Table 14.4: Distribution of Land Leased-in by Households According to Labour Use Classification of Households

(* *in acres*)

Classification	*No.*	*Area**	*Share in total land leased*
Agriculture labour	6	11.50	1.80
Poor Peasant	155	313.25	49.10
Middle Peasant	78	186.25	29.19
Rich Peasant	19	93.50	14.66
Non-Cultivating households	3	33.50	5.25
All households	261	638.00	100.00

Source: Field Survey.

Here one finds an interesting relation between the land market and land lease market. In the land market land is changing hands in favour of the non-cultivating households. These households are not cultivators so these households have to identify method of organization of production. These households lease land in the lease market and so these households become demand points in the land market but are supply points in the land lease market. The poor peasants are demand points in the land market also but due to the incompletely formed credit market, their demand is not realized in form of purchases in that market. This leads then to become demand points in the land lease market. Because one does not have rich peasantry as an active player either in the land market or the land lease market, does not imply a non-growing external economy. Part of the inactivity by the rich peasantry may be due to ceilings on land holdings.

Generally land market, an active market, is one of the indicators of development where the market does re-allocate the important factor of production, namely land from inefficient producers to efficient producers. This is supposed to increase the overall efficiency of the system. In the absence of an active land market, the land lease market is supposed to perform the task of re-allocation. The land lease market, being a short run adjustment process, may give static efficiency but raises questions of incentive to invest in soil and land development. Considerable body of literature exists which highlights such incentive problems as a case of regulating/abolishing of tenancy. Such literature looks at the incidence of tenancy as an arrangement between large landholders (non-cultivating households) and small landholders cum agricultural labourers. However, recent literature on tenancy makes a comparison between owner operated cultivators and pure tenants as well as mixed tenants categories to study the efficiency implications of tenancy arrangements. A case can be made out for such study if market oriented rich peasants enter the tenancy arrangements with scale-wise inefficient smaller units or a non-cultivator. Such arrangements can lead to greater efficiency and also may solve some incentive problems. In the literature, it is sometimes referred to as reverse tenancy, with small landholders leasing out to big rich peasant households. Tenancy, per say, if contextualized, can play different role. In this context, the study of nine villages shows some interesting observations.

Resource Endowments and Land Lease Market

Irrigated villages among the nine villages, there are two villages, namely Mentipudi and Kothapalli, which are in West Godavari district. The villages have a history of more than hundred years of canal irrigation with the provision of water for irrigation for two crops per year. Consequently, the village recorded the highest value of output per acre and has lowest variation in output per households among different villages. These two villages record the highest incidence of tenancy with more than fifty per cent of land cultivated being operated under tenancy. Further, the form of tenancy is also uniform with fixed-kind rent contract being the only form. The crop grown is invariably paddy for both the seasons. The rent as a proportion of output works out to around 35 per cent in one village (Mentipudi) and more than 50 per cent in the other village (Kothapalli). Importantly, it is the poor peasants and agricultural labourer who are entering into the tenancy market as tenants. More that 50 per cent of the tenants belong to this category in these two villages. Further, substantial chunk of agricultural labourers without land are the tenants. For example, in Mentipudi 32 per cent of the tenants are households without land. In the absence of tenancy market, these households could have participated only in the labour market. In the other village, Kothapalli the situation is far worse, with 75 per cent of the tenants belonging to the poor peasant category. Further 62 per cent of these tenants are households without land. Given that these villages represent a highly irrigated double-cropped area and belong to the most developed districts, the re-appearance of tenancy in a massive scale calls for a serious economic analysis on the one hand and serious policy implication on the other hand. If we look at all the ten villages, these two villages alone contribute to about 47 per cent of the total leased-in land.

Rainfed Village

Tenancy is important in another village, namely, Jonanki in Srikakulam district. This is generally a drought affected area with only tanks as source of irrigation. Around 30 per cent of the land is leased. There are 43 contracts of tenancy and majority of them are share cropping contracts, and the average rent works out to be around 55 per cent of the output. Here again, it is the poor peasants forming around 76 per cent who enter the lease market. 21 per cent of these peasant households do not own any land.

Ground Water and Commercial Crops

Compared to these canal irrigated and dry villages, another village which is typologically different also presents a high incidence of tenancy. This village, namely Seethampet, in the replaced areas of West Godavari, has tenancy contracts which are in the form of fixed cash. The crop grown is tobacco. This village is a dry village but has irrigation provided by private tubewells. Around 16 per cent of the land is under tenancy operations and there are 28 tenancy contracts, out of which interestingly the poor peasant participation as tenants is as low as 25 per cent and the households without land entering into the tenancy market is around 14 per cent.

Others

In the rest of the five villages tenancy is not of great importance. The area operated under tenancy works out to around 7 per cent. Out of the 89 contracts, 41 contracts, i.e. nearly 46 per cent are entered by the poor peasants as tenants, while only 8 households without land also lease-in. Interestingly, in all these villages, there is no homogeneity in the type of rent contracts. There are 28 contracts which are of fixed-kind type, 18 are fixed-cash contracts and 43 are of share tenancy (Table 14.5).

There is always a notoriety associated with the data on tenancy as agents do not reveal the actual lease data and also the form of contract. Within the limitation, the above presentation does indicate that with more development via an irrigation system tenancy seems to be revisiting the economy. In such circumstances, rents are also abnormally high. In the absence of migration as alternative, the poor peasants and agricultural labourers are trapped in the village and enter the lease market. Thus not only posing the problem of incentives for investment but also a depressive situation for the generation of an active labour market. We return to this point in the next section.

Labour Market

The potential suppliers of labour in the market are agricultural labourer households and poor peasantry. These households form nearly 71 per cent (1241 households) of the total households in the villages surveyed. The analysis of the labour market depends on the demand as well as the supply behaviour.

Table 14.5: Share of Tenancy, Forms of Contract and Nature of Agents Leasing-in the Surveyed Villages

(land in acres, output and rent in rupees)

Village	Land owned (reported)	Proportion of land leased to operated land	No. of contracts			% number of tenant households who are		Average output	Rent as a share of output
			Fixed rent (Kind)	Fixed rent (cash)	Share cropping	Poor peasants	Landless labour		
Mentipudi	118.7	52.54	37	0	0	45	32	19,789.51	35
Kothapalli	116.45	66.18	78	0	0	75	62	14,548.80	52
Seethampet	375.14	15.86	1	26	1	25	14	10,987.48	51
Arepalli	1015.75	5.41	16	2	0	72	22	8,371.44	42
Tatiparti	723.82	8.45	3	8	4	66	0	2,139.55	10
Chinnapur	269.52	17.80	2	3	23	28	3.5	9,794.27	42
Nagaram	378.55	7.98	4	2	14	25	5	8,644.75	32
Jonanki	271.27	29.83	3	4	36	76	37	7,401.22	55
B.Koduru	406.79	7.67	3	3	2	62	25	10,227.66	27
Total	3702.99	16.64	147	48	80	57	32		

The demand for labour in the market is from non-cultivating households and the rich peasants. The middle peasants mostly use their own labour. The suppliers of labour in the market are agricultural labourers and the poor peasantry. The extent of demand would depend on the amount of land owned by the two segments of rich peasantry.

The rich peasant households form a dominant section in the villages under study, one would witness a dominance of casual form in the labour market. A non-cultivating household does not cultivate the land so he has to either lease-out the land or cultivate using attached labour. These two categories who depend on hired labour own only 36 per cent of the land in the villages. Nearly 64 per cent of the land is owned by households who do not demand labour from outside the household. So the size of the demand for labour is also small. In addition, 5.5 per cent of the households are non-cultivating households in the study villages and they own 20 per cent of the land. These households will not demand labour in the casual labour market but have an indirect demand for labour. Their demand for labour is mediated via the land lease market. The direct demand for labour is from the rich peasantry who form 4.5 per cent of the households and own 16 per cent of the land. So the demand for labour in the casual labour market is even smaller (Table 14.1).

The supply of labour is from the agricultural labour households and the poor peasantry. The agricultural labour households depend completely on the casual labour market, while the poor peasants operate some land as well as enter the casual labour market. The poor peasant could either be owning some land or could be leasing-in land or could also be attached labour. The choice of a household supplying labour could be to enter the casual labour form or to enter the lease form or to be attached labour or to migrate. 71 per cent of the households depend on the supply of labour in the economy. The proportions of households who are poor peasants are more than the agricultural labour households. In other words, one has households who enter the labour market partly are the dominant group. Table 14.6 gives the information on the choice of these two segments in the economy.

Migration

One sees that migration is a dominant feature for these two segments in the economy (Table 14.6). Nearly 20 per cent of the households have at least one migrant from their households in each size group. Permanent farm servants are not a very dominant choice in the survey villages but are relatively important choice for agricultural labour households. Land leasing-in is relatively important choice for the poor peasant households. Given this pattern we are interested to see if choice as casual labour market is a dominant choice from the supply side. The formation of the labour market needs the dominance to casual form of labour contract. If this is a preference towards poor peasantry this would imply non-casual labour contract to be the preferred choice and by implication a constraint to the formation of the labour market. All the villages have 752 households who were identified as poor peasants. In these there are 156 households who lease-in land. In these 156 households who have leased-in land, 90 are landless who have leased-in land or who are called as pure tenants. So one has landless households who want to lease-in land and become poor peasantry giving the impression that poor peasantry is a preferred choice. In other words, these households who are part of the agricultural labour get some access to land and become poor peasantry. This implies there is land hunger, and households given a choice prefer to lease-in land and become poor peasantry. The second option is migration wherein agents move but hold on to the land and have preference to some day come back to the villages.

Table 14.6: Choice of Poor Peasant and Agricultural Labour Households in the Study Villages

Category	*Migration*	*Permanent Farm Servants*	*Land Lease*
Agricultural labour households	98 (20.04)	31(6.33)	6 (1.22)
Poor peasantry	156 (20.74)	6 (0.79)	157 (20.87)

Note: Figures in brackets are percentage of households who have made this choice to total number of households in that class.
Source: Field Study.

Credit Market

In the village economy one sees that there exists a large segment of households called the poor peasants who have a desire to purchase land but lack the corresponding purchasing power. One source of funds for purchasing land is the past savings of the households. The second source is credit from the banks and financial institutions. A well developed market for credit may be able to solve this problem of the household. Credit market also has two hands, the demand and the supply side. Let us consider the demand side factors.

Demand for credit could be broadly classified into demand for credit for consumption purpose and demand for credit for production purpose. Here we introduce current production needs (crop loans) as well as for capital investment by household into production purpose. Consumption purpose consists of loan for family consumption, housing, health, education, livestock and marriage. The share of consumption loan in total loan is approximately 55 per cent, i.e. major share of the credit is taken for consumption purpose in the study village.

Table 14.7: Distribution of Credit Taken and Purpose for Credit taken by Labour Use Classification

(*In 000's)

Classification	*Number of House-holds*	*Total loan taken**	*Loan per House-hold*	*Loan per acre*	*% of Non-Agricultural loan in total loans*
Agricultural labour	490	645	1.32	Not applicable	95
Poor peasant	752	1873	2.49	1.37	58
Middle peasant	323	1172	3.63	1.14	40
Rich Peasant	76	603	7.94	1.00	25
Non-Cultivating Household	96	273	2.84	0.33	65
All villages	1737	4565	2.63	1.18	55

Source: Field Study.

Does this trend exist for all size groups in the economy? In case of agricultural labourer the share of consumption loan is 95 per cent. This is expected as these households do not have any productive investment and so any loan has to be for consumption purpose. The poor peasant share of loan for consumption is 58 per cent and from that class group all higher class groups have less that 40 per cent loans taken for consumption. The non-cultivating households are the next important group who take loans mainly for consumption purpose, i.e. 65 per cent of the loans taken by this class is for consumption purpose. In the demand side, consumption loans dominate at the aggregate level while more that 50 per cent of the loans taken by agricultural labourer and poor peasantry is for consumption purpose (Table 14.8).

Table 14.8: Distribution of Non-institutional Credit and its Share in Total Credit According to Labour Use Classification

(*in 0000's)

Classification	*Non-Ins. Amount**	*Share in Total Credit*	*Avg. loan per acre**
Agricultural labour	613	95	Not Applicable
Poor peasant	1435	77	1.05
Middle peasant	770	66	0.75
Rich Peasant	270	45	0.45
Non-Cultivating Household	216	79	0.26
All villages	3303	72	0.86

Source: Field Study.

The total credit transacted in all the villages is 4.6 crores. In this amount of loan transacted the share of loan of agricultural labourer 14 per cent and the share of poor peasant is 41 per cent, i.e. the share of loans in of poor peasantry and agricultural labourer is 55 per cent. So in the total loans transacted in the villages 55 per cent of the loans are to agricultural labourer and poor peasantry and 55 per cent of the loans in the village are for consumption purpose. In the consumption purpose the dominant need is by the agricultural labourer and poor peasantry. [The high share of consumption loan in total loans is true for agricultural labour and poor peasant in all villages individually also. Two of the villages, which were selected from the delta region also, showed the same trend. So irrigation by itself does not solve the problem]. If the demand points of credit are these two segments a feature which is important is that they do not have a credible collateral and so are not able to approach the institutional sources. In addition, credit market transactions have an important information problem making the institutional sources a non-viable source of credit. This makes the credit market localized and personalized.

The main demander in the market influences the supply of credit and as they lack credible collateral and there exist information problems in the economy the non-institutional sources are the main supplier of credit in the market. Out of the total loans nearly 72 per cent of the loans are by non-institutional sources. The share of loans being advanced to agricultural labourer in the non-institutional sector is 18 per cent while the share of poor peasantry is 43 per cent. The share of credit advanced by non-institutional sources to agricultural labour household and poor peasant is 61 per cent.

But is the share of non-institutional credit in total credit an important feature. The agricultural labourer take 95 per cent of the loans from non-institutional sources while the share of poor peasantry is 77 per cent.

In case of the credit market one has the situation where the main demander of land are agricultural labourer and poor peasantry and they take credit for consumption purpose and so the supplier of credit are non-institutional sources thus constraining the formation of the credit market[5].

Inter-relationship between Markets

Given the context of the non-growing rest of the economy, the rich peasant are not the main player in the market and the main demanders of land are non-cultivating households. As these households are the main demander of land in the land market but are not actual cultivators and so these households would lease-out land, i.e. these households would be supply points in the lease market. Another potential demand point in the land market is the poor peasantry but their demand can not be realized due to credit market constraint. As these households are not able meet their consumption due to uncertainties in the labour market they are demand points for land in the lease market. Thus in the general context of non-growing outside economy the land market is incompletely formed with non-cultivators purchasing land. As these households cannot cultivate the land lease market becomes active with poor peasantry leasing-in land to meet subsistence.

In case of labour market the demand for labour is by rich peasantry and non-cultivating households. The rich peasant need an active labour market but there share of land in the village economy is small and so their demand is small which increases the uncertainty in the market for supplier of labour. The second demand point is non-cultivating households but they do not directly demand labour in casual labour market but have an indirect demand for labour, i.e. through the lease or attached labour. Given that rich peasant are a small segment the uncertainties with respect to labour market would be high and so labour supplying households would not prefer to enter the labour market but will look for alternative methods of supplying labour like lease or attached labour or will migrate out of the village. As the labour-supplying households do not have a preference to enter the labour market but look for alternate institutions to earn income the labour market is incompletely formed. The land lease market connects the land and the lease markets.

If the labour market is incompletely formed poverty gets concentrated in the agricultural labour and poor peasant households. So these households need credit to meet their consumption and so consumption credit becomes an important feature of the credit market. The poor peasantry and agricultural labour households are the main demanders of credit in the market and this credit is supplied by non-institutional sources. So one has a credit market where non-institutional credit dominates and they lead to consumption purpose only. This leads to the credit market to become localized and personalized.

IV
LAND MARKETS AND POVERTY

Ever since the publication of the results of the study by Dandekar and Rath on Poverty, almost three decades ago, estimation of extent of poverty and methods to eliminate poverty are an important agenda for research and policy formulation. To the extent it is a recurrent theme, poverty indicates that it is both a long run structural problem as well as a temporary shock related adjustment problem. In the later category come situations like a drought/famine, where market for food grains goes for a disequilibrium position indicating high prices of foodgrains or which is the same thing as lack of foodgrains at the previously available prices. The survey period is one such period when the agricultural sector in Andhra Pradesh was passing through repeated shocks of lack of rainfall. As a result most of the households independent of the resource position, report poverty like situation. The estimation of poverty line and the numbers below that line for a long time remained at level where the human being will not be in a position to reproduce biologically, i.e. in terms of work effort, without a state intervention in supplying the minimum calories food requirement. The 2000 calorie requirement determining the poverty line thus speaks of one dimension of poverty. Translated into a policy framework, the calorie-norm gets into what is called the white cards in Andhra Pradesh. A white card holder gets food grains at a subsidised price.

This paper does not attempt to study independently the measurement of the number of households below the poverty line. However, we present information on the households possessing white cards as an indicator of poverty. Any 'indicator' has in built bias more so in case of white card holders as indicator of poverty. The allotment of the cards is at the local level and based on subjective valuations. Any rule has enormous subjectivity and this subjectivity gets reflected in political, administrative implementation of the rule. Given the limitation of the indicator, in the following table, we present data on the distribution of white cards across households, classified by class and village.

Tables 14.9 and 14.10 presents the data from the survey discussed above. 66.27 per cent of the households reported possessing white cards. The figure varies from around 54 per cent in Mentipudi in West Godavari district to about 90 per cent in Tatiparti in Mahboobnagar. Among the different classes naturally, the poorer sections of the households, namely agricultural labour and poor peasant households have a substantially higher share of white cardholders. Surprisingly around 17.5 per cent of the rich peasant households and 47 per cent of the middle peasant households possess white cards. Even the non-cultivating households have a 33 per cent of white cardholders.

If one takes a figure of 30 per cent as a number of people below poverty line in rural areas, an easier thumb rule could be to locate households belonging to agricultural labour who do not own any land, this figure also works out at 30 per cent of the households. The survey records that in this class nearly 75 per cent of the households could avail the facility of white cards.

Table 14.9: Class-wise Distribution of B.P.L. Households in Survey Villages

Classification	*Number of B.P.L. Households*	*Total number of households*	*Proportion of BPL households in Total Households*
Agricultural Labourers	410	545	75.22
Poor Peasants	594	759	78.26
Middle Peasants	167	352	47.30
Rich Peasants	14	80	17.50
Non-cultivating households	34	102	33.34
Total	1219	1838	66.27

Source: Field Study.

Table 14.10: Village-wise Distribution of B.P.L. Households in Survey Villages

Name of the village	*Number of B.P.L. Households*	*Total number of households*	*Proportion of BPL households in Total Households*
Mentipudi	49	90	54.44
Kothapalli	154	208	74.03
Seethampet	97	170	57.05
Arepalli	195	669	57.52
Tatiparti	196	216	90.74
Chinnapur	143	216	66.20
Nagaram	71	170	41.52
Jonanki	110	151	72.84
Bontalakoduru	142	177	80.22
Cheldiganipalli	62	101	61.38
Total	1219	1838	66.32

Source: Field Study.

Poverty, apart from being a temporary phenomenon, also exists as a long terms phenomenon, indicating a structural causation. The present paper is an attempt to understand the nature of structures that guide the agricultural sector of the economy. Poverty, in terms of structures arises when there is an inflexibility in the structures to absorb the resources of the individual agent, thus keeping the agents in the margin without offering a scope for the agent to reproduce the activity not to speak of expanded reproduction. The structures we studies in the paper are market structures for the various resources of the agents. In that context, if the labour market is inflexible, with say, a downwardly rigid wage structure, the agent whose only resource is labour meant for sale, the system can produce underemployed labour whose human reproduction can be only through "doles" or some sort of unemployment insurance/relief by the state outside the market structures. This poverty generated by the inflexibility in the structures can be a long term phenomenon, if the structures themselves cannot be flexible, evolving into newer structures.

Given that the Indian economy is following a capitalist/market structure, an element of inflexibility gets introduced in the structure if one of the resources, namely land, does not follow the rules of the market or to say the same thing differently, the land market is inactive. To the extent that any agent who has a desire to buy (sell) land can do so at a price, the market is active and has a self-regulatory capacity to adjust for any disturbance causing a disequilibrium. An active land market has both the seller and the buyer expressing their preferences for land through a price indicator. In the absence if an active land market, the rest of the markets are also likely to be constrained either by the supply side factors or demand side factors generating conditions where the resources of the agents cannot be absorbed by the structures, leading to a poverty situation which is structure related and hence has a long term implication.

An inactive land market thus imposes inflexibility in the system and can cause poverty. However, it is important to note that there are three market based solutions for the removal of poverty. They are as follows:

(i) An active land market would facilitate the transfer of land to the efficient land user. Given the general context wherein the small farmers are said to be more efficient than the large farmers, one would expect land to be transferred to the small farmers. But the market is not transferring the land to the efficient small farmer. In addition, it was seen in the study villages that net transfer of land is not to the cultivators but to the non-cultivators in the economy. A non-cultivators purchases land as a store of value and not as a productive asset and so would not have any incentive to increase productivity in the short or in the long run. So the land market transactions in the study villages are not in favour of agricultural labour households and/or the poor peasantry but to the non-cultivating households. Secondly, if the land transfers are towards the rich peasantry, i.e. the demanders of labour, one would have expected an increase in employment and reduction of poverty but this process is also not taking place.

(ii) A second process to decrease poverty by the markets is if the external economy (i.e. the economy outside the village economy) is growing fast. In this case the interim transaction would be converted into permanent transaction and land as a productive asset would dominate over land as a store of value.

(iii) The third process is one where the lease market plays an important role in the context of inactivity of the land market.

> The literature on lease market identifies that in the general context of inactive land market households adjust their resources in the lease market. In the process the households have access to land (at least in the short run as they can not own land due to the nature of the market) and this would mitigate the problem of poverty of the households. In the study areas one did sec the important role played by lease in the rural economy. In some villages more that 50 per cent of the land is under lease (Mentipudi, Kothapalli). Does the lease market mitigate the problem of poverty for the agricultural labourers and poor peasantry households? In the short run, under conditions of excess supply of households from poor peasantry and agricultural labour households who would like to lease in land (as this provides food security) the rental rates would be very high and the lease-in households will be at their subsistence level and any random shock on to the household (like sickness or marriage) will push the households to below poverty line. Given the excess supply of households to enter the lease market and non-written nature of the contract the tenants is vulnerable in the short and also have effects on the long run. In a lease arrangement without written contract both the agents may not have any incentive to invest and so the long-term growth process is affected. So in the short run the households is pushed to subsistence level or even below it while in the long run the economy may be stagnant affecting the long-term demand for labour. So though lease provides access to land but it may not mitigate the problem of rural poverty.

The thrust of the paper is that the village economy has a structure in terms of the five classes. The specific result of the structure is the constraints to the formation of the land, labour and credit markets. In the structure described there are no processes that can generate the market or change the structure. This structure is self-reproducing under conditions of non-expanding external economy and/or the output market. One process, which can change the structure, is if the rich peasants are more dominant in the economy. This segment are the market friendly segment and if the output market is expanding this segment can change the structure and also facilitate the formation of the land, labour and credit markets in the agrarian economy. But a non-expanding output market does not allow this segment to play that role. If the rich peasants do not play an important role, this structure is self-reproducing, and there are no other internal processes to bring a change in the structure.

If the structure is self-reproducing, the poverty if it exists, is structural. Rural studies show that poverty is concentrated in two size classes in the economy. One is the agricultural labour and the second is the poor peasantry. In the village studied they form nearly 71 per cent of the households. It is these segments who have 'land hunger', and so are the dominant leasing-in agents in the village. These segments do not prefer to enter the labour market but look for other institutions to sell their labour. These segments are also dominant players in the credit market and take loans for consumption purposes. Given the context where markets are not completely formed, the only solution is a land reform policy.

The striking structural feature of the village is the large extent of land owned by non-cultivating households, and the land-hunger of the poor peasantry and agricultural labour. If a land reform policy transfers land to the poor peasantry and agricultural labour households, this will have two effects. One, the poverty in these segments would decrease. Two, there is a potential for the development of market for land, labour and credit, leading to a situation wherein land reform is a necessary condition for the generation of active rural markets.

END NOTES

1. This is expressed as the primary concern in papers on the need for property rights reforms in China [For instance, Zhu and Jiang (1993)].
2. It may not be unusual in such instances for agents to opt for a sale in this area and repurchase in some non-irrigated area. Here, an interim transaction will actually be attained, but the final seller in this sequence of transactions, would have to be a regular seller.
3. A further source of discrimination between agents could be the uneven access to knowledge about the new technology, which could involve not only different cultivation techniques but also new crops. The lack of information here could imply that learning could prove to be a costly process for some agents.
4. Raghavalu (CPM, Andhra Pradesh State Secretary) in a study conducted in Ugutuluru village in Krishna Delta Region of AP, says that this village

has 591 household and the land cultivated in the village is 813 acres. The total numbers of households leasing-out are 114 out of which 64 stay outside the village. The total land leased-out forms 68 per cent of the land.

5. Given the structure of the credit market in the nine villages one should be careful before providing policy interventions. Post elections it is recognized that agriculture sector is in crisis and there is need to address some of the issues related to the agricultural sector. One policy is to increase availability of credit to farmers so that these farmers can invest in agriculture and the issue of poverty would be solved. But the poverty is maximum in the agricultural labour households and poor peasantry and they can access institutional credit (Vijay and A.V.N. Sunder, 2004).

REFERENCES

Alchian, A. A (1965). "Some Economics of Property Rights." *Il Politico* 30, pp. 816-29.

Alston, L. J., G. D. Libecap and R. Schneider (1995). "Property Rights and the Preconditions for Markets: The Case of the Amazon Frontier", *Journal of Institutional and Theoretical Economics*. 151(1), pp. 89-111.

Bardhan, P. K. (1984). *Land, Labour and Rural Poverty*, Columbia University Press.

Barzal, Y. (1989). *Economic Analysis of Property Rights*, Cambridge University Press, Cambridge.

Basu, K. (1986). "The Market for Land: An Analysis of Interim Transactions", *Journal of Development Economics*, 20 (1), pp. 163-77.

Bliss, C. J. and N. H. Stern (1982). *Palanpur: The Economy of an Indian Village*, Oxford University Press, Delhi.

De Alessi, L. (1980). " The Economics of Property Rights: A Review of the Evidence." *Research in Law and Economics*, 2, pp. 1-42.

Demsetz, H. (1967). " Toward A Theory of Property Rights." *American Economic Review*, Papers and Proceedings, 57, pp. 347-59.

Dreze, J. (1997). "Palanpur 1957-93: Occupational Change, Land Ownership and Social Inequality" in Breman, J., Peter Kloos and Ashwani Saith (1997) edited volume *The Village in Asia Revisited.*

Eggertsson, T. (1990). *Economic Behaviour and Institutions*, Cambridge University Press. Cambridge.

Eirik, G. Furubotn and Rudolf, Richter (2001). *Institutions and Economic Theory: The Contribution of the New Institutional Economics*, The University of Michigan Press.

Eswaran, M. and A. Kotwal (1995). "A Theory of Contractual Structure in Agriculture", *American Economic Review*, 75(3), pp. 352-67.

Fujimoto, A. (1996). "Rice Land Ownership and Tenancy System in South Asia: Facts and Issues based on Ten village studies", *The Developing Economics*, 34(4).

Furbotn, E. G. and S. Pejovich. (1972). "Property Rights and Economic Theory: A Survey of Recent Literature", *Journal of Economic Literature* 10, pp. 1137-62.

Klaus, Deininger and Gershon, Feder (2001). "Institutions and Land Markets" in *Handbook of Agriculture Economics*, Vol 1, pp. 288-324, (Ed.) B. Gardner and G. Rausser, Elsevier Science. B. V.

North, D. C. (1981). *Structure and Change in Economic History*. New York and London: Norton.

North, D. C. (1990). *Institutions, Institutional Change, and Economic Performance*. Cambridge University press, Cambridge.

Ostrom, E. (1990). *Governing the Commons: The Evolution of Institutions for Collective Action*. Cambridge University Press, Cambridge.

Pant, C. (1983). "Tenancy and Family Resources: A Model and Some Empirical Analysis", *Journal of Development Economics*, 12(1-2), pp. 27-37.

Rakshit, M. (1989). "Underdevelopment of Commodity Credit and Land Markets: Macroeconomic Implications", In Rakshit M. (1989) (Ed.) *Studies in the Macroeconomics of Developing Countries*. Oxford University Press, Delhi.

Rao, R. S. and Bharati, M. (2004). "Comprehensive Study on Land and Poverty in Andhra Pradesh: A Preliminary Report" submitted to Society for Elimination of Rural Poverty (Velugu), Government of Andhra Pradesh.

Rao, V. M. (1972). "Land Transfer: Finding in a Ryotwari Region", *Economics and Political Weekly, Review of Agriculture*. 7(30).

Renkow, M. (1993). "Land Prices, Land Rents, and Technological Change: Evidence from Pakistan", *World Development*. 21(5), pp.791-803.

Sarap, K. (1991a). *Interlinked Agrarian Markets in Rural India*, Sage Publication India Ltd, New Delhi.

Sarap, K. (1995). "Land Sale Transactions in Indian Village: Theories and Evidence", *Indian Economic Review*. 30(2), pp. 223-240.

Shaufias, E. (1995). "Households Resources, Transaction Cost and Adjustment Through Land Tenancy", *Land Economics*, 71(1), pp. 42-56.

Sreenivasulu, Y. (2002). "Rural Labour Market: Nature of Fragmentation: An Investigation into Kondaiahgaripalli Village", Unpublished, M. Phil thesis submitted to University of Hyderabad.

Sunder, A. N. V. S. (2003). "Nature of Rural Credit Market: An Investigation of Eight Villages in Andhra Pradesh". Unpublished, M. Phil thesis submitted to University of Hyderabad.

Vijay, R. (1992). "Models on Agrarian Relations and the Need for Land Reforms", Unpublished, M. Phil thesis submitted to University of Hyderabad.

Vijay, R. (2000). Review Article "Development Microeconomics" Published in *Artha Vijnana*, 42(4), pp. 385-97.

Vijay, R. (2002). "Land Market Activity: A Framework" in *Indian Journal of Agricultural Economics*, 57(4), pp. 714-721.

Vijay, R. and A. N. V. S., Sunder (2004). "Rural Credit Market in Andhra Pradesh: A Study into Structural Constituents" forthcoming in the book titled *Agrarian Transformation in Orissa*: Issues and Evidence edited by K. Sarap. P. K. Tripathy, S. S. Rath and B. Mishra, publishers P.G. Department of Economics, Sambalpur University.

Vijay, R. and Y., Sreenivasulu (2003). "Fragmented Labour Market: An Investigation into a village labour market" in *Agrarian Transformation in Orissa: Issues and Evidence* edited by K. Sarap. P. K. Tripathy, S. S. Rath and B. Mishra, publishers P.G. Department of Economics, Sambalpur University.

Vijay R. and Y., Sreenivasulu (2004). "Functioning of Labour Market in Andhra Pradesh: A Study into the Constraints" forthcoming in the book titled *Agrarian Transformation in Orissa: Issues and Evidence* edited by K. Sarap, P.K. Tripathy, S. S. Rath and B. Mishra, publishers P.G. Department of Economics, Sambalpur University.

Vijay R. and Y., Sreenivasulu (2004). "Household Resources and Adjustment in Factor Markets: Investigation into a Village Economy" communicated to *Indian Journal of Labour Economics.*

Walker and Ryn (1989). *Village and Household Economics in India's Semi-Arid Tropics*, The John Hopkins University Press.

Zhu, Ling and Jiang, Zhongyi (1993). "From Brigade to Village Community: The Land Tenure System and Rural Development in China", *Cambridge Journal of Economics*, 17, pp. 441-461.

Chapter 15

Changing Land-Caste-Class Relations and Rural Poverty in Bihar

ANUP K. KARAN

I
INTRODUCTION

The purpose of this paper is to analyse salient features of the agrarian change and its impact on rural poverty, which have taken place in Bihar over the last two decades or so. The paper is largely based on a comparison of two sets of data generated through two primary surveys, the first during 1981-82 and the second in 1999-2000. The survey and the re-survey cover the same 12 villages, spread over six districts of the state[1]. On the basis of the data collected at two points of time, it is argued in this paper that Bihar agriculture is in a phase of fast transition from semi-feudal mode of production[2] to market based peasant capitalist mode with the emergence of a definitive and assertive peasant class[3]. The observation is based on the changing pattern of caste-class relations, land distribution pattern, tenancy relations, and increasing private investment in agriculture. Moreover, it is argued in the paper that although agriculture in Bihar has moved closer to market, the pace of penetration of market forces is constrained by the virtual absence of state support and consequent lack of infrastructural development.

Agrarian change has been widely discussed in literature. In the simplest terms, the Marxian literature focuses on the way a peasant economy changes into capitalist agriculture through a dialectical process. The central argument in Marxian theoretical framework on agrarian change concerns about the transition from the feudal to the dominant capitalist mode of production. However, the persistence of peasantry has raised some dissonance within the Marxian framework itself. In the classic Marxist position pressure on peasants created by capitalist production relations result in their disappearance as distinct form of producers (Ellis, 1988, Breman and Mundle, 1991). An opposing line of reasoning is that family farm production, of which peasants comprise a major type, possesses an internal logic which permits it to resist the pressure of capitalist production relations and thus to reproduce itself indefinitely (Scott, 1976; Bernstein, 1979; Harriss, 1982). Further, many of the reasons advanced for the survival of peasant production are reasons for the persistence of family farm production under capitalism. In this connection, Friedman (1980) notes that capitalist farming is not the only path of agrarian change; an alternative route is transition from peasant farming to commercial family farming in a context of fully developed output and input markets. While analysing the situation in Asia, and particularly in India, Byres' (1991) discerns six paths of agrarian transition[4] with or without full development of capitalism in agriculture. Despite several limitations of his study, Byres' brings out possibilities of interplay of various forces, ranging from class struggle to state supported emergence of peasantry, in shaping the future of capitalist mode of production. In fact, in practice it is the interplay between these forces rather than complete dominance of one or another, which determines the fate of peasant societies. In certain conditions the forces of disintegration are observed to dominate; in others the forces of stability or persistence seem to prevail. In contemporary agrarian societies the relative strength of these opposing forces is influenced, in turn, by two factors: (i) intensity of the pressure imposed on peasants to yield surplus, which is captured by other social groups, and (ii) role of the state in contributing to the stability or instability of peasant production (Ellis, 1988).

The present paper analyses the situation in Bihar from this perspective and tries to discern the level of capitalist development in agriculture and its impact on agricultural development. The paper is divided into three sections. After the introduction, the second section presents changing social relations, and the resulting changes in the nature and causes of emerging class conflicts in rural Bihar. The third section presents an analytical perspective of land distribution pattern and the changes therein. The emerging tenancy pattern in the light of changing land structure is discussed in detail in this section. This section also addresses a number of tenancy related issues with the perspective of increasing penetration of capital in subsistence agriculture. The fourth section tries to briefly present the linkage between changing agrarian relation and rural poverty in Bihar.

II
CHANGING SOCIO-ECONOMIC RELATIONS

The agrarian situations of Bihar, based on share-cropping and 'debt slavery' of the poor peasantry, forcing them into 'unequal exchange' and distress sale, has been characterised by Prasad (1990) as 'semi-feudal'. Accordingly, Prasad (1990) pointed out to the inescapable debt-binding of the peasant of Bihar to the landlord who, besides leasing out land, performs usury and trade. Similarly, according to Bhaduri (1983), the carry over of the pre-capitalist mode of production is resulting in the 'semi-feudal' form of agrarian structure of Bihar, in which the interest of the landlord class is best served by holding agriculture backward. He characterises the agriculture of Bihar as 'semi-feudal' also because the process is carried out under the compulsion of the debt trap while the production is actually catering to the capitalist market demand. The 'unequal exchange' between the appropriators and the producers is causing polarisation along with primitive accumulation. A wide ranging study conducted during early 1980s by a group of researchers from A.N. Sinha Institute of Social Studies (ANSISS) and International Labour Organisation (ILO) (hereby referred to as ANSISS/ILO study) found that "the essential conditions of capitalism is yet to take root in Bihar's agriculture in its historical process of development, where.......... the bulk of surplus value is appropriated by big peasants and landlords through tenancy (especially share cropping tenancy), usury, and labour process (using in part non-free labour)". The study also noted that there is *prima-facie* case of interlocking of the 'land', 'labour', and 'credit' markets in rural Bihar (Prasad *et al.*, 1988).

Since then a lot of changes have taken place on the agrarian front of the state. Explaining the features of one village of Purnea in Bihar, Rodgers and Rodgers (2000) finds that the situation of the village seemed to be well captured by the model of semi-feudalism. However, they also noted a number of changes in social and economic institutions at the village level. In fact, the period of 1980s onwards has been marked by stiff and sporadic class struggles, rising trends of real wages, declining patron-client relationships, increasing casualisation of rural labour, growing mechanisation, commercialisation and diversification of agriculture, increasing trends of seasonal and temporary migration, increasing positive role of remittances in rural economy, and workforce diversification to non-farm sectors are the new features of the rural economy of Bihar[5]. Some scholars have called these changes in the rural areas as 'stylised shifts' in rural society[6] but others (Rodgers and Rodgers, 2000; Sharma *et al.,* 1999 and 2002) see these changes as a result of the process of breaking the shackles of semi-feudalism, though at a limited scale.

Social Conflicts: Class Struggles and Resilience

The meeting of semi-feudal traditions with the modern market forces in rural Bihar has led to stiff social conflicts marked by sporadic incidence of violence in rural areas[7]. The most striking feature of these class struggles has been that in recent years it has been of more overt nature. Rural labourers are now increasingly able to assert what they perceive to be their rights[8]. While conflict and struggle between the poor and dominant classes has never been absent from rural scene in Bihar, the recent forms of class struggles and assertiveness of rural poor entered into a new phase. The phenomenal ascendance of 'middle castes' to the seat of political power of the state, particularly during the 1980s and 1990s has been attributed to major transfer of land in favour of these castes through 'sale' and 'lease' markets. On a number of occasions, now poor agricultural labourers have a direct conflict with this 'rural neo-elite' and faced several forms of 'extra-economic' sanctions against them[9] in the same way as they faced historically at the hands of upper castes.

The direct access of the middle castes to the seat of state political power reinforced the tendency for surpluses to be diverted away from agriculture in the areas of incipient peasant capitalism and into what has been called 'primitive accumulation' through corruption and crime (Wilson, 1999; see also Das, 1992). However, the major balance of power and controls not only continued to remain firmly with 'dominant castes' (mainly *Brahmin, Rajput, Bhumihar, and Kayastha*)[10], but also, in order to stall the changes, which are fast taking place in rural Bihar, they started to resort to various types of criminal retaliation[11]. The poor peasants', and labourers' livelihood, on the other hand, remain precarious as they continue to carry land lease at very low returns to their labour, often pay very high interest rates especially for consumption loans and face insufficient and uncertain employment in the labour markets.

However, the class struggle has brought positive, although limited, changes for rural labourers and poor peasants. As for example, during the last two decades or so, there have been changes in production and social relations, wage structure, local power and political structure, living status, etc. which go in favour of the rural labourers. Moreover, the struggles have intensified, and in spite of counter actions by middle and big peasants, the position of labourers has strengthened in comparison to that in the past. Now the rural labourers are found open and enthusiastic supporters of different ultra-left political parties such as CPI(ML), MKSS, Party Unity, PWG and their movements pose a direct threat to the power of dominant rural class. One of the most important benefits of these struggles has been net rise in real wages both in agriculture as well as non-agriculture. It is important to note that the real wages have increased by approximately 60 to 80 per cent during the last one decade or so (Sharma *et al.*, 2002). Although, the emancipatory process of rural labourer has been analysed in different perspectives by different scholars[12] (Kapapdia and Lerche, 1999), in rural Bihar it led to sordid form of resilience by the landowners by deploying criminal gangs against the landless poor. In this respect the role of state also has been dubious. The rural elite as well as neo-elite most of the time connived with the state power and used the state machinery in order to 'stall' the forces of change. Lack of political wills in implementing the land reform measures, minimum wages law, targeting of welfare measures, installing of Panchayati Raj Institution (PRI) etc. are only a few reflections of this. Concerted efforts to destroy rural infrastructure in order to make rural poor more dependent on rural dominant classes—through lease of land, power, and machinery, and credit—have been yet another example of this phenomenon.

The issue of social conflicts in rural Bihar, hence, can be seen against the backdrop of stiff class conflicts and changing 'land' and 'labour' relations in a transitional society where "semi-feudalism meets the market"[13].

Changing Class Structure

These changes have strong implications for the agrarian relations in Bihar. On the basis of the two surveys mentioned earlier, certain changes are easily discernible. First, there is a growing tendency towards 'landlordism'[14] and 'non-agriculturai class' in general. Second, the growth of landlordism is although more pronounced among middle and big peasants who also belong largely to middle and upper castes respectively, there is growing tendency of landlordism also among lower classes such as agricultural labour largely belonging to lower caste. Third, although there is no increase in the agriculture labour, there is phenomenal increase in the proportion of non-agricultural labour class, resulting into net increase in the casualisation of labour (Parthasarthy, 1996; Sharma, 1996). Fourth, there is almost complete elimination of long term attached labour system in agriculture, although peak season short term contractual arrangement continues and might be on increase in many areas of acute labour shortage during the peak season. Fifth, in view of the growing casualisation and landlessness, out-migration of labour class has phenomenally increased from Bihar. During the reference intervening periods the intensity of out-migration of workers has increased from less than 10 per cent in 1981-82 to approximately 19 per cent in 1999-2000 (Karan, 2004)[15].

The paradox of increasing landlordism and increase in the proportion of non-agricultural class shows increasing tendency of disassociation from agriculture in general. The process of dis-association from agriculture is known in literature as 'de-agrarianisation' rather than 'de-peasantisation' (Bryceson, 2000). The survey figures also suggest that in aggregate terms the growth of landlord and non-agriculture class in Bihar during the last two decades has been largely contributed by a decline in the agriculture labour class and not by decline in peasant class. Moreover, the growth in the landlord class is not a reflection of strengthening of semi-feudal or feudal forces as the growth is depended more on a capitalist calculation of minimising the cost of cultivation. In the context of landlessness and persistent land-leaser on the part of the poor and the resulting higher demand for land lease on the one hand and in view of increasing cost of cultivation on the other, leasing out of land (particularly on fixed rent basis) may be a more profitable business in comparison to self-cultivation either by employing family labour or by using hired labour. This also reduces risk factors in cultivation and ensures assured supply of labour to a great extent. In fact in the region, where impact of green revolution has been limited, particularly in terms of technological penetration, the growth of capitalism is not always reflected by 'severe blow to landlordism' (Moij, 2000) but it is more reflected in terms of changing nature and composition of landlord class. The changing nature of landlord class in rural Bihar is reflected by the fact that more and more households from middle and lower caste hierarchy on the one hand and agriculture labour class on the other, are joining the landlord class. As a result, the landlord class now controls comparatively smaller size of holdings. The survey data reports that in Bihar there is more than 50 per cent fall in the average land holding size of the landlord class between the two survey periods. Although owing to continuous fragmentation of land holding due to demographic pressure the decline in the average size of land holding is widespread across all classes, the decline is more prominent among agricultural labour and landlord classes. The fall in the average size of land holding of landlord and agricultural labour classes has been more than 50 per cent (Table 15.1).

Table 15.1: Class-wise Changes in the Average Size of Holdings, 1982-1999

Class	*Average size of owned land (acre)*		*Percentage fall in average area*
	1999	*1982*	
AL	0.45	1.08	58.02
PMP	0.83	0.73	-13.66
MP	1.02	1.48	31.56
BP	2.99	4.78	37.42
Landlord	2.93	6.13	52.31
Total	1.80	3.42	47.52

AL: Agricultural Labour, PMP: Poor Middle Peasant, MP: Middle Peasant, BP: Big Peasant
Source: Survey data, 1982 and 1999.

This sharp fall in average land holding of landlord and agricultural labour classes has been largely accounted for by a shift in favour of poor middle peasant class. Hence on the one hand landlord now controls smaller size of land and on the other agricultural labourers are close to landlessness.

Caste-Class Linkages

Caste class linkage in agrarian relations has been widely discussed in both theoretical as well as empirical researches in India[16]. Empirical researches have shown that caste is an important social institutions, which play its vital role in determining social as well as class status of households. The congruence has been found stronger particularly at the lower levels of caste hierarchy, especially among *dalit* castes. However, there is a broad agreement that in the post colonial period typical connection between caste and occupation was eroded by factors such as expansion of cash economy, industrialisation, the spread of western education, etc. Although a broad disruption of caste and class relationship is perceptible in all parts of post-independence India (Beteille, 1975; Bose, 1975), the relationship has been found stronger in the areas of 'permanent settlement' (Prasad, 1987; Rodgers, 1983; Sharma, 1995; Chakravarty, 2001).

Accordingly, social distinction between those who perform wage labour on other's land and those who limits themselves to the cultivation of their own holdings is an extremely sharp factor throughout Bihar. For agricultural labourers the correlation between class position and caste status is very strong. The high degree of correspondence between caste and class (Sharma *et al.*, 1999) has led to concentration of rural labour among a few castes belonging to lower strata of the caste hierarchy. Prasad *et al.* (1988) finds that "caste traditions are reflected in occupational structure in the plains of rural Bihar. According to time honoured caste tradition, upper caste Hindus are forbidden to touch plough and women of upper caste Hindus cannot work outside their own dwellings. Traditionally, upper caste Hindus also do not work as agricultural labourers........ as agricultural labour happens to be low status work." Chakravarty (2001) also notes that "the circumstances of birth into a low-ranking caste.... tend to determine their social and material conditions". The term '*mazdoor*' or labourers connotes a position in both hierarchies (Wilson, 1999), in terms of class as well as caste. However, despite the deep-rooted caste stratification still prevalent in Bihar, there have always been interactions across the caste groups related mainly to wage employment. People from the lower castes generally work as agricultural labour in the fields of upper caste groups. In addition to this the lowest caste groups have also been known to work as attached labour—*halwaha, charwaha, kamiya* etc. However, despite the strong caste-class correspondence, over the years there has been substantial change in the class affiliation of different caste groups.

In order to show the changes in the caste class linkage, the same categorisation of caste and agrarian class as used in the ANSISS/ILO study has been used[17].

One of the major changes worth mentioning, related to the caste class linkage, is the upward mobility of the middle castes such as Kurmi, Koeri, and Yadav towards the higher classes in the hierarchy. In case of Kurmi the vertical mobility is noticeable towards both big peasants and landlords, while in case of Koeri the mobility is exclusively towards landlord. Yadav has consolidated more as big peasants. OBC I have also consolidated over the years and a substantial proportion from them has ascended to the rank of middle peasant. In fact, proportion of landlord households has increased in general in rural Bihar reflecting an increasing tendency of leasing out of land (Table 15.2). Similarly, proportion of non-agricultural class has also increased. Increase in the proportion of these two classes is largely contributed by upper and middle castes (except Yadav). In case of SC and Muslim also some changes can be observed. In view of the declining patron-client relationships in labour markets these groups have substantially changed their status from attached agricultural labour to free agricultural labour.

In general, the proportion of agriculture labour households has declined among these caste groups, which has been offset by an increase in the proportion of peasant and non-agricultural class among them. This is also corroborated by the fact that over the years, more and more upper caste households are joining the ranks of poor middle peasant, middle peasant, and also agricultural labour classes. Hence, the social taboo of 'not touching the plough' is breaking among the upper castes. This phenomenon has been known as 'peasantisation of upper castes' (Prasad *et al.,* 1988; Sharma *et al.,* 1999 and 2002). In contrast to this, the proportion of middle caste households falling under these lower class categories has been declining (Table 15.2).

The caste-class analysis on the basis of the data set of the two surveys data sets clearly shows that although caste-class correspondence still exists in Bihar, there is considerable movement among the caste groups towards re-alignment of class positions. The most interesting fact that emerges from the comparison of the two surveys is the accretion of households of upper caste group to the class of agriculture labour as well as to that of landlord. The accretion to the class of agriculture labour is of course a manifestation of land alienation from peasant classes. But the accretion to the class of landlord is the outcome of land-loss and migration.

Table 15.2: Class Affiliation of Different Caste Groups in 1981-82 and 1999-2000 and Changes therein

Main class affiliation in 1981-82	*Caste groups*	*Main class affiliation in 1999-2000 and changes over 1981-82*	
Big peasants Landlord	Upper caste	Big peasants	(decline)
		Landlord	(increase)
		Non-agriculture	(increase)
		Some also agriculture labour	(new)
Big peasant	Kurmi	Big peasants	(increase)
Middle peasant		Landlord	(increase)
Agriculture labour		Non-agriculture	(new)
Middle peasant	Yadav	Middle peasant	(no change)
Agriculture labour		Big peasants	(new)
		Agriculture labour	(decrease)
Middle peasant	Koeri	Landlord	(new)
Poor middle peasant		Middle peasant	(decrease)
Agriculture labour		Poor middle peasant	(decrease)
Non-agriculture		Agriculture labour	(decrease)
		Non-agriculture	(decrease)
Landlord	Other OBC II	Landlord	(increase)
Non-agriculture		Non-agriculture	(decrease)
Middle peasant		Agriculture labour	(decrease)
Agriculture labour			
Agriculture labour (also attached)	OBC I	Middle peasant	(increase)
Non-agriculture		Agriculture labour (largely free)	(decrease)
		Non-agriculture	(increase)
Agriculture labour (also attached)	SC	Agriculture labour (largely free)	(decrease)
Non-agriculture		Non-agriculture	(increase)
Middle peasant	Muslims	Landlord (new)	
Big peasant		Big peasant	(increase)
Agriculture labour (also attached)		Non-agriculture	(increase)
		Agriculture labour	(decrease)

The upper caste peasants, who have lost their land to the point where the land cannot produce a surplus, find themselves unacceptable as members of the upper caste. They can neither meet wage demands nor take to the plough for fear of caste opprobrium. Hence, they opt for renting out land and migration. Even the non-cultivating backward castes and even scheduled castes who have some land, migrate in search of a better future. Educated landowners by and large migrate for jobs in urban centres.

III
LAND DISTRIBUTION PATTERN AND TENURIAL RELATIONS

Land Distribution Pattern and Caste-Class Linkage

The land distribution pattern in rural Bihar has become less skewed over the years. Although still there is a large concentration of households among the landless and marginal farmers, concentration of land in the larger land class categories has come down considerably. A comparison of the two data sets (1981-82 and 1999-2000) shows that during the last 18 years landlessness has increased by nearly 3 percentage points (from 40 per cent in 1982 to 43 per cent in 1999). The proportion of marginal farmers with less than 1 acre of land has also increased by 5 per cent during the same intervening periods. On the whole, proportion of landless or households having less than one acre of land has increased from 66 per cent in 1981-82 to 73 per cent in 1999-2000. However, within the same period the proportion of households having 10 acres or more land has come down from 13 per cent in 1981-82 to 6 per cent in 1999-2000. Fig. 15.1 shows the change in the land structure over the last 18 years for the two extreme land classes.

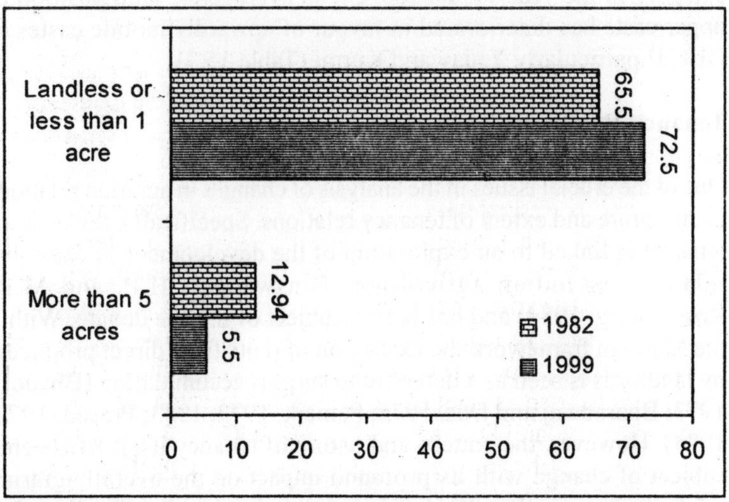

Fig. 15.1: Percentage of Households in Two Land Classes in 1981-82 and 1999-2000

A comparison of the two surveys also indicates that concentration of total land in the marginal and small holding has increased from 16 per cent in 1981-82 to more than 30 per cent in 1999-2000. This has been a result of slip of large chunk of land from big peasants and landlords to marginal and small landowners. Among the middle landholders also (between 2.5 to 10 acres of holding) the proportion of land concentration has increased over the years.

There is also considerable movement of different caste groups across land holding classes. It can be seen from Table 15.3 that there has been all round increase in landlessness except in case of Yadav and other OBC II. Among these two caste groups landlessness has decreased but there has been comparatively larger concentration in the marginal land size group. The landholding position of forward castes has slipped from big land owners to slightly lower land class. Over the years although proportion of households in higher land classes has decreased among all caste groups, Kurmis have maintained their older land position among the bigger land classes. There seems to be acute deterioration in terms of land distribution among Muslims and SCs. It is important to note that in 1981-82 slightly less than one-fifth of the upper caste households held land of the size 10 acres or more, which has been reduced to a negligible proportion in this category in the year 1999-2000. On an average the land position of upper caste has deteriorated in favour of upwardly mobile castes of OBC II particularly Yadav and Kurmi (Table 15.3).

Tenancy Relations

One of the crucial issues in the analysis of changes in agrarian relations is the nature and extent of tenancy relations. Specifically, the issue of tenancy is linked to an exploration of the development of capitalist relations in Indian agriculture (Binswanger, H.P. and M.R. Rosenzweig, 1984) and has been a subject of intense debate. Within the Marxian framework the extraction of rents from direct producers by landlords is seen as a deterrent to surplus accumulation (Bhaduri, 1973; Bharadwaj and Das, 1975; Patnaik, 1972, 1983; Prasad, 1973, 1974). However, the pattern and nature of tenancy itself has been a subject of change with its profound impact on the overall agrarian relations. In agriculturally developed states such as Punjab, Haryana, and Western Uttar Pradesh there has been increasing incidence of self-cultivation, emergence of fixed rent tenancy, participation of medium and large households in the lease market as lessees, etc. (Singh, 1989; Bhalla, 1983; Srivastava, 1989; Siddiqui, 1999).

Table 15.3: Percentage Distribution of Households by Owned Land Size Class From Different Castes, 1981-82 and 1999-2000

Caste	*Land size (in acres)*							
	Land-less	*0-1.0*	*1.0-2.5*	*2.5-5.0*	*5.0-10.0*	*10.0-20.0*	*20+*	*Total*
				PANEL I : 1981-82				
Brahmin	4.94	16.05	13.58	27.16	19.75	14.81	3.7	100
Bhumihar	6.67	25	23.33	16.67	10	15.00	3.33	100
Kurmi	4.17	16.67	16.67	20.83	37.5		4.17	100
Yadav	19.35	32.26	29.03	16.13		3.23		100
Koiri	11.11	59.26	22.22	3.7	3.7			100
Others	50.00	22.22	11.11	3.7	7.41	3.7	1.85	100
OBC II								
OBC I	61.62	30.3	4.04	1.01		3.03		100
S.C.	69.53	25	5.47					100
Muslim	50.85	20.34	18.64	5.08	1.69	3.39		100
Total	39.89	25.53	12.77	8.69	6.56	5.14	1.24	100
				PANEL II : 1999-2000				
Brahmin	15.66	22.89	25.9	19.28	12.05	3.01	1.2	100
Bhumihar	9.09	36.36	25.0	19.32	6.82	2.27	1.14	100
Kurmi	17.86	14.29	32.14	21.43	7.14	7.14	0	100
Yadav	17.31	53.85	19.23	7.69	1.92	0	0	100
Koeri	20.00	66.67	3.33	6.67	3.33	0	0	100
Others	37.50	44.44	8.33	6.94	2.78	0	0	100
OBC II								
OBC I	61.29	24.52	11.61	1.94	0.65	0	0	100
S.C.	73.23	23.74	2.02	1.01	0	0	0	100
Muslim	64.79	23.94	4.23	5.63	1.41	0	0	100
Total	42.65	29.85	13.36	8.64	4.15	1.01	0.34	100

Likewise in Eastern states also recent studies report qualitative changes in tenancy relations (Chadha and Bhaumik, 1992; Swain, 1999). With capitalist development in agriculture (or weakening power of landlords in less developed areas) self-cultivation by capitalist peasants and capitalist tenant is on the rise (Reddy, 1997; Haque, 2000; Srivastava, 2000). This implies that large capitalist cultivators lease in land from small land owners (referred to as 'reverse tenancy' in literature). This phenomenon of reverse tenancy was first witnessed in North-Western and Western states (Vyas, 1970;

Laxminarayan and Tyagi, 1977) and became soon widespread in other parts of country. The phenomenon of reverse tenancy is seen as a mechanism of sidestepping of land legislation by capitalist cultivators (Srivastava, 2000). Moreover, this is also taken as beneficial for large cultivators in order to reap the benefits of emerging economies of scale in agriculture. Hence, the present tenancy relations cannot be equated with traditional feudal tenancy relations, as there is now a notable absence of the appropriation of surplus in the form of unpaid labour services through extra-economic coercion (Bardhan and Rudra, 1980). Accordingly, with the introduction of modern and formal credit institutions in rural areas the phenomenon of interlocking is also on decline. Moreover the interlocking of land labour and credit market has also witnessed a qualitative change as now most of the interlockings take place largely through credit markets instead of land markets.

The available official data show that the incidence of leasing at the All India level has substantially declined over time. At the time of Independence, nearly 35.7 per cent of the total cultivated area was under tenancy. According to various rounds of National Sample Survey (NSS), this proportion gradually declined to 20.3 per cent in 1953-54, 11.6 per cent in 1971-72, 8.3 per cent in 1991-92 (Haque, 1986, 2000). It is only during the 1980s, i.e. between 1981-82 and 1991-92 that the proportion increased marginally from 7.18 per cent in 1981-82 to 8.28 per cent in 1991-92. During the 1990s some of the states, which registered major increase in the leased-in area are Haryana, Punjab, Andhra Pradesh and Madhya Pradesh. The states such as Bihar and West Bengal reported a fall in the leased-in area during the 1990s. Recent household survey data collected by the National Sample Survey (NSS), 1999-2000 (NSSO, 2000) shows further decline in the proportion of total leased-in area to approximately 5 to 6 per cent in all the states except the states such as Bihar, Kerala and Orissa. The NSSO, 2000 household survey shows an increase in the proportion of leased in area in states like Bihar. The proportion of leased in area in Bihar was 4 per cent in the year 1991-92 which increased to approximately 8 per cent[18] in 1999-2000. This is despite the fact that tenancy is legally banned in Bihar and the data related to leasing is supposed to be fraught with gross underestimation in general[19].

Besides this, it is also argued that general household survey at macro levels may not be able to capture the real intensity of tenancy and this leads to underestimation of tenancy practice. Instead, a more focused and particularly longitudinal village surveys give better estimation of leasing practice in comparison to those conducted at the macro-level in general (Srivastava, 2000). That is why the two primary sources data as mentioned above show much higher intensity of tenancy in Bihar. The proportion of leased in area as reported by the two primary sources is as high as 25 per cent in both the periods with slight increase in the latter period (Table 15.4).

Table 15.4: Percentage of households Leasing-in, and Percentage Leased Area in Different Land Classes, 1999 and 1982

Land size (in acres)	*Percentage of household leasing-in to*		*Percentage area leased in to total area cultivated*
	All households	*Cultivating households*	
		PANEL I: 1981-82	
Landless	34.53	100.00	100.00
0-1.0	53.57	60.98	62.63
1.0-2.5	36.99	41.54	37.52
2.5-5.0	34.48	36.36	18.87
5.0-10.0	10.00	10.53	4.21
10.0-20.0	3.85	4.17	1.97
20+	0.00	0.00	0.00
Total	36.23	52.99	24.59
1999-2000		PANEL II: 1999-2000	
Landless	22.63	100.00	100.00
0-1.0	36.09	52.51	58.15
1.0-2.5	28.57	40.96	27.62
2.5-5.0	5.19	6.90	3.88
5.0-10.0	0.00	0.00	0.00
10.0-20.0	11.11	12.50	5.04
20+	1.17	2.50	1.98
Total	22.67	41.84	25.47

Table 15.4 reveals that at present more than 22 per cent of all the rural households and approximately 42 per cent of the cultivating households lease in land for cultivation. The proportion of leased in land is approximately 25 per cent of the total cultivated land. The corresponding figures in the year 1981-82 were 36 per cent, 53 per cent, and 26 per cent respectively. This suggests a substantial fall in the proportion of leasing in households but a marginal increase in the leased area over the two reference periods. The two primary surveys

show that over the years there has been two important changes in the practice of tenancy in rural Bihar. First, although there has been marginal increase in the proportion of total leased area, the proportion of leasing-in households has sharply declined. This has resulted into increase in average size of leased in land in general. Second, the extent of tenancy (proportion of households leasing in) across different land size class shows that the fall in the proportion of leasing-in households has been largely contributed by substantial fall in the proportion of leasing-in households from lower to marginal land size and landless households. In the higher land size category, particularly those with more than 10 acres of land, there has been phenomenal increase in the proportion of households leasing in as well as proportion of leased in area. The proportion of leasing households in this category increased by nearly 4 times with more than two times increase in the leased in area.

Caste-wise analysis of leasing pattern shows that Yadav is the most prominent followed by OBC I, who almost dominate the entire lease-in market (Table 15.5).

Table 15.5: Percentage of households Leasing-in, and Percentage Leased Area in Different Castes and Classes, 1999 and 1982

Caste	*Percentage of household leasing-in to*		*Percentage area leased in to total area cultivated*
	All households	*Cultivating households*	
		PANEL I: 1982	
Brahmin	13.58	15.71	3.49
Bhumihar	23.33	25.00	5.74
Kurmi	25.00	25.00	4.90
Yadav	70.97	73.33	61.87
Koeri	59.26	64.00	33.84
Other OBC II	25.93	40.00	31.75
OBC I	42.42	72.41	55.66
S.C.	42.19	75.00	73.85
Muslim	42.37	67.57	55.65
		PANEL II: 1999	
Brahmin	11.45	19.00	6.21
Bhumihar	13.64	23.53	11.88
Kurmi	21.43	31.58	16.64
Yadav	57.69	68.18	50.91
Koiri	13.33	22.22	27.27
Other OBC II	23.61	58.62	46.00
OBC I	27.10	67.80	52.04
S.C.	23.88	55.81	58.17
Muslim	24.24	60.00	42.03

Approximately 58 per cent of all the Yadav households are involved in leasing in with as high as 51 per cent of their total cultivated area as leased in area. In case of SCs although the percentage of leasing in households is much lower in comparison to Yadav the proportion of leasing in area to total cultivated area the highest among them (more than 58 per cent). This is because SC households have poor land base and leasing in of land, for the purpose of cultivation, is an important coping up mechanism for them. Koeri was also one of the important castes involved in leasing in 1982, however, their participation in the lease in market has reduced considerably in 1999. Among them the proportion of leasing in households has fallen by a margin of 45 per cent with a decline in the proportion of leased-in area by a margin of 7 per cent between the two intervening periods.

Kurmi and Other OBC II followed by Forward Castes show the tendency of increasing the proportion of leased in land over the years. The increase in the proportion of leased in area has been 14 per cent and 11 per cent in case of Kurmi and other OBC II. In case of upper castes the increase in the proportion of leased in area has been approximately 4 to 5 per cent.

In both the surveys some practice of leasing out of leased in land by landlord class was identified. Approximately 7 and 2.5 per cent of the landlord households are involved in leasing-in the two surveys. However, these landlords do not cultivate the leased in land of their own but generally lease out the same piece of leased in land to other households for cultivation. The landlord in such situation is involved in the supervision work and earns the benefit of middleman. However, over the years this phenomenon has also declined, because of growing absenteeism among them, and now very few landlords are involved in such types of activities.

Changing forms of Tenancy

Changing nature of tenancy, reflected by changing terms and conditions, is one of the most important indicators of capitalist development in agriculture. The whole argument of changing contractual relations in land is centred around the question "what is the most productively efficient system of cultivation?" (Binswanger and Rosenzweig, 1984; see also Cheung, 1968 and 1969 for further exploration in this[20]). In the classical models the existence of share tenancy has been argued "on the basis of a combination of more than one factor which include risk-aversion, incentive benefits, asymmetric information and transaction cost" (Srivastava, 2000). The classical economists believed that 'sharecropping', one form of tenancy is an efficient system of cultivation as compared with self-cultivation with the help of wage labour. However, the classists also believed that the sharecropping provides the workers with less incentive than a fixed-rent tenant or self-cultivator. Doubts have been raised over classical explanations of risk sharing benefits of sharecropping *vis-à-vis* coexistence of 'fixed rental' and 'self-cultivation with the help of hired labour' on two sub-plots simultaneously (Newbery and Stiglitz, 1979). However, Newbery and Stiglitz (1979) provide solution of persistence of 'sharecropping' as an efficient system under more complex situation of risk such as wage rate risk in the labour markets[21]. Within the Marxian framework, it has been argued that development of fixed rent type of tenancy is an outcome of expanding market economy wherein cultivators resort to more risk-bearing in order to reap the benefit of higher surplus. This type of tenancy is directly linked to increasing entrepreneurial capacity of peasantry. Hence, contractual arrangement in land makes a *tenancy ladder*[22] with the level of capitalist development. However, recent literature on land relations shows co-existence of different forms of contractual arrangements even within a small region either with a higher or lower level of development[23]. Binswanger (1980) and Sillers (1980) note that workers of the same region may differ in many respects such as ability, management skills, capital endowments etc. leading to coexistence of different forms of contractual arrangement within a region at the same point of time[24]. Moreover, technological development may be yet another strong reasons of choice of forms of tenancy[25]. The implications of the form of tenancy, hence, have to be analysed in very specific context as the choice contractual arrangement itself may differ widely within the same region at every level of development.

Analysing the contemporary Indian scenario, Srivastava (2000) finds that during the 1960-61 and 1981-82, rental tenancy (both cash rent and fixed rent in kind) showed a declining trend, but between 1981-82 and 1991-92, the percentage of leased area under fixed rent doubled[26]. Sharma (2000) also finds that during the 1980s the proportion of fixed rent tenancy increased in all the Indian states with the exception of a few states such as Assam, Kerala and

Rajasthan, where the proportion remained constant. In most of the eastern states such as Bihar, Orissa, Uttar Pradesh, and West Bengal although sharecropping remains a dominant form of contract, fixed rental tenancy has increased in all of these states. Although because of paucity of empirical data[27] at the national level, major trends in forms of tenancy has not been discerned, many of the micro studies[28] show that during the 1990s sharecropping has been on fast decline in the states like West Bengal and Bihar.

Recent data on choice of tenancy in Bihar shows a phenomenal increase in fixed rental tenancy. The proportion of leased in plots on the basis of fixed rent in 1999-2000 is approximately 24 per cent, which was less than 5 per cent during 1981-82 (*see* Fig. 15.2). Accordingly, the proportion of sharecropping declined by approximately 13 per cent from 88 per cent in 1981-82 to 74 per cent in 1999-2000. Apart from sharecropping, leasing in against labour service (labour tying for tenancy) was one of the important modes during 1981-82, which has almost vanished by 1999-2000. The interlocking of labour-land market, which was up to 8 per cent in 1981-82, came down to approximately 2 per cent in 1999-2000.

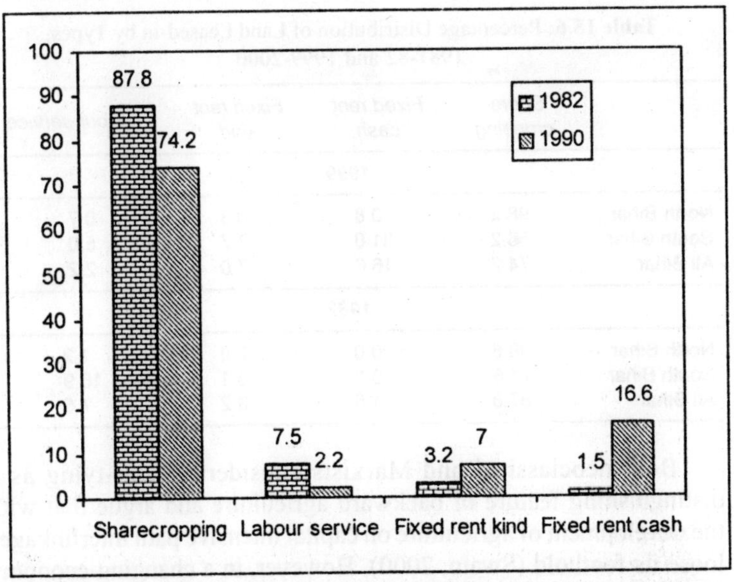

Fig. 15.2: Percentage Distribution of Leased in Plots by Terms of Leasing-in

Anaysing the data of 1981-82 Prasad *et al.* (1985) noted that there is a *prima facie* case of interlocking of and labours and credit in Bihar agriculture[29]. Use of labour tying in tenancy although involved monitoring cost, the surplus was maximised by ensuring a judicious mix of labour tying and rental modes of tenancy[30]. Bhaduri (1983) has shown that the simultaneous operation of two methods of surplus extraction in the form of rent as well as usurious extraction tends to increase on total claims on peasants' produce by expropriating class.

Changes in the types of tenancy shows a regional contrast within the state of Bihar. In North Bihar, a region of largely backward agriculture, sharecropping has been the most dominant form of tenancy and there has been very little change in the scenario during the past two decades or so. In contrast to this, the region of South Bihar has shown fast changes as in some of the pockets of this region there has been complete shift to fixed rental from sharecropping tenancy (Table 15.6). It can be recalled that majority part of the South Bihar region, comprising the districts of Rohtas, Arah, Patna, Naanda, etc. has been known for one of the earliest interventions of state supported modern technology in agriculture[31], and the region is characterised by high agricultural productivity (Prasad, 1982; Sharma, 1995).

Table 15.6: Percentage Distribution of Land Leased-in by Types, 1981-82 and 1999-2000

	Share-cropping	*Fixed rent cash*	*Fixed rent kind*	*Labour service*
		1999		
North Bihar	98.2	0.8	0.3	0.7
South Bihar	56.2	31.0	7.7	5.0
All Bihar	74.2	16.6	7.0	2.2
		1982		
North Bihar	98.8	0.0	0.0	1.2
South Bihar	71.6	3.2	8.1	16.9
All Bihar	87.8	1.5	3.2	7.5

Both neoclassical and Marxists considers labour-tying as a distinguishing feature of backward agriculture and argue that with the development of agriculture on capital intensive path interlinkages loose its foothold (Swain, 2000). However, in a changing economy like that of Bihar, it is interesting to note that in the agriculturally developed region of South Bihar, labour tying in tenancy was quite prevalent both during 1981-82 and 1999-2000, although its intensity has decreased over the years. In this context it important to note that during the initial phases of agricultural development, apart from the argument of judicious mix of 'fixed rental' and 'self-cultivation with the help of wage labour', there is argument of peak season labour demand. In case of green revolution areas in Haryana, Bhalla (1976) attributes this trend to increased labour demand, increased demand for timeliness operations, and tight labour markets. Accordingly, Bardhan (1981) and Bardhan and Rudra (1981) show that the need to secure timely peak-season labour supply, in tight labour markets may be the most important determinant of the use of tied labour in tenancy. The argument holds true also in case of South Bihar, where short-term peak season labour tying is still prevalent as the basis of tenancy.

IV
AGRARIAN STRUCTURE: LAND REFORMS AND THE POOR

Given the rural predominance of Bihar, access to land still continues to be an important means for the livelihood, social status, and security. Though there has been considerable change, rural Bihar continues to be associated with the problems of land reforms. The district of West Champaran is still known for a few landlords holding vast areas of land. Central Bihar, which has witnessed several radical political struggles, is still known, though to a lesser extent, for a few landlords in a few villages occupying public land denying access to the landless poor. We have seen in the above sections that landlordism appear to have taken a commercial path of parcelling out of large holdings through sale as well as lease markets to local cultivating caste households, access to land by poor remains largely unresolved. Yet there has been considerable change in the landholding structure over the years. Although there is still a large concentration of households among the landless and marginal farmers, concentration of land in the larger land class categories has come down considerably.

It implies that, apart from land reforms, there have been three important factors contributing to land transfers. Some of the lower caste groups who have been migrating in large numbers from rural Bihar have been remitting one-third to one fourth of their earning to the villages of their origin.

Table 15.7: Percentage Distribution of Households from Different Caste Groups by Class in 1981-82 and 1999-2000

Caste	*Agricultural labour*			*Peasant*			*Landlord*	*NAG*	*Total*
	ALF	*ALA*	*AL*	*PMP*	*MP*	*BP*			
					PANEL I : 1981-82				
Brahman and Kayasth	3.70	0	3.70		2.47	54.32	32.10	7.41	100.00
Bhumihar and Rajput	6.67	0	6.67	1.67	6.67	56.67	23.33	5.00	100.00
Kurmi	8.33	4.17	12.50		50.00	29.17	8.33		100.00
Koiri	25.92	3.7	29.62	18.52	33.33	3.70		14.81	100.00
Yadav	35.48	0	35.48	6.45	48.39		6.45	3.23	100.00
Other OBC II	18.52	0	18.52	5.56	14.81	14.81	14.81	31.48	100.00
Backward I	63.63	10.1	73.73	3.03	7.07	5.05	3.03	8.08	100.00
S.C.	60.15	23.44	83.59	4.69	3.13	0.78	1.56	6.25	100.00
Muslim	50.85	1.69	52.54	3.39	11.86	10.17	6.78	15.25	100.00
Total	36.70	7.62	44.32	3.90	12.06	18.79	10.99	9.93	100.00
					PANEL II : 1999-2000				
Brahman and Kayasth	7.23	0	7.23	0.6	1.81	40.36	37.35	12.65	100.00
Bhumihar and Rajput	1.14	0	1.14	1.14	2.27	43.18	43.18	9.09	100.00
Kurmi	14.28	0	14.28	3.57	17.86	39.29	17.86	7.14	100.00
Koiri	23.34	0	23.34	10.00	26.67	3.33	26.67	10.00	100.00
Yadav	23.08	3.85	26.93	7.69	42.31	15.38	5.77	1.92	100.00
Other OBC II	26.39	1.39	27.78	1.39	9.72	12.5	23.61	25.00	100.00
Backward !	51.61	1.3	52.91	4.52	16.77	5.16	7.1	13.55	100.00
S.C.	71.14	7.47	78.61	3.98	5.97	1.99	0.5	8.96	100.00
Muslim	39.39	1.01	40.40	1.01	8.08	17.17	16.16	17.17	100.00
Total	35.57	2.36	37.93	3.03	10.44	18.29	18.07	12.23	100.00

Besides meeting consumption needs, in some cases these remittances have been the main source of land acquisition by the lower castes in recent years. Second, many of the members of the upper or middle caste or skilled labour households who have migrated as professionals, as formal sector employees and as businessmen have been selling their lands. Much of these land transfers are in favour of middle or lower caste households who are trying to acquire some land. The third source of acquiring land in many of the villages of the plains of Bihar appear to be outright encroachment of public lands like river banks, and households of all castes are involved in this process of gaining access to land.

Besides this, over the years tenancy has shown an increasing trend in the state. This is despite the fact that Bihar is one of those states where tenancy is legally banned. Approximately 22 per cent of all the rural households and as much as 40 per cent of the cultivating households are involved in leasing of land. The total leased in area is approximately 25 per cent to the total cultivated land. Moreover the practice of leasing out is on the rise as it is not only the big land owners who lease out land but also many of the small and tiny landholders are increasingly resorting to the practice of leasing out. Seeing the overall practice of tenancy in the state, the IHD study finds that while leasing-in of land has been a source of livelihood for a number of land-poor households, in view of rising cost of cultivation leasing out is becoming an alternative option of sustaining agricultural practices. The increasing trend of tenancy is coupled with changing terms and conditions. Although sharecropping continues to dominate the lease market, over the years there has been marked increase in the proportion of fixed-rent leasing, while the leasing on the basis of labour services has almost vanished. There is room in tenancy reforms to learn from the experience of the neighbour of the state.

END NOTES

1. The study is part of a larger study, *viz.* "Dynamics of Employment, Poverty and Human Development in Bihar" conducted by the Institute for Human Development in the year 2000-2002.
2. Semi-feudalism is a pre-capitalist stage of mode of production in which social forms and organisations are developed on the basis of unequal distribution of land, tenancy, labour tying, and indebtedness. All these mechanisms ensured dependence of the labouring classes on the village

land-owning elite, permitting the persistence of highly unequal distribution of incomes and opportunities (Rodgers and Rodgers, 2000). The model of semi-feudalism in case of Bihar was developed by Bhaduri (1973) and was tested with the help of empirical data by Pradhan H. Prasad in case of Bihar. See Prasad, (1985) and other writings by the same author for an analytical framework of the model.

3. Scott (1976), Bernstein (1979), Harriss (1982) etc. notes that family farm production, of which peasants comprise a major type, possesses an internal logic which permits it to resist the pressure of capitalist production relations and thus to reproduce itself indefinitely. Further, they also argue that many of the reasons advanced for the survival of peasant production are reasons for the persistence of family farm production under capitalism.
4. For a discussion over the six paths discussed by Byres' see Reddy, 2002.
5. A detailed account of these positive changes has been documented by Sharma *et al.* (1999) at macro level and by Rodgers and Rodgers (2000) at micro level.
6. *See* for example Rao, Mohan, 1999, and Byres, 1999.
7. For a detailed account of the violence in rural Bihar see Bhatia, 1999.
8. Srivastava, 1999 also finds in the context of Uttar Pradesh that in recent years, overt forms of conflict seem to have been increasing.
9. Sharma *et al.*(1999) and Rao, Sharma, and Srivastava, (2000) document such incidents on the basis of case studies of a few villages in Bihar, see also Lieten and Srivastava (1999).
10. However, some of the 'middle castes' such as Kurmi, Yadav, and Koeri have also joined the hands with the upper castes in different regions of Bihar depending upon their numeric and political strengths.
11. One private army of upper castes landowners *Ranvir Sena* led a series of massacres of low castes labouring family in rural areas of Bihar is the example of these criminal retaliations.
12. As for example, Jan Breman (1993) and Tom Brass (1994) give two different explanations of the process of emancipation of rural labour on the experience of their long term studies of two different states of India. Breman argues that following the rise of free labour relations 'a groundswell of social emancipation' has taken place. Brass, however, does not see such a link. On the basis of his field work in Haryana, he argues that such types of the process of emancipation of the labourers may legitimise 'communal discourses and practice' instead of creating at least, 'pre-figurative socialist forms'.
13. The caption "semi-feudalism meets the market" is due to Rodgers and Rodgers, 2000.
14. Here the term 'landlordism' has been used in traditional Marxian framework for the purpose of comparability across the two surveys mentioned earlier. All those households who resort to leasing out of land and are not engaged in self-cultivation have been defined as landlord.
15. *See* also Singh and Karan, 2002, for caste class linkage of out-migration of workers.

16. *See* for example, Dumont (1972); Beteille (1975); Bose (1975); Habib (1995) etc.
17. The categorisation designed by the ANSISS/ILO study priorities the labour exploitation criterion developed by Patnaik (1987). However, this takes into account some of the specific conditions prevailing in rural Bihar. It should be noted that all the households with any member engaging in agricultural wage labour are categorised as 'agricultural wage labour' households, and all those leasing out any land are categorised as 'landlord' households.
18. The data taken here is related to erstwhile Bihar for the purpose of comparability. The present geographical region of Bihar shows higher intensity of tenancy of about 12 per cent of leased in area.
19. In some of the states such as Bihar, Uttar Pradesh, etc. tenancy is not legal. Because of this households surveys are supposed to underreport the practice of tenancy. However, it is supposed that the information related to leasing in is likely to be better estimate as there may be less problem related to under reporting of leasing-in.
20. Cheung's (1968, 1969) work has the basis for more recent sharecropping literature because it established the major reasons for share tenancy and the major issues to be addressed.
21. According to Newbery and Stiglitz (1979), since the Cheungian mode considers wage rates as exogenously given, it does not explain the persistence of share tenancy under the situations of the coexistence of the other two forms of contractual arrangements.
22. For a detailed analysis on tenancy ladder see Binswanger and Rosenzweig, 1984.
23. Binswanger and Rosenzweig (1984) offers at least explanations for the coexistence of tenurial and contractual arrangements: (i) differences in risk aversion, (ii) screening of workers of different quality, and imperfect markets for input other than labour.
24. See also Hallagan (1978), Bell-Zusman (1979), Jaynes (1982), Newbery and Stiglitz (1979) etc. on the choice of contract between landord and workers.
25. For a review of literature on role of technological innovations in choice of forms of tenancy see for example, Kikuchi *et al.,* (1984), Rao (1975), Bhalla (1976), Bardhan and Rudra (1980), Singh (1981) etc.
26. Based on the NSSO data Srivastava (2000) finds that between 1981-82 and 1991-92, the percentage of leased area under cash rent increased from 10.9 per cent to 19 per cent while the percentage of area under fixed rent in kind increased from 6.3 to 14.5.
27. One of the most important sources of data related to tenancy has been that from NSSO. Till now the NSSO has published tenancy data only up to 1991-92. This is why most of the studies on tenancy in India at date have been limited to analyse the empirical data only up to 1980s.

Fellow, Institute for Human Development, New Delhi. Author is thankful to D. Narshimha Reddy for his extensive comments on the earlier draft of the paper. However, the usual disclaimer applies.

28. *See* for example Haque (1999), Sharma *et al.*, (1999), and Sharma *et al.* (2002).
29. *See* also Prasad (1975, 1987) and Rodgers (2000) for use of labour-tying in Bihar agricullture during 1970s.
30. The judicious mix of labour tying and rental tenancy is reflected by the fact that the both the systems were prevalent in a small region say in a village, where full-fledged market led fixed rental tenancy was not developed.
31. The majority part of the region falls under command area of Sone river. The Sone command was developed during late 1970s covering the south western part of the state. The region is marked by good government investment in irrigation by developing network of canal system. This led to massive transformation of agriculture of this region from primitive to highly capital intensive mode of production.

REFERENCES

Bardhan, P. and A. Rudra (1980). 'Terms and Conditions of Sharecropping Contracts: An Analysis of Village Survey Data in India', *Journal of Development Studies,* Vol. 16, April.

Beteille, A. (ed.) (1974). *Studies in Agrarian Social Structure*, New Delhi: Oxford University Press.

Bhaduri, A. (1984). *The Economic Structure of Backward Agriculture*, Macmillan Press, New Delhi.

Bhaduri, A. (1973). 'A Study in Agricultural Backwardness under Semi-feudalism', *Economic Journal*, March.

Bhalla, Sheila (1976). "New Relations of Production in Haryana Agriculture", *Economic and Political Weekly,* Vol. 11, No. 13, *Review of Agriculture*, March 27, pp. A-23-A-30.

Bhalla, Sheila (1983). "Tenancy Today: New Factors in the Determination of Mode and Level of Rent Payments for Agricultural Land", *Economic and Political Weekly,* Vol. 18, Nos. 19, 20 and 21, *Annual Number*, March, pp. 832-854.

Bharadwaj, K. and P. K. Das (1975). "Tenurial Conditions and Mode of Exploitation: A Study of Some Villages in Orissa", *Economic and Political Weekly,* Vol. 10, Nos. 5, 6 and 7, *Annual Number*, February, pp. 221-224 and *Review of Agriculture*, Vol. 10, No. 25 and 26, June 21-28, 1975, pp. A-49-A-55.

Binswanger, H. P. and M. R. Rosenzweig (1984), "Contractual Arrangements, Employmet and Wages in Rural Labcur Markets: A Critical Review", pp. 1-40, in H. P. Binswanger and M. R. Rosenzweig (Eds.), *Contractual Arragements, Employment and Wages in Rural Labour Markets in Asia*, Yale University Press, New Haven and London.

Bryceson, Deborahfahy (2000). "Peasant Theories and Smallholder Policies: Past and Present" in *Disappearing Peasantries: Rural Labour in Africa,*

Asia and Latin America, (Eds.) Deborah Bryceson, Cristoba Kay and Jos Mooij published by Intermediate Technology Publications.

Bose, N. K. (1975). *The Structure of Hindu*, Longman, Delhi.

Brass, T. (1994): "Post Script: Populism, Peasants and Intellectuals or What's Left of the Future? New Farmers Movements in India", *The Journal of Peasants Studies*.

Breman, J. (1993): *Beyond Patronage and Exploitation: Changing Agrarian Relations in South Gujarat*, Oxford University Press, Delhi.

Byres, T.J., Kapadia, K., Lerche, J.C. (1999): Rural Labour Relations in India, Taylor & Francis Ltd., New Jersey.

Chadha, G. K. and S. K. Bhaumik (1992), "Changing Tenancy Relations in West Bengal: Popular Notions, Grassroot Realities", *Economic and Political Weekly*, Vol. 27, No. 19, May 9.

Chakravarti, Anand (2001). *Social Power and Everyday Class Relations: Agrarian Transformation in North Bihar*, Sage Publications, Delhi.

Das, Arvind N. (1992). *The Republic of Bihar*, Penguin Books India, Delhi.

Dumont, Louis (1972). Homo Hierarchicus, Paladin, London.

Habib, Irfan (1995). *Essays in Indian History: Towards a Marxist Perception*, Tulika, Delhi.

Haque, T. and A. S. Sirohi (1986). *Agrarian Reforms and Institutional Changes in India*, Concept Publishing Company, New Delhi.

Haque, T. (2000). "Contractual Arrangements in Land and Labour Markets in Rural India" *Indian Journal of Labour Economics*, Vol. 55, No. 3.

Harriss, John (1982). *Capitalism and Peasant Farming: Agrarian Structure and Ideology in Northern Tamil Nadu*, Oxford University Press, Delhi.

Karan, Anup K. and Singh, Manjeet (2002). *Rural Labour Migration in Bihar, Study sponsored by Ministry of Statistics*, Institute for Human Development, New Delhi (mimeo).

Laxminarayan, H. and S. S. Tyagi (1977). "Inter-State Variations in Types of Tenancy", *Economic and Political Weekly*, Vol. 12, No. 39, *Review of Agriculture*, September 24.

Mooij, Jos (2000). "Changing Peasantries in Asia", *Disappearing Peasantries: Rural Labour in Africa, Asia and Latin America*, (Eds.) Deborah Bryceson, Cristoba Kay and Jos Mooij published by Intermediate Technology Publications.

Patnaik, Utsa (1972). "Development of Capitalism in Agriculture", *Social Scientist*, Vols. 2 and 3.

Patnaik, Utsa (1983). "On the Evolution of the Class of Agricultural Labourers in India", *Social Scientist*, July.

Patnaik, Utsa (1987). *Peasant Class Differentiation—A Study in Method with Reference to Haryana*, Oxford University Press, Delhi.

Prasad, Pradhan H. (1975). "Agrarian Unrest and Economic Change in Rural Bihar. The Three Case Studies," *Economic and Political Weekly*, June 14.

Prasad, Pradhan H. (1987). "Agrarian Violence in Bihar," *Economic and Political Weekly*, June, 30.

Prasad, Pradhan H., Gerry Rodgers, Alakh N. Sharma and S. Gupta (1986). *Dynamics of Poverty and Employment in Bihar*, A. N. S. Institute of Social Studies, Patna (mimeo).

Rao, C. H. Hanumantha (1975). *Technological Change and Distribution of Gains in Indian Agriculture*, Macmillan of India, Delhi.

Rodgers, Gerry and Janine, Rodgers (2000). *Semi Feudalism Meets the Market: A Report from Purnea*, Working Paper No.6. Institute for Human Development, New Delhi.

Sharma, Alakh N. (1996). 'Development, Economic Reforms and the Poor: The Case of Bihar', paper prepared for the IDPAD seminar on 'Liberalisation and the Poor: Impact, Opportunities and Barriers', Hyderabad, February 7-9.

Sharma, Alakh N., Actionaid India (2002). *Project Report on Dalit Situation in Bihar*, (Memio), Patna.

Sharma, Alakh N. (1995). "Political Economy of Poverty in Bihar", *Economic and Political Weekly*, Vol. 30, Nos. 41 and 42, October.

Sharma, Alakh N. (1999). *People on the Move: ……and Pattern of Migration in Bihar*, Vikas Publishing House, New Delhi.

Sharma, Alakh N., A. K. Karan, V. Gayathri, Pushpendra and S. Sarkar (2001). *Dynamics of Employment, Poverty and Human Development in Bihar*, Institute for Human Development, New Delhi (mimeo).

Sharma, Alakh N., Anup K. Karan and Sandip Sarkar (2002). *Dynamics of Employment, Poverty and Human Development in Rural Bihar* (Part II), Institute for Human Development, (mimeo).

Sharma, Alakh N., Anup K. Karan, Sandip Sarkar, V. Gayathri, and Pushpendra (1999). *Dynamics of Poverty, Employment and Human Development in Bihar*, Phase I, (mimeo), IHD, New Delhi.

Siddiqui, Kalim (1999). "New Technology and Process of Differentiation: Two Sugarcane Cultivating Villages in U.P.", *Economic and Political Weekly*, Vol. 34, No. 52, December 25-31.

Srivastava, Ravi (1989). 'Tenancy Transactions During Transition: A Study Based on Fieldwork in Uttar Pradesh (India)', *Journal of Peasant Studies*, Vol. 16, No. 3, April, pp. 339-95.

Srivastava, Ravi (1999). "Rural Labour in Uttar Pradesh: Emerging Features of Subsistence, Contradiction and Resistance", *Journal of Peasant Studies*, Vol. 26, Nos. 2 and 3, January and April.

Swain, Mamata (1999). "Agricultural Tenancy and Interlinked Transactions: Neoclassical and Marxist Approaches, I & II", *Economic and Political Weekly*, Vol. 34, Nos. 37 and 38, September 11 and 18.

Vyas, V. S. (1970). "Tenancy in a Dynamic Setting", *Economic and Political Weekly*, Vol. 5, No. 26, June 27.

Wilson, Kalpana (1999). 'Patterns of Accumulation and Struggles of Rural Labour: Some Aspects of Agrarian Change in Central Bihar', *The Journal of Peasant Studies*, 26(2 and 3): 316-54.

Chapter 16

Land Reforms and Land Policy Issues in the Context of Karnataka

R. S. DESHPANDE

I
INTRODUCTION

The focus and emphasis on land policy changed during the last five decades, but the core issues remained revolving round a just distribution of land resources. Land reforms have predominated the land policy issues during the first three decades after independence. The abolition of intermediaries aimed to eliminate the land rights of intermediaries who held large share of the land resources. Close on the heels were the tenancy reforms that began on the hypothesis of 'tenant efficiency' and an expected increase in the capital formation. In addition to these economic goals, the tenancy reforms were taken as an intervention to provide tenants more secure and profitable rights to land. Ceilings on the size of land holdings were addressed to reduce the concentration of wealth in the hands of few and providing means of living to others. The second important intervention that superimposed on the ongoing process of land reforms came in the form of the area-based programmes like Drought-prone Area Programme and Desert Development Programme. Both the programmes focused on building the land resources in the ecologically fragile regions and to provide employment opportunities to the inhabitants. Another similar land policy intervention came from the policy emphasis on soil and water conservation through a massive watershed development programme. Wasteland Development

Programme that intended to restore the ecology and environment in drought prone areas was the next to follow in terms of National Wasteland Development Board. It is, however, quite clear that land reforms dominated the entire land policy scenario dwarfing the other initiatives till the interventions centred on watershed development occupied the central stage. Even then the thinking about the next phase of land reforms and consequent debate is knocking on the policy door.

Land as a basic production resource in the agricultural sector has various uses in the other sectors as well. Management of land resource, therefore, involves inter-sectoral economic linkages as well as intra-sectoral influences caused by different land uses. Broadly speaking, we can classify land use into five main categories. The first is land under agricultural crops especially seasonal crops, where use pattern as a dynamic connotation becomes the most important category for any land use policy. Within this category we find land is allocated to foodgrains as also to the non-foodgrain (commercial) crops. The allocation decision between these two sectors depends largely upon relative prices and price elasticity of demand of different commodities. In addition to this, the income elasticity of demand for various commodities also has significant influence on the land-use pattern. However, in a broader sense, to obtain future projections of land-use patterns, it is necessary to arrive at land resources required for different purposes of food and commercial crop economy based on the trends in consumption of these crops. The second use of land relates to forests, in which forest land is defined as land legally allocated to the forest department. Quite often legal ownership and actual use of land in this context are confused. Recently, the Forest Department with the help of the National Remote Sensing Agency has completely mapped the forest area to arrive at different categories of forests. In addition to this, we have orchards and plantations which are ecologically similar to forest lands. The third important component of the land-use policy relates to land for dwelling purposes, urban uses and industrial uses that depends upon the growth of population, rate of change in employment, sectoral composition of employment, and growth as well as changing structure of the industrial sector. Given the process of liberalisation it is more likely that the pressure of population as well as demand for industrial use of land is likely to increase substantially. Fourth, we have large land mass being under-utilised with respect to its economic capability. This group includes fallows, cultivable wasteland and land used for miscellaneous tree crops. These lands have good potential for alternative use but are in the category for various reasons. Lastly, we have vast patches of degraded land spread across each of the categories and also existing separately.

In this paper, we have tried to analyse the land reforms as an intervention to deal with poverty. The discussion is more towards the philosophy that dominated the contours of reforms during those formation years. This is also viewed in the light of the experience gathered so far. The national and international influences on the land policies is discussed in the context of Karnataka. This is followed by a section on land policy and poverty issues. The impact of these policies on the land use pattern is the core of the discussion in the next section. This also includes pattern of land use in Karnataka from the perspective of evolving a long-term policy directing use of land resources in the State. We have analysed this at the district level for all the districts of Karnataka over the last four decades. Finally, we have presented land policy contours for Karnataka State that includes reforms and land use issues.

II
LAND REFORMS AS AN INTERVENTION TO DEAL WITH POVERTY

While in the earlier phases of land reforms thrust was given more on the food production, through area approach, extension of technology, and abolishing regressive institutions, poverty as an issue was not explicit. Raj Krishna grouped land reform measures based on the theme and implementation of reforms into four groups, namely liberative, distributive, organisational and developmental reforms (Raj Krishna, 1961). The liberative measures aimed at the emancipation of the actual tillers of the land from the burden of the landlord. This was to be achieved by conferring the land title or occupancy rights on the tenant. Fixing of rent was undertaken in a few states, e.g. West Bengal's 'Operation Barga', where tenancy was recorded. The distributive measures on the other hand were meant to achieve this by providing the material resources to the poor as promised by the Constitution of India, especially those who required land as a productive resource. This was to be achieved by redistributing land in ownership from large landholders to the landless specifically from socially weaker sections. The tenancy reforms and ceiling on land holding represented liberative and distributive measures in the categorisation of Raj Krishna (1961), whereas, the organisational reforms aimed at choosing and setting in place a particular form of agricultural production organisation with the help of technological change that was introduced in mid-sixties. Thus, the three components together had put pressure on the land resources provoking need for developmental reforms. Development reforms as the fourth component encompassed other interconnected issues with land policy. These impacted the overall development of the agricultural sector. All four components taken together form a part of distributive and development images that were taken immediately after the independence in the country. Even though Raj Krishna wrote this chapter almost at the beginning of the first phase of land reforms, the description aptly gives a clear theoretical view of the reforms that preceded.

Immediately after the independence four important components of land reforms were thought of as major policy interventions in building the land policy. These included: (1) abolition of intermediaries; (2) tenancy reforms; (3) fixing ceilings on land holdings; and (4) consolidation of landholdings. These were taken in phases as the ground preparation and the political will was to be built for their wider acceptance. By 1960, the whole process of legal enactment of the abolition of intermediaries was completed. This was the most successful component of the land reform process.

The tenancy reform component of the land reforms was relatively less successful. Tenancy was widespread at the time of Independence. The discrepancy between the ownership and operational holding was a major malady of Indian agriculture. At the time of independence it was felt that conferment of ownership on the tenant or at least some measure of tenure security coupled with rent regulation would be an important intervention to avoid tenants' exploitation. It was felt necessary as this would increase employment, consumption standards and enhance the market participation of the poor tenants.

The major aspects of tenancy reforms included security of tenure, termination of tenancy, resumption for personal cultivation by the landlord, regulation of rent, and confirmation of ownership rights. Various state laws were enacted between 1960 and 1972. These differed across the states and territories. Owing to the diverse and complicated nature of social and agrarian structure in the countryside, no uniform guidelines could be formulated for the country. However, some broad guidelines were given in addition to the directives given in the successive plan documents. The consensus on the policy of tenancy reforms favoured neither complete expropriation of landlordism nor interest of the tenants. In the national guidelines the quite a few measures were communicated to the state governments for incorporating in the State level legislation: (i) Security of the tenancy to be conferred on the actual cultivator, (ii) Fair rent to be fixed between 1/4th and 1/5th of the gross produce, (iii) Landowners may be permitted to cultivate land for the personal use, (iv) The surrender of the tenancy rights with mutual consent, (v) In respect of some of the area, the landlord-tenant nexus to be ended and the tenant cultivator be brought directly under the contact with the state, (vi) Disabled persons, defence personnel and other such exemptions be allowed to lease their land, (vii) The term "personal cultivation" should be clearly defined if landlords are allowed to remove tenants in order to resume cultivation, and (viii) Tenancy records should be corrected and oral tenancies should be abolished.

Because land is a state subject in India and that the production relations dictating land relations varied from state to state, the national policy recommendations resulted in differing tenancy reform laws in each state. Some of the basic differences in the tenancy reform laws are outlined in Table 16.1.

As it is well known that there are variations and interesting exceptions across States. Tenancy is completely prohibited in some States whereas it is completely free in a few others. Punjab and Haryana have not prohibited tenancy whereas Karnataka has a near-complete ban on tenancy. Some states have conferred ownership rights on tenant cultivators except for sharecroppers, whereas West Bengal chose to provide owner-like rights only to the sharecroppers. Some states such as Maharashtra and Orissa chose to provide different tenancy reform regimes for different areas within the state. Many states allowed tenancy only for certain limited classes of persons, often broadly termed as "disabled". Orissa law considers a landowner owning less than 3 standard acres of land as a disabled person. In Rajasthan a student pursuing studies in an educational institution and having age less than 25 years is also a disabled person. In Uttar Pradesh such student is disabled if his father is dead. In Uttar Pradesh all minors, women and unmarried daughters are not treated as disabled but whose husband or father is dead are treated as disabled. In Bihar a public servant whose salary is below the given norm is treated as disabled. The ultimate step in providing tenure security was to confer ownership rights on the tenants from a specified date. Some states declared the tenants as deemed to be owners on the payment of the reasonable price fixed as compensation to the owner as fixed earlier. The legislation in Assam, Gujarat, Himachal Pradesh, Karnataka, Kerala, Manipur, Madhya Pradesh, Maharashtra, Orissa, and Rajasthan allowed for conferment of ownership on certain tenants, although most laws contained exceptions that weakened the actual impact.

Table 16.1: Trends in Land Holdings in Karnataka 1970-1990

(*Area under holdings in 000 ha*)

Sl. No.	*Size Class*	*1970-71*	*1976-77*	*1980-81*	*1985-86*	*1990-91*	*1995-96*
1.	Marginal	549	638 (16.2)	733 (14.9)	866 (18.2)	1,072 (23.7)	1,248 (16.4)
2.	Small	1,221	1,319 (8.0)	1,543 (17.0)	1,888 (22.4)	2,308 (22.2)	2,480 (22.3)
3.	Semi-Medium	2,205	2,288 (3.7)	2,572 (12.5)	2,880 (11.9)	3,200 (11.2)	3298 (11.1)
4.	Medium	3,792	3,858 (1.7)	4,018 (4.1)	3,881 (-3.4)	3,770 (-2.9)	3,489 (-7.45)
5.	Large	3601	3,254 (-9.6)	2,880 (-11.5)	2,364 (-17.9)	1,971 (-16.6)	1,593 (-16.6)
6.	Total	11,368	11,357 (-0.01)	11,746 (3.4)	11,879 (1.1)	12,321 (3.7)	12,109 (-1.7)

Note: Figures in brackets are percentage increase/decrease over previous censuses.

Source: Agricultural Censuses of Karnataka for the respective years.

Among the various exceptions given under the tenancy acts, provisions allowing the landlords to remove tenants in order to resume personal cultivation assumed greater importance as the dominant landlords took advantage of this clause. The clause was entered with a view to induce the landlord to undertake personal cultivation and also to control absentee landlordism. Tenancy acts in almost all the states allowed the landlord to resume lands for personal cultivation, but the terms and definitions differed. The National policy recommended that residence of the owner or members of his family be one of the essential conditions for personal cultivation. Some states such as Maharashtra and Karnataka have required that in order to resume personal cultivation, a landlord must both reside within a certain distance of the land and the produce from the land must be the principal source of income. In some states, landlords with a certain economic status (such as those paying income tax) were not eligible to resume cultivation. Other differences in provisions allowing for landlord resumption included: the definition of family holding, economic holding or basic holding (relating to how much land the landlord could resume); how much land should be left with the tenant after resumption of cultivation; the time limit for resuming cultivation; and the consequences of not cultivating. In all cases, these provisions could be and were utilized by the landlords to their advantage.

Most tenancy reform laws also contained provisions concerning the ability of tenants to voluntarily surrender the land back to the landlord. These provisions were also misused by landlords to weaken the laws' impact. In most states the surrender of land falls in the jurisdiction of the revenue authorities. The authorities allowed such surrender after verification of the voluntary element in the process. The strong nexus between landlords and revenue officials often allowed the landlords to skirt the law's intention (Deshpande, 1999). Punjab, Kerala, Karnataka, Gujarat, Tripura and Andhra Pradesh (Telangana area) did not provide for any surrender by the tenant to the landlord. A few of these states did allow for surrender to the State. Tenants in some states were also given the right to purchase the land. For example, in Maharashtra, where tenancy is not prohibited, the tenant acquires the right to purchase the land after one year from the date of tenancy.

The types of tenancy contracts are also changing over the last three decades beginning with 1971-72. There are fluctuations in Cash Rents and Rents in terms of Fixed Produce over years and across states, but Rents in terms of share of produce show a consistent decline. The picture has different shades across regions/states. The regulation of rent levels was an important aspect of the tenancy reform legislations. The prevailing rent levels differed across the states in the country. The National policy recommended that fair rent payable by a tenant shall be subject to mutual agreement but should be limited to 20 to 25 per cent of the produce. Individual states recalculated this for the purpose of their legislations, some using land revenue as a basis and others using the gross value of produce. Most states using the gross value of produce set the maximum rent levels in the range of 25-33 per cent of the gross value of the produce. Therefore, the variations in the tenancy contracts across states is not unexpected so also the changes over the decades in these contracts.

The most controversial and debated provision of the tenancy reforms has been the complete or near-complete ban on tenancy existing in many states. Some of the states where tenancy is legally allowed the tenancy reform laws also provided for the termination of tenancy under various circumstances. The laws commonly provided for termination of tenancy on five grounds: (i) tenant has failed to pay rent for the year within the time stipulated in the law; (ii) tenant is using land for purpose other than agriculture; (iii) the land is made unfit for cultivation; (iv) the tenant failed to personally cultivate the land; and (v) the term of lease period is over or the landlord has resumed the land for personal cultivation (e.g. Deshpande, 1998). It must be noted that even where tenancy is technically allowed, provisions that give long-term and protected rights to tenants can have the same impact as a ban as they prevent landowners from leasing out their land. The National Commission on Agriculture has asserted that under India's present ratio of agricultural land per capita, tenancy as such cannot and should not be totally banned (National Commission on Agriculture Part 15). Experience and field studies have shown that prohibition on tenancy is not entirely effective. Tenancy continues to exist and some observers note that the ban on tenancy have negative impact on the landless and land-poor (Shah and Sah, 2002). It is interesting that all these restrictions have given rise to a refractory tenancy market. Concealed tenancy and reverse tenancy have proliferated as new forms of tenancy (Nadkarni, 1976; 2002).

On paper, the enactment of tenancy legislations between 1962-1977 appears to have resulted in a sharp decrease in tenancy. National Sample Surveys record a dramatic fall in the area under tenancy from 23.34 per cent during the year 1952-53 to 10.7 per cent during the year 1961-62 and further down to 7.2 per cent in 1982. This settled down to 8 per cent by 1991 as revealed by 48th NSS round (*see* Table 16.2). Three important notes here. First, at least part of the decrease in tenancy resulted from landlords evicting their tenants either in anticipation of the laws or using loopholes in the laws. One estimate is that tenancy reform laws led to evictions resulting in the rural poor losing access to about 30 per cent of the operated area in India (Appu, 1996).

Second, the National Sample Surveys almost certainly undercount tenancy due to the fact that both landowners and tenants are often afraid to reveal tenancy relationships because of the existing legal

Table 16.2: Land Reforms Implications and Likely Changes

Sl. No.	*Land Reform Measure*	*Implications and Likely Changes*
1.	Abolition of intermediaries	Successful but this is likely to re-emerge in other forms
2.	Abolition of tenancy	Partially successful. Gave rise to un-recorded tenancy and reverse tenancy. Land tenancy market will have to be opened up
3.	Ceiling on land holdings	Partially successful but unlikely to sustain in near future
4.	Agrarian reorganisation including consolidation of holdings and prevention of sub-division and fragmentation	Consolidation of holding either through state efforts or by co-operation likely to emerge strongly.
	Proposed Changes	
1.	Organisation of co-operative farms	Small and marginal farmers are likely to form consortiums not in the co-operatives way.
2.	Increased ceiling limit for specific purposes (educational institutions, industries, housing, horticulture)	Land concentration in the hands of resourceful individuals is likely to increase.
3.	Widening the definition of agriculture	Misuse of the provision is more likely.
4.	Allowing non-agriculturists to hold land	This was happening earlier. Land concentration is likely to change.

restrictions. The question of concealed tenancy has been debated and it is recorded that anywhere between 15 to 25 per cent tenancies in the country is illegal and concealed. NSS data shows that informally leasing of land is dominated by smaller and marginal farmers. More than 80 per cent of the leased-in land is held by this group. Since the tenancy is oral and sharecroppers are weak both economically and politically, they rarely get their due. They only have a tenuous hold on the land that they cultivate and invariably have to hand over the land to the owner at any time he demands.

Third, the tenancy laws did help tenants to acquire ownership or owner-like rights in about 4 per cent of the operated area. These benefits were concentrated in a small number of states including Kerala, West Bengal, Karnataka, Assam, Gujarat, Jammu and Kashmir, and Maharashtra (GoI, Ministry of Rural Development Annual Report, 2000-2001).

In the present context, tenancy in India should be seen as a mechanism for resource adjustment, access to credit, sharing of risk and entrepreneurship, avoiding transaction costs, leasing out by the poor in favour of others if it becomes difficult to invest capital, and leasing out the distant plots which are difficult to cultivate.

III
IMPACT OF INTERNATIONAL AND NATIONAL POLICIES ON LAND USE: A CASE OF KARNATAKA

The global and domestic economic scenario is changing fast, responding to the policies favouring liberalisation and globalisation. Land being the major economic resource in a developing country like India, policy changes at the international level as also interventions from the domestic economic parameters influence variations in land use. Therefore, it becomes essential to address the issue of responses of the land-use to global and domestic policy changes. Since independence, land use in India largely remained unaffected by international policies and will continue to be so in future also. However, other policies do impact the land use indirectly. Trade is one such process through which land use gets altered in favour of trade-concentrated commodities. Trade policy is one of the most important international policies that has the potential to impact the domestic land-use policy. Provisions of the WTO like removal of quantitative restrictions and imposition of tariff barriers can influence land-use. Even after these policies become operative, the contribution of foreign trade to gross domestic product in India may remain between 9 and 10 per cent (9.6% in 1996, 9.3% in 1997, 8.8% in 1998 and 10.8% in 2000-01). Agricultural exports presently form about 2 per cent of the GDP (1.95% of GDP in 1996, 1.83% in 1997, 1.62% in 1998, and 1.52% in 2000-01). The contribution of agriculture to India's foreign trade has been decreasing and it is around 19 per cent (20.4% in 1996, 19.5% in 1997, 18.5% in 1998 and 13.3% in 2000-01) (GoI, Economic Surveys, 1996-98, 2000-01). Considering the enormity of the landmass and land use categories, coupled with the meagre contribution of agricultural trade, changes in international trade may not impact land-use very significantly. Heuristically, in Karnataka, even with the largely varying domestic prices, land-use has remained largely inelastic, dominated by the food crops. Thus, even if India's (or Karnataka's) land use is exposed to international prices, which are relatively stable compared with domestic prices, land-use will continue to be inelastic at macro level. This trend will continue as long as food grain production continues to dominate the priorities in Karnataka and in India. Our marginal propensity to consume food commodities is still on the higher side and the proportion of people below the poverty line is still around 33 per cent of the population. The available empirical evidence clearly demonstrates that Karnataka's land use will continue to be more responsive to domestic demand pressures rather than international policies. It is clear that international trade and price developments do not appear to have much influence on land allocation decisions. Therefore, it would be interesting to explore the impact of domestic developments on land-use, especially those dealing with institutional changes.

Interventions from institutions matter in the land-use pattern both as incentive creator as well as land-use modulator. A large number of institutions have direct as well as indirect influences on land-use pattern. Institutions that influence land-use include formal, informal, state initiated and locally generated institutions. The influence occurs through a legal or modulated framework as well as from the creation of incentive structure or a regulatory body. These are the vehicles by which regulations are made and implemented, business and commerce are organised, and individuals and communities participate in and influence trends. They may be formal or informal, ephemeral or long term, public or private, constituted for a particular purpose and operates at local, community, regional, national or international level. Institutional shortcomings have been frequently recorded as causes of development failure (Chadha *et al.*, 2002). This indicates the need for strengthening institutions and their building capacity to discharge their functions more effectively. With the need to reduce public expenditure, and to improve national economic performance, many functions and institutions currently in the public sector are planned to be moved into private control.

Karnataka Land Revenue Manual, Land Acquisition Act of Karnataka and Land Reforms Acts and Karnataka State Land Use Board are the major legal institutional instruments governing land-use pattern in the State. Among the non-state informal village institutions, the most important ones are: caste (*jati*) panchayats, village panchayat (non-PRIs), traditional village administrative structures (Gowda, Patel, Shanbhog, Kulkarni, Patwari etc.). These institutions directly or indirectly influence patterns of land-use. We can group them among legal institutions, monitoring institutions, and incentive-creating institutions. The main institutions influencing, the land-use patterns in Karnataka can be categorised into four groups: each of them has a major bearing on the ultimate land-use patterns of the state (Burns and Deshpande, 2001):

(i) Institutions governing land ownership and monitoring land-use.
(ii) Institutions for development of technology and transfer/dissemination of the technologies developed.
(iii) Institutions covering supply of credit and finance to the farming community.
(iv) Institutions that help marketing of agricultural commodities.

These four components directly or indirectly monitor the use of land resources and tone the agrarian structure[1] in the State. One of the important interactions is the following:

> Land reforms is an integrated programme of measures designed to eliminate obstacles to economic and social development arising out of defects in the agrarian structure. Land reforms constitute an important component of the overall programme of agrarian development including modification in rural credit, land division, land taxation, marketing facilities, co-operative organization, agricultural education and advisory services. Land reforms aim at providing greater equity in income and wealth. Following the directives from the National Government, Government of Karnataka also introduced land reform legislation and modified them from time to time.

The main objectives of land reforms are to achieve greater equality and efficiency in use of resources (Government of Karnataka, 1993). Karnataka's Land Reform policy was developed with the twin objectives of (i) conferring ownership on erstwhile tenants, and (ii) redistribution of surplus lands available after land ceiling to the deserving. This policy has relatively achieved its objective by fixing a ceiling on land holdings and conferring ownership to tenants. Up to the latest amendment in 1995, land reforms did not promote land lease. The purpose of land reforms was to make more rational use of the scarce land resource by affecting condition on holdings, imposing ceilings on holdings so that cultivation can be done in the most efficient manner without any waste of labour and capital. It is a means of redistributing agricultural land in favour of the less privileged classes and of improving the terms and conditions on which land is held for cultivation by the actual tillers, with a view to ending exploitation (Aziz and Krishna, 1997).

Land reforms in Karnataka are considered to be better-implemented reforms as compared with those in many other states in the country not only by analysts from Karnataka but by others also (Sinha and Pushpendra, 2000). The reforms in Karnataka are certainly pragmatic in their content but the process of implementation leaves a large area unattended to. The major achievements include the acquisition of surplus land, abolition of intermediaries and abolition of tenancy, at least the recorded old tenancy. The main failures listed by the analysts in the context of reforms are the distribution of surplus land, the quality of the surplus land, economic viability of the distributed land and conduction of check on concealed tenancy (Thimmaiah and Aziz, 1984). Among the major failures of land reforms, concealed tenancy, reverse tenancy and marginalisation of holdings are the most important ones. Land going out of agricultural sector for non-agricultural uses and interestingly the other sectors have no land ceilings.

There are a few interesting observations, which emerge out of the broad trends shown in Table 16.3. Marginalisation of land holdings is occurring very fast and this may result in bringing down the viability of small and marginal farms (Aziz and Krishna, 1997). With this pace of marginalisation of land holdings, it is feared that a large number of small and marginal farmers are likely to go out of business, swelling the ranks of the urban poor. The area under large and medium farms is fast decreasing, though this has not shown any significant effect on the production probably due to inverse size-productivity relationship. However, this it is likely to be problematic in future in the context of the fast changes that are taking place in the agricultural sector. In Karnataka, the number of holdings operated by different size groups are; 26.10 lakh marginal, 17.07 lakh small, 12.04 lakh semi-medium, 5.94 lakh medium and 1.06 lakh large holdings. The land concentration is 0.685 as against the all India level of 0.713. The average size of holdings is 1.95 ha and the number of holdings with land less than 1.0 ha accounts for the maximum share of 42 per cent of the total holdings in the State, which in itself is cause for concern. The ceiling limit on land holdings in Karnataka is 4.05-8.10 ha for irrigated land with two crops, 10.12-12.14 ha for irrigated land with one crop and 21.85 ha for dry land.

Table 16.3: Policy Interventions and their Perceived Impact

Policy Interventions	*Poverty Alleviation*	*Conflict Management/ Equity*	*Environmental Management*	*Sustainable Economic Growth*	*Production Efficiency*
Abolition of Intermediaries	Sig	Sig	Par	Sig	Sig
Tenancy Reforms	Sig	Sig	Neg	Par	Sig
Ceiling on Size of Holding	Sig	Sig	Neg	Sig	Par
Consolidation of Holdings	Neg	Neg	Par	Par	Sig
Computerization of Land Records	Neg	Sig	Neg	Neg	Par
Drought Prone Area Development Programme and Desert Development Programme	Neg	Neg	Sig	Sig	Par
Watershed Development Programme	Sig	Sig	Sig	Par	Par
Waste Land Development	Par	Neg	Sig	Par	Par

Note: Impact levels are perceived as Sig—Significant, Par—Partial, Neg—Negligible.

The Karnataka Land Reforms Amendment Bill, 1995 has brought about major changes in agrarian relationship in the following areas:

(1) Allows lease of agriculture land for aquaculture for a period of 20 years in the districts of Dakshina Kannada and Uttara Kannada up to 40 units (around 220 acres).
(2) Agricultural land can be bought or inherited by any one whose income from non agricultural source is below Rs. 2 lakh.
(3) Up to 108 acres of agricultural land can be bought for industrial development purpose.
(4) Up to 28 acres can be bought for educational institutions.
(5) Up to 54 acres can be bought for places of worship.
(6) Up to 54 acres can be bought for housing projects.
(7) Up to 108 acres can be bought for horticulture including floriculture and agro based industries.

After this amendment, Government has permitted leasing out land up to 40 standard acres for aquaculture, 20 standard acres for industrial development, 4 standard acres for educational institutions recognised by the State, 20 standard acres for housing projects; and 20 standard acres for horticulture including floriculture and agro-based industries. This policy has brought about changes in land use especially in the urban fringes and in semi-urban areas, where absentee landlords are promoting floriculture/horticulture. In fact, instead of leasing out land, farmers have resorted to total sale of their land, and this in many cases has resulted in farmers becoming tenants (or even wage labourers) on their own land, due to poor portfolio management. The probable implications of the changes in land policy of the earlier vintage and with the 1955 amendments are summarised in Table 16.2.

The main purpose of the amendment is to supplement the objectives of the new agricultural policies of the Government of Karnataka and augmenting the process of liberalisation and globalisation initiated by the Government of India. Karnataka State, on the policy front, is getting into the process of liberalisation in a big way and the state has initiated a good number of interventions to boost these. However, the inter-sectoral competition in the land-use still needs to be critically looked into and analysed rationally.

IV
LAND, POVERTY AND POLICY ISSUES

In the present context, it is clear that the small and marginal farmers are not competing well in either the domestic or foreign markets. The competition is hampered due to the crop they produce on their farms as well as due to the market imperfections and lack of information available to them. In this context, many analysts argue that there has not been level playing field for the farmers of India *vis-a-vis* the farmers of the western world. The factors that inhibit India's farmers in the competitive world markets include the small size of landholdings, size of production, and market imperfections. It is difficult for the small and marginal farmers to grow the commodities that have good demand in the world market mainly because of the high cost of cultivation of such commodities as well as their limited know-how about such commodities. In order to overcome this problem it is essential to create the larger size of entrepreneurs groups so that such groups can take the risk of entering into competition to grow the crops and commodities which have better demand both in domestic as well as in the world market.

The nexus between the land policy initiatives and growth is quite clear. Though one cannot implicate one-to-one correspondence between land policy and agricultural growth, the available evidence is significant enough to suggest such a nexus. Because the majority of India's population depends upon land for their livelihood, poverty issues are also closely associated with land policy. A study by Besley and Burgess gave robust evidence of a link between poverty reduction due to tenancy reforms and abolition of intermediaries. They also inferred that land reforms also benefited the landless (Besley and Burgess, 2000).

The poor in rural India are located mostly among the landless agricultural labourers, marginal and small farmers. NSS data indicates that landless is the best predictor of poverty in India. In a cross-section analysis of the states in India, the empirical data suggest that marginalisation is on a fast increase. The trends differ across the various regions and social groups, but it is clearly visible that the land-based poor are becoming poorer due to the process of marginalisation. I have made use of empirical data across the states in the country to buttress these points and to bring forth the land policy-poverty nexus in Table 16.3.

India's land policy interventions during the last five decades can be assessed based on their impact on various parameters, including alleviation of poverty, conflict management and equity, sustainable economic development, environmental impact, and production efficiency. The land policy interventions have had varying impacts across the states, depending in large part on the agrarian situation and the extent to which a given policy was implemented. In Table 16.3 we have presented the perceptions gathered from the literature about various policy interventions (Appu 1996; Sinha and Pushpendra, 2000; Das, 2000; Joshi, 1975, 1987 and various state volumes published by Sage publication under the series editor Yugandhar, B. N.) we have taken the overall impact on three point scale, namely significant (sig), negligible (neg) and partial (par). An important limitation of this approach is the subjectivity associated with the judgement but that was weeded out on the basis of discussion with knowledgeable people. We can see poverty alleviation could be impacted by the first three measures significantly, but DPAD and

DDP made little inroads here. Similar results are seen in respect of the conflict management and equity but a significant change was recorded in this area due to computerisation of land records. DDP, DPAP, and Waste Land Development Programmes could impact environmental management significantly. Similarly, these could influence sustainable growth in some pockets. But major contributor to sustainable growth came from the abolition of intermediaries and ceiling on land holdings that together have put a pressure on the use of resources. It is true that production efficiency is not a direct derivative of land policy, but the components of land policy help in achieving higher level of efficiency. Abolition of intermediaries, land ceiling and consolidation of holdings (wherever it could be done) have certainly helped in production efficiency. Watershed development programme has been one of the important land policy interventions in the recent past and has impacted poverty alleviation, conflict management and environmental management significantly. Its influence on production efficiency is not very prominent (Deshpande and Narayanamurthy, 1999).

The concept of land reforms may have to be reviewed in line with the concepts of the new economic policy. Although abolition of tenancy has been the ideal of many land reform movements, it is debatable whether tenancy can ever be entirely abolished even if the man-land ratio in agriculture is favourable for its abolition. A variety of circumstances may necessitate its continuance to some extent in all situations. Even if redistribution of land is carried out, every rural family cannot possibly be given a piece of land sufficient to provide even subsistence. In the short run, the only realistic course of policy is to recognise the inevitability of some tenancy and to legalise and promote the most productivity oriented form of this tenancy, and not attempt to outlaw it. Empirical research is required to determine the precise manners in which alternative tenancy arrangements affect input use and productivity.

END NOTE

1. Agrarian structure refers to the manner in which man-land relationships are governed and covers the way in which land is held and cultivated. In addition to this, it also covers the rights and privileges enjoyed by different categories of people who have access to land.

REFERENCES

Appu, P. S. (1996). *Land Reforms in India*, Vikas Publishing House, New Delhi.

Aziz, Abdul and Sudhir Krishna (1997). *Land Reforms in India: Karnataka Promises Kept and Missed*, New Delhi: Sage.

Behuria, N. C. (1997). *Land Reforms Legislation in India*, Vikas, New Delhi.

Besley, Timothy and Robin, Burgess (1998). "Land Reform, Poverty Reduction and Growth: Evidence from India", *The Quarterly Journal of Economics*, May.

Burns, Tony and R. S. Deshpande (2001). *Karnataka Rural Policy Review: Land Administration, Agricultural Development and Rural Transformation Unit*, Institute for Social and Economic Change, Bangalore.

Chadha, G. K., Sucharita Sen and H. R. Sharma (2002). *Land Resources in India Agriculture: Policy, Use and Future Strategic Choices*, A Report for the Millennium Study on Indian Agriculture, New Delhi.

Deshpande, R. S. (1998). Land Reforms and Agrarian Structure in Maharashtra, *Journal of the Indian School of Political Economy*, Vol. 10, No. 1, January-March.

Deshpande, R. S. and A. Narayanamoorthy (1999). *An Appraisal of Watershed Development Programme Across Regions in India*, Gokhale Institute of Politics and Economics, Pune.

Deshpande, R. S. and K. V. Raju (2001). *Rural Policy for Growth and Poverty Reduction, Agricultural Development and Rural Transformation Unit*, Institute for Social and Economic Change, Bangalore.

Government of India (1976). *National Commission on Agriculture*, Part XV, Agrarian Reforms.

Government of India (1996, 1997, 1998, 2000a, 2001). *Economic Survey*, Ministry of Finance, New Delhi.

Government of India (2000). *Land Use Statistics and A Glance, 1995-96 and 1996-97*. Ministry of Agriculture, New Delhi.

Government of India (2001). *Annual Report of the Ministry of Rural Development*, Government of India, New Delhi.

Government of Karnataka (1993). Report of the Expert Committee on Stagnation of Agricultural Productivity in Karnataka during 1980s (Chairman: Shri T. R. Satishchandran), Bangalore.

Government of Karnataka (2001). Perspective Land-use Plan for Karnataka–2025, Institute of Agriculture Technology, State Land Use Board, Government of Karnataka, Bangalore.

Nadkarni, M. V. (1976). Tenants from the Dominant Class: A Developing Contradiction in Land Reforms, *Economic and Political Weekly*, Vol. 11, December.

Nadkarni, M. V. (2002). Land Reforms—A Bus That India Missed which May Never Come Again, *Indian Journal of Agricultural Economics*, Vol. 57, No. 4, October-December.

Raj Krishna (1961). Land Reform and Development in South Asia, in Walter Frochlich (ed.), *Land Tenure, Industrialisation and Social Stability: Experiences and Prospects in Asia,* The Marquette University Press, Wisconsin.

Rao, V. M. (1992). "Land Reform Experiences: Perspective for Strategy and Programmes." *Economic and Political Weekly*, June 27th.

Shah, Ghanshyam and D. C. Sah (2002). Land Reforms in India: Performance and Challenges in Gujarat and Maharashtra, Sage, New Delhi.

Sinha, B. K. and Pushpendra (2000). *Land Reforms in India: An Unfinished Agenda*, New Delhi: Sage.

Thimmaiah, G. and Abdul, Aziz (1984). *The Political Economy of Land Reforms*, New Delhi: Ashish Publishing House.

Chapter 17

Conceptualizing Land and Rural Poverty Linkages with Some Reflections on Madhya Pradesh and Chhattisgarh

PRAVEEN JHA

I
INTRODUCTION

It would hardly be an exaggeration to say that of all the issues confronting the contemporary developing countries, arguably among the most important, with profound implications for the material well-being of the masses in the countryside, is the agrarian question. Unfortunately, for policy makers across several countries in Asia, Africa and Latin America, i.e. the continents housing the overwhelming proportion of the world's miserable indigents, this question has been a most challenging one, almost an impossible nut to crack. Furthermore, as is well-acknowledged, at the core of the agrarian question lies the land question. This paper is a modest attempt to explore some of the critical connections between land and poverty at a conceptual plane and look at some of the relevant issues in rural Madhya Pradesh and Chhattisgarh, the latter of very recent origin, as a state, being carved out of the former in 2000. The undivided Madhya Pradesh itself came into being in 1956 and included the five erstwhile regions of Mahakoshal, Madhya Bharat, Vindhya Pradesh, Bhopal and a small area of the Sirohi region of Rajasthan. Given that the state of Chhattisgarh is of very recent origin, and that much of the relevant data from large scale official sources refer to undivided

Madhya Pradesh, it may be preferable to treat the two entities as the earlier combined one; thus in this paper, Madhya Pradesh (henceforth MP) refers to the undivided entity prior to November 2000, inclusive of Chhattisgarh.

MP, located in India's centre, is geographically among the largest and, as per the 2001 census, accounts for 7.9 per cent of the country's population. Like much of India, and more than most other states, it is primarily rural, with almost three-fourths of its population residing in rural areas, and overwhelmingly depending on agriculture for livelihood. Apart from being among the least industrialised/urbanised, MP also belongs to the infamous club of states called BIMARU (literally meaning sick), Bihar, Rajasthan and Uttar Pradesh being other members, with well-below national average per capita income and well-above average incidence of poverty, compared to major states of India. In fact, as per the estimates based on the 55th round of NSS, three states, namely Uttar Pradesh (including Uttarakhand), Bihar (including Jharkhand) and Madhya Pradesh (including Chhattisgarh), housing about one-third of India's population between them, accounted for almost half of the country's officially defined poor. In each of these states, the share of poor was substantially larger than the share of population. Going beyond the conventional economic indicators of well-being also, it clearly emerges that MP happens to be at the bottom rung among the major states of India.

II
LAND AND RURAL POVERTY

Of course, there is no single, straightforward explanation for the persistence of poverty in contemporary developing countries. However, it is easy to identify the obvious structural correlates of economic well-being. These are:

(i) assets (a) tangible like land and (b) intangible or embodies like specific skills,
(ii) employment availability, and
(iii) rate of return to labour power.

A process of economic transformation which improves the prospects with reference to these correlates for the masses is bound to have promising implications for their economic well-being. Thus, central to an understanding of the problem of poverty is the specific linkages connecting the nature of an economic transformation—i.e. its pace, structure and the above noted correlates. It is our contention that a robust agricultural transformation, through a variety of mechanisms, has extremely positive implication for such correlates.

In this context, it may be useful to elaborate a little the argument hinted at the outset regarding the significance of addressing the agrarian question, before we come to a closer examination of the case of MP. History of 'modern economic growth', to use the expression made famous by Simon Kuznets, offers an unambiguous lesson as regards the significance of successful agricultural transformation in facilitating overall economic transformation[1]. Sure enough, a multiplicity of patterns emerge when it comes to the processes of agricultural transformation[2] as well as to its linkages with overall economic transformation. Nonetheless, the centrality of agricultural transition in the early to middle stages of modern economic growth, is clearly evident. Thus the message for the poor countries of Asia, Africa and Latin America, seeking escape from economic backwardness is obvious enough. In fact, historical experiences would suggest that the need for addressing their respective agrarian questions for these countries is even more urgent as some of the critical inputs that facilitated economic transformation of many among the contemporary developed countries in their early stages, in particular colonialism/imperialism and massive migration, are simply not available to the latecomers. Furthermore, the range of trajectories of agrarian transition for the latecomers has also got constrained in significant ways. Specifically, it has become increasingly clear that for countries in the Third World, where large sections of the population are dependent on agriculture for their livelihoods, feasibility of successful agricultural transformation through the landlord road, or by any other road that ignores the issue of land reform, is highly suspect. There is a great deal of evidence from countries in Asia, Africa and Latin America that the agricultural policies pursued in the post-World War II era, (i.e. period when most of these countries got the political space to embark on trajectories of relatively autonomous economic development), generally neglected thoroughgoing land reforms. By and large, the strategies adopted by them resulted in betting on the strong and excluding the weak. Not surprisingly, across these continents, agrarian structure has either remained, or has evolved towards, what Barraclough (1997) has described, with reference to the Latin America agriculture, as 'bimodel', or what Joshi (1987) calls, with reference to the Indian agriculture, as 'structural dualism'. Such a characterization does seem useful for much of the Third World, with suitable qualifications for country-specific differences and varying degrees of complexity, and does capture one of the fundamental traits of most of these countries: that a large section of the rural population is almost trapped in agriculture for livelihood, much of it barely surviving, with no means of escape. This huge mass of people is subjected to what de Janvry has described as a 'double (under)—developmental squeeze'—on the one hand, a land squeeze and on the other, an employment squeeze (de Janvry quoted in Kay, 1997). Much of this mass of people forms the hardcore of persistent rural poverty globally.

Thus, the process of agricultural transformation in much of the Third World, even though it may have pockets of substantial achievements, can hardly be considered as being on a successful trajectory, even in terms of the conventional kinds of paradigm thrown up by the early literature in Development Economics regarding the contribution of the agricultural sector to a country's economic development. In the case of latecomers to modern economic growth, the limited success, or even abject failure in many cases, in terms of agricultural transformation can be traced to their inability to confront squarely the structural constraints related to inequalities in access to land, and substantial masses of landless populations in several instances, with insecure tenancies.

A comprehensive programme of land reforms may well be the *sine qua non* for an agricultural transition geared towards rapid economic transformation, and particularly so if one is interested in issues such as expansion of productive employment, and equity. It is possible to argue that this may well be among the most important lessons emerging from development experience in the post-World War II era. The economic performances of the so called Asian miracle cases, such as Japan, South Korea and Taiwan are very impressive examples of extremely effective land reforms and its contribution to agricultural transition and economic development. It is generally well-acknowledged that the class of emancipated and economically empowered small peasant producers played a key role in the agricultural revolutions in these countries. In India a variety of regional and sub-regional politico-economic patterns have emerged since independence and here too, it would appear that, although there are contrasting styles, the relatively successful agricultural performances have often been via the peasant route: for instance, the early green revolution belt in India, i.e. Punjab, Haryana, Western Uttar Pradesh and some other pockets can be described as a version of the 'capitalism from below', where the middle and rich peasants played a leading role; more recently, in West Bengal the Left Front Government's land reforms initiatives empowered small and marginal farmers who have played a key role as growth agents in the state's agricultural performance. Given that the initial conditions, in-terms of agrarian structure, were particularly challenging in case of West Bengal due to the history of the Zamindari system, its performance is indeed quite creditable. After the Left Front Government assumed power in 1977, within a couple of decades more than 9,13,000 acres of land was redistributed benefiting 19,93,660 households, of which a large proportion happened to be either landless or land-poor to begin with. Through 'Operation Barga', tenancy arrangements were secured giving the much-needed relief and incentive to close to 1.44 million share-croppers in the state. These initiatives contributed to creating an environment which resulted in the most impressive agricultural performance for West Bengal, among major states of India, in the 1980s and 1990s, and creditable reduction in the incidence of poverty over the same period. Gradually, a variety of other positive spin-offs have also unfolded over the years.

As mentioned earlier, the Indian case throws up quite a diversity at sub-national levels but this paper does not go into those details. The assertion here is that a degree of seriousness in addressing the agrarian question, in particular access to land for the masses, generally leads to a variety of positive outcomes. Of course, this has been a very well established position among the radical social scientists; it is interesting to note that in the recent times similar views have been frequently echoed from unexpected quarters, such as the World Bank, or mainstream neoclassical economists. For instance, the World Bank has come out with several reports in the last few years, the most recent one published in June 2003, titled 'Land Policies for Growth and Poverty Reduction', making a strong case for strengthening poor people's land rights and treating access to land for the dispossessed masses in the countryside as being central to development. However, the problem with such studies, or several others coming from neoliberal institutions and individuals, is that generally they tend to advocate 'market-based' land reforms, which to put it mildly, may be a contradiction in terms. Nonetheless, the recognition of access to land being central to the well-being of masses in the countryside across the Third World, in however convoluted way it may get advocated, is welcome from mainstream at a time when neoliberal economic policy has been ascendant globally.

Thus, the ardent advocates of neoliberalism may find very jarring the conclusion advanced by a World Bank study, that: 'much emphasis was placed on economic growth in explaining the decline of poverty in India. While our results—emphasize that redistributive effort has also played its part ...Implementing a land reform has a similar effect on poverty to a 10 per cent increase in per capita income' (World Bank, 1997, quoted in Thompson, p. 413, 2003). Likewise, Bharat Dogra refers to a study by FAO which estimates that redistribution of only 5 per cent of farmland in India, coupled with improved access to water, could reduce rural poverty levels by 30 per cent compared to what they would otherwise be (Dogra, 2002). Besley and Burgess (2000), in their recent empirical work on the subject, make a persuasive case and argue that land reforms in India, as and where implemented, have had a robust impact in reducing poverty. There are several other studies in the recent years, coming from the stable of mainstream economics which have rediscovered the virtuous implications of land reforms. Given the current global economic conjuncture and the nature of the dominant economic policy discourse, this rediscovery of the wheel may be welcome, as most governments in the developing world seem to consider the institutions like the World Bank repositories of invaluable wisdom! It is indeed ironical, if not positively sad, that policy makers in countries like India, where theoretical and empirical discussions on land reforms have been of the highest quality since the early days of independence, need to be reminded of its importance by the institutions like the World Bank. But such are the quirks of history.

There are a couple of other points which may be worth stating here. First of these is that the need for a holistic view, as against a segmented view, of land reforms is greater than even before. The conventional view of land reforms has typically tended to accord centrality to its distributive aspects, along with tenancy reforms. However, the experiences gained over the past few decades have made it increasingly clearer that a land reform package can hardly succeed in the absence of a supportive macroeconomic policy framework for the intended beneficiaries of such reforms. Such a framework should address among others, issues relating to the provisioning of production and consumption credit, supply of necessary inputs, technical and marketing assistance, and appropriate price policies. Moreover, the other supportive actions of the state, particularly in the area of infrastructure and facilitative political means that register and respond to people's needs, are obviously crucial ingredients in improving the efficiency of redistributive endeavours. It is also equally important to note that a land reforms programme should be designed and implemented in conjunction with the policies relating to the other important natural resources, especially, water. Anyone familiar with India's agricultural landscape knows that in large parts of the country, particularly in the dry land regions, the issue of water rights is as critical as that of land rights.

The second important point that is made here relates to the conception of agricultural transformation itself in terms of its final destiny. As suggested earlier, in terms of conventional understanding, agricultural transformation is supposed to be complete and successful, as and when the weight of agriculture in a country's total economic output and labour force becomes negligible. Such an outcome has indeed materialized for the developed world. However, the prospect of any substantial shift in occupational structure away from agriculture in most developing countries seems remote in the foreseeable future, as it was argued in some detail elsewhere (Jha, 2003). Eric Hobsbawm, one of the most celebrated historians of the post World War II era, seems quite optimistic that within a few decades humanity will cease to be an essentially rural species (Hobsbawm, 2005), as the countries in the Third World are well on course in terms of emulating the advanced countries in this respect. The Indian experience suggests that Hobsbawm's optimism is quite misplaced. In fact, much of the shift out of agriculture in developing countries is caused by 'push' factor as the sheer logic of survival forces many households from rural areas to diversify their livelihood strategy, with little chances of absorption in the formal secondary or tertiary sectors. Those expelled from agriculture often end up in the drudgery and squaller of the urban informal sector, many of them seasonally also scrounging for work in rural areas as well, either in their own villages or elsewhere, doing a variety of odd jobs.

Thus, in retrospect, it seems to me, that the 'dual economy' models and other 'modernization' paradigms, that had hypothesized a sure and not-too-distant transition in occupational structure, may have been far too optimistic. In the countries of the Third World, even where increases in industrial output have been rapid, growth of employment in modern industries have been far from impressive. In recent years, studies have shown that there is little to choose across the developed and developing countries as regards the employment intensity of aggregate manufacturing value added (for details, see Jha, 2003 and the references cited there).

The simple point is: in terms of labour absorption in the modern manufacturing or services sector, developing countries are not as favourably placed as the countries of the first world in their comparable phases. In addition to the two very critical differences mentioned earlier (e.g. colonialism/imperialism and migration), this is partly linked to the differences in the availability of technology options in the respective stages under consideration. In any case, in large parts of the developing world, a major decline in dependence on agriculture, and a rapid transfer of labour into decent livelihood options elsewhere does not appear likely in the foreseeable future. Furthermore, the routes of such a diversification that have emerged in these countries appear to be limited, bumpy and often quite ugly.

It should be evident from the foregoing observations that the vision of an inclusive and democratic development in economically backward countries can hardly ignore carefully designed land reform packages. In the absence of such packages, it is difficult to visualize how significant headway can be made, for substantial sections of the masses, to break free from the poverty trap. It should also be clear from the preceding discussion that the conventional view of successful agricultural transformation, and its prospects in developing countries, need to be qualified in important ways. Furthermore, as hinted earlier, India's academia and policy practitioners have provided extremely valuable contributions to the subject of land reforms and some of the important concerns raised here have been extensively discussed by them in the light of the Indian experience. Any attempt to provide a comprehensive overview of this literature here would probably be preposterous. The limited purpose in the preceding discussion has been to flag a couple of issues which appear to be critical in conceptualizing the agenda of land reforms and its linkages to poverty in the present context, that may be particularly relevant to backward economies.

III
LAND AND RURAL POVERTY IN MADHYA PRADESH AND CHHATTISGARH

As mentioned at the outset, MP came in to being in 1956 and five different regions became part of one administrative unit at the level of a state. However, as in most of India, the history of British colonial rule had left its indelible marks in this state. Regional patterns notwithstanding, one of the most significant outcomes of the colonial revenue settlements happened to be a fundamental distortion of peasant land rights culminating in the gradual conversion of a large body of peasant proprietors into mere tenants-at-will and landless labourers. The other side of the coin was the emergence of a largely parasitic body of rich landed proprietors who exploited the growing land-hunger of the masses to the hilt and looked for relatively easy avenues of profit, such as rack-renting, using etc. In a nutshell, the British revenue policies were critical in unleashing processes that resulted in a progressive increase in the hold of the colonial State and its allies on various land and non-land resources and, adversely, dispossession and economic disenfranchisement of the bulk of the rural population from such crucial resources, MP has been among the richest regions in the country in terms of forest, and currently houses almost a quarter of India's 'scheduled tribes', must of whom have been historically, and continue to remain, dependent on forests; thus, in this case, policies towards forests were quite important in the dynamics of accumulation, exploitation and dispossession[3].

Thus, on the eve of independence from the British rule, bulk of the masses in rural India had either been stripped of their productive assets, or their access to such assets had been seriously curtailed (as in the case of forests). Sure enough, the widespread discontent experienced by them had been an important input in the struggle for independence and, as it happens, the leaders of the national movement often made promises couched in the socialist rhetoric in which actual tillers' of land were supposed to become its owners; those deprived of other natural resources were promised better access to it; and so on. Central to all these promises was the idea of an equitable socio-economic order and a decent economic deal in terms of ownership of assets, livelihood options, etc. for the bulk of the rural masses. To move towards such a socio-economic order, land reforms were viewed as among the most important state-mediated instrument. The well-known reports of the Congress Economic Programme Committee of 1948, and the Congress Agrarian Reforms Committee of 1949 provided the basic frameworks of the envisioned reforms. Subsequently the Indian Constitution, adopted in 1950 authorized the state governments to legislate on all matters related to the administration of land. By the end of the 1950s, almost all the states had enacted land-reform legislations, (which were further amended, modified etc. in the later years), and were generally much diluted versions of the agenda advocated in the 1940s.

By now, there is a very substantial literature evaluating experiences of land reforms in different states of India. The general thrust of this literature is very well known: in a few important respects (e.g. abolition of the intermediaries, securing of land rights for the better-off layers among erstwhile tenants etc.), the achievements at the all India level may be considered modest successes, but in other respects, miserable failures; further, there are only a couple of states where land reforms can be said to be reasonably successful with reference to the legislated provisions. It is neither necessary nor feasible here to enter into a detailed discussion of the evaluation of land reforms in various states; there are a number of excellent overviews on the subject (e.g. Joshi, 1987; Appu, 1996; among others). However, a brief remark on the experience of MP based on a couple of recent studies are in order here.

By and large, the literature on the experience of land reforms in MP does not offer much to cheer about. In a study that I had the privilege to put together as editor (Jha, 2002), a number of eminent contributors attempted to investigate and analyse the promises made and missed regarding the issues of equity with reference to the land and non-land resources in rural MP. One of the contributions in this volume, prepared by the Land Reforms Unit of the Lal Bahadur Shastri National Academy of Administration, Mussoorie, was a very detailed, field-based study conducted in the late 1980s and early 1990s, on three key aspects of land reforms—namely, ceiling, tenancy, and the distribution of government and community land. In terms of geographical catchment, the study was very impressive, capturing every major region of the state, and the size of the sample of respondents was also more than substantial. The conclusion of this study, to put if mildly, was that the implementation of the relevant programmes, with respect to each of the above noted aspect, was far from satisfactory.

Another recent field-based study done by a well-known organization called Samarthan, working in MP for a decade now arrives at a similar conclusion. This study was conducted towards the end of 2002, and was carried out in two districts Damoh and Panna—in the Bundelkhand region of MP, and in all covered 182 respondents spread over 8 villages. Focal concern of the study happened to be some of the distributive aspects relating to grazing land to SCs and STs, and it finds several serious gaps in the implementation of the existing provisions (for details, see Samarthan, 2003).

Among the most significant people's movement working for the land rights of marginalized sections in MP, (as well as in some other states) in Ekta Parishad. Through a series of field-based studies, Ekta Parishad has brought out that the majority of Scheduled Caste and Scheduled Tribe population in MP, dependent on casual wage labour, sustenance agriculture, forest related activities, livestock rearing and a variety of other small time activities, suffer from very serious socio-economic deprivation. It would appear from the field-accounts of Ekta Parishad that such vulnerable sections have probably been net losers, in terms of access to land and land rights, since independence. In fact, throughout this period, at the all India level, and in almost every major state of India, it emerges clearly that of the total population of the SCs and STs, the share of cultivators declined significantly whereas the proportion of agricultural labourers has gone up substantially. Clearly, land alienation, due to distress, as well as because of governments' policies itself (for instance acquisition of land for public purpose)[4]. Apart from distress-driven pauperization, in states like MP that are rich in forest resources, wholesale classification of large tracts of tribal areas as state property and lack of coordinated functioning between the forest department and revenue department has led to massive losses of land, and rendered large tracts of land as disputed territories, inflicting very serious livelihood deprivations for millions of tribal population.

Based on a careful perusal of several of Ekta Parishad's consultations, and research studies, Harris and Sharma (2005) arrive at a severe indictment of the implementation of land reforms in MP. They reach a startling conclusion that of about 65 per cent of households who are supposed to be owners of some sort of land in the state, only approximately 10 per cent actually hold effective entitlement as well as possession of land. Further, they reiterate almost all the major failures reported by the earlier research on the subject.

In sum, the above cited researches bases on field-based accounts, are further substantiation of the fact that the implementation of land reforms is easily among the worst in the country and it continues to be in dire state. The different dimensions of this failure have been subjected to searching scrutiny by the contributors in the edited volume mentioned earlier (Jha, 2002).

Going beyond the distributive dimensions of land reforms, which are clearly extremely important, these accounts are also insistent in their reminder that an isolationalist view of land in MP, has not, and can not take it very far towards addressing the livelihood issues. For instance, in her perceptive piece on the material context of survival strategies of the tribals, Prasad concludes that, 'giving them ownership and rights over land will only be meaningful, if the productivity of these lands is increased. .....[T]his can only be done through a consolidation of holdings and provision for financial and technical assistance by the state' [Prasad, p. 274, in Jha (ed.) 2002]. Likewise, in the same volume, P. S. Vijay Shankar and Mihir Shah, based on their extensive field-involvement in MP, argue that apart from redistribution of land, security and fair terms of tenancy, the agenda of land reforms must include total watershed planning approach, land-record reform and access to common property resources. The thrust of the other contributions of in the said volume is very much characterized by a strong advocacy for a comprehensive view of land reforms along the lines emphasized through this paper.

Unfortunately, as is well-known, even the limited agenda of land reforms has not been receiving much attention, beyond the ritual lip-service, for more than a couple of decades now, particularly during the so called liberalization era since the early 1990s. In fact, during this period, it may well be the case that we are witnessing a reversal of even the limited achievements of the yesteryears and the interests of the poor are getting seriously subverted through extension of the liberalization agenda to the land, water and common property related issues. Removal of restrictions on conversion of agricultural land for non-agricultural purposes, prospects of easing the ceiling limits and the easing of tenancy laws, growing contractualization and corporatization of agriculture, forests, water etc. are some of the key issues to have emerged in the recent years which may unleash a variety of adverse mechanisms for the large sections of the rural population, and the writing already seems to be there on the wall. Micro-level surveys from different regions in the country have been reporting increased leasing in by large farmers from small landowners, as also loss of land by many small and marginal peasants over this period. It clearly emerges from the National Sample Survey data that during the liberalization period there has been a substantial increase in the degree of concentration in terms of operated holdings. At the all India level the share of landless households, in total rural households, increased from around 35 per cent in 1987-88 to as much as 41 per cent in 1999-2000, and this growing landlessness can be traced, in large measure, to the various changes that have occurred in the countryside over this period.

The change in the macroeconomic policy regime has meant a very substantial contraction of credit, increase in input costs, mainly due to decline in subsidies, and a variety of other mechanisms which have resulted in the reduced viability of small farms. These changes are very well documented by now and there is wide agreement among researchers that the changed macroeconomic policy regime has resulted in vast sections in rural India getting caught in a serious crisis (for further details on these, see Chandrasekhar and Ghosh, 2001 and Patnaik, 2003). Thus, it is hardly surprising that the greater landlessness, during 1987-88 to 1999-2000, is reported from every major state of India. By way of concluding one may only note that such processes imply not only dumping the unfinished agenda of land reforms, but actively undoing it. This does not bode well for the economic well-being of the large sections of the masses in the countryside, and states like MP are likely to get hit where it hurts most.

END NOTES

1. There is a substantial literature on this subject from a variety of alternative analytical perspectives for a brief overview of this literature, see Jha (2002) and the references cited here.
2. Typically, as the process of modern economic growth unfolds a stage is reached when the share of agriculture in a country's total economic output as well labour force starts declining; the faster this decline, the more successful and complete is supposed to be the process of agricultural information.
3. As it happens, even after close to six decades of independence from the British rule, government's policies towards forests continue to be heavily titled against the tribals, and we will return to this point later.

4. According to Central Government's draft national policy on tribals put in the public domain recently (i.e. in 2005), close to 85.39 lakh tribals had been displaced until 1990 on account of some mega project or the other, reservation of forests as National Parks etc. Tribals constitute at least 55.16 per cent of the total displaced people in the country.

REFERENCES

Appu, P. S. (1996). *Land Reforms in India*, Vikas Publishing House, New Delhi.

Barraclough, S. C. (1997). 'Obstacles to Increasing Sustainable Agricultural Productivity in Latin America', in Bhaduri and Skarstein (eds.). *Economic Development and Agricultural Productivity*, Edward Elgar, Cheltenkam, U.K.

Besley, T. and R. Burgess (2000). 'Land Reform, Poverty Reduction and Growth: Evidence from India', *The Quarterly Journal of Economics*, May.

Bhaduri, A. and R. Skarstein (eds.) (1997). *Economic Development and Agricultural Productivity*, Edward Elgar, Cheltenham, U.K.

Chandrasekhar, C. P. and Jayati, Ghosh (2001). *Market That Failed: A Decade of Neoliberal Reforms in India*, Leftword, New Delhi.

Harris, Jill Carr, and P. K. Sharma (2005). A National Land Rights Proposal Including Five States Concept Note (Mimeo).

Hobsbawm, E. (2005). 'War, Peace and Hegemony at the Beginning of the 21st Century', *The Book Review*, Vol. 29, No. 2.

Jha, Praveen (2003). 'Issues Relating to Employment in India in the Era of Globalization', *Social Scientist*, Vol. 31, Nos. 11-12.

Jha, Praveen (ed.) (2002). *Land Reforms in India: Issues of Equity in Rural Madhya Pradesh*, Sage Publication, New Delhi.

Joshi, P. C. (1987). *Institutional Aspects of Agricultural Development*, Allied, New Delhi.

Kay, C. (1997). 'Cement' in Bhaduri and Skarstein (eds.). *Economic Development and Agricultural Productivity*, Edward Elgar, Cheltenkam, U.K.

Patnaik, Utsa (2003). Republic of Hunger, SAHMAT, New Delhi.

Samarthan—Centre for Development Support (2003), *Land to Dalits: Myths and Realities*, Samarthan, Bhopal.

Thompson, H. (2003). 'Reviews', *Journal of Contemporary Asia*, Vol. 33, No. 3.

World Bank, (2003). *Land Policies for Growth and Poverty Reduction*, World Bank, Washington D.C.

Chapter 18

Land Distribution and Tenancy in Orissa

R. K. PANDA and S. TRIPATHY

I
INTRODUCTION

The possession of land, the most valuable asset in rural economy is, not only important from the point view of social status but also from its significant contribution to raise the standard of living of poor people. One of the hidden objectives of land reforms policies is the optimal use of land resources. So land reforms policies not only are confined to reduce inequality in land holding pattern and create egalitarian society but also to increase agricultural productivity and to reduce poverty level. There are many examples, which show dividing large farms into smaller units result in more food production per hectare. So safely it can be inferred that land reform can increase both employment and income in addition to creating an egalitarian society. Owning land, how small it may be, helps a household in many ways as small farms employ more people per hectare than the larger units, often to the benefit of the landless and unemployed. And owning land means that family farmers often secure the bank credit that was previously denied them. In Orissa around 62 per cent of people depend on agriculture for their livelihood, but most of them have ownership rights though in many cases of very little land. Many of the cultivators are not having legal rights to the land they farm, they mostly cultivate land as tenants. Besides this, there are agricultural labourers, who work as hired labour on large farms. Cultivated land area remaining more or less fixed, with increase in population the land-man ratio has worsened over time. The per capita availability of cultivated land which was 0.39 hectare in 1950 has been drastically reduced to 0.17 hectare in 1999. Percentage of cultivators to main workers has decreased from 57 per cent in 1960 to 44 per cent in 1990. By contrast the percentage of agricultural labourers to main workers has increased from 17 per cent in 1960 to 29 per cent in 1990. Thus, within a span of three decades the ratio of agricultural labourers to cultivators has increased substantially from about 3:7 in 1960 to 6.5:3.5 in 1990. This is primarily due to increase in landlessness or near landlessness on account of population growth and subdivision of land holdings among legal heirs.

Despite of the fact that tenancy is completely banned in Orissa, except special cases, concealed tenancy is widely practiced. Generally tenants are poorer than owners. This does not hold true in all the cases. Land may be lease out by poor households if they do not have the labour or livestock to farm it. For instance, Mearns and Sinha (1999) find that 80 per cent of leasing activity is by small and marginal farmers on both sides of the market. So far as land holding pattern is concerned, the degree of inequality has been fairly steady (John Mackinnon, 2002). According to the figures published by NSS 48th Round, there are 13.8 per cent of landless households in the state. Some have argued that land alienation has been a major problem for tribal groups. One study in 1987 found that over a 25-30 year period, tribal groups in four districts lost 56 per cent of their land for reasons including indebtedness, mortgages and forcible possession (Mearns, Sinha, 1998 and Viegas, 1987). Pradhan *et al.* (1997) report that over 100,000 members of Scheduled Tribes and Castes has been displaced by large projects in Koraput, and that 25,000 people are displaced by each major irrigation project. But Agricultural Census does not capture such data for calculating the extent of landlessness. According to a report prepared by John Mackinnon (2002) for DFID and Government of Orissa, there are a number of possible ways of reconciling this apparent disparity between the data and well-documented reports of alienation. First, people displaced may have become landless, and therefore, be landlessness do not appear to confirm this. It is possible that some of the new landless have migrated outside the state in search of work. Secondly, tribal people who have been displaced may have become illegal occupants of other land. This would not necessarily reduce the amount of land they farm, but would reduce the security of their land rights and is, therefore, a concern. Thirdly, the land possessed may have been common land, for instance land periodically cultivated by shifting cultivation (known as '*podu*'). This would usually have been omitted from the census and NSS estimates of landholdings. Similarly, land on a gradient over 10 per cent was classified as 'wasteland', leading to its alienation from tribal groups. Finally, people may have become impoverished if the land they have received in compensation is inferior in quality or infrastructure to the land they have lost.

Land being the most valuable asset in rural Orissa, inequality in land ownership may be an important determinant of overall inequality. In the first section of this paper both NSS and Agricultural Census data are considered to assess inequality in land holdings and land ownership pattern in Orissa. It is also important to study the land holding in terms of the social groups and region specific variations in land holding patterns, because of the existing disparities among various castes/tribes and regions of Orissa. So in addition to inequality in land holding and ownership pattern, social group-wise and region-wise variations in land distribution pattern is also discussed in this section.

In a formal sense all land is owned by the government and the recorded persons in the record of rights are tenants of the Government of Orissa. So while we talk about tenancy, we are basically talking about the sub-tenancy. Practices sub-tenancy or share cropping without any type of security is detrimental to investment in agriculture and to agricultural productivity too. Over the years with increase in the population growth and rise in income level the demand for land has increased. This is a general perception that land market has become active and with the expectation of rise in land prices, many economically advanced families in rural areas of Orissa are purchasing land. However, all of them are not involved directly in agricultural activities. So it has lead to a rise in the practices of tenancy. Another matter of concern is that with the rising agricultural wage and lack of family labour has made agricultural activities a very costly affair. So many rural landowners prefer to share cropping instead of self-cultivation. According to Agriculture Census Data (1991), there are 22,000 landless farmers in Orissa. There may be more landless farmers in Orissa, and landless farmers engaged in cultivation are mostly tenants. Section two discusses various issues such as extent of tenancy, terms of tenancy and leasing period details. In the third section, some village level findings regarding tenancy practices in Orissa as documented in the Village Study Reports submitted by the Officer Trainees of Indian Administrative Services will be presented. This village level findings may be quite interesting, because of the reason that concealed tenancy is widely being practiced in Orissa. The only limitation of these village level information is that the villages covered are mostly located in the southern part of the state. In the concluding section, in addition to the overall situation in the state regarding inequality in land holdings and tenancy, a brief introduction to the land reforms Acts, which are relevant in the context of tenancy will be documented.

II
LAND HOLDING STRUCTURE IN ORISSA

There are two major sources, viz. Agricultural Census (Ministry of Agriculture, Government of India) and National Sample Survey (NSS) from where one can access secondary data with respect to land holdings in India. The basic objective of this part of the paper is not only to examine the inequality in land holding pattern in Orissa but also to find out the extent of variations in land distribution pattern as revealed by data published by NSS and Agricultural Census. The trends and patterns in inequality in landholdings is analysed on the basis of data from Agricultural Census as well as NSS survey.

Mackinnon (2002) mentioned: "less than 5 per cent of land is in holdings over 10 hectares and about 20 per cent in holdings over 4 hectares. There is very little change in the distribution over the early 1990s, and the changes observed may reflect increasing population size rather than any major shift in inequality". In addition to his reference, analysis has been done to assess the preliminary status of various types of landholders with respect to land leasing. This can be observed from Table 18.1 that marginal farmers (< 1 hectare) are in the possession of largest share in operational holdings, whereas their share in area operated is smaller than small and semi-medium farmers. This is because of the fact that the marginal farmers are large in number as compare to other categories. Marginal farmers' shares in operational holdings and area operated are 53.6 per cent and 19.7 per cent respectively. In contrast to this, large farmers (above 10 hectares) are having 0.4 per cent share in land holdings and 4.8 per cent in area operated. The share of area operated has remained almost constant in case large farmers during 1990-91 and 1995-96 implying that large farmers are less active in land lease market. But, for medium class farmers it can be seen that share in area operated has declined over the years 1990-91 to 1995-96. Similarly in case of semi-medium farmers, area operated has marginally declined.

Table 18.1: Changes in Landholding Structure in 1990s

	1990-91		*1995-96*	
	Share in Holdings	*Share in Area Operated*	*Share in Holdings*	*Share in Area Operated*
< 1 hectare	53.6 (20.81)	24.43 (10.28)	54.1 (21.45)	20.7 (10.64)
1-2 hectares	26.2 (10.21)	9.65 (4.06)	27.9 (11.06)	29.6 (15.22)
2-4 hectares	15.0 (5.85)	36.57 (15.39)	13.7 (5.44)	28.2 (14.51)
4-10 hectares	4.7 (1.82)	23.62 (9.94)	3.9 (1.56)	16.8 (8.64)
Above 10 hectares	0.4 (0.15)	5.73 (2.41)	0.4 (0.15)	4.7 (2.43)

Note: Figures in parenthesis indicate lakh holdings and lakh hectares for holdings and area respectively.

Source: Agricultural Census 1990-91 and 1995-96.

The decline in area operated by medium and semi-medium farmers probably hints that these groups are leasing out land. The evidences of leasing out of land by medium and semi-medium farmers will be concrete once we deal with land ownership data or data related to leased in and leasing out in the tenancy section. Area operated has increased over the two agricultural census periods in case of small farmers. So at this preliminary stage it can be assumed that medium and semi-medium classes of farmers are leasing out land and small farmers are leasing in. However, land market (sale and purchase) has a significant impact in affecting the changes in the share of area operated by different farm sizes.

Table 18.2 presents the pattern and trends of inequality in land holding pattern among different classes of farmers. One thing is clear, that share of area operated in percentage of large farmers has declined between 1981-82 and 1990-91, indicating that inequality in terms of area operated is reduced. However, inequality in land holdings in terms of area operated had increased during 1970-71 to 1980-81, as there has been a rise in the percentage area operated by large farmers.

Table 18.2: Change in Percentage Distribution of Operational Holdings and Area Operated in Rural Orissa

Year/ Farm Sizes	Marginal		Small		Semi-Medium		Medium		Large	
	No.	Area	No.	Area	No.	Area	No.	Area	No.	Area
1970-71	54.52	18.60	25.78	27.32	13.90	27.06	5.25	21.56	0.55	5.46
1981-82	54.45	17.02	26.11	26.48	14.08	26.16	4.63	17.84	0.73	12.50
1990-91	59.99	22.09	24.34	30.16	12.02	27.87	3.36	16.20	0.29	3.68

Source: Various NSS Rounds, *Sarvekshana*, Vol. XX (January-March, 1997).

The rise in percentage of area operated by large farmers over the decade 1970-71 to 1980-81, is quite consistence with the fact that percentage distributions of area operated among all other farm sizes have declined. During the period 1980-81 and 1990-91, the percentage of operational area has sharply declined in case of large farmers and percentage distributions of area operated have increased in all other categories like marginal, small and semi-medium. This indicates that a rise or fall in percentage of area operated by large farmers is directly linked to rise/fall in area operated by marginal, small and semi-medium farmers. One can argue that rise in the number of operational holdings may be due to increase in the population growth, but the same is not true in case of rise in area operated. The variations in share area operated are arising because of—land leasing, land purchase, land possessed by other means or property divisions among the divided joint families of large land holders.

Fluctuation in area operated mostly reflects the reality of lease markets or land possessed by other means. Figures of NSS data on area operated shows that in early 90s marginal farmers are gaining in terms of area operated and this holds true to a little extent in cases of small and semi-medium farmers too. Agriculture sector as such not much remunerative in Orissa, so land owning households, without much family labour support prefers to land leasing out. Small farmers are having largest share in area operated as per figures given by 48th NSS Round. Semi-medium farmers are having second highest percentage share in area operated. NSS data also shows that semi-medium farmers have gained in terms percentage share of area operated during (1980-81 and 1990-91). Large farmers share in area has declined and this may be possible because of rise in population and number of households, thereby many large farmers have joined in the groups of either medium or semi-medium categories. Gini coefficient so far as land ownership is concerned has declined during 1971-72 to 1982 and there has been a fall in the percentage of landless households in the state, where as gini coefficient of land ownership and percentage of landless households have increased during 1982 and 1992.

Social Groups and Land Holdings

Table 18.3 shows distribution of landownership among the main social groups in Orissa. While overall small-marginal farmers together account for 77 per cent of holdings and 55 per cent of the cultivated area, for Scheduled Castes almost 98 per cent of holdings and 66 per cent of area owned are in the category of small-marginal farmers. One can interpret the same as Scheduled Caste farmer means marginal farmer or at the most small farmer. They also dominate the landless category. The situation regarding Scheduled Tribes is different because the average size of holdings for this group is larger but the location of their lands are invariably in the hills and remote areas. Data for early 1990s shows there are changes in the relative position of different classes within SCs and STs.

Table 18.3: Size-Class and Caste Distribution of Ownership Holdings in Orissa 1991-92 (Percentages)

Sl. No.	*Size-Class (hectares)*	*Scheduled Caste*		*Scheduled Tribe*		*All*	
		Households	*Area*	*Households*	*Area*	*Households*	*Area*
1.	Marginal (< 1.00)	89.81	38.34	58.82	23.88	63.16	26.37
2.	Small (1.01 to 2.00)	8.09	27.40	17.27	26.53	14.42	27.16
3.	Semi-Medium (2.01 to 4.00)	2.87	18.27	10.02	27.93	7.34	25.99
4.	Medium (4.01 to 10.00)	1.07	15.99	3.27	19.24	2.40	18.08
5.	Large (> 10.00)	—	—	0.16	2.43	0.12	2.40

Source: NSS, 48th Round as reported in *Sarvekshana*, Vol. XX, No. 3, January-March, 1997.

In contrast to the earlier findings, in cases of both the SCs and STs it is found that large farmers have gained and medium class farmers have lost in terms of area operated. So it can be inferred that large farmers are more active in lease market and Land Market in cases of both social groups. {It is not clear how land owned by one group but farmed by tenants from another group is treated in this data, but the Scheduled Castes are often sharecroppers in coastal areas (Pradhan *et al.*, 1997)}. However, these data suggest that the relative poverty of tribal groups may not be due to lack of access to land, but due to lack of access of infrastructure, markets or information, and to non-agricultural occupations. This also cannot be rule out that land holdings by tribal groups is of lower quality than other groups.

Regional Disparity in Land Distribution in Orissa

It is well known that land transactions influence land distribution. Studies reveal that land transactions are very much region specific and the prevailing local conditions shape and influence the land transactions and hence land distribution among different farm sizes. Taking into account the historical background and agro-climatic conditions Orissa can be divided into two broad regions—the Coastal Plain and the Inland Region. The Coastal Plain comprising 14 districts are mostly belongs to the erstwhile Mugalbandi region of the British period ruled directly by the British Government/East India Company. It is mostly a plain and fertile tract with better irrigation and developed infrastructure. The Inland Region on the other hand is the previous Garhjat Region (Land of Forts) ruled by tributary rulers under British jurisdiction. Major portions of land area of this region are uneven with mountains and forest covers. Irrigation and other infrastructural facilities are less developed in this region. In view of the disparity noticed between these two regions we have made here an attempt to discuss the prevailing land distribution pattern between the two regions along with possible explanations thereof. Table 18.3 presents data in this respect.

For simplicity, the state of Orissa is broadly divided into two broad regions, coastal region comprising 14 districts and remaining 16 districts are included in Southern-cum-Inland region. Taking the region-wise data on land distribution it is observed that in the Coastal region the small farmers are in the possession of highest (32.2%) area operated of total area operated of this region, whereas in Southern region, semi-medium farmers are having highest operated area (29.4% of total area operated in the Southern region). Area operated by marginal and small farmers jointly in coastal region constitute around 57 per cent of area operated of the total area operated of the coastal region and the inland region it is about 44 per cent of total inland region's area operated. So marginal and small farmers are holding more land as operated area in coastal region. As inland districts are larger in number, this is not surprising that more land is located in this region. However, if come to compare inequality in terms of area operated, it seems inequality is more pronounced in inland region. This is reinforced by the fact that large farmers are having only 2.9 per cent of area operated in coastal region as compare to 6.3 per cent of total inland (southern part) are operated belongs to large farmers. Thus, between the two regions, the Coastal Plain has more egalitarian land distribution compared to the Inland Region. This fact is also proved, when one observes that semi-medium and medium size classes constitute around 49.4 per cent of total area operated in the inland (southern) region, where as in the coastal region it comes to be 40 per cent only.

To find out the possible reasons for the differences existing in the land distribution we provide two explanations. One relates to the land/revenue system inherited from the British period and other, the disparity in current development indices. It is observed from history that the land system prevailed in Garhjats during British rule was very much hierarchical with various interests in land. There was no systematic revenue laws to regulate the land system and tenancy in various forms were in vogue (Rath, 1955). In contrast, the land system in Mugalbandi was more systematized by regular surveys and settlement. More so to regulate tenancy in the region, Bengal Tenancy Act, 1885 was enacted for the first time to record the rights of the tenants. Thus the land system prevalent in Mugalbandi was more congenial for the farming community than that was found in Garhjats. The present land distribution in the Coastal Plain and Inland Region being inherited from the previous land system of Mugalbandi and Garhjats, and because of poor implementation of various land reforms measures in the state in the post-independence period (Mishra, 1990) there lies disparity in the land distribution between the two regions. Secondly, if we compare the two regions on the basis of current development indicators like percentage of literacy, percentage of area under irrigation to net sown area, percentage of village electrified, the road length per 1000 sq. km of area, average population per bank branch office, etc., we find that the Coastal Plain is in a higher development scenario compared to Inland Region. Agriculture is more advanced (in terms of area under HYV cultivation, cropping intensity and yield of major crops) in the coastal plain than that in the Inland Region. Prevalence of lease cultivation is more in Coastal Plain than in the Inland (Southern) Region. The Agriculture Census, 1995-96 reveals that the percentage of lease-in land in the Coastal Plain to total lease-in land of the state comes to more than 70 per cent. This has raised the share of marginal and small farms in the total operational area and thus reduced interclass inequality in the land distribution in the region.

III
LAND LEASE MARKET IN ORISSA

Informal land leasing or concealed tenancy is one of the worst practices, which defeats the main objectives of land reforms (tenancy reforms aims at abolition of tenancy and vest land ownership with the actual tiller of land). The unrecorded tenants without any security to land are mostly prone to exploitations. Due to uncertainty in tenure of possession of land most of tenants, who have leased in land are not in a mood to invest or to adopt measures, which are required for a sustainable rise in agricultural productivity. So land leasing is discouraging private capital formation in agriculture. Most of the cases the tenants also adopt very short-term productivity enhancing agricultural technologies, which are not sustainable and this results in decline in the quality of land. There are many problems in case of land leasing without any tenurial security. In the anticipation of loosing rights over land and control over the tenants, the landowners most of the cases prefer to change the sharecroppers for the same price of land. On the other hand there are arguments, which favour the practices of share tenancy. Many protagonist, of share tenancy argue that, it is the second best response to missing, thin and imperfect markets for land, credit, labour, management, information and performs some very important functions, which have to fulfilled by other institutions it is neither necessarily inefficient nor a barrier to adoption of technology, tenancy contracts often play an important role in matching land, labour and capital endowments. They are not necessarily explotive, but where they are, owing to the unequal bargaining power between agents, attempts to 'fix' relation in one sphere can lead to compensatory shift in other contracts to leave tenants net worse off (Mearns, 1998). Agriculture sector in Orissa is dominated by mono-cropping (paddy cultivation) practices. The paddy grown by most of the farmers in Orissa is not of very good quality, so it does not fetch a good price in market. Hence, land, as one of the factors of production does not significantly contribute to the household's income. Lack of assured irrigation, non-existence proper market linkages, rise in agricultural wages and low agricultural productivity are major factors, which are making agriculture a very un-remunerative occupation. So most of the land owners prefer to lease out land in the absence of adequate family labour support. But land selling by large farmers except extraordinary cases is not taking place due to the fact that land selling many times, hampers social prestige. This is a known fact that income from agriculture sector is not taxed, so many families in the higher income group are interested in purchasing land rather that selling. However, it is see that area operated by large farmers has not changed significantly in 1990s. So it can be inferred that land selling and purchasing is taking place, it is mostly confined to other categories like medium, semi-medium, small and marginal farmer. With the help of data from Agricultural Census and NSS Rounds presented below, we will be able to throw more lights on land leasing and probably will be successful in drawing inferences on land transactions through market.

According to Agricultural Census 1995-96, 83.76 per cent of total operated area was under ownership cultivation, so around 16 per cent of land is under categories of completely leased, partly leased in. So it can be said that due to the prevalence of concealed tenancy and unavailability of desegregated data on partly leased in, partly owned and partly otherwise possessed, there is no clarity regarding extent of tenancy practices in the state. Land located and leased in by a landowner in other villages is mostly included in the category of partly leased in. Hence, partly leased in area should be included in the category of area leased in, but the segregated data on partly leased in is not available. Out of the total area operated by the marginal farmers, 85.68 per cent is under self-cultivation and wholly owned, so 14 per cent of area operated by marginal farmers not under ownership cultivation. So far as wholly leased in area is concerned, it may include the landless families, who are only leasing in land and by virtue of the area operated by them, they are included in different categories like marginal, small, semi-medium, etc. it is very difficult to say anything concretely about the size of classes, which are actually leasing out land and others which are leasing in land.

In order to investigate further into the prevalence of tenancy in Orissa NSS data on land leasing in Orissa with respect to 48th NSS Round (1990-91) is presented in Table 18.4. If we consider size of classes of holdings 0.002 to 0.02, 0.21 to 0.50 and 0.51 to 1 hectare, which can be clubbed into a single class i.e. marginal farmers, percentage of area owned is around 80 per cent and leased in varies from 7.5 to 13 per cent and it seems marginal farmers are in the second positions in terms of land leasing in.

Table 18.4: Size-wise Distribution of Operated Area by Type of Possession in Orissa 1991-92

Broad Size Class of Operational Holdings (ha.)	*Percentage of Operated Area by Type of Possession*				
	Owned	*Leased in*	*Otherwise Possessed*	*N.R.*	*All*
0.002-0.20	79.77	7.35	3.91	8.97	100.00
0.21-0.50	83.65	7.39	6.37	2.50	100.00
0.51-1.00	81.05	12.99	2.93	3.03	100.00
1.01-2.00	78.26	14.35	4.31	3.08	100.00
2.01-4.00	87.35	7.97	1.85	2.83	100.00
4.01-10.00	93.99	2.98	0.44	2.59	100.00
10.01 & above	86.49	0.26	0.10	13.15	100.00
All Sizes	84.41	9.48	2.77	3.34	100.00

Source: NSS, 48th Round.

Small farmers (with 1.01-2.00 hectares of holding) are having the highest percentage (14.35%) of area operated in leasing in form. Similarly the semi-medium farmers (with land holding size 2.01-4.00 hectares), has a share of 7.97 percentage of operated area in the form of land-leased in. Broadly, it can be said that mostly, marginal, small and semi-medium farmers are leasing in land. However, these estimates, like Agricultural Census data, are also underestimates. However, the NSS data is considered more reliable as it is based on independent household surveys. Practices of informal tenancy in a state like Orissa, where tenancy is banned, likely to be underreported because of lessors tend to understate the leased out area owing to in anticipation that tenants will stake claims in favour continued right of cultivation and in order to escape from clutches of Orissa Land Reforms Act, which prohibits sub-letting, regulates rents and confer security of tenure.

Tenancy—Among Different Social Groups

In this part the incidences of tenancy among different social groups, are analysed on the basis of Agricultural Census data only, as social group-wise land leasing figures are not available from NSS 48th Round Survey. Taking all size of classes together, among the SCs and STs wholly owned and self-cultivated areas as the percentage of total area operated are 79.39 and 82.48 percentage respectively. Similarly, wholly leased in holdings as percentage of total area operated among SCs and STs are 4.74 and 1.24 per cent respectively. Hence, it can be opined that practices of tenancy is more prevalent among the SCs as compare to STs. Like all social groups, among SCs and STs, it is observed that small and marginal farmers are mostly leasing in land. However, it is again found that compare to all other social groups including SCs, the instances of wholly leased in land (0.44%) is higher among the large farmers belonging to ST category.

Terms of Tenancy

As tenancy is banned in the state, concealed tenancy is broadly prevailing in the state. In case of concealed tenancy, informal agreements or mutual agreements are made between the land lessor and land lessee. But conventionally, the terms of lease are (i) fixed money, (ii) fixed produce, (iii) share of produce, (iv) share of produce with other terms, (v) usufructuary mortgage, and (vi) from relatives: no specified terms. Generally, share of produce is one of the prominent terms of lease (9.79%). Fixed money terms of leasing is also being adopted by 3.78. Share of produce as terms of leasing in is mostly practiced by small farmers and marginal farmers. In Orissa, share of produce vary from crop to crop and generally for kharif season paddy crop it is shared 50:50 basis. However, for high yielding variety, the share of produce differs and a higher share is gone in favour of tenants and the produce without any input contribution by the landlord, is shared 75:25. Generally, the disputes regarding rent payment by a tenant, where oral agreements are made are not brought into limelight.

In case of large farmers, it is observed that the terms of lease from relatives without any specified terms is mostly prevailing. Service contract type of leasing term is not found at all, but it is commonly reported that tenants borrow money from their landlords and repay the loan with labour contributions. It cannot be ruled out that some factor markets may be interlinked to land lease market so far as terms of leasing is concerned. According to figures given by Agricultural Census survey, out of the different terms of leasing-in of land above, the operational holders preferred the term share of produce commonly as 82 per cent of the total leased-in land was taken on lease under the above term. The contribution of "share of produce term" for small and marginal holdings accounted for maximum with 85 per cent and 83 per cent respectively. Broadly, the NSS and Agricultural Census give similar kinds of conclusion. During 1990-91 census, the term "share of produce" was also remained as major term of leasing in the state as it accounted for 70 per cent. With respect to large farmers, it is found from the NSS survey that, terms of leasing mostly confine to leasing to relatives without any specified terms, but from Agricultural Census it is seen that large farmers mostly adopting share of produce type terms of tenancy. Terms of leasing are highly correlated with input sharing, cropping pattern, factor market linkages and period of leasing too.

Tenure of Leasing

Tenure of leasing in the context of the fact that tenancy is banned in the state is very important. As a tenant, who has been in practical possession of a plot of land for a period of 12 consecutive years, may acquire legal occupancy rights, the landowners mostly prefer to short term contracts. Short-term contracts that too oral many times give landlords leverage with respect to bargaining power against the tenants and landowners become more exploitative. In addition to this, short terms contract also discourage the tenants in terms of taking long-term measures to increase agricultural productivity.

Around 5 per cent area is found to be leased in for period of 12 years or more and it is again found that marginal and small farmers are mostly leasing in for such longer period. Generally, the absentee landlords prefer to lease out land for longer period. Normally period of leasing is short, due to the fact the landowners believe that the same tenant leased in once, may not cultivate properly, if he leased in land second time. In Orissa land mostly leased in for kharif crop, i.e. for one season only. In many cases land is leased in for a period of cultivation of one crop only.

IV
MICRO LEVEL EXPERIENCE OF LEASE MARKET

Mukundpur Village, Anugul District

In Mukundpur village of Anugul district, a few cases of unrecorded sharecropping are noticed. Some of the landlords of adjacent villages engage the landless cultivators for the purpose of share cropping on a 50:50 ratio. From the report of the village, it is observed that Narayanpatna and Bandhugaon blocks of the district which border Andhra Pradesh, the soil is very good for cotton. But the local tribals, the landowners of the area, are not aware of the price that cotton fetches in the market. They also do not have means and skills necessary for cotton cultivation. Taking advantage of these factors and extreme poverty of the tribals, people from Andhra Pradesh come to this side and take the land of tribals on lease. They pay about Rs. 200 for one acre of land. The cultivators from Andhra Pradesh do cotton cultivation on the land of tribals and tribals work as farm labourers on their own lands. This form of reverse tenancy is prevailing in the border areas.

Khadiyadiha Village, Keonjhar District

In Khadiyadiha, tenancy is widely prevalent and it is in all the cases concealed tenancy. On interaction with the villagers it was found that the landless persons and tribals who had land less than 20 cents were generally opting for being tenants. Farmers having one acre of land or more were not interested in cultivating as tenant. However, this is not a general rule. Because, during the agricultural season, they were too busy sowing their own fields and since the working persons in their families were limited and their financial position did not allow them to hire labour, they could not spare time for further cultivation as tenants. The small and marginal farmers in Khadiyadiha do not plough their fields because they don't have plough and oxen. They prepare their fields by the spade which is a time consuming process. Obviously, therefore, it would be difficult for them to spare any time for more than a small piece of land. The second reason is that small farmers did not have enough resources to provide for inputs. It was very difficult for them to provide for the inputs for their own fields. Apart from this, sometimes the lands are far apart and it becomes difficult to manage two fields at separate places.

The lease period of the tenures is without exception annual in this village. The landowners generally do not give the land for cultivation on tenurial system, to the same person the next year. It meant that they were not aware of the provisions that if a person had been tilling the same land for the past three years then he could apply to the settlement authorities for getting a raiyati status for that plot of land. The landowners on their part had devised this effective means of tenurial system to suit their interests. Generally, only those landowner give land on lease, who either have more land than what they can actually cultivate or those who are old and do not have helping hand to undertake the cultivation on their own. By giving land on an annual lease basis the landowner ensures that no tenant cultivates the same land for three years. Landowners change tenants every year, and for the tenant, landlord changes annually.

The rates of lease prevailing in Khadiyadiha are Rs. 300 for 4.0 cents of unirrigated land and Rs. 450 for irrigated land. These rates vary from village to village, and are determined by the landowners depending on the revenue assessment of the village. The rent in Khadiyadiha is paid in cash. Earlier the landlords used to agree for rents in kind, but these days they demand only cash. This amount the tenant has to pay before tilling the soil. It means that once a landowner agrees to give land on rent, the tenant has to pay the rent before he actually starts cultivating the field. This puts the tenant under tremendous financial pressure, and this partly explains why the marginal farmers do not cultivate on lease. According to the tribal farmers, during the agriculture season, they had to take loan in order to pay the rent and to buy seeds and other inputs. This cycle of debt repeated itself every year and many of them were unable to clear off their debts in full. This implied that they got entangled into the vicious cycle of debt trap. Once the landlord is paid the rent, the landowner ceases to bother about crop and does not have any role to play in cultivation.

V
CONCLUSIONS AND POLICY IMPLICATIONS

Land distribution has been progressive towards marginal and small farmers and their share in total operated area of the state has increased over time. The rise in the share of marginal and small farms in the total operational area is partly due to more of lease transactions, and partly due to disintegration families of semi-medium, medium and large farmers with an increase in the population growth and number of households. The role of ceiling surplus land is doubtful. The social group-wise analysis shows that inequality in distribution of operational holdings is more among the SCs and STs. Between the two regions, the Coastal Plain, the relatively developed region, exhibits more egalitarian land distribution as compared to Inland Region, and this is due to the greater prevalence of lease-in cultivation among marginal and small farms in the former region than in the latter and partly because of larger holdings in dry and hilly regions. This corroborates the earlier findings in this regard that tenancy is higher in agriculturally leading states as compared to agriculturally laggard states (Swamy, 1988). Forces like land system inherited from the British period and disparity in the current development indices are found influencing land distribution between two regions in the state.

Concealed tenancy is widespread in the state. Legally tenancy is banned in the state. Reverse tenancy is not widespread, as agriculture sector is not developed and commercialization of agriculture has not taken place in the state. Rent is mostly paid as share of produce and terms of tenancy is generally in favour of lessors and the rent is in excess of the legally fixed rent, i.e. one-fourth of the gross produce. Marginal and small armers are mostly leasing in land in spite of concealed tenancy's harmful effects. Tenancy, though concealed is at least working as a means for the rural poor to gain access to land. Tenancy is some what leading to optimal use of land resources. Most of the leasing contracts are for very short period and informal and this is detrimental to agricultural productivity. Keeping all these in the backdrop, one can argue in favour of liberalization of tenancy with proper protection to the tenant as well as small-marginal farmers who lease out. Deregulation of tenancy will help in preventing concealed tenancy and will be favourable for the lessors to give land lease for a longer period. In view of the above findings it is suggested that the existing tenancy legislation needs to suitably amended to legalize tenancy in the state.

REFERENCES

Birthal, Pratap Singh and R. P. Singh (1991). "Land-Lease Market, Resource Adjustment and Agricultural Development", *Indian Journal of Agricultural Economics*, Vol. 46 (3), July-September.

Jodha, N. S. (1981). "Agricultural Tenancy: Fresh Evidence from Dry Land Areas in India", *Economic and Political Weekly*, Vol. 16 (52), December 26.

Government of India, *Census of India 2001*, Director of Census Operations, Bhubaneswar.

Government of Orissa, *Agricultural Census of Orissa*, (Various Issues), Board of Revenue, Cuttack.

Government of Orissa, *Economic Survey of Orissa*, (Various Issues), Directorate of Economics and Statistics, Bhubaneswar.

Haque, T. (2000). "Contractual Arrangements in Land-Labour Market in Rural India", *Indian Journal of Agricultural Economics*, Vol. 55 (3), July-September.

Kumar, Srendra (1993). *Land Reforms Assignment, Khadiyadiha Village of Keonjhar District*.

Mackinnon, John (2002). *Assessing the Impact of Fiscal and Structural Reforms on Poverty in Orissa*, Report for DFID, Delhi, and the Government of Orissa.

Mearns, R. and S. Sinha (1999). *Social Exclusion and Land Administration in Orissa*, India, Policy Research Working Paper No. 2124, World Bank.

Pradhan, J., B. Panda and G. Menon, (1997). *Facets of the Irony: Emerging Development Trends and Directions in Orissa*, Development Resources and Training Centre, Bhubaneswar.

Rao, V. M. (1972). "Land Transfers in Rural Communities—Some Findings in a Ryotwari Region", *Economic and Political Weekly*, Review of Agriculture, September.

Rath, B. C. (1995). *Land System in the Native States of Orissa*, Arya Prakashan, Cuttack.

Sarangi, Santosh (1994). *Land Reforms Assignment*, Mukundpur Village of Anugul District.

Sarvekshana, Vol. XX, No. 3, 70th Issue, January-March 1997, National Sample Survey Organization, Department of Statistics, Ministry of Planning and Programme Implementation, Government of India.

Swamy, Dalip S., "Agricultural Tenancy in the 1970s", *Indian Journal of Agricultural Economics*, Vol. 43 (4), October-December.

Viegas, P. (1987). "Land Control and Tribal Struggle for Action", *Social Action* 37, 4, 325-44.

Vijay, R. (2002). Land Market Activity: A Framework, "*Indian Journal of Agricultural Economics*, Vol. 57 (4), pp. 714-722.

Chapter 19

Land Relations and Conflicts in North Eastern India: A Look at Modernisation, Immigration and Livelihood Loss

WALTER FERNANDES

I
CUSTOMARY COMMUNITARIAN RIGHTS AND 'MODERN' INDIVIDUAL

Legal Rights Over Land

Much of India knows the North East only for its ethnic conflicts which some call secessionist and others terrorist, thus oversimplifying a complex phenomenon that requires a deeper analysis. In order to better understand the issues involved we did a study with the indications got from our past research as its starting point. The studies showed that among their causes are changing land relations caused by the adverse impact of the changes that the modern legal system introduces in the tribal tradition and by encroachment of their land by the immigrants. The lacunae in the formal law facilitates the latter. These external inputs do not necessarily begin the conflicts but are crucial in exacerbating those existing already.

In order to test this hypothesis we studied six tribes and a non-tribal group. After getting secondary data on them and on conflicts around land, we discussed the issues with knowledgeable persons, held 60 group discussion sessions with men, women and the youth of these ethnic groups and interviewed 662 of their families. The ethnic groups studied are the Aka of Arunachal Pradesh, the *Adibasi,* Boro, Dimasa and ethnic Assamese of Assam, the Garo of Meghalaya and the Rongmei of Manipur. The study confirmed our belief that the conflicts are on one side linked to lack of investment in the secondary sector in the Northeast by the outsiders who control the economy and on the other, changing land relations because of encroachment by immigrants and class formation caused by the interaction of their customary law with the individual based State administration and the modern legal system.

Land Relations Among the Tribes Studied

A major criterion in choosing the tribes was their closeness to their customary law and inclusion in the Sixth Schedule that recognises community control over land and forests (CPRs). Our studies had indicated a close relationship between their customary law, equity and a higher status of women than in caste societies without them being equal to men. We also found indications that modernisation and commercialisation without measures to counter their negative impact combined with the interaction of the Sixth Schedule with the individual oriented administrative and financial systems had resulted in class formation and had strengthened patriarchy in some of their societies (Fernandes and Barbora, 2002a: 117-119). In the present study (Fernandes and Pereira, 2004) aimed at understanding this process, we chose some tribes that are close to their tradition, some that have experienced modern inputs and are governed by the Sixth Schedule and others that do not have a customary law and are not covered by the Sixth Schedule. The ethnic Assamese were a control group.

Among the tribes studied the Aka of West Kameng district in Arunachal Pradesh are close to their tradition and govern themselves according to their customary law but the Sixth Schedule does not apply to them. So the law does not recognise their community ownership and the CPRs though it is their practice (Sinha, 1962). This *jhum* practising tribe lacks the very concept of land ownership and only has the tradition of community control and the concept of usufruct right over the CPRs. In the *jhum* season every family cultivates as much land as it needs. After it the land reverts to the community. However, slow change is visible among them. Two respondents claimed individual ownership but three others with a salaried jobs called themselves landless since they do not practise *jhum* any more, as such have abandoned their right over the CPRs (Fernandes and Bharali, 2002: 7-8).

The Dimasa of North Cachar Hills in Assam have been exposed to the dominant cultures since their Hinduisation by the Bengali administrators who accompanied the British colonial rulers but have retained their internal autonomy, continue to be governed by their CPR based customary law, come under the Sixth Schedule and have a district autonomous council. Many of their clans have dual descent with property inheritance through the male line and the clan and family name coming through the female line (Bordoloi, 1984). So the husband and wife have different family names and belong to two different clans, unlike in most other tribes in which the wife is co-opted into her husband's clan. However, their elite is moving towards individual *pattas.* One of their leaders owns over 200 acres (Barbora, 2002: 1287). Our study also put us in contact with a village in which a voluntary agency has introduced oranges and some other commercial crops without changing their land ownership pattern. Some families that have accepted individual land ownership have conferred the inheritance right also on women. If more villages accept this system it can become a model for tribes that follow their customary law to change their land use without abandoning equity.

The Garo of Meghalaya are governed by their customary law and the Sixth Schedule. Their tribe is matrilineal but patriarchal (Marak, 1997: 60-69). The families we studied in the East Garo Hills have begun to show signs of class formation and of strengthening patriarchy, an important reason being the introduction of rubber plantations that got them to interact with the administration which gives subsidies and loans only to individual owners and "heads of families" that most financial institutions understand as male. However, the twenty families we studied in West Garo Hills continue their CPR culture but have not planted commercial crops. As such we do not consider them models of combining the modern with the traditional that the Dimasa families can become if more accept the changes they have introduced.

On the other side, the *Adibasi* of Jharkhand origin whom the British brought to Assam in the 19th and 20th centuries as indentured labour to work in its tea gardens are not included in the Schedule though they speak of a customary law which has very little value today. So they represent the type of modernisation that results in impoverishment and exploitation (Fernandes, Barbora and Bharali, 2003: 33-34). Studies show that they are impoverished at present and marginalised in the long run. Landlessness is the highest among them and literacy the lowest. So they have very few possibilities of improving their livelihood even in the next generation (Toppo, 1999: 133-134). Though they have lived in Assam since the second half of the 19th century, they continue to be considered non-indigenous. As late as the May 2004 general elections a candidate appealed to the voters to reject the candidate belonging to the plantation labourer community as non-indigenous and vote for himself since he was indigenous Assamese (*The Telegraph*, May 5, 2004).

The Boro, a plains tribe not under the Sixth Schedule, have won a Boro Territorial Council (BTC) after a struggle but till recently their community based customary law was not recognised (Roy, 1995: 16-17). As a result they have almost fully internalised the ideology of individual ownership in the sense that those living on common land call themselves encroachers while others like the Aka and Dimasa consider themselves CPR dependants. The Boro have been in conflict with the Santhals for land and it has led to some massacres like those of Kokrajhar in 1996. The BTC has recognised their right partially but does not seem to have granted them Sixth Schedule status.

The Rongmei are a Scheduled Tribe of Bishnupur district in Manipur but are not governed by the Sixth Schedule. Several have lost their land to ethnic conflicts and some to the Loktak project but have not even been compensated since much of what they sustained themselves on was CPRs that the law does not recognise as their community livelihood. They thus represent the interaction of their CPR based customary law with the individual based administration. Some of them have founded new villages by encroaching on the CPRs of others or sharing this resource with them and are trying to retain their control over it. Simultaneously they put their land to commercial use as a step in a search for non-land based alternatives of education and jobs in the administration (Fernandes and Bharali, 2002: 16-17).

The ethnic Assamese of Nagaon district have passed through the political process of the Assam Movement of 1979-1985. Land loss to the immigrants was its main cause (Baruah 1999: 132-135). However, later studies show that today they are moving in the direction of the Rongmei. They have invested much in their children's education and are giving more importance to jobs in the administration than to tilling their land, but want to retain its ownership. So some of them employ immigrants, mostly of Bangladeshi origin, to cultivate it. Others rent it out for a season on a sharecropper basis. Thus they too represent the type of ambiguity visible among the Rongmei (Fernandes and Barbora, 2002b: 76-79).

II
MULTIPLE DIMENSIONS OF DEMOGRAPHY, SOCIAL PROCESS AND LAND RELATIONS

The number of members in each family showed a close relationship between the demographic and social processes and land relations. Studies show that subsistence farmers tend to have around five children since that is the number they need for their agriculture based economy (Mehta, 1993: 341-342). The average family size of 5.97 in our sample tallies with it but it is higher among the Aka because some of their leaders practise polygamy and have large families. But most Aka families keep to the agricultural norm. The Assamese are moving towards non-land occupations and have relatively small families. The family size and sex ratio have implications for land relations, so we studied them by the ethnic group because among six of the seven groups studied land is inherited by all the sons. So a bigger than average family can lead to conflicts. The sex ratio is 963 for the sample but is close to 1,000 among the Garo and is low among the *Adibasi* who being impoverished send many teenaged girls to middle class families as domestic helpers (Fernandes and Barbora, 2002a: 79-80).

Population growth is relatively high in the region also because of immigration from Nepal, the Hindi region and Bangladesh. The feudal system and lack of land reforms in their places of origin have pushed them to the fertile plains of the Northeast where many of them occupy land that is the local people's livelihood. Some say that the Hindu Bangladeshi migrate because of persecution but others hold that this justification is legally untenable and some question even its ethical basis. During the negotiations leading to the Assam Accord those who were agitating against the immigrants did not accept this justification, so this issue remained inconclusive (Baruah, 1999: 132-133). The focus today is on Bangladeshi Muslims. Even the Bangladeshi Hindus are ignored and the fact that probably two-thirds of the immigrants are from the Hindi speaking region is rarely mentioned. At times they are mentioned within a communal perspective because of which some deny the very existence of Bangladeshi immigrants while others exaggerate their numbers and put it at more than 40 lakhs (Bhattacharyya, 2001: 120-121). The somewhat reliable figure seems to be 12 lakhs (Bhuyan, 2002). They would thus be a third of the immigrants, the rest being from the Hindi region.

The origin or religion of the immigrants makes no difference to those who lose their land. Most immigrants, whatever their origin, were agricultural labourers in their places of origin and know the cultivation techniques. Many encroach with impunity on the CPRs of the local communities since the formal law does not recognise them as the people's livelihood. They then prosper by using the agricultural techniques that they bring with them to grow three crops. On the other side, the ethnic Assamese and most other people of the Northeast have lived in a single crop culture. The *zamindari* and sharecropper systems that had developed in regions like Assam had deprived their peasants of motivation to grow a second crop since half or more of what they grew went to the *zamindar* (Majumdar 2002: 107-108). Also *jhum* on which the hill regions depended kept them at a single crop culture.

Immigration is an encounter of these two histories. With shortage of land resulting from encroachment, a contradiction develops in the local people's attitude towards it. Most of them need viable non-land alternatives because the educational status in most States is higher than the national average but very few jobs are created in the secondary sector since those who control the economy have neglected investment in industries and have treated the region mainly as a supplier of raw materials like tea, oil and coal. The seven States together have only 166 industries, many of them sick. Simultaneously the present type of education takes them away from land. In the absence of jobs in the secondary sector, their dependence on land and jobs in the administration is high and both are becoming scarce. Around 75 per cent of the workforce in many States of the region depends on land and 23 per cent on the tertiary sector against 66.75 per cent and 20 per cent respectively in India as a whole (D'Souza, 1999: 9).

Moreover, in the North East the primary sector is mainly land and forests while in the rest of India it includes components such as mining. The tertiary sector is mainly jobs in the administration while in much of India it includes tourism, commerce and the information technology. Encroachment causes land shortage and very few new jobs are created in the administration. The anti-foreigner Assam movement of 1979-1985 (Baruah, 1999: 133-135) and the anti-Bihari riots of November 2003 (Fernandes, 2003) show how the resultant shortage of land and jobs lead to competition and ethnic conflicts. Thus conflicts are caused not by immigration in itself but by encroachment and competition for scarce land and jobs.

Ambiguity Around Land Relations

As a result of the shortage and conflicts, ambiguity develops among the local people around land. As stated above, the Rongmei or the ethnic Assamese want to retain control over it and also to move away from it as a livelihood. It is true also of some of the *Adibasis* and to some extent Boro who have lost much of their land to ethnic conflicts but not of the Aka, Dimasa and others who live by their CPR based customary law with land as their sustenance. The Rongmei seem to have given up hope in land as long-term security and use it as a tool in their search for alternatives. It is visible in the high investment they make in their children's education and the manner in which they mortgage or sell it in order to bribe government officials and get jobs in the administration. Despite their tradition of a symbiotic relationship with land and forests, they have lost hope in these resources as their sustenance and are ready to part with them for an alternative. Thus ethnic conflicts that have their origin in the shortage of land also result in changes in land relations.

Also the formal law that does not accord recognition to the customary law in most States affects land relations. It recognises the CPRs only in the Sixth Schedule areas. Meghalaya and two districts of Assam come under the Sixth Schedule. Article 371A protects the customary law of Nagaland and Article 371G that of Mizoram. No such recognition is accorded to the remaining tribes of Assam and of Arunachal Pradesh, Manipur and Tripura. AP is run according to the British administrative rules. Other administrative rules govern the hill or tribal areas of Manipur. Tripura has some autonomous councils formed as reaction to the insurgency (Barooah, 2002) but the law does not protect the customary law and CPRs.

Land relations change even in the Sixth Schedule areas where the CPRs are accorded legal protection, because of the individual orientation of the administration. It encourages the processes leading to an individual *patta* that is alien to their culture. For example, the

State and the financial institutions give loans and subsidies for commercial crops to *patta* owners alone, thus encouraging a transition to individual ownership with no protection against class formation. Because of such modernisation without protective measures, land that was their livelihood and the centre of their culture and identity tends to become a commodity alone to be sold or leased to the highest bidder. Their communities begin to lose the sacredness attached to it in their tradition and absorb a new worldview that they are not familiar with, as seen among others, in the fact that much of the mortgaging and sale is within the community (Fernandes and Barbora, 2002a: 50-52). Its result is class formation in their egalitarian society.

Commercialisation and Land Relations

Thus what leads to conflicts is not immigration itself but land encroachment and other attacks on their livelihood. Laws that recognise only individual ownership facilitate this process of alienation. Thus the people have to interact with encroachment on one side and on the other, with low investment in productive jobs and the high level of education. In other words, encroachment is facilitated by the legal system that does not accord recognition to their CPR based customary laws. So the land losers do not have any legal protection. To this one may add corruption in the administrative machinery. For example our 2002 study in the Nagaon district of Assam showed that many Bihari immigrants have *pattas* in its Lanka sub-division but their land is in the neighbouring Karbi Anglong district which comes under the Sixth Schedule that protects tribal CPR ownership (Fernandes and Barbora, 2002b: 65-66).

To this anomaly should be added the role of the economic decision makers from outside the region who have neglected the secondary sector. So the only jobs outside the agricultural sector are in the administration. Thus, their economy remains predominantly agrarian with *jhum* as its main form in the hills. Conflicts arise because in the context of shortages caused by encroachment and the failure to create productive jobs every group views the limited land and jobs as its exclusive right. Given their symbiotic relationship with land, the community views the resultant conflicts as defence of its culture, identity and livelihood. The local people resent the fact that, many immigrants prosper on this land by using the agricultural techniques they bring from their place of origin and cultivating three crops while they themselves are left behind. So the changes have both intensified traditional rivalries and created new ones with outsiders and within the region (Baruah, 1999: 29-32).

A crucial issue in them is commercialisation of land and forests and the resultant transition of most ethnic groups from subsistence to a commercial economy and of their land from livelihood to a commodity. The administration supports the transition to a commercial commodity by insisting on individual *pattas* for subsidies and loans. From this transition results the changeover from an egalitarian to a class society and strengthening of patriarchy since the administration by and large recognises only the man as the owner. The commercial processes thus weaken the traditional tribal culture that gave some decision-making power to women in the family. Today more power than in the past is transferred to men even among the matrilineal tribes like the Garo who took to commercial crops with no safeguards against these hazards. As a result, men who had till now shared power with women in the task of producing riches, are slowly taking over all decision-making in the family and society (Fernandes and Pereira, 2004: 45-46). Also the patrilineal tribes had traditionally allotted an important role to women without making them equal to men. As long as the resources were community owned, the woman had some control over them since she was in-charge of the family economy and cultivation. Individual ownership deprives them of their relatively high status since decisions on land begin to be taken only by men (Menon, 1995: 101-105).

Customary Laws, Land and Conflicts

We saw instances of this situation also among the tribes we studied. The Rongmei had lost much of their land to the Naga-Kuki conflict or to a development project. That led to the ambiguity towards land described already. For a decade they had fought to protect their land or had protested when the State alienated their livelihood for the Loktak project but they lost out in both the cases. Also most Santhals of the Bodo area in Western Assam lost their land in an ethnic conflict and some *Adibasi* respondents of Lakhimpur to the airport. However, their reaction differed from that of the Rongmei. As stated above, they were brought to Assam as indentured labourers. Because of their regimented work structure for over a century and landlessness forced on them, they seem to have lost their tribal identity and have imbibed a psyche of dependence and helplessness (Fernandes, Barbora and Bharali, 2003: 2-3). Their reaction to the loss of their little land is a feeling of greater helplessness.

The Rongmei, on the other hand had a strong sense of identity attached to their CPRs that displacement and the ethnic conflict alienated from them. During the study they told us that the realisation that they could not recover what they had lost brought them closer as a community and got them to form new organisations and develop new norms for their tribe, one of them being to give a new meaning to their land as a tool in their search for non-land alternatives such as education and salaried jobs. All their children below 20 are at school. To earn money for their education and to bribe officials for a job some of them have mortgaged or sold their land. Thus land continues to be their livelihood but as a tool of transition.

Among other conflicts around land is the Assam Movement in which land was a basic issue (Behal, 2002: 145-146). Also the Tripura tribes had a strong identity linked to the CPRs whose ownership the law did not recognise in the absence of the Sixth Schedule. So when the CPRs were under threat, they tried to defend them at first and then reacted strongly by rebuilding a new sub-national identity. The Boro too had a land-based identity that they had rebuilt through conversion to Brahmo Hinduism or to Christianity that reformed their society without alienating them fully from their past. However, they have internalised the ideology of individual ownership and speak of themselves as encroachers. They have re-written their history to lay exclusive claim to the region to the exclusion of the Santhals who have lost their identity and are unable to defend their livelihood (Fernandes and Pereira, 2004: 95-96).

III
SEARCH FOR SOLUTIONS

Though not the only cause of conflicts, the economic factor is crucial. Land should be seen in the context of people's livelihood. So the first step is to deal with their livelihood resources. The economic and political decision-makers have to recognise that the secondary sector has been neglected and that the region has been treated as a supplier of raw materials of tea, coal and petroleum and a market for the finished products from the rest of India. They need to work towards non-land alternatives that their high level of education demands and deal with unemployment that is a major cause of unrest. With its rich raw material base of natural and mineral resources, the secondary sector should have generated many jobs in the region. Instead, its raw materials are exported and finished products imported. The first step should thus be stable income generation through new jobs.

Our study indicates that the Dimasa village of Chottowaphu may be able to show a direction. A voluntary agency helped it to introduce some commercial crops like oranges that they can grow and sell locally without changing their community land control system. They have changed their land use but not its ownership pattern. By growing fruits they have added a commercial angle to their view of land while retaining its role as sustenance and identity. Those who have accepted individual ownership have reinterpreted their customary law in a gender friendly context. Their custom allows daughters to acquire inherited land while clan land can be inherited only by sons. A family in this village that did not have sons allowed daughters to inherit it and a second one allowed equal distribution between sons and daughters. The rest of the village did not object to it. This trend needs to be encouraged.

Rebuilding the community involves control over land and the rest of the economy including production and marketing. Much of the economy is in the hands of outsiders. The local people will not be able to wrest complete control over it overnight. Processes have to be put in place that can strengthen them by training them to go beyond agricultural production to processing and marketing the produce to deal with the debilitating effect of the middleman grabbing the lion's share of the income from them. The lack of control over the economy and the role of the middlemen point not merely to the poor marketing facilities but also to the fact that, focus has been on the individual and production, not on the community and marketing.

The Rongmei and Dimasa experiences show that when some individuals take new steps, others follow them if they see them succeeding. Eventually the community internalises the need for change. The Dimasa have internalised it to such an extent that the families that grow new crops refer to themselves, not to the lead farmers, as change agents. It was possible because the new crops were chosen according to their capacity. They also changed their community and its approach to land changed but not its ownership system. The Garo had to undo the damage done, so they built on their community ethos while retaining individual ownership and dealt with the gender issue. They show that, a cooperative approach can be combined with individual ownership by adapting the community ethos to new needs.

We have studied in this paper, the processes that have in some cases strengthened and in others weakened the community and the land ownership pattern based on it. Our analysis of the conflicts that ensue, shows that, going back to the past is not the solution but one has to build on their past. Their communities and customary laws need to be modernised but not rejected. Modernisation has to be based on the value system that their communities represent. The civil society, people in education in particular, can assist these communities in this task. The school is probably the best tool if it becomes a place where children are encouraged to work as a community and take new initiatives such as growing new crops that can improve their nutritional status. The children can thus absorb the value of using their land to rebuild their community and economy. This process can be strengthened through community work, by growing new crops and tilling land as their livelihood. The children thus become "lead farmers" who motivate the community to rebuild itself by accepting new practices and earn an income for new needs and not transfer the fruit of their work to a middleman.

REFERENCES

Acharya, S. K. (1990). "Ethnic Processes in North-Eastern India," in D. Pakem (ed). *Nationality, Ethnicity and Cultural Identity in North-East India.* New Delhi, Omsons Publications: pp. 69-108.

Barbora, Sanjay (1998). Plantation Systems and Labour Movement in North Eastern India. Unpublished M. Phil. Thesis. Delhi: Department of Sociology, Delhi School of Economics.

Barbora, Sanjay (2002). "Ethnic Politics and Land Use: Genesis of Conflicts in India's North-East," *Economic and Political Weekly,* 37 (n. 13, March 30), pp. 1285-1292.

Baruah, Sanjib (1999). *India Against Itself: Assam and the Politics of Nationality,* New Delhi: Oxford University Press.

Behal, Monisha. 2002. "Women's Collectives in Assam: A short History of their Status and Present Day Realities," in Walter Fernandes and Sanjay Barbora (eds). *op cit.* pp. 138-148.

Bhattacharyya, Hirnya Kumar (2001). *The Silent Invasion: Assam* versus *Infiltration.* Guwahati and Delhi: Spectrum Publications.

Bhaumick, Subir (2003). "Tripura's Gumti Dam Must Go," *The Ecologist Asia* 11 (n. 1, January-March), pp. 84-89.

Bhuyan, Jogesh Ch. (2002). "Influx from Bangla: Demographic Change in NE," *The Sentinel,* May 4.

Bordoloi, B. N. (1984). *The Dimasa Kacharis* of *Assam.* Guwahati: Tribal Research Institute.

Bordoloi, B. N. (1986). *Alienation* of *Tribal Land and Indebtedness,* Guwahati: Tribal Research Institute.

Datta, Brijendranath (1990). "Ethnicity, Nationalism and Sub-Nationalism, with Special Reference to North-East India". In D. Pakem (ed), *Nationality, Ethnicity and Cultural Identity in North-East India.* New Delhi, Omsons Publications, pp. 36-44.

D'Souza, Alphonsus (1999). *North East India.* Jakhama: Kohima Jesuit Region (Mimeo).

D'Souza, Alphonsus (2001). *Traditional Systems of Forest Conservation in North East India: The Angami Tribe of Nagaland.* Guwahati: North Eastern Social Research Centre.

Fernandes, Walter (1999). "Conflict in North-East: A Historical Perspective," *Economic and Political Weekly,* 34 (n. 51, December 18-24), pp. 3579-3582.

Fernandes, Walter (2003). "Why is Assam Burning?" *The Hindu,* December 8.

Fernandes, Walter. 2004. "Limits of Law and order Approach to the Northeast." *Economic and Political Weekly,* 39 (no. 42, Oct. 16-22), pp. 4609-4611.

Fernandes, Walter and Sanjay Barbora (2002a). *Modernisation and Women's Status in North Eastern India: A Comparative Study of Six Tribes.* Guwahati: North Eastern Social Research Centre.

Fernandes, Walter and Sanjay Barbora (2002b). *The Socio-Economic Situation of Nagaon District: A Study of Its Economy, Demography and Immigration.* Guwahati: North Eastern Social Research Centre (mimeo).

Fernandes, Walter and Gita Bharali (2002). *The Socio-Economic Situation of Some Tribes of Bishnupur and Palizi.* Guwahati: North Eastern Social Research Centre (mimeo).

Fernandes, Walter, Sanjay Barbora and Gita Bharali (2003). *Primary Education of Plantation Labourers in Assam.* Guwahati: North Eastern Social Research Centre (mimeo).

Fernandes, Walter and Melville Pereira (2004). *Changing Land Relations in North Eastern India: A Comparative Study of Six Tribes and One Non-Tribal Community.* Guwahati: North Eastern Social Research Centre (mimeo).

Lianzela (2002). "Internally Displaced Persons in Mizoram," in C. Joshua Thomas (ed). *op cit.* pp. 241-251.

Majumdar, Anindiyo J. (2002). "Human Movement and the Nation State: Dimensions of an Indian Crisis in its North-Eastern Region," in Joshua Thomas (ed). *op cit.* pp. 91-111.

Marak, Caroline (1997). "Status of Women in Garo Culture" in Soumen Sen (ed) *Women in Meghalaya,* New Delhi: Omsons Publications, pp. 56-72.

Mehta, B. C. (1993). "Economics of Fertility Decisions in the Tribal Areas of Rajasthan," Social Action 43 (N. 3, July-September), pp. 339-357.

Menon, Geeta (1995). "The Impact of Migration on the Work and Tribal Women's Status," in Loes Schenken-Sandbergen (ed). *Women and Seasonal Labour Migration.* New Delhi: Sage, pp. 79-154.

Roy, Ajay (1995). *The Boro Imbroglio.* Guwahati: Spectrum Publishers.

Roy Burman, B. K. (1985). "Foreword" in Gangmumei Kabui. *Anal: A Transborder Tribe of Manipur.* Delhi: Mittal Publishers, pp. xi-xiv.

Roy Burman, B. K. (1992). "Historical Process in Respect of Communal Land System and Poverty Alleviation Among Tribals," in Walter Fernandes (ed). *National Development and Tribal Deprivation.* New Delhi: Indian Social Institute, pp. 21-48.

Sanyu, Visier (1996). *A History of Nagas and Nagaland: Dynamics of Tradition Village Formation.* New Delhi: Commonwealth Publishers.

Sen, Sipra (1992). *Tribes of Mizoram: Description, Ethnology and Bibliography.* New Delhi: Gian Publishing Company.

Toppo, Hippolytus (1999). "Violation of Human Rights in the Tea Plantations of Assam and West Bengal," in Thomas Pullopillil (ed). Identity of Adivasis of Assam. Delhi: Indian Publishers Distributors, pp. 129-156.

Chapter 20

Land Holdings and Tenancy in North-Eastern States

S. TRIPATHY

INTRODUCTION

The economy of the North Eastern (NE) States is mainly rural and agrarian. The region offers scope for cultivation of a wide variety of agricultural crops because of its diversity in topography, altitude and climate conditions. Land is a critical resource in many of the NE States, and availability and management of land for agricultural activities are essential for raising the region's overall agricultural production and productivity. In the North Eastern region there are two types of land such as hill land and plain land. The extent of cultivable land in the NE region varies from state to state. In the states of Arunachal Pradesh, Nagaland, Meghalaya and Mizoram there is a dearth of sufficient plain land suitable for permanent cultivation. Whatever plain land is available is too little for the requirement of the people for wholesome subsistence. Hence in these states shifting cultivation is being practiced. Of the total gross cropped area 74.7 per cent is in Assam alone, leaving very little for the rest six states. The percentage of cultivable area in the geographical area of the NE is 24.69 per cent which is less than the national average of 59.22 per cent. The percentage of cultivable area in the geographical area is highest in Meghalaya (47.88%) and lowest in Arunachal Pradesh (3.50%). The percentage utilization of cultivable area in the NE regions (62.04%) is less than the national average (73.05%) and mono cropping is the predominant method of cultivation. In the absence of multi-cropping is the predominant method of cultivation. In the absence of multi-cropping, little or no surplus is generated in the agricultural sector. The utilization is lowest in Meghalaya (19.18%) and highest in Tripura (89.35%). Among all the NE States, Assam takes the highest position both in terms of available cultivable area and new sown area. The paper is divided into three sections. The first section provides a broad overview of land use and land holding structure in the North-Eastern States. The second section presents the tenancy system in the North-East as revealed by field reports of IAS Probationers. The third section presents a brief conclusion on the tenancy in the North-East.

I
LAND RESOURCES AND LAND HOLDING PATTERN

Land Use

The net sown area in the North-Eastern region has increased by 3.4 per cent during the period from 1980-81 to 1988-89. The net area sown has increased by 53.6 per cent in Arunachal Pradesh during the same period, whereas in Nagaland and Tripura, the rate of increase was 17.6 per cent and 9.8 per cent respectively. However, the increase in net area sown was negligible in rest of the NE States. The area available for cultivation in the total geographical area in the NE ranges from 3.5 per cent in Arunachal Pradesh to 47.88 per cent in Assam. The net sown area is much less than area available for cultivation, indicating the potential for increasing use of land for agriculture. Irrigated area as a percentage of total gross cropped area in the NE region is only 16.17 per cent, whereas at all India level irrigated area as a percentage of gross cropped area is 38.33 per cent.

Operational Holdings

About 80 per cent of the farmers in the NE region belong to the small (<1.44 ha) and marginal (<0.40 ha) category. Moreover, with increase in population, the average size of holdings is gradually reducing over the years. The average size of land holding for the NE States (1.60 ha) is higher than the all India (1.57 ha) average.

Table 20.1: Geographical Area and Land Used for Agriculture in NE

State	Total Geographical Area (000' ha)	Cultivable Land (000' ha)	(3) as % of Geographical Area	Total Cropped Area (000' ha)	Area Sown more than once (000' ha)	Net Sown Area (000' ha)	(7) as % of Cultivable Area	Gross Irrigated Area (000' ha)	(9) as % of Gross Cropped Area
(1)	(2)	(3)	(4)	(5)	(6)	(7)	(8)	(9)	(10)
Arunachal Pradesh	8374.3	293	3.50	244	59	185	63.14	36	14.75
Assam	7843.8	3387	43.18	3938	1158	2780	82.08	572	14.53
Manipur	2232.7	164	7.35	182	42	140	85.37	75	41.21
Meghalaya	2242.9	1074	47.88	247	41	206	19.18	45	18.22
Mizoram	2108.1	445	21.11	109	0	109	24.49	9	8.26
Nagaland	1657.9	626	37.76	228	17	211	33.71	72	31.58
Tripura	1048.6	310	29.56	426	149	277	89.35	60	14.08
All NE	25508.3	6299	24.69	5374	1466	3908	62.04	869	16.17
All India	328726.3	194680	59.22	186561	44346	142215	73.05	71510	38.33

Source: CMIE Report on Agriculture, 1997 and 1998.

Among the NE States the average size of land holding is highest in Nagaland (6.92 ha) and lowest in Tripura (0.97 ha). Overall, most of the farmers are small. This is primarily because hilly terrain constitutes nearly two-thirds of the region's geographical area, and large sized holdings are not feasible. The average plot size is too small for mechanization of agriculture and adoption of modern farming practices. Subsistence farming, therefore, is predominant in the NE region and there is hardly any commercial surplus.

In most of the hill areas of the NE the community as a whole owns land. Individual ownership of land recognized in certain areas is usually confined to homestead and settled farmland. Of late, because of the inherent contradictions in the communal ownership of land, privatization is gradually emerging as the main form of ownership. Lands under shifting cultivation, are still under communal ownership. Under this system each village operates in a particular demarcated area and the power of distribution of land to individual families is vested in the headman or village council. Due to non-fixity of tenurial rights, the farmers naturally do not take interest in the improvement of land for future use. A tendency for improvement is noticed in areas where land is privately owned. The issue of agrarian relations and land reforms in the hilly tracts of North-East needs to be treated differently, because of the fact that historically inherited agricultural practices, customary land ownership rights are generally not conducive for the proper implementation of land reforms polices.

II

TENANCY AND LAND HOLDINGS : EXPERIENCES FROM VILLAGES OF NE STATES

Assam

Various legal measures have been taken in the state since Independence against exploitative tenancy. According to 48th Round NSS survey report, the proportion of tenanted land in total operated area in Assam had increased from 6.4 per cent in 1981-82 to 8.9 per cent in 1991-92. This implies incidence of tenancy is growing in the state. As the tenants are not coming forward for recording, unrecorded tenants are increasing in number. In such a situation the costs are not shared proportionately. The following case studies reveal that unrecorded tenancy far exceeds recorded tenancy and tenancy is widely prevalent mostly in the form of sharecropping in the state.

Village: Kalitakuchi, Kamrup District of Assam

A person who occupies the land for more than three years acquires the status of a tenant. A tenant acquires the status of landholder by paying 50 times the land revenue to the landlord. According to official record, there are fifteen occupancy tenants in the village, together occupying 27 bighas or 12.231 acres of land. However, the real situation is that there are numerous other unrecorded tenants. Most of the unrecorded tenants are from poorer sections like SCs and STs, and households below poverty line. The rent is not fixed, although payment may be either in cash or in the form of grain. The term for this kind of arrangement is called *Adhiar*, and the produce is usually shared between the tenant and the landowner on a 50 : 50 ratio. The cost of ploughing and other labour work is borne by the tenants but the costs of seed and fertilizers are shared by the tenant and the landowner. The tenants are evicted whenever the landowner needs the land for his own purposes. A few of the landowners are absentee landlords who live in urban areas. Agreement between the tenant and the landlord is oral, and based on personal trust and faith.

Village: Pachim Matia, Goalpara District of Assam

According to official record there is no tenant in the village but as per the field observation, it was found approximately 58 tenants are there in the village and these tenants have been working since last 10 to 15 years, but their tenancy is not recorded in the *chitha*. As per land Manual, Lot Mandals are supposed to record name of the tenants, in column 9 of *chitha* of the tenancy. But such type of record is not updated by the Mandals as per the observation approximately 90 acres of land in the village was under tenancy. All the tenants are below poverty line households, and they are mostly landless and belong to SC or ST community. People are not aware of any tenancy Act. The rent is not fixed, and the rent payment share is settled between owners and tenants. In the whole village, the system is called *Adhiar*, because all the produce is shared on a 50 : 50 basis. Ploughing and other labour work is contributed by the tenant. The tenants are evicted when owner needs his land for other purpose or for his own cultivation. Sometimes, *Adhiar* hire the labour from outside and pays for it. Sometimes he takes loan from the owner to pay the labourer, and in lieu of loan he sells a share of final produce. Most of the landlords are absentee owners and they live in big cities like Guwahati. No written agreement exists. Tenancy is oral.

Village: Silberchak, Karimganj District of Assam

Village Silberchak has cases both of recorded as wells as non-recorded tenancies. The later is widely prevalent due to peculiar nature of the borrowing system (credit facility) in the village, which is linked to the direct mortgaging of land for one or more reasons depending on the amount borrowed. There were six cases of recorded tenancy. All the tenants are residents of the village. They are all in possession of small pieces of their own land, and additional land has been leased in they them to make their operations slightly larger. The leased in area ranges from 0.1 acres to 0.63 acres, and the total area operated by a tenant ranges from 0.33 acres to 2.28 acres, thus showing most of the tenants are marginal farmers.

In the village all the tenants have been evicted. The reasons for eviction is either transfer of ownership (66%), or due to the landlord deciding to cultivate the land himself (33%). In all the cases the rent arrangement was half of the crop share. All the lessees are marginal farmers. No inputs were given to the lessees by the landlord at all. Although the legal rent was 1/5th of the produce, these rules merely exist on paper and they are not complied with. Surprisingly most of the villagers know about these rules and regulations. All of the leasing out has been done by Muslim landowners but the tenants include both Muslims and Hindus.

Non-Recorded Tenancy

Although the number of non-recorded tenancy could not be ascertained with exact precision, the number was approximately 30. Usually, the area leased out varies from 2 to 10 bighas (0.9 acres to 4.53 acres). The terms and conditions are very clear under such cases. The rent to be paid is half of the crop output with no inputs from the landlord or not any managerial help usually. The land is usually given for one to two years, and if land is given once to a person, it is not given to the same person again. The reasons of leasing out land to the lessees are linked to the lack of infrastructure of the owner in terms of labour or he is being involved in some other non-agricultural activities which takes most of his time.

Land and Credit Market Interlocking

The credit system in the village is very peculiar. All the villagers own land in varying extent, the small landowners are usually at the receiving end due to financial hardships. On such occasions, they usually turn to larger landowners for financial assistance. The repayment mode is then worked out. For a financial assistance upto Rs. 2000, usually a bigha (0.453 acres) of land is surrendered to the lender for a fixed period of time, usually a year. In this piece of land the original owner is to cultivate and the produce is appropriated by the owner himself. After the completion of the time period the loan repayment is made and if it is defaulted the piece of land changes ownership and the lender becomes the owner. In some cases about 1/10th of the produce is given to the lender, but this is not prevalent everywhere. All these go unrecorded and the revenue officials are very much aware of such practices. This practice has been in operation for a long period of time and seem to suit the villagers because they do not have to pay and interest money in the form of cash transaction. Also, the village leaders claimed that since they are Muslims they are not expected to claim interest money as it is against their religious teachings. There has not been any discordant note or unnecessary tension between the villagers because of this arrangement. It just seems to suit all.

Tenants do not come forward to get their names as recoded tenants either because of the strong amicable understanding amongst the villagers or because of the fact that they do not want to enter into unnecessary interaction with the revenue officials whom they eye rater contemptuously. Unrecorded tenants, whoever the interviewer met, seem to be aware of their rights *vis-à-vis* tenancy laws and other legislations. However, there seems to be a conspicuous practice of rotational sharing of the fields, in the sense that once a tenant cultivates a certain field he is usually not given another one again. As far as unrecorded tenancy is concerned, there seems to be no cases of forceful eviction though nothing concrete can be concluded on account of lack of the evidence.

Tenancy in Sonitpur District, Assam

Tenancy in terms of *benami* is still prevalent. The normal procedure followed is the *Adhiar* system, where the owner and the cultivator share the produce equally. Area under self-cultivation is very small for large farmers and nearly for all the small farmers who not only cultivate every possible inch of their land but also resort to tenancy. There were two exceptions among the large farmers who not only cultivated their complete land but also took other people's land for *Adhiar* cultivation. For example, there was a government employee who with the support of his alternative source of income was engaged in large scale farming activities with about 30 bighas (13.59 acres) of his own land and 45 bighas (20.385 acres) of leased in land. He was using modern means like tractor, power tiller, HYV seeds and was also leasing the implements on hire.

Arunachal Pradesh

Land ownership pattern in Arunachal Pradesh is by and large communal but there is private ownership as well to a limited extent. There is no tenancy legislation in the state and there are also no land records. The ownership of land is governed by traditional customs. The Jhum Land Regulation, 1947, only recognizes the ownership to a piece of Jhum Land. According to a study there are three types of land ownership: (i) Clan or community ownership, (ii) Private ownership, (iii) Mixed type of ownership. In recent years it is observed that the traditional patterns of ownership are fast changing and giving place to private ownership of land in all areas, owing to a number of factors. Another recently observed fact is that frequent transfer of land or change of ownership is taking place in the state. But the most important thing is that in most of the cases of transfer of land are not registered or recorded. Before any land reform measures are implemented in the state, cadastral survey must be taken up so that proper land records will be available for land reforms measures. Land ownership legislations should be introduced in rural areas. Land transfer and transactions should be officially registered. The modification of the Jhum Land Legislation Act (1947) could be amended to include the provisions for conversion of Jhum land into settled cultivated land.

Manipur

Details about landholding in Manipur are available for only 1970-71. Assuming that not much has happened to agrarian structure since then, Manipur is essentially a small-marginal farmer dominated agriculture, much more than the rest of India. Marginal farmers (< 1 ha) constitute about 40 per cent of holdings and account for 19 per cent of cultivable area. Small farmers (1-2 ha) account for 42.9 per cent of holdings and 44 per cent of area, whereas semi-medium (2-4 ha) holdings account for 14.9 per cent of holdings and 31.6 per cent of area. Even medium size holdings (4-10 ha) account for a very small proportion in number (1.2%) or area (5.5%) of holdings. Large holdings (>10 ha) are exceptional, only 0.026 per cent in number and 0.5 per cent in area. According to Section 2 (c) of the MLR & LR Act, 1960, an agricultural holding with an area of on hectare is called a basic holding and a person holding land equal to a basic holding or less is called a landless person (*vide* Rule 2 of The Allotment Rules). So according to this definition, two-fifths of the total number of holders of lands in Manipur Valley would be landless in the eyes of law, for the purpose of allotment of land. Taking together all the three groups, namely marginal, small and semi-medium, we find that 98.7 per cent of holdings in Manipur are below 4 hectares and they cover an area, which forms 94.5 per cent of the total area of all holdings. As the lower limit of ceiling area is 5 hectares, we cannot escape the conclusion that there is very little surplus land left in Manipur for acquisition under the ceiling law.

Tenancy System More Prevalent in Manipur

The reason for the comparatively wide prevalence of tenancies in Manipur, is that abolition of intermediaries has not been one of the initiative of the State Government as it has been done in the case of Assam and Tripura. In Manipur, emergence of new intermediaries has been prevented by banning creation of future tenancies, but old tenancies have not yet been converted to full ownership and so the old intermediaries continue as before. Though there is provision (*vide* Section 127) for declaring all tenants as owners from a specified date, no such declaration has in fact been issued till now. However, there is a provision for the right of pre-emption (Section 132) in favour of the tenants whenever a landlord intends to sell his land and it is understood that advantage has been taken of this provision by many tenants. This is a redeeming feature, though it is a milder form of land reforms.

Manipur is far away from the main channels of communication with the outside world. There is no rail communication to the State, no river transport and no major road transport. So there is less scope people to be involved in commercial activities. In addition to this, more than twelve lakh people are inhabiting in area of about two thousand sq. kms. There is thus a heavy pressure of population on land. Besides there is no scope for investment in other spheres of economic activities. Those who have funds to spare, invest them generally in lands. On account of all this, prices of land in Manipur rule high.

Land Rights

Rights over land are acquired in three general ways, namely (i) by transfer from a previous owner, (ii) by inheritance from a previous owner or (iii) by allotment of new land by Government. Transfer includes sale, gift, mortgage and lease (sub-letting). The maximum acquisition of land was by transfer, which may be attributed to the fact that in ancient time, the Maharaja of Manipur used to give land to various people as revenue-free tenure and revenue-payable tenures. The ownership of most of these lands changed a number of hands. The lands acquired by clearing jungles without allotment for Jhum (shifting cultivation) by tribals are of their own. The acquisition by allotment is somewhat less because the right and obligations of allottees are somewhat restricted. Purchase seems to be a common and regular phenomenon. The existence of records of rights, commercially active nature of the people and gradual disappearance of available waste land in the valley seems to have contributed to the wider prevalence of this form of transfer, i.e. purchase. Mortgage, though prevalent, seems not to be very popular gift is not insignificant.

Tenancy: Village Level Experiences

In the five villages studied in the plain area of the district of Senapati as many as 38 plots out of 93 transferred plots were found to be clearly under subletting. Out of 38 tenanted plots, 11 were recorded in the records of rights and the tenants were given Khatians. The remaining 27 tenancies were unrecorded.

Apart from what was during field studies, which were done in terms of holdings, it is pointed out that as per the figures collected during World Agricultural Census of 1970-71, the total rented area in Manipur formed 8.8 per cent of the total cultivated area whereas in Assam and Tripura the percentage was 5 per cent and 4.2 per cent respectively.

Land Rent

One pot is equivalent to 43.3 kgs and one pari is equivalent to one hectare. In the villages visited, the rates of rent varied from 12 pots per pari to 18 pots per pari. That is to say, the range of rates of rents is from 6.39 quintals per hectare to 9.59 quintals per hectare. In terms of maund per bigha, which is still the common measure prevalent in Assam Valley, the above rents of Manipur would vary from about 1.5 maunds per bigha to 2.5 maunds per bigha. According to the prevailing practice in Assam, the fixed rent ranges from 1 maund to 2 maund per bigha. The rates of crop rent prevalent in Manipur are, therefore, slightly higher than in Assam but not unreasonably higher.

In one village, namely Saikul of Senapati District, the rent was found to be unusually higher, i.e. 30 pots per pari (hectare). This is almost double of the rates prevalent elsewhere. The reason for the higher rate of rent was said to be, firstly, that the land was more fertile and secondly, because the tenants were mostly Nepalis who were prepared to pay any rent for land because they wanted to have a foothold by any means. Thirdly, these lands were close to Saikul Sub-Divisional Headquarters and there was a prospect of converting them to non-agricultural use, e.g. trade, where the rents were fantastically high. For example, in Saikul bazar, a few plots measuring 50 ft × 20 ft each with a small thatched house standing on it, attracted a rent of Rs. 300 per month.

Rents on *Adhiar* terms (i.e. 50% share of the crop) were found to have been paid in 7 plots of village Saikul, but not the same is prevailing in other villages of the sample. Barring this, the rent system is not very unreasonable. The Land Reforms Law, i.e. Section 112 of MLR & LR Act restricts the rent to a maximum of one-fourth and one-third of the produce. The rent of 12 pots per pari appears to be within the legal limit.

There is no uniformity pertaining to period of leasing. In village Saikul, tenants are changed every year, though renewal of tenancy is done upto 10 to 12 years. In village Purm Likli, landlords do not change tenants every year. In practice the duration of leasing is one year. Thus, generally speaking, there is no statutorily fixed minimum period of tenure.

Ejection

Ejection is not uncommon. An agricultural tenant rarely goes to the court for filing objection against ejection. In village Saikul, it has already been shown that the tenants were allowed to cultivate for only one year and though renewal of tenancy occurred in some cases, the changing of the tenant was the usual practice. Thus, the safeguard provided by section 119 is not very effective. Neither the tenant nor the landlord seemed to know about such provisions, but even if they knew, the custom predominated rather than the law.

Though it is not true for all villages, in a number of cases tenanted lands belonged to absentee landowners. Absentee ownership is often attributed to the vestiges of post landlords. Of late there has been active land markets in Manipur. In the five villages studies, as many as 93 land transfers were noticed. Though in 59 out of 93 cases, the transfer is by delivery of possession, in 34 cases it was by proper written documentation. Further, out of 93 cases of transferred land 7 cases were from tribal to non-tribal and in all these cases previous permission of the Deputy Commissioner was taken, whereas in 49 cases lands were transferred from tribal to tribal. It is interesting to note that none of the tribal of these villages was found to have purchased any land of non-tribals, whereas it can be noted that the number of transfer from non-tribal was found to be quite large, i.e. about 39.8 per cent.

Plain Area

Plain areas are those where MLR & LR Act, 1960 is applicable. Data on land transfers in five plain villages in Senapati district were collected. Land transfer through purchase is around 20 per cent, and another 24.5 per cent land is also leased out. Thus, around 45 per cent land is in the purview of either sales or lease market. In any way in plain areas of Manipur, land market is quite active. Further, 3.2 per cent land is under mortgage system. Land market is vital from the point view of access to land as around 50 per cent land is being transacted through leased market, sales and mortgage.

Quite surprising to note here that 63.4 per cent land in these villages are transferred without any formalities. This means land lease market and mortgage type transactions are taking place. In many cases it is also quite true that lack of proper land records is facilitating the process of land transfer in informal way. Land purchase and sales are taking place in a concealed manner.

Sikkim

The economy of Sikkim is mainly based on agriculture and animal husbandry. Approximately, 11 per cent of the total geographical area is under agriculture. Agriculture is of the mixed type and still at the subsistence level rather than commercial level. The female participation rate in Sikkim is also much higher than the national average. This is an important aspect of the hill economy. As the productivity is low, all the able-bodied people are employed in agriculture and other activities. Cultivators account for the greater majority of the people in the state; their percentage is 57.84 per cent. Agricultural labourers as a whole constitute only 7.81 per cent of the workers in the state. Households and other industries are negligible, but other workers (Tertiary Sector) at the state level represent a good percentage of population. The decreasing ratio of workers at the state level indicates the low level of economic diversification. The importance of agriculture can be judged by the high percentage of population approximately 65 per cent engaged in it. Animal husbandry is an integral part of the household economy of the region. There are certain household industries also which substantially add to household income. The past one and half decade has witnessed a tremendous upward swing in various development programmes giving a new thrust to the Sikkim economy. This process has increased wage employment opportunities. Though most of the inhabitants are basically engaged in agriculture, they have diversified into tertiary jobs such as government services.

Tenancy in the State

Tenants of Sikkim could be divided into four categories—(a) *Adhiars*, (b) *Kutidars*, (c) *Chakureys*, (d) *Phakureys*. The *Adhiars* and *Kutidars* are found in large numbers through out the state whereas the *Chakureys* and *Phakureys* are mostly found in Monastery Estates and the Private Estates. The *Adhiars* are mostly advanced type of tenants because in case of *Adhiar* system the basic principles of tenancy are universally accepted. The *Adhiars* have to pay 50 per cent of the produce to the landlords and there is hardly any remission of the landlord's share in case of crop failure. The second type of tenants *Kutidars* account for more than 50 per cent of the total households in agriculture sector in Sikkim. In the *Kutidar* system of tenancy, there are no definite lease terms, the terms of tenancy mostly decided by the landowners and in addition to high rent to be paid to the landlord, the tenants under this system also bear some other burden. The tenants of this type many times are actually sub-tenants as the middleman known as '*Thois*' is given large area of land by the landlords on the basis of definite terms and the '*Thois*' leased out land to sub-tenants. So the *Kutidars* (tillers) have no direct relationship with the landlords. The middleman normally does not give any concession to the Kutidars during the time of crop failure. The landowners in some cases, where the produce is not enough to meet the fixed amount rent extracts the rent by depriving the *Kutidars* of his cattle and owned land. The *Chakurey* and *Phakurey* types of tenants are provided land by the Monastery and individual Lama in lieu of the services of manual labour rendered by them to the Monastery. Since there are no terms and conditions laid down for this compulsory labour, normally the tenants send one family member of their family for such daily labour or as per the requirement of the Monastery. In this order the term mortgage means mortgaging the whole or part of holdings on the *biyaz* or *masikata* system and term sublet means subletting the whole or part of the holding on the *Pakhuria* system.

Biyaz means mortgaging land to another person who enjoys the produce of the land as interest so long as the principle loan remains unpaid.

Masikata means mortgaging of fields to creditor who enjoys the produce of field as an annual installment towards the loan.

Pakhuria means subletting, where a *raiyat* allows another *raiyat* to settle, upon a portion of his own land holding, generally receiving from him some rent in cash and some assistance in cultivating his own fields. The Sikkim Cultivators Protection Act, 1985. The Act provides protection against termination of cultivation. No owner shall have right to terminate the cultivation of his land by a cultivator except in execution of an order made by the prescribed authority, i.e. District Collector. The prescribed authority shall not make an order for termination of the cultivation by a cultivator except on one or more of the following grounds and on no other ground, namely:

(a) The cultivator has, without any reasonable cause, failed to cultivate the land or a part of land exceeding one-fourth of the total area of land in any agricultural year;
(b) The cultivator has failed to pay the rent in cash or in kind or a share or a fixed quantity of the produce from the land within the period as stipulated in any contract or in the absence of any contract within a period of two months from the date of harvest of any particular crop;
(c) The cultivator has sublet the land to another person for cultivation;
(d) The owner having no land other than the land which is being cultivated by the cultivator desires to cultivate the land personally and gives at least six months notice to cultivator; and
(e) The cultivator has erected or caused to be erected a residential house or any other permanent structure on the land without the written permission of the owner.

Tripura

Tripura is located at the south-west extremity of Assam and is surrounded on three sides by Bangladesh. To the North-East are the states of Assam and Mizoram. The area is 10,491 sq. kms. About 60 per cent of the land area is hilly, while the remaining 40 per cent constitutes plain land. Tripura has a sub-tropical climate with on average annual rainfall of 2100 mm. The state has an area of 10491 sq. km. The net sown area comprises 25 per cent of the total area. The effect of rapidly growing population on the limited cultivable land available is dwindling the average size of operational holdings. This has come down from 1.25 hectare (3.09 acres) per holding in 1976-77 to 0.97 hectare (2.40 acres) per holding in 1991-92. 88.6 per cent of the holdings are marginal and small. The distribution of surplus land is no doubt a major issue among the farmers; and to satisfy the needs of landless and homeless, the government has adopted the policy of distributing khas land among them. The land reforms Act provides for allotment of land belonging to the government for agricultural purposes or for construction of dwelling houses and preference is given to *jhumias*, landless agricultural workers and members of the Scheduled Tribes and Scheduled Castes in allotting land. It has been estimated that so far about 30,000 hectares of *khas* land has been distributed among 48,000 landless and homeless families. Many poor tribals have still not got the benefit of land allotment, and allotment, therefore, continues to be a major issue occupying the minds of landless.

Tenancy in the State: Bargadars Records of Rights

In 1979, by an amendment of the TLR & LR Act, 1960, a summary procedure was laid down in Section 46-A. According to this procedure, each bargadar will have separate *khatian* and the name of the bargadar will also be mentioned in the *raiyats khatian*. In many villages, bargadars have been recorded. Bargadar is defined as "*a person who, under the system generally known as adhi, barga, bhag or any other term, cultivates the land of a person on condition of delivering a share of the produce of such land to that person*". Bargadar is not recorded as under-*raiyat* in the normal records-of-rights and their records are put in a separate register. The Government launched the programme "Operation Barga" on the pattern of West Bengal, for recording of Bargadars' rights. Till November 1983, barga rights of about 4085 bargadars had been recorded. The Government also started a scheme of giving legal aid to Bargadars upto Rs. 350 per case, to enable them to prove their rights but the performance has not been very impressive in this respect. Large number of Bargadars have been recorded especially during Revisional Survey Operations. These Bargadars enjoy the benefit of Security of Tenure. However, even now, there are many unrecorded bargadars, who are operating under oral/informal tenancy agreements and who have not come forward to record tenancy. The landowners prefer to cultivate the land themselves, with the help of family members or by engaging some labourers, if necessary. They avoid engaging bargadars for fear of loosing lands. No precise estimate is available of the extent of lands cultivated under Barga. However, around 10 per cent of total area under operational holdings is under tenancy in Tripura. As regards Regulation of Rent, the implementation of laws have been very ineffective. Although maximum rate of rent has been fixed between 20 per cent to 25 per cent of the produce, the actual rate continues to be about 50 per cent of produce. Surprisingly, even recorded bargadars, who can claim protection under TLR & LR Act, continue to pay rent at rates much higher than prescribed rates. The reasons for such high rent appear to be the general social acceptance for the prevailing high rates of rent, desire of the bargadar to avoid conflict with the landowner and ignorance of the bargadars about legal provisions.

Experiences from Village Paschim Champamura, District West Tripura

In Paschim Champamura, a total of 184.8 hectares of land is under cultivation. Of this, 149.9 hectares is under self-cultivation of 551 raiyats and 34.8 hectares is under tenancy. Thus, we find that almost 20 per cent of cultivable land in the village is being cultivated by tenants. A total of 125 tenants were found in the village of which only two were recorded. The recorded area under these two tenants was 0.8 hectare. However, the remaining 34 hectares was found to be under cultivation by unrecorded tenants. What is to be noted here is the extremely small size of the tenant holdings.

Village survey reveals that the following terms and conditions of tenancy were being practiced in the village:

(i) 50 per cent of the produce is to be provided by the tenants to the landowner, where inputs are supported by the landowner. This clearly violates Land Reforms Act which prescribes a maximum of 25 per cent of the produce is to be shared with the landowner.

(ii) 25 per cent of the produce to be given to the landowner, where inputs are not provided by the landowner. This also neglects the Land Reforms Act which prescribes 20 per cent produce are to be shared with the landowner where inputs are not provided to the tenant.

(iii) Fixed cash rent system is followed, where Rs.700 per kani per year (2.5 *kani* = 1 acre) is given as rent to the landowner. In this case also, all expenditures are borne by the tenant. This also violates the norms of Land Reforms Act which prescribes average land revenue at the rate of Rs. 8.5 per *kani* and hence four times of this comes to be Rs. 34 per *kani*.

From the village surveyed, it was observed that share cropping is the main form of tenancy and most of the tenants are marginal or landless farmers. The landowners also do not encourage long tenure for tenancy. Maximum tenancy period ranges from one to two years.

III
CONCLUSION

Land Reforms Policies, without a proper institutional and organizational arrangements have been handicapped to attain minimum equality in the distribution of land and other resources among the rural mass. Land records are not properly maintained in North-Eastern States. In most of the cases, communal ownership system prevails and customary ownership rights of lands are conferred. Survey and settlements are not done in many states. So it is very difficult to capture the dynamisms of land transactions in North-Eastern States. Land Markets in the areas, where customary rights are prevailing is operating in a very informal manner. Traditional agricultural practices are also adopted. However, land grabbers have succeeded in taking possession of land and many communal lands are becoming private lands. Ultimately hidden land market is helping the rich class of people, and more and more people are loosing their rights over communal lands. So in this context, attempts should be made to gear up survey and settlement in North-Eastern States to maintain proper land records. Tenants and absentee landlords are widely found in these states. Terms and conditions of tenancy are mostly favourable to land owners and are very exploitative in most of the cases. Land reforms Acts are violated and not properly followed. This is probably happening due to lack of appropriate institutional and organizational arrangements. Limited success has been achieved to curb the exploitations through leased market in the state of Tripura, because of introduction of Operation Barga in the state. However, there are even then many unrecorded tenants in the state.

IAS Probationers' Assignments that Served as the Basis for the Paper

1. Baihata, Kamrup, Assam: Kailash Chand Sharma, 1995
2. Siberchak, Karimganj, Assam: Donanld P. Wahlang, 1995
3. Hatkhula Gaon, Dibrugarh, Assam: Mukesh Chandra Sahu, 1996

4. Kalitakuchi, Guwahati, Assam: Caralyn Khongwar, 1996
5. Paschim Matia, Goalpara, Assam: Krishna Kumar Dwivedi, 1996
6. Kamrup, Assam: Manish Thakur, 1998
7. Tungjoy, Senapati, Manipur: Paulunthang Vaiphei, 1991
8. Thingra, Tamenglong, Manipur: Prashant Kumar Singh, 1993
9. Chawainamei Khuno, Senapati, Manipur: Vivek Kumar Dewangan, 1993
10. Uttar Takmachara, South Tripura, Tripura: Shikhar Agrawal, 1993
11. Baishyamani Revenue Village, South Tripura, Tripura: Anil Garg,1994
12. East Champacherra, West Tripura, Tripura: Sheo Shekhar Shukla, 1994
13. South Mirza, South Tripura, Tripura: J. K. Sinha, 1996
14. Deorachhera, North Tripura, Tripura: Nitin Kulkarni
15. Bagaban Nangar, North Tripura, Tripura: Atish Chandra
16. Kameswar, North Tripura, Tripura: Subba Reddy
17. Satchand, South Tripura, Tripura: Sanjeev Kumar, 1998
18. Bomidila, West Kameng, Arunachal Pradesh: Santosh D. Vaidya, 1998
19. Tsiese Basa, Kohima, Nagaland: V. Shashank Shekhar, 1996
20. Pekhulakha, Sikkim: Vishal Chauhan, 1998
21. Chumbi, East Sikkim, Sikkim: B. Ashok, 1998
22. Paschim Champamura, West Tripura, Tripura: Ankur Garg, 2004

REFERENCES

1. Bordoloi, G. and Neog, A. K. (1986). *Economy of North East India*, Vol.-I, LBS Publication, Guwahati.
2. Dutta, N. C., (1968). *Land Problems and Land Reforms in Assam*, S. Chand & Co., New Delhi.
3. Dasgupta, M. (1991). *Impact of Land Reforms in North East India*, Omsons Publications, Guwahati.
4. Goswami, P. C.: *The Economic Development of Assam*, Kalyani Publisher, New Delhi.

Chapter 21

State and NGO Interventions in the Distribution of Land to the Poor: A Study of Tamil Nadu

M. THANGARAJ

I
STRUCTURE OF LAND HOLDINGS

This is a modest attempt to analyse the roles of State and NGOs in Tamil Nadu in the distribution of land to the weaker sections. State intervention in enabling the weaker sections, presently classified as Scheduled Castes, to access land has a long history in Tamil Nadu, dating back to colonial times. The post-independence period witnessed assignment of ceiling-surplus as well as government lands to the SCs and others. Recently, certain NGOs have come forward to acquire land through market purchases and allot the same to the SC households. The paper is divided into four parts. The first part provides a brief account of landholding structure in general and that of the SCs and STs in comparison with others in the State. The second part discusses the land assignment programmes by the State since the pre-independence days. The third part documents the recent NGO initiations in the assignment of land to the SCs through market purchases. The last is the concluding part.

The distribution of the number and area of operational holdings as given in Table 21.1 clearly shows that the total number of operational holdings has increased significantly during the period from 1985-86 to 1995-96 in Tamil Nadu. The increase in the number of holdings was confined only to the marginal size groups up to 1.00 ha. (Hectare) and the area operated was confined only to the marginal and small holdings, whereas the middle level holdings above 2 ha. showed a decline both in terms of number and area. The increase in the area in the marginal and small size holdings was at the cost of middle and large size holdings. The average size of holdings has declined marginally from 1.01 ha. in 1985-86 to 0.93 ha. in 1990-91 and to 0.90 ha. in 1995-96. The main reason for the increase in the number and area under small size holdings may be due to the operation of land market, sub-division of land among the family members due to population explosion, redistribution of surplus land to the landless through the Land Ceiling Act and other re-distributive measures.

Table 21.1: Distribution of Operational Holdings by Size Groups in Tamil Nadu (Number in thousands and area in thousand hectares)

Size of Groups	*1985-86*		*1990-91*		*1995-96*	
	Number	*Area*	*Number*	*Area*	*Number*	*Area*
Marginal	5498	2018	5848	2118	5951	2210
(Below 1 ha.)	(71.34)	(25.88)	(73.11)	(28.34)	(74.28)	(30.26)
Small	1260	1772	1275	1794	1234	1721
(1 to 2 ha.)	(16.35)	(22.72)	(15.93)	(24.01)	(15.40)	(23.57)
Semi-medium	649	1778	618	1687	601	1623
(2 to 4 ha.)	(8.42)	(22.81)	(7.72)	(22.57)	(7.50)	(22.22)
Medium	261	1508	228	1301	200	1135
(4 to 10 ha.)	(3.38)	(19.34)	(2.85)	(17.41)	(2.50)	(15.54)
Large	39	720	31	574	26	614
(10 ha. & above)	(0.51)	(9.24)	(0.39)	(7.68)	(0.32)	(8.41)
All sizes	7706	7796	8000	7474	8012	7303
	(100)	(100)	(100)	(100)	(100)	(100)

Note: Figures in brackets indicate percentages.

Sources: 1. Agricultural Situation in India, August, 1995.

2. Tamil Nadu Agricultural Census, 1995-96.

Landholdings by Social Groups

Land is closely associated with the caste system. Socially and economically dominant castes own most of the land and socially disadvantaged people belonging to the Scheduled Castes own less or no land. In Tamil Nadu, the area operated by Scheduled Castes was only 7.1 per cent both in 1985-86 and 1990-91 and 7.2 per cent in 1995-96 but the proportion of the Scheduled Castes population to the total population was 19.18 per cent (Table 21.2). The STs who account for about 1 per cent of the population, have a share of over 1 per cent of the share in landholdings but much of their land could be in hilly tracks. The SCs and STs, who together constitute over 20 per cent of the population, account for only 8 per cent of the total land holdings. This clearly indicates that the land operated by the social groups has been disproportionally lower than their share in the total population in Tamil Nadu.

Table 21.2: Distribution of Operational Holdings by Social Groups: Tamil Nadu

Social Groups	*Percentage of Population*	*Number ('000)*			*Area in ha. ('000)*		
	1991	*85-86*	*90-91*	*95-96*	*85-86*	*90-91*	*95-96*
1. Scheduled Castes	19.18	876 (11.4)	904 (11.3)	911 (11.4)	557 (7.1)	534 (7.1)	527 (7.2)
2. Scheduled Tribes	1.03	58 (0.8)	67 (0.8)	62 (0.8)	87 (1.1)	87 (1.2)	77 (1.1)
3. Others	79.79	6772 (87.9)	7029 (87.9)	7039 (87.9)	7152 (91.7)	6853 (91.7)	6699 (91.7)
Total	100.00	7706 (100)	8000 (100)	8012 (100)	7796 (100)	7474 (100)	7303 (100)

Note: Figures in brackets indicate percentage.

Sources: 1. World Agricultural Census, Tamil Nadu, 1979-80.
2. Tamil Nadu Agricultural Census, 1995-96.

II
STATE AND LAND DISTRIBUTION TO SCs AND STs

Panchama Lands

Tremenhere, the then Collector of Chengalpattu District during the British period submitted a memorandum to the British government about the plight of the depressed classes in Chengalpattu district and the need for distribution of land for them in 1891. The British government conceded his demand and enacted a law in British Parliament to distribute land for cultivation purpose to the Untouchables in India to improve their socio-economic status. The government order numbers 1010 and 1010A dated September 30, 1892 specified that land would be assigned to the Depressed Classes by the government. Under this Act, agricultural land was distributed to the Depressed Classes from 1892. Margu study on Panchama land shows that 633 acres of land was distributed to the Depressed Classes in Karanai village, Chengalpattu district in 1933 (District Collector, Chengalpattu; Order RIDIS 5560, Dated 19th November, 1933). These lands are known as 'Depressed Class Land' (D.C. Land) or 'Panchama Land'. While distributing the land to the Depressed Classes, the British government made certain conditions and hence they are known as conditional assignments. These conditions were: (i) These lands cannot be sold or mortgaged to any one for ten years, (ii) These lands may be sold or mortgaged after 10 years to the Depressed Classes only, (iii) Any breach of these conditions would invite cancellation of land assigned. In this process a lot of Pariahs took possession of land. Sundari (1991) views the attempt made by the British government to provide land to the Pariahs thus, "The rise of Parayans in the agrarian hierarchy is an important phenomenon especially since it was a break from centuries' old tradition and social restriction". A study conducted by Margu on Panchama land struggle shows that the British government distributed 12 lakhs acres of land to the Depressed Classes. The leader of the 'Save Panchama land movement', Mr. Karuppan, a former civil servant, says that about 2.5 lakh acres of Panchama land have been illegally occupied by the non-SCs/STs in Tamil Nadu.

Distribution of number and area of Panchama land is presented in Table 21.3. It is to be noted from the data that the extent of Panchama land was more in Thiruvannamalai and North Arcot districts as compared to other districts in Tamil Nadu. Information relating to Panchama land given in Table 21.3 is incomplete, as the data on Panchama land could not be collected completely from all districts and the data on Panchama land by districts was not made available for all districts in Tamil Nadu. Another sources shows that the total land assigned under the scheme upto 1930-31, was to the tune of over 123000 acres (Table 21.4).

Land Colonization Cooperative Society for Adi-Dravidas

The Government of Tamil Nadu established the land colonization cooperative societies for Adi-Dravidas in 1960 with a view to providing agricultural land with necessary inputs for Adi-Dravidas (SCs). The Government of Tamil Nadu allotted cultivable wastelands for this scheme. The beneficiaries of this scheme can cultivate the land but are not allowed to have any right over the land cultivated.

Share capital, seeds, fertilizers, plough bullocks, digging of wells were all financed by the Government. Totally 56 societies were established across districts in Tamil Nadu. Total area of 56 societies was 14262.64 acres with 2516 beneficiaries (2285 beneficiaries belong to the SCs and the rest 231 non-SCs). Name of the society, number of members and extent are given in Table 21.5. It is also important to note that such scheme was also being implemented in other states, viz. Karnataka and Kerala.

Table 21.3: Distribution of Panchama Lands and the Extent under Occupation of Others

Districts	Panchama Lands (Acres)		Extent under occupation of others (Acres)
	No.	Extent	
1. Coimbatore	1683	3191.02	503.01
2. Chengalpattu	2968	950.52	661.22
3. Chidambaranar	—	—	—
4. Dindigul	830	1892.39	275.43
5. Dharmapuri	5842	9004.55	803.41
6. Kanyakumari	—	—	—
7. Kamarajar	94	109.42	—
8. North Arcot	16969	21316.75	2081.48
9. Nagapattinam	222	155.62	—
10. Pudukottai	—	—	—
11. Pasumpon	—	—	—
12. Periyar	—	—	—
13. Ramanathapuram	—	—	—
14. South Arcot	893	987.70	—
15. Salem	8180	13601.95	703.12
16. Thanjavur	544	287.17	8.97
17. Tiruvannamalai	19923	22398.31	5805.90
18. Villupuram	4597	11102.08	—
19. Nilgiris	—	746.33	—
Total	62745	72142.16	10219.42

Note: The data given in this Table was obtained by the "Save Panchama Land Movement and Dalit Joint Action Committee" of Tamil Nadu from the Government of Tamil Nadu. The Movement leader Mr. Karuppan has stated the data given in this Table is incomplete, as the Movement was unable to obtain the statistical information from all Taluks of all districts in Tamil Nadu.

Source: Laws relating to the redemption of Panchama Lands, Dalit Joint Action Committee and Save Panchama Land Movement, Chennai as quoted in M. Thangaraj, (Ed.) *Land Reforms in India—Tamil Nadu: An Unfinished Task*, Sage Publications, New Delhi, 2003.

Table 21.4: Statement Showing the Extent of Land Assigned to Adi-Dravidas (Acres)

District	Patta land total (1930-31)	Area Assigned (Percentage)	
		Upto 1927-28	Upto 1930-31
North Arcot	1235913	38696 (3.1%)	56560 (4.6%)
South Arcot	1615961	15202 (0.9%)	22968 (1.4%)
Chingleput	696187	3575 (0.5%)	5683 (0.8%)
Coimbatore	2290833	6473 (0.3%)	9003 (0.4%)
Madura	1185803	8226 (0.7%)	6748 (0.6%)
The Nilgiris	228456	46 (0.0%)	27 (0.0%)
Ramnad	324490	476 (0.1%)	573 (0.2%)
Salem	1163567	7115 (0.6%)	9456 (0.8%)
Thanjore	1163567	965 (0.1%)	980 (1.0%)
Tinnevelly	1229294	3224 (0.3%)	4386 (0.4%)
Trichinopoly	1481844	4096 (0.3%)	6882 (0.5%)
Total	12615915	88094 (0.7%)	123266 (1.0%)

Source: G.O. No. 2778L., Public Works and Labour Department, 5 Novervmber 1928, p. 62, Statement VII; G.O. No. 3218L, Public Works and Labour Department, 21 December 1931, p.30, Statement VII; Jamabandi Report for Fasli 1340 (1930-31), p.79, as quoted in Yanagisawa, Haruka. *A Century of Change—Caste and Irrigated Lands in Tamil Nadu: 1860s—1970*, Manohar, 1996.

Table 21.5: Land Colonization Cooperative Societies for Adi-Dravidas

District	Name of the Land Colonization Cooperative Society	Number of Members	Area (Acres)
1. Kanchipuram	1. Karanaipuducheri	—	—
	2. Karunguzhipallam	—	94.39
	3. Ponpadi	—	268.87
	4. Nemalur	70	224.08
	5. Thammanur	—	104.00
2. Vellore	6. Perungalathur	—	—
	7. Ipedu	—	—
	8. Cangavaram	—	—
3. Salem	9. Navalur	—	—
	10. Nathakarai	—	—
	11. Siruvachiyur I	—	—
	12. Siruvachiyur II	—	—
	13. Peryieri	—	—
	14. Manmalai	—	—
	15. Thammanpatti	—	—
	16. Singipuram	—	210.00
	17. Unathur	—	—
	18. M. Pudupatti	—	—

(*Contd.*)

(*Contd.*)

District	Name of the Land Colonization Cooperative Society	Number of Members	Area (Acres)
4. Dharmapuri	19. Manithahalli	80	402.88
	20. Kakkanpuram	52	150.59
	21. Thalli	82	251.30
5. Coimbatore	22. Vadugapatti	161	464.06
	23. Brough Nagar	—	—
	24. Chickarasamplayam	35	140.00
6. Nilgiris	25. Mavanahalla	—	66.35
	26. Erumad	—	—
7. Thanjavur	27. Pichagotagam	—	—
	28. Kodiyalamparavathur	30	104.90
	29. Sanaurapatti	30	76.23
8. Cuddalore	30. Killiyanur	11	80.00
	31. Indili	97	457.00
	32. Bangaram	77	291.00
	33. Maravanatham	—	654.34
	34. Moongilpadi	135	661.00
	35. Kuhaiyur	66	325.00
	36. Pakkampadi	27	94.00
	37. Thenponparappi I	40	200.00
	38. Thenponparappi I	49	228.50
	39. T. Vellore	17	140.60
	40. Pullur	36	180.00
	41. Rayarpalayam	—	285.00
9. Trichy	42. Nergunam	—	—
10. Madurai	43. Poonjuthi	30	176.91
	44. Kottakudi Pathinettangudi	42	116.92
	45. Chinmainayakkankottai	—	266.47
	46. Kesmpatti	37	142.20
	47. Kallangadu	—	266.12
	48. Santhaiyur	—	114.00
	49. Gopalapuram	—	—
11. Thirunelveli	50. Pidaneri	—	—
	51. Panangudi	—	—
	52. Karandhaneri	—	—
	53. Kottaikarungulam	24	118.13
12. Ramanathapuram	54. Anuppanendal	—	—
	55. Tharaganendal	—	—
	56. Velangulam	—	—

Note: 1. Data relating to Members of Society and Land were collected from the Directorate of Adi-Dravida, 2. In Pakkambadi village, the data includes 36 acres of land cultivated by 16 non-members of the Society.

Source: G.O., Ms. No. 2007, 10-8-1984, Department of Social Welfare, Government of Tamil Nadu as quoted in M. Thangaraj, (Ed.) *Land Reforms in India—Tamil Nadu: An Unfinished Task*, Sage Publications, New Delhi, 2003.

In the recent past, the Government of Tamil Nadu has received several complaints from the Land Colonization Cooperative Societies for Adi-Dravidas that they are unable to run the societies due to non-functioning effectively and incurring loss. The Government has constituted a committee consisting of the Registrar of Cooperatives and Secretary of Adi-Dravidas and Tribal Welfare Department to find out the working of these societies. The Committee has recommended that (i) Societies which are not functioning effectively may be closed down, (ii) The Government may write off all loans given to the society members, and (iii) Whoever is cultivating the society's land may be given patta. The Government has accepted their recommendations. Finally, the Government of Tamil Nadu gave permission to abolish the Land Colonization of Cooperative Societies for Adi-Dravidas, which are not functioning effectively and incurring losses. The number of societies, which were abolished, is not readily available.

Distribution of Ceiling Surplus Land

Redistribution of ceiling surplus land as given in Table 21.6 shows that the total area declared as surplus was 204495 acres (as on 31.3.04). Out of this, 10185 acres of land was reserved for public purposes. The total area of land distributed to the beneficiaries was 184945 acres. The ratio of total area of surplus land distributed to beneficiaries to the total operated area was only 1 per cent. The break up of the beneficiaries by social groups is available for the period upto 31st March, 2004. Out of the 146633 beneficiaries, 65198 (44%) persons belonging to Scheduled Castes and 69743 (37.7%) acres of ceiling surplus land was distributed to them. Thus the above data unmistakably suggest that the Land Ceiling Act could not alter the agrarian structure. It is significant to note that the guidelines for the distribution of the ceiling surplus land show that preference will be given to the agricultural labourers belonging to Scheduled Castes and Scheduled Tribes. But looking at the data on the distribution of ceiling surplus land reveals that 61 per cent of the land was distributed to others (Non-SCs and STs). This clearly shows that the implementing officers have vested interest and hence the benefit of ceiling surplus land could not fully reach the target groups.

Table 21.6: Statement Showing the Progress in the Distribution of Ceiling Surplus Land under the Land Ceiling Act in Tamil Nadu

Description	*Acres (as on)*			
	1.2.90	*31.8.95*	*31.3.99*	*31.3.04*
1. Area declared surplus	173100	189738	198680	204495
2. Area covered by stay before initiating proceedings for distribution	9334	21655	13880	
3. Area for which proceedings for distribution initiated	163766			
4. Area covered by stay after initiating proceeding for distribution	16881			8663
5. Net area for distribution	146885	168101		195832
6. Area yet to be distributed	1012		1789	702
7. Area for which distribution completed	145873	167720		195130
(a) Area for which distribution completed	9976	9724	9976	10185
(b) Distributed to eligible persons:				184945

Categories of Beneficiaries	*No. of Beneficiaries*			*Area Distributed (acres)*			
	As on			*As on*			
	1.2.90	*31.8.95*	*31.3.04*	*1.2.90*	*31.8.95*	*31.3.99*	*31.3.04*
1. SC	50293	58625	65198	54452	61518	—	69743
2. ST	93	180	205	136	234	—	275
3. Others	60454	72996	81270	81309	96244	—	114927
Total	110840	131801	146633	135897	157996	173035	184945

Source: Short Notes on Land Reforms, Directorate of Land Reforms, Government of Tamil Nadu.

Distribution of Cultivable Government Land

Every year a considerable amount of government land is being distributed to the beneficiaries by the Government of Tamil Nadu. Data on distribution of cultivable land was collected for the latest year (2003-2004) only, as the data are not readily available for many years. It is significant to note that a study conducted by the author on "Land use pattern in Tamil Nadu" reveals that about half of the total geographical area is unsown, which clearly indicates that there is a vast scope for further increase in the area of land under cultivation.

Table 21.7: Assignment of Cultivable Lands: as on 31.3.2004 (acres)

District	SC		ST		MBC		BC		Others		Total	
	No.	Area	No.	Area	No.	Area	No.	Area	No.	Area	No.	Area
1. Chennai						*Ban in force*						
2. Coimbatore	13	14.79	0	0	17	14.15	31	23.02	0	0	61	51.96
3. Cuddalore	165	77.14	0	0	380	223.42	188	110.3	2	3	735	413.86
4. Dharamapuri	82	42.49	0	0	183	62.77	102	37.36	0	0	367	142.62
5. Dindigul	17	9.6	0	0	57	19.55	133	84.96	0	0	207	114.11
6. Erode	14	9.02	0	0	3	3.36	26	17.64	0	0	43	30.02
7. Kancheepuram	98	55.3	0	0	4	0.59	30	9.79	3	0.75	135	66.43
8. Kanniyakumari	0	0	0	0	0	0	57	13.82	0	0	57	13.82
9. Karur	6	26.56	0	0	0	0	23	52.7	0	0	29	79.26
10. Krishnagiri	23	10.55	0	0	44	17.64	16	6.59	0	0	83	34.78
11. Madurai	81	26	0	0	37	44.15	146	134.77	0	0	264	204.92
12. Nagappattinam	27	24.9	0	0	15	10.08	35	11.82	68	15.14	245	61.94
13. Namakkal						*Category-wise figures not furnished*						
14. Perambalur	55	37.64	7	4.95	211	137.15	224	144.82	4	2.5	501	327.06
15. Pudukottai	420	134.84	0	0	255	109.22	751	196.65	0	0	1426	440.71
16. Ramanathapuram	30	17.3	0	0	58	35.87	84	53.75	0	0	172	106.92
17. Salem	0					*Category-wise figures not furnished*				0	0	21.41
18. Sivaganga	106	32.25	0	0	197	82.50	213	152.32	0	0	516	267.06
19. Thanjavur	173	50.88	0	0	158	31.76	344	85.57	73	11.55	748	179.76

(*Contd.*)

(*Contd.*)

District	SC		ST		MBC		BC		Others		Total	
	No.	Area	No.	Area	No.	Area	No.	Area	No.	Area	No.	Area
20. The Nilgiris					Ban in force							
21. Theni	4	3.11	0	0	14	35.42	11	16.34	0	0	29	54.87
22. Thoothukudi	59	50.62	0	0	36	45.33	158	195.85	0	0	253	291.8
23. Tiruchirapaili	112	127.05	10	14.1	105	51.06	409	393.72	25	26.28	661	612.21
24. Tirunelveli	69	57.27	0	0	97	84.08	110	96.85	11	7.11	287	245.31
25. Tiruvallur	2	3	0	0	0	0	3	1.5	0	0	5	4.5
26. Tiruvannamalai	140	115.7	29	33.92	276	198.00	258	157.27	15	13.96	718	518.85
27. Tiruvarur	50	22.00	0	0	11	2.50	92	65.00	73	36.50	226	126
28. Vellore	130	131.67	0	0	201	121.58	147	127.17	5	2.81	483	383.23
29. Villupuram	370	166.88	0	0	893	306.99	494	177.52	8	1.49	1765	652.88
30. Virudhunagar	41	0	14	0	69	0	0	0	0	0	124	100.31#
Total	2287	1246.56	60	52.97	3321	1637.17	4085	2367.1	287	121.09	10040	5525.17

Note: Target fixed as per G.O.Rt. No.345, Revenue, dated 15.7.2003—3000 acres. Target achieved upto 31.3.2004 was 5747.76 acres. The achievement of target was 192 per cent.

\# Break-up of data on area of land by social group is not available for Viruthunagar district; hence columns total may not tally with the total area of land.

Source: Commissioner, Land Administration, Government of Tamil Nadu, Chennai.

Data on distribution of cultivable land (assessed and unassessed wastelands) by the government of Tamil Nadu as given in Table 21.7 clearly shows that a considerable area of land has been distributed to the beneficiaries during the year 2003-04. The district level data further shows that there exists an uneven distribution of cultivable land in Tamil Nadu. It is significant to note that about one-fifths of the land was distributed to the SCs and about 70 per cent of the land was distributed to the BCs and MBCs. It is significant to note that the target achieved was more than the target fixed for the year. Assuming about 5000 acres of Government land is assigned every year to about 2000 families, the total extent would have been more than the ceiling surplus land, that is about 1 per cent of the total cultivated area. This shows that still considerable scope exists for the assignment of Government land to poorer households in Tamil Nadu.

III
NGOs AND LAND PURCHASE SCHEME

Land purchase scheme is a laudable scheme in Tamil Nadu. Two Non-Governmental Organisations (NGOs), viz. LAFTI and DAPSY have done a commendable job in providing land to SCs with the support of Tamil Nadu Adi-Dravidas Housing and Development Corporation (TAHDCO) during 1990. Now TAHDCO has come out with a new land purchase scheme in 2004, on its own.

LAFTI (Land for Tillers Freedom), a voluntary non-government organization was formed by the followers of Acharya Vinoba Bhave in East Thanjavur district (now in Nagapattinam district) in 1985. The founder Secretary was Padmashri Krishnammal Jaganathan. The main objective of the LAFTI was to obtain cultivable lands from landowners at the existing market value and distribute the same to the most deserving landless poor belonging to the SCs.

LAFTI initiated the project during the year 1989-90 and purchased 980.66 acres of land and distributed to 980 SCs from 18 villages (Table 21.8), at the cost of Rs. 71.29 lakhs. IRDP subsidy and the term loan from National Scheduled Castes Development Corporation (NSFDC) through TAHDCO were sources of funding for the project. NSFDC sanctioned term loan Rs. 43.23 lakhs and IRDP subsidy was Rs. 28.03 lakhs. The average cost of the land works out to Rs. 7500 per acre.

Table 21.8: Distribution of Beneficiaries Assisted by the LAFTI (1989-1990)

Sl. No.	*Name of the Block*	*Name of the Village*	*No. of Families*	*Extent of land in Acres A.C.*
1.	Kilvelur	Karugudi	89	88.64
		Serunallur	58	57.99
		Odachery	34	33.50
		Odhiyathur	34	34.03
		Senbagapuram	26	25.75
2.	Nagapattinam	Mahadanam	22	22.14
		Pappakovil	33	33.03
		Ettukudi	93	92.89
		Venmanalcheri	63	63.06
3.	Thirumarugal	Sirkali	85	84.94
		Kuthalam	50	50.26
4.	Thiruvarur	Vepathangudi	123	122.79
5.	Koradachery	Agarathirunallur	42	41.69
		Vadugagudi	71	71.00
6.	Kottur	Kurichimulai	29	29.11
		Naruvalikalappal	30	30.00
		Seelathanallur	80	79.84
		Kullamanickam	20	20.00
		Total	982	980.66

Source: TAHDCO, Chennai.

In the second phase, LAFTI purchased 1029.12 acres of land and distributed to 1029 families (Table 21.9) from 17 villages from Nagapattinam and Thiruvarur districts at the cost of Rs. 111.33 lakhs. The average cost works out to Rs. 10200 per acre. NSFDC sanctioned the term loan of Rs. 59.88 lakhs in 1991 and IRDP subsidy was of Rs. 51.45 lakhs for this project.

DAPSY (Dr. Ambedkar People Society) was established in 1990. Shri P. Muthusamy was the President of the Society. The objective of the DAPSY was to purchase lands from landowners and assign the same to the most deserving families belonging to the SCs on loan and subsidy basis. NSFDC sanctioned Rs. 90.94 lakhs as loan and IRDP subsidy was of Rs. 2267866 in 1992. Average cost of the land was Rs. 20500 per acre.

DAPSY purchased 564.49 acres of land and distributed to 550 landless SC beneficiaries spread over 28 villages in 6 blocks, viz. Myladuthurai, Kuttalam, Sembanarkoil, Sirkali, Kollidam and Nannilam in Nagapattinam district. It is worth noting that the NSFDC has sanctioned similar projects in Andhra Pradesh and Karnataka (Tenth Five Year Plan).

Table 21.9: Distribution of Beneficiaries Assisted by the LAFTI (1991)

Sl. No.	Name of the Block	Name of the Village	No. of SC beneficiaries families	Extent of land in Acres A.C.
1.	Kilvelur	Porkalakudi	166	165.92
		Kokur	63	62.83
		Vadakarai	50	50.00
		Irunchiyur	25	25.00
		Shenbagapuram	16	16.00
2.	Koradacherry	Perumpukalur	20	20.00
3.	Kodavasal	Nemmeli	197	197.28
4.	Thalainayar	Sathiyakulam	48	47.65
		Thalainayar	83	82.75
5.	Tiruvarur	Vappathankudi	13	13.35
		Nannarimanagalam	8	8.26
		Vaipur	51	51.22
6.	Thirumarugal	Perunsathangudi	27	27.00
7.	Koliidam	Kumarakkudi	94	93.60
8.	Thiruthuraipoondi	Kokkaladi	18	18.26
9.	Nannilam	Dhoothukudi	100	100.00
		Sagadaimangalam	50	50.00
		Total	1029	1029.12

Source: TAHDCO, Chennai.

The government of Tamil Nadu wanted to implement the LPS and enacted G.O. Ms. No. 36; AD&TW Dept. dated 30th March, 1995 to benefit 1000 beneficiaries with a subsidy outlay of Rs. 1.00 crore. Under this scheme maximum unit cost of land was fixed at Rs. 20,000 per acre and 50 per cent (Rs. 10,000) was to be provided as subsidy. Each beneficiary was to be given 1 acre of dry or 0.5 acre of wetland. But the scheme was implemented only in Nagapattinam and Thiruvarur districts and only 21 beneficiaries got benefited.

During the financial year 2002-03, as part of the district action plan under agricultural activities, land purchase scheme was promoted for the benefit of self-help groups. In 2002-03, it was planned to provide land to 185 persons at a total assistance outlay of Rs. 50.55 lakhs. Out of which Rs. 25.12 lakhs was given as subsidy.

A new land purchase scheme was announced during the budget for 2003-04 [G.O. (Ms) No. 15] by the Government of Tamil Nadu. The objective of the scheme was to help landless SCs and STs to become owners of the land and to make the marginal and small holdings economically viable. Under this scheme, each beneficiary can purchase and own a maximum of 5 acres of dry land or 2.50

acres of wetland including the land, already owned by each beneficiary.

Table 21.10: Distribution of Beneficiaries Assisted by the DAPSY (1990)

Sl. No.	Name of the Block	Name of the Village	No. of families	Extent of land in Acres A.C.
1.	Mayiladuthurai (Mayiladuthurai Taluk)	Mannipallam	13	12.80
		Mclanallur	6	6.37
		Porvasanallur	29	31.11
		Varathampattu	3	2.94
		Kidakkam	1	1.63
		Kizhai	16	16.19
		Maharajapuram	6	6.19
		Aruvapadi	4	4.07
		Total	78	81.30
2.		Kuttalam	13	12.68
		Umayambalpuram	6	6.50
		Sengudi	43	43.98
		Porumbur	3	2.67
		Total	65	65.83
3.		Akkur-Pandarvadai	11	11.47
		Mamakudi	8	7.58
		Thirukadaiyur	6	6.13
		T. Manalmedu	27	27.42
		Neduvasal	4	3.68
		Visaloor	4	4.58
		Kudaloor	29	29.17
		Total	89	90.17
4.	Sirkazhi (Sirkazhi Taluk)	Agani	24	22.17
		Kathiruppu	15	14.84
		Thennampattinam	64	64.62
		Vanagiri	92	99.54
		Keezhaperumpallam	26	26.20
		Total	221	227.37
5.	Kollidam (Sirkazhi Taluk)	Sothiyakudi	13	13.80
		Total	13	13.80
6.	Nannilam (Nannilam Taluk)	Pillur	3	3.34
		Keeranur	11	10.95
		Koothanoor	70	71.24
		Total	84	85.53
		Grand Total	550	564.00

Source: TAHDCO, Chennai.

The maximum unit cost is Rs. 2 lakhs of which maximum of 1 lakh is for the purchase of land and a maximum of 1 lakh for other components such as land development, minor irrigation, etc. The pattern of financial assistance is 50 per cent as term loan and

50 per cent as subsidy. Subsidy will be met by TAHDCO from Special Central Assistance (SCA) to Special Component Plan fund for SCs and Tribal Sub Plan fund for STs. In the first year of the implementation 6000 SC women and 1000 ST women will be benefited by this scheme. Subsidy outlay was Rs. 30 crores for 6000 SC and Rs. 5 crores for ST beneficiaries respectively. No funding is required from the state government for the implementation. The term loan will be provided by the commercial banks.

The foregoing analysis clearly exhibits the prevalence of unequal distribution of landholdings. The data on landholdings by social groups discloses the fact that there was a problem in getting access to land by SCs. An attempt to provide land by the government through re-distributive measures have really helped SCs to consolidate their position to hold the land, although marginally. If the government had given preference to SCs while distributing the ceiling surplus land and assignment of cultivable land, the land cultivated by SCs would have been much higher by now. The NGOs and government should come forward to help the SCs and other poor in bringing equality in the distribution of land. As land is the backbone for the economic development, equitable distribution of land to the vulnerable section of the society would ensure holistic development of the society.

REFERENCES

Government of India, *Tenth Five Year Plan—2002-2007*, Vol. II, Sectoral Policies and Programmes, Planning Commission, New Delhi.

Margu, (1995). *Panchami Nila Pore (Tamil). (Struggle for Panchama Land)*, Muhil Publishers, Madurai.

Sundari, T. K. (1991). *Caste and the Agrarian Structure*, Oxford and IBH Publishing Co. Pvt. Ltd. New Delhi and Centre for Development Studies, Trivandrum.

Thangaraj, M. (2003). *Land Reforms in India—Tamil Nadu: Un-finished Task*, Sage Publications, New Delhi.

Thangaraj, M. (1992). "Land Use Pattern in Tamil Nadu", MIDS Working Paper No. 107, June.

Chapter 22

Globalization and Contract Farming: The Experience of Some States

K. GOPAL IYER

The concept of "contract farming", which is being projected as an answer to most of the woes of the Indian farmers, is not at all new to out agriculture. 'Contract Farming' has been practiced in the sugar cane sector on a large scale and for a long time. The manner in which the policy makers ignored the experiences of this practice is surprising. According to a report in *Business Line*, the sugar mills in the country owe farmers a staggering Rs. 230 crores (of the total dues of Rs. 1325 crore) as payment of arrears for the cane supplied during the 2001-02 crushing season. Apart from the issue of non-payment, there are also reports of malpractices in grading and weighing farmers' produce. With the entry of mighty agribusiness multinationals whose annual incomes are far more than the GDP of many developing countries, we can well visualise the fate of the meek and weak Indian farmers. This paper discusses contract farming experiences of Punjab in two phases, in Andhra Pradesh and Karnataka.

I

FIRST PHASE OF CONTRACT FARMING IN PUNJAB AND SMALL FARMERS

Contract farming is being suggested in policy circles as the major answer to the existing problems of farmers in marketing their produce. Contract farming has relatively a recent history in India but it has a longer history in United States and Europe. The experience of the success and failure in these countries can be of some relevance to our countries but we have to be more concerned about the ground level realities of its viability for the marginal and small farmers in India. Contract farming can be defined in terms of a system for the production and supply of agricultural and horticultural produce under forward contracts. *It can be described as a halfway house between independent farm production and corporate/captive farming.* It basically involves four things: pre-agreed price, quality, quantity and time. Contract farming in India is currently being practiced by multinational firms like Pepsi, HLL, ITC, Cargill, besides domestic corporates like BIL (WIMCO), VB, Nijjer Agro, Tarai Foods and various state agencies and public sector agencies especially seed production and perishables like vegetable.

Contract Farming is essentially a means of allocating the distribution of risk, between processor and grower. The latter assumes the risks associated with production while the former assumes the risks of marketing the final produce. Development of contract farming in India is likely to proceed only as long as the rewards perceived to be associated with these risks by both parties are commensurate with the risks assumed. Hence, the challenge is to create such an enabling environment. The broad objectives of promoting contract farming are:

(a) To reduce the load on the central and state level procurement system.
(b) To increase private sector investment in agriculture.
(c) To bring about a market focus in terms of crop selection by Indian farmers.
(d) To generate a steady source of income at the individual farmer level.
(e) To promote processing and value addition.
(f) To prioritize micro agro climatic zones and crops for promotion of contract farming.

Contract farming in an organized way was started in Punjab with the establishment of Tomato Processing Unit by Pepsi in 1989. Vegetables cover one per cent of the gross cropped area and the share of the tomato crop is 7 per cent of the total area under vegetable in the state. As food was not the priority area for Pepsi, it sold its unit to Brooke Bond India Ltd., which in turn sold it to the Hindustan Lever Ltd. (HLL) in 1995.

To ensure regular supply of fresh tomatoes to the plant, the farmers were ensured a remunerative price by the company. This arrangement was helpful to both farmers as well as the company. It had fixed the net profit of Rs. 12,000 per acre. Before establishment of this unit at Zahura, tomato yields at farmers' level were low and the cost of production was high. A two pronged strategy was designed to help farmers to improve yield and develop new technology to reduce cost of production. This helped both the tomato producers and the processors to improve the profitability. The HLL made contract with 325 to 388 farmers annually during the period 1994-95 to 1997-98 and area planted varied from 2500 to 3000 acres annually. The study by Rangi and Sidhu (2000) showed that the fresh tomatoes procured by the company was 34262 tonnes in 1995-96 which came to a low of 8075 tonnes in 1997-98. The climatic conditions affected the yield as well as production of tomato crop. In lieu of low production the open market price of tomato was high. The contract farmers delivered major portion of the produce to the market and only partially delivered the tomato to the plant. After establishment of the tomato processing plant at Zahura there was a quantum jump in the area under tomato which rose from 845 hectares in 1988-89 to 3117 hectares in 1990-91 and further increased to 6000 hectares in 1997-98.

Similarly, the Nijjer plant had made contract with 500 to 800 farmers annually during the period, 1994-95 to 1997-98 and area planted varied from 1400 to 1800 acres. Bot the Zahura and Nijjer units provided seedlings of tomato to the farmers and guidance was given to them by their technical staff. Most of the contract farmers were in the large land size category. The average size of their operational holdings was 24.04 acres as compared to the state average of 9 acres. The holding size of sample farmers were 2.7 times higher. The per cent gross return of tomato crop was higher than the other crops, namely, wheat and paddy. Contract farming proved beneficial to Punjab tomato farmers. Some farmers had better management of crop, and therefore, they got higher yield in comparison to others. Some of the farmers did not follow the technical advice given by these processing companies. This had adverse effect on the productivity of the crop (Sidhu and Rangi, 1998).

The study brought out that 46 per cent of the contract farmers operated between 10 to 20 acres, 20 per cent between 20 and 30 acres and 24 per cent more than 30 acres. Only 10 per cent of the contract farmers operated between 5 to 10 acres. None of the sample farmers were in the small and marginal category having less than 5 acres of operational holding. The study points out that it has a wider policy implications because *a big chunk of the marginal, small and medium farmers have been totally ignored by the contract farming in the state.*

II
AGRICULTURAL DIVERSIFICATION AND CONTRACT FARMING

Agrarian Crisis' in Punjab: The Second Phase

Punjab agriculture over the years has witnessed rising costs, deteriorating productivity, degradation of land and water resources and steep fall in profitability resulting in serious crisis. The fundamental problems are linked with the cropping pattern and water salinity. The rice-wheat farming system has been over exploiting the underground water resources of the state. The water table in the Punjab, where rice is the predominant Kharif crop, is going down at the rate of 23 cm per annum resulting in increased power requirement. About 60 per cent of the blocks are estimated as dark blocks in Punjab. On the other hand, in some pockets of the south-western region in the state, the water table is rising leading the problems of salinity and waterlogging. Due to the predominance of rice-wheat and cotton-wheat rotations, incidence of weeds diseases and insect-pests has increased. New weeds, pests and diseases have appeared. Pests like Heliothis and weeds like Phalaris minor have developed resistance. As a result the marginal and small farmers are not able to get out of poverty cycle. There is strong evidence of reverse leasing in Punjab. The small farmers are increasingly leasing out their farms to bigger farmers and there is ample evidence of acute indebtedness of small farmers. There are also incidences of small and marginal farmers committing suicides in Punjab.

In 2000, Government of Punjab appointed an advisory committee to suggest suitable agricultural production pattern adjustments in order to replace substantial area from under wheat and rice to crops. The Committee recommended crop diversification and alternative institutional arrangements like contract farming. It suggested cultivation of crops which are replacements/alternatives to wheat and rice on a larger scale such as oilseeds, specially rapeseed and mustard in Rabi and groundnut and soyabean in Kharif and also pulse crops and cotton need to be encouraged. There has to be a policy stance, which creates conducive market environment to sustain the production effort.

State Initiated Contract Farming Programme

The Punjab Government has entrusted the responsibility of crop diversification and contract farming to Punjab Agro Industries. The Punjab Agro Industries has evolved a 'Total Five Year Contract Fanning Plan' to extend crop diversification to begin with 3 lakh acres in 2003 and ultimately reach 19.35 lakh acres by 2007.

The crops to be brought under Contract Farming and total area to be involved under each crop in the five year period, is as follows:

Crop	*Target (acres)*
Hyola	8,00,000
Barley	1,65,000
Winter Maize	1,60,000
Dururn Wheat	1,69,000
Sunflower	5,02,500
Spring Com	73,500
Basmati	4,00,000
Kharif Corn	5,30,500
Other/New Crops	83,500

The contract fanning plan of different district show that the major area under various crops would be grown in the districts of Hoshiarpur, Jalandhar, Nawanshar, Ludhiana, Ferozepur, Amritsar, Gurdaspur, Kapurthala and Ropar. These districts are located in sub-mountainous (Kandi) region in Central Punjab and partly in the Malwa region. Though the Government of Punjab has proposed in its target to include 3.80 lakh acres under Contract Farming Plan for the year 2003 but its preparedness is limited to the following crops and areas indicated against them.

Area under Contract Farming for Different Crops during 2002-03

The Punjab Agro-Industries Corporation Ltd. (PAICL) has taken up many initiatives in the ambit of Contract Farming including entering into agreements with various agencies for providing seed, agricultural extension services and buy back of the produce. For example, for the Basmati Crop Rice agreement has been signed with M/s United Riceland Pvt., M/s Rallies India Ltd. and M/s L.T. Overseas Ltd., for providing seed, agricultural extension services and buy-back of the produce. For the maize crop arrangements have been made with Advanta India Ltd. Syngenta India Ltd., Sukjit Starch and Bharat Starch Ltd. PLICS is also working with other players including HAFED, Mahindra and Mahindra, Pepsi, United Breweries and Cargill for other crops. The Punjab Government is ensuring that the Punjab farmers do not have to resort to distress sale at below MSP prices and will provide adequate returns to the farmers (*The Hindus Business Line*, April 3, 2003).

Sl. No.	*Name of crop*	*Area under Contract Farming (in acres)*
1.	Spring Sunflower	7041
2.	Barley	840
3.	Hyola (rapeseed mustard)	10,000
4.	Kharif Maize	10500
5.	Winter Maize	1500
6.	Spring Maize	1250
7.	Basmati	64000

The Punjab Government has decided to drastically cut taxes on all new economically friendly crops like barley, maize, durum, wheat, oil seeds and basmati. This is expected to make procurement cheaper for companies in Punjab while encouraging farmers into shifting out of wheat, paddy to the local APMC board and the Development Fund charge of 2 per cent will be cut to just 0.25 per cent each for these crops. The companies buying these alternative crops may be shelling out less than 2 per cent in taxes. The state otherwise charges more in taxes for procurement of crops like wheat and rice from local mandies. A large number of corporates have evinced interest in procuring a wide range of new crops from Punjab. Punjab Agro Industries Corporation and Marked are acting as facilitators in bringing together companies and farmers (*The Economic Times*, 7 May, 2003, p. 10).

III
CONTRACT FARMING PRACTICE IN ANDHRA PRADESH

Corporate and contract farming at Kuppam revolves around "Israel Cooperative Model of Agriculture" (Chaudhary *et al.*, Hyderabad,

2000). Kuppam area is part of D.P.A.P. Block and chronically drought affected. Around 85 per cent of the population lives below the Poverty-line. Only a small portion of the gross cropped area is under assured source of irrigation. The soil is saline as also composed of gravel and stones of varying sizes with low level of organic matter. A team consisting of experts and social activists undertook a study of 'Contract Farming at Kuppam' from February 17 to 19, 2000. They interviewed the officials of M/s BHC Agro (India) Ltd., the farmers who were taken over for Israeli Demo Project, Japanese International Cooperative Agency and workers engaged in the Kuppam Project. To facilitate the demonstration on corporate/contract farming Chabdipalle, Joint Fanning Cooperatives Society' was formed. The summary of the findings are presented here.

Small and marginal farmers are involved in large numbers in this enterprise. The members of the society have no knowledge of the functioning of society. They also do not know that the Society has entered into a contract with corporate body for farming. All the nine directors of the society are employers working with the Corporate Body (MIS BHC Agro (India), Ltd.). The farmers said that it was the government that took their lands voluntarily to the Corporate Body. None of the farmers know the details of the contract though the Israeli Company claims that the Demo is contract farming. Only the Government of AP signed the contract with the Israeli Company; the members on any decision relating to the demonstration on the fields. No element of cooperation, not even symbolic was involved either in the formation of the Mutually Aided Joint Farming Cooperative Society or in signing the contract. The lands taken over from the farmers are being managed by the corporate body at all stages. The average cost of cultivation is Rs. 20,000 per acre. The labourers get employed only when there is work on the farm. The employers claimed that so far the income accrued to the farmers was Rs. 17,000 per acre. The crops grown were mainly vegetables: gherkin, onion, tomato, potato, water-melon, sweet-melon, capsicum, chillies, beans, peas, carrot, ocra and field crops like groundnut, baby com, popping com and sunflower. The major crop was gherkin. The local foods crops have almost been eliminated. Farmers were never consulted before deciding on the crops to be grown. It is the government and not the company, which is making payments to the farmers for the lands taken over for the demonstration. At the time of procuring the lands the farmers were promised to be paid Rs. 30,000 to Rs. 50,000 per acre per annum. In practice, they were paid Rs. 3000 per acre in the first year, Rs. 4000 per acre in the second year and Rs. 10,000 per acre in the third year. The farmers were very unhappy because of the big gap between what was promised and actual payment. The farmers indicated that the government was diverting the DRDA funds to pay to the farmers.

The adopted Israeli Technology consists of intensive irrigated cultivation, use of heavy machinery and high input. The farmers are worried about the sustainability and productivity of their lands. The deep bore wells are leading to the steep depletion of the ground water. The only positive point about the Israeli cultivation is the use of drip irrigation. The other positive point is that the agricultural labour families are employed in the fields as labourers. Absentee landowners favour corporate farming. Farmers are worried about the productivity of their lands and its boundaries. If the model is replicated the alternative employment of the displaced family becomes a serious threat.

There are not many such references in the state. Other examples in Andhra Pradesh include Gherkin in a limited way and seed companies in some parts of the state. Otherwise, there is no spread of contract farming to other crops and regions in the state.

IV
CONTRACT FARMING IN KARNATAKA

This Indian Gherkins Exporters Association is 100 per cent export driven Industry located in Karnataka. This industry is cited as one of the most successful example of contract farming in India. Gherkin industry sources 100 per cent of its requirement by backward linkage. It has established the practice of entering into agreements not with each and every farmer but alternately either with 25 farmers or any multiple of 25 for contract farming. It believes that it is virtually impossible to take legal action against a small farmer and the system has to work on trust, continued good performance and group pressure in case of a default. Hence it draws agreements on plain paper as the farmers are wary of signing on a stamp paper.

Gherkin Industry is a major industry engaging on contract several thousand farmers for their requirement of raw material, i.e. 'Gherkins'. It operates in a manner so as to make contract farming simple, transparent, accountable and beneficial to the farmers, etc. A study group consisting of five experts from MFPI< APEDA, Tecsok, Kappic and HABARDI listed the Gherkin Industry from 20th-22nd February, 2003 interacted with group of farmers at Hunasenah in Sirsa Taluka of Tumkur District and M/s Global Green Company Ltd., Exporters of Gherkins and Gherkin Processors/exporters. This industry is highly labour intensive and cannot be undertaken by mechanised cultivation. The high labour cost prevailing in the West has made the industry shift towards India as the labour is cheap here. Gherkin can be grown in Karnataka in all the three seasons whereas in the West it can be grown in only one season. The companies provide the farmers with seeds, fertilizers, pesticides and advise them on the package of practices to be followed. The extension persons of the company visit the farmers' fields right from the preparation of the land for sowing till the material is harvested and taken by the company at the doorstep on a pre-contracted price. In view of this, farmers are not put to any hardship in procuring seeds, inputs, marketing etc. The selection of farmers is based on this suitability of land, irrigation facility, farmers ability to put in hard work and commitment. Passbook is maintained by the company showing the details of inputs supplied, produce given by the farmers, payment details and final settlements of the company enters into agreements with 7000 farmers. It is the success story of small companies, small Gherkins and small farmers. Gherkin industry has engaged about 30000 small and marginal farmers for the cultivation of Gherkins. If there is any disturbance to the contract farming, the industry will collapse. In some cases the farmers drop out due to which companies face problems in recovering the cost of inputs. In such cases the assistance of backward linkage scheme has become a boon to the entire Gherkin processing companies. The farmers had no problem in signing contract with the processors. Gherkin seed is not grown locally. It has to be imported as per taste of the importers. By signing the contract the farmers feel morally and legally bound to supply Gherkin to the processors on contract price. (Report of the Study Group on Backward Linkage Assistance of MFPI to Gherkin Industry from 20th-22nd February, 2003).

V

The experience of contract farming in India is limited to a few crops in a few regions which constitute an insignificant proportion of agricultural production. The entry of small farmers appear to be highly risky. There is hardly any regulatory mechanism that minimizes either farmers or those of contracting firms. If the system were to benefit large majority of small-marginal farmers, the primary necessity is a strong institutional structure. The Punjab experience of recent years needs to be analysed from the point of view of small-marginal farmers. Grassroots level farmers' organizations will ensure adequate bargaining power and better returns to farming community.

REFERENCES

Bhalla, G. S. and B. D., Talib (1979). "Agrarian Structure and Peasant Movement" (mimeo), New Delhi: CSRD, Jawaharlal Nehru University.

Gill, Sucha Singh (1978). "Agrarian Transformation in a Punjab Village", *Mainstream*, 16 (27): 12-17.

Government of Punjab, (1973). "Report of the Inquiry Committee of Legislators, Appointed by Government to Probe into the setting up of Sizeable Agricultural Farms on Evacuee Lands by Officers, their relatives and Other Influential Public Men" (Harchand Singh Committee Report) Chandigarh: Department of Rehabilitation.

Shergill, H. S. (1986). 'Land Sales and Land Prices in Punjab' 1952-53 to 1978-79, *Economic and Political Weekly*, 21 (38, 39): A 125-30.

Singh, Baldev (1982). *Land Market: Theory and Practice in India*, New Delhi: Agricole Publishing House.

Singh, Iqbal (1989). "Reverse Tenancy in Punjab Agriculture: Impact of Technological Change", *Economic and Political Weekly*, 24 (25) L A 86-92.

Talib, B. D. (1986). "Agrarian Tensions and Peasant Movement in Punjab", in A. R. Desai (ed.) *Agrarian Struggles in India After Independence*, New Delhi: Oxford University Press.

Index

A.N. Sinha Institute of Social Studies, 273
Absentee landlords, 5, 16, 62, 135, 161, 313, 345, 368, 381
Adhiar, 368-369, 371, 374, 377
Adi-Dravidas and Tribal Welfare Department, 390
Agrarian crisis, 402
Agrarian development programme, 310
Agrarian institutions, 245
Agrarian revolution, 24, 26-27, 190
Agricultural census, 3, 19, 72, 90, 152, 163, 166, 246, 333-336, 342-345, 374
  survey, 345
  data, 334
Agricultural labourers, 24-25, 61, 128, 144, 148, 161, 251, 253-255, 257, 266, 274, 277-278, 314, 328, 332-333, 355, 390
Agriculture and tenancy, investment in, 58
Agriculture labour group, 248
Agro-processing, 7, 9
Alfred Marshal's Principles, 88
Allotment rules, 372
Aman paddy, 144
Ambiguity around land relations, 356
Amit Bhaduri's, Model of, 51, 53-54
Animal husbandry, 52, 376
Anti-Bihari riots, 356
Anti-foreigner Assam movement, 356
APEDA, 406
APMC board, 404
Asian miracle cases, 321
Assam accord, 354

Backward agriculture, 49, 53-56, 59, 61, 228, 290
Bargadars, 17, 81, 141-143, 379-380
Below the poverty line, 263, 309
Benami ceiling surplus land, 22
Bengal Tenancy Act, 340
Bhave, Acharya Vinoba, 394
Bihar Tenancy Act, 66
BIMARU, 319
Boro Territorial Council (BTC), 353
British administrative rules, 356

Capitalism, 23-24, 272-273, 276, 322
Cash income, 7
Cash renting, 129, 131
Caste (*jati*) panchayats, 309
Caste-class Linkages, 277
Casual labour markets, 257-258, 261
Cauvery delta zone, 180-181
Ceiling legislation, 2, 5, 18
Ceiling surplus land, 18, 45, 139, 144, 348, 390-391, 394, 398
  distribution of, 45, 390
  redistribution of, 390
Centralization, 23-24
Changing class structure, 275
Charwaha, 278
Cheap credit, 55
Class struggles, 18, 273-274
Coastal regions, 339-340
Commercial crops, 11, 255, 352, 357-358, 360

Commercial tenancy, 133
Commercialisation and Land Relations, 357
Concealed tenancy, 2, 35, 131, 133, 152, 180, 306-307, 311, 333, 335, 341-342, 344, 348
Conditional assignments, 386
Conflict management, 314-315
Congress Agrarian Reforms Committee, 140, 327
Congress Economic Programme Committee, 327
Contract farming, 11, 15, 399-407
  encouragement to, 11
Contractual arrangements, 132, 215, 288
Cooperative farming, 2
Credible collateral, 260
Credit constraints, 217
Credit institutions, forms of, 53
Credit market, 47, 53, 57, 60, 76, 210, 212, 215-217, 220-221, 241-242, 244, 248, 253, 258-262, 266-267, 284
  imperfections, 212, 216-217, 220-221
Credit shortage, 54, 75
Crop
  agricultural, 300, 364
  exportable, 39, 44
  growing, 361
  losses, 74-75, 84
  performance, 171
  share, 180, 183, 186, 369
  sharing rights, 141, 143
  tomato, 400-401
Cultivable area, 364-365, 372
Cultivable government land, distribution of, 391
Cultivable land, 19, 72, 95, 165, 171, 364, 380, 391-392, 394, 398
Cultivation, 8, 81-82, 85, 175, 186-187, 276-287, 311, 347, 365, 377-378, 380
  cotton, 346
  direct, 37, 49
  efficient system of, 287-288
  predominant method of, 365
Customary law, 351-352, 356-358, 360-361

Daimyo, 32
Dalit castes, 278
Dalits, 21
Delivery systems, improvements in, 11
Democratic revolution, 15, 24
Department of Rural Development, 64
De-peasantisation, 276
Depressed class land, 386
Depressed classes, 385-386
Desert development programme, 299
Development fund, 404
Development planning, 76, 78
DPAP block, 405
Dr. Ambedkar People Society (DAPSY), 394-395
Drought-prone area programme, 299
Dryland villages, 131

East India Company, 339
Economic
  reforms, 126, 128, 173
  transformation, 163, 319-320
Egalitarian society, 332, 357
Ekta Parishad, 328
Employment generation, 245
Employment Guarantee Bill, 10
Encroachment, 94, 224, 231, 233, 293, 350-351, 355-357
Entirely leased-in holdings (ELIH), 94
Environmental management, 315
Era of reforms, 75
Ethnic Assamese, 351, 353, 355-356
Ethnic conflicts, 350, 353, 356

Fair rent, 37-38, 176, 187, 303, 305
Family farm production, 272
Farm servants, 246-248, 258
Fertiliser consumption, 108-109, 112

Finance capital, 15, 23-25
dominance of, 15, 23-25
Financial
markets, 205, 208, 210, 216, 235
support, 10
Five Year Plan, Ninth and Tenth, 79
Fixed money, 91, 96, 344
Fixed rent tenancy, 51, 56-57, 88-89, 96, 98-99, 107, 111, 231, 282, 288
Floriculture, 312-313
Food and Agriculture Organization, 191
Forest department, 300, 328
Formal credit, 209
Fragmentation, 132, 191, 198, 202, 227
Free lease markets, 10

Garhjat Region (Land of Forts), 339
Garibi hatao, 18
GATT agreement, 42-43
Gherkin industry, 406-407
Gini coefficient, 3, 178, 338
Global conjuncture, 26-27
Globalized finance, era of, 24
Government wastelands, 19
Gramin banks, 141
Green revolution, 63, 73, 144-145, 152-153, 160-161, 163, 165, 276, 291, 322

HABARDI, 407
Halwaha, 278
Handlooms and powerlooms, 44
Higher-value cropping pattern, 38
Household responsibility system, 7
HYV, 36, 38, 152, 244, 341, 371

Immigrants, 350-351, 353-355
Immigration, 354-357
Imperfections, 204, 212, 217, 219-220
Imperialism, 25, 320, 325
Income inequality, 123-124
Indebtedness, 53-54, 62, 71, 333, 402
Indian Association of Social Science Institutions, 21
Indicator of poverty, 263
Inequality, 3, 58, 64, 123, 126-127, 177-178, 196, 206, 233, 334-336, 340
in land distribution, 166, 205, 233
Infant mortality rate, 42
Informal tenancy, 179, 343
Institutional credit, 26, 38, 41, 44, 55, 80, 84, 143, 232-233
access to, 44, 55, 80, 232
Institutional gap, 205, 211-212, 233
Institutional protectionism, 60
Institutional reforms, 144, 147
Institutionalized tenancy, 79
Insurance markets, 212, 220
International Labour Organisation (ILO), 273, 279
IRDP, 394-395
Israel cooperative model of agriculture, 404

Jaganathan, Padmashri Krishnammal, 394
Jhum Land Legislation Act, 371
Jhum, 351-352, 355, 357
Joint fanning cooperatives society, 405
Jotedars, 140
Junker, Prussian, 32

Karnataka Land Reforms Amendment Bill, 312
Karnataka Land Revenue Manual, 309
Karnataka State Land Use Board, 309
Kharif season, 77, 141, 344
Khud-kasht ('home farm'), 17

Labour market, 48
imperfections, 212, 220-222
Labour shortage, 50, 158, 160
Land Acquisition Act, 309
Land and credit market interlocking, 370
Land assignment programmes, 383
Land Ceiling Act, 128, 384, 390
Land colonization cooperative society, 386, 390

Land development banks, 5, 11
Land distribution
  pattern of, 138, 167
  programme, 227, 233
Land for Tillers Freedom (LAFT), 394-395
Land lease market, 78-79, 100, 129, 133, 152, 172, 179, 183, 198, 202, 232, 251-253, 257, 261-262, 336, 341, 345, 376
Land markets
  active, 165, 209, 243, 253, 265, 375
  agrarian economies, 210
  agricultural, 241
  competitive, 162
  depresses, 224
  failure of, 219
  hidden, 381
  inactive, 217, 265
  informal, 209
  liberalizing, 14
  restricting, 4
  rural, 85, 212, 219-220, 224, 235
Land monopoly, 21, 26, 31, 33, 36
Land reforms, 1-3, 5, 8-9, 11-19, 21-26, 31, 33, 41, 45-46, 65, 73, 128, 138-140, 148-149, 153, 155, 175, 190, 192, 201, 204-205, 208, 211, 216, 222-223, 225, 228, 291, 299-302, 309-311, 314-315, 320-330, 332, 335, 340-341, 354, 367, 371, 373-374, 379-381, 387
  act, 309, 335, 379-381
  failure of, 204, 222, 224
  law, 374
  programme, 139, 148, 324
  reemergence of, 18
Land relations among the tribes, 351
Land rent, 205, 208, 210-215, 230, 233-235, 374
Land rental, 205, 212-214, 233
Land rights, 15, 133-134, 207-208, 218, 224, 299, 322, 324, 326-328, 333, 373
Land tenurial rights, 134
Landless and marginal farmers, employment for, 10
Landless farmers, 10, 161, 191-192, 334, 381
Landless person, 346, 372
Landlessness, 20, 25, 108, 225, 233, 276-277, 281-282, 330, 333, 353, 358
Landlordism, 25, 140, 276-277, 291, 303
Landlord-tenant
  nexus, 303
  relationship, 162
Leased markets, 376, 381
Leased-in area (LIA), 94
Leasing-out land, 129, 154, 156, 158, 160-161, 232, 251
Left Front Government (LFG), 139
Legal rights over land, 350
Liberalisation era, 82, 329
Liberalization, privatization and globalization (LPG), 21

Mackinnon, John, 333
Mahajan, 53
Major irrigation, 243, 333
Marginal
  farmers, 10
  groups, 57, 224, 233
  holdings, 6-7, 9, 72, 127, 134, 142, 168, 173, 345
Marginalisation of peasantry, 134
Market imperfections, 205, 211, 233, 313
Market support, 43
Marshallian inefficiency, 88
Middle peasant group, 247
Ministry of Rural Development, 17, 19, 22, 155, 307
Minor irrigation, 397
Mixed holdings (MH), 94
MLR & LR Act, 372, 374-375
Money lenders, 5, 75-76, 85
  regulation of, 75
  tax paying registered, 76

Mutually Aided Joint Farming Cooperative Society, 405

NABARD, 11
Naga-Kuki conflict, 358
National Commission on Agriculture, 154-155, 306
National Institute of Rural Development, 21
National remote sensing agency, 300
National Sample Survey, 3-4, 19, 33-34, 39, 48, 63-64, 72, 90-91, 103, 105-106, 110-111, 113, 116, 130, 149, 152, 177-179, 284, 306-307, 314, 319, 330, 333-335, 337, 342-345, 367
National Wasteland Development Board, 300
New economic policy, 41-42, 315
Non-agricultural income, 9, 242
Non-institutional
  credit, 77, 260-262
  lenders, 76-77
  sources of finance, 71, 77, 85
Non-recorded tenancy, 369
North Eastern Zone, 180-181

Occupancy tenancy, 161
Operation barga, 13, 34, 37-38, 79, 138, 140-141, 147, 176, 213, 301, 322, 379, 381
Orissa Estate Abolition Act, 228
Orissa Land Reforms Act, 228, 343
Ownership cultivation, 342

Panchama land, 385-387
Panchayati Raj Institution (PRI), 148, 275
Panchayati raj system, 141, 144
Patnaik, Prabhat, 15, 24
Patwari circles, 193
PDS, 41, 45, 78
Peasant based agriculture, problems of, 74
Peasant groups, 247-248
Peasant holdings, 7
Peasant households, 248, 254, 258, 262-263
Peasantry, 16-18, 23-25, 128, 134, 246, 272, 288
  poor, 25-27, 248, 251-252, 255, 257-262, 265, 267
  rich, 25, 253, 257, 261, 265
Pepsu Abolition of Ala Malkiyat and Talukdari Rights Act, 154
Pepsu Tenancy and Agricultural Land Act, 154
Personal cultivation, 17, 35, 52, 79, 82, 154, 228, 302-306
Petty farmers, 134, 148, 161
Planned economy era, 123
Planning Commission, 42, 133
Podu, 334
Poor peasants, 23-25, 32, 252-255, 257-258, 274-275
Post-harvest operations, 9
Post-independence era, 190
Post-reform era, 223
Post-World War II era, 31, 320-321, 324
Poverty alleviation, 190, 204, 314-315
Poverty eradication programme, 128
Poverty line, 8, 197, 262-263, 266, 309, 368
Pre-green revolution era, 152
Price-cost conditions, 36-37
Primitive accumulation, 273-274
Private institutional finance, 60
Private investment, 58-60, 62
Productive assets, 20, 233, 242, 247, 265, 326
Public investment, collapse of, 26
Punjab Abolition of Ala Malkiyat and Talukdari Rights Act, 154
Punjab Agro-Industries Corporation Ltd. (PAICL), 403
Punjab Occupancy Tenants (Vesting of Proprietary Rights) Act, 154
Punjab Security of Tenure Act, 154
Pure tenants, 35, 253, 258

Quantitative restrictions (QRs), 42

Radical policies, 81-82
Rainfed village, 254
Redistributive reform, 15, 26
Regional disparities, 123, 125, 339
Regression analysis, 109-110
Rental markets, 85, 212-214, 217
  activation, 221
Rental tenancy, 288
Resource endowments, 149, 253
Resource use efficiency and tenancy, 55
Reverse tenancy, 47, 57, 60, 68, 90, 101, 106-107, 111-112, 133-134, 149, 152-153, 157, 159-160, 162, 212, 214, 252-253, 283-284, 306, 311, 346
Revisional survey operations, 379
Revolutionary land reforms, 14
Rich peasants, 247, 249-252, 257, 261, 266-267, 322
Rights on land, 207
Risk mitigation, 11
Rural conflicts, 224
Rural development, 1, 15, 19, 22, 65, 144, 176
Rural industrialisation programme, 11-12
Rural infrastructure, 26, 53, 275
Rural labour, casualisation of, 274
Rural labourers, 144, 274-275
Rural neo-elite, 274
Rural poverty, 31-32, 41, 70, 138, 142, 145, 213, 234, 266, 271, 273, 318-319, 326
Ryotwari, 1, 3, 17, 94, 241 *see also* Zamindari

Samarthan, 328
Self-cultivated holdings, 94, 231
Self-cultivation, 49, 51-53, 56, 135, 152, 155, 165, 276, 283, 288, 291, 334, 342
Self-help groups, 22, 396
Semi-feudal traditions, 274
Semi-feudalism, 273-275
Sharada Act, 38
Share cropping, 62, 96, 228, 231-232, 334, 346, 381
Share tenancy (ST), 96
  determinants of, 109
Sharecropping
  contracts, 184, 215
  tenancy, 175, 290
Sikkim Cultivators Protection Act, 377
Singh, Tarlok, 128
Social conflicts, 274-275
Social revolution, 16
Special component plan, 398
State of food insecurity, 191
Structural adjustment programme, 128
Sustainable development, 12, 79-82
Sustenance agriculture, 328

Tamil Nadu Adi-Dravidas Housing and Development Corporation (TAHDCO), 394
Tamil Nadu Agricultural Lands Record of Tenancy Rights Act, 176
Tamil Nadu Cultivating Tenants (Payment of Fair Rent) Act, 176
Tamil Nadu Cultivating Tenants Arrears of Rent (Relief) Act, 176
Tamil Nadu Cultivating Tenants Protection Act, 176
Tamil Nadu Record of Tenancy Right Act, 188
Tax equivalent, 88
Technological upgradation, 53
Tecsok, 406
Telangana Act, 82
Tenancy
  Abolition of, 18, 228, 311, 315, 341
  changing forms of, 287
  credit market and, 53
  -depressed markets, 53
  -landlord relationship, 228
  legislation, 5, 17, 68, 78, 132-133, 154-156, 176, 306, 348, 371
  problem of, 31

relations, 88-90, 107-108, 110-113, 139, 223, 231, 271, 282-284, 306
terms and conditions of, 57, 64, 142, 380-381
Tenant landlord relationship, 101
Tenanted
area, 35, 72, 179
holdings, 67, 72
Tenure of Leasing, 345
Tenurial rights, 131, 135, 367
Terms of tenancy, 68, 90-91, 96, 98, 111, 156, 186, 228, 231-232, 329, 334, 344-345, 348, 377
Thois, 377
TLR & LR Act, 379-380
Transaction costs, 88, 211, 213, 215, 217-218, 220-221, 234-235, 308
Tribal groups, 333-334, 339
Tubewell investment, 38

UP Zamindari and Land Reforms Act, 198
Upper castes, peasantisation of, 279
Usurious income, 53, 59

Village panchayat, 309
Village study reports, 335
Voluntary surrenders, 17
Waste land development programmes, 315
Water table, 402
Watershed development programme, 299, 315
West Bengal type tenancy reform, 80
White cards, 262-263
World Bank, 14, 212, 219, 322-323
World War II, 32
WTO, 42-43, 308

Yield differences, 157

Zamindari, 16-17, 90, 94, 138, 140, 355
abolition of, 128
Zamindars/jotedars, 140